GOVERNMENT FINANCE:
ECONOMICS OF THE PUBLIC SECTOR

THE IRWIN SERIES IN ECONOMICS

Consulting Editor
LLOYD G. REYNOLDS
Yale University

Ames   *Soviet Economic Processes*

Anderson, Gitlow, & Diamond (eds.)   *General Economics: A Book of Readings*   rev. ed.

Balassa   *The Theory of Economic Integration*

Beal & Wickersham   *The Practice of Collective Bargaining*   3d ed.

Blaug   *Economic Theory in Retrospect*   rev. ed.

Bornstein (ed.)   *Comparative Economic Systems: Models and Cases*   rev. ed.

Bornstein & Fusfeld (eds.)   *The Soviet Economy: A Book of Readings*   rev. ed.

Buchanan   *The Public Finances*   rev. ed.

Cartter   *Theory of Wages and Employment*

Cartter & Marshall   *Labor Economics: Wages, Employment, and Trade Unionism*

Davidson, Smith, & Wiley   *Economics: An Analytical Approach*   rev. ed.

Davis, Hughes, & McDougall   *American Economic History: The Development of a National Economy*   3d ed.

Doll, Rhodes, & West   *Economics of Agricultural Production, Markets, and Policy*

Drummond   *The Canadian Economy: Organization and Development*

Due   *Government Finance: Economics of the Public Sector*   4th ed.

Due & Clower   *Intermediate Economic Analysis*   5th ed.

Fellner   *Probability and Profit: A Study of Economic Behavior along Bayesian Lines*

Ferguson   *Microeconomic Theory*   rev. ed.

Gambs & Komisar   *Economics and Man*   3d ed.

GOVERNMENT FINANCE:
ECONOMICS OF THE
PUBLIC SECTOR

JOHN F. DUE

Professor of Economics
University of Illinois

Fourth Edition • 1968

RICHARD D. IRWIN, INC., Homewood, Illinois

Irwin—Dorsey Limited, Nobleton, Ontario

FOURTH EDITION

First Printing, May, 1968
Second Printing, September, 1968
Third Printing, May, 1969

Library of Congress Catalog Card No. 68-23342

PRINTED IN THE UNITED STATES OF AMERICA

To Jean, Allan, and Kevin

PREFACE

This edition has been entirely rewritten to reflect changing orientation and emphasis in the field of governmental finance in the last decade, to incorporate new material that has appeared in recent years, to adapt the organization to changes in material, and to raise the level of analysis.

One major change in public finance has been the great increase in emphasis on decision making for governmental activities and expenditures, integrating the work of political science, administrative theory, and economics. As a part of this development, increased attention has been given to cost-benefit analysis and to budget systems, with particular emphasis on program budgeting. These trends have been greatly influenced by the writings of Paul Samuelson, J. M. Buchanan, Gordon Tullock, and Anthony Downs, by the work at RAND and elsewhere on national defense programming, and by the studies of Otto Eckstein and others in the water resources field. The first five chapters of this edition have been developed in light of this newer analysis; I am greatly indebted to the work of the persons named above and to others in the field.

A second major change in the book has been the reorganization of the structure to allow unified treatment of economic effects of expenditures, debt, and revenue sources in a single section, Chapters 6 through 9. This section reflects particularly the work of Richard Musgrave and the empirical studies in recent years of effects of various expenditure and tax programs. Analysis of distributional effects (shifting and incidence) still leaves much to be desired. The conflicting results of the various econometric studies of the distribution of burden of the corporate income tax have added confusion, at least temporarily, to the picture.

This analysis of economic effects leads to a discussion of various policy questions: fiscal and debt policy, intergovernmental fiscal questions, and the use of charges for financing. The intergovernmental chapter reflects the work by George Break in the Brookings studies. Chapter 14 considers the role of various major taxes in the overall tax structure in light of assumed objectives of society, and Chapters 15 and 16 review issues relating to the structure of these major taxes. The space allocated to income taxation has been reduced from the previous editions, in conformity with changing emphasis in the field. These tax policy chapters have benefitted from the various Brookings studies, particularly the general surveys by Pechman, Goode, and Netzer. The final chapter of the book considers the relationship of economic development and public finance with emphasis on the developing economies, and reflects in part the work of Hinrichs. Some of the issues that were of primary emphasis a decade ago, such as the shifting of debt burden to future generations, forward-versus-backward shifting of sales taxes, and integration of personal and corporate income taxes, receive less attention, in view of greater agreement in the disputes and changing emphasis.

Throughout the book the attempt has been made to improve the unity of treatment of the material and to hold down unnecessary empirical detail which contributes little to the student. The level of analysis has been raised in some sections, but the book is still based upon the assumption that the student has had only a year of Principles—although additional work in micro and macro theory is obviously helpful as a background.

I would like to express particular appreciation to Dr. Alice Vandermeulen, Senior Lecturer in Economics in the University of California, Los Angeles, for her suggestions about organization of material and emphasis, and for her comments on the first drafts of a number of the chapters—although the final product bears little resemblance to the book she would write in this field. I am also indebted to students in public finance courses at the University of Illinois and UCLA (in which portions of the new material were used in duplicated form) for their comments; and to my colleagues at the University of Illinois, and particularly Professor Jane Leuthold, for assistance. As in previous editions, I would like to express my deep appreciation to Professor Malcolm M. Davisson of the University of California, Berkeley, who first interested me in public finance when I took his course in the field as an undergraduate at Berkeley.

I would also like to express appreciation for their comments to various users of previous editions of the book and to Professor Lloyd Reynolds, Editor of the Irwin Series in Economics. Mrs. Paulette Graziano, who compiled and checked data and sources and read the manuscript, and Mrs. Dorothy Sullivan and Mrs. Wendy Alguero of the University of Illinois who typed, respectively, the first and the final drafts of the manuscript, greatly facilitated the work.

Urbana, Illinois   JOHN F. DUE
April, 1968

TABLE OF CONTENTS

xi

PART I

Governmental Decision Making

Chapter	THE RATIONALE OF
1	GOVERNMENTAL ACTIVITY

In any society, persons have various goals or objectives, with relative priorities or preference schedules for these goals. They likewise have preference schedules for alternative means of satisfying these objectives. Thus a person seeks to stay alive, an objective to which he usually attaches very high priority. To do so he must eat; in turn, he has relative preferences for various foods that will enable him to attain this basic goal. Some of the goals are ones involving the individual alone; others relate to groups and to the entire society itself, such as international prestige. The precise preference schedules for goods and means vary widely among persons in a particular society, within a society over time, and among societies. Many preference schedules relate to activities that the person can provide for himself within the household, as, for example, sleeping. In a primitive society most desires are satisfied within the household, village, or tribal unit, without exchange. In the modern complex economy, most goods to meet these preferences must be acquired either through the market mechanism from private enterprise producers or through the government— the central organization of society.

The economies of the world today can be grouped into two classes on the basis of the relative importance of these two methods of supplying goods: the market economies, characterized by primary reliance upon private enterprise and the price system, and the centralized economies, characterized by the conduct of most production activity by government. The market economies, however, by no means confine economic activity to private enterprise; while the governmental sectors may be small compared to those in the centralized economies, they are not unimportant. This study is concerned with the determinants that influence the size and nature of the government sector in the market economies, with decision making in the governmental sector, and with the influence of the governmental sector upon the private sector. The initial primary question is twofold: (1) in any economy in which the market system with private enterprise is accepted

3

as the preferred form of economic organization, why do governments now play significant roles and (2) what criteria can be employed to judge the optimal size and scope of the governmental sector? The answers are to be found through an analysis of the nature of preferences and the relative effectiveness of private and governmental activity in satisfying them.

Major Objectives in Preference Schedules

Contemporary society emphasizes two primary objectives. The first is maximization of per capita real income. This goal requires optimal adjustments of production in terms of individual preferences for various goods and services, maximum efficiency in the allocation and use of resources so that output per unit of resources is maximized, full employment of resources, and an optimal rate of economic growth, given the preferences of society between present and future consumption.

Secondly, society has certain preferences relating to equity in the distribution of income among the members of society. The exact nature of these preferences is difficult to define. On the one hand some correlation between income and economic activity—contribution to production—is considered desirable. On the other hand the high degree of inequality of income that develops in a market economy is regarded as excessive. The exact concept of an optimal distribution varies widely in time and place. Preference schedules relating to income distribution necessarily involve value judgments about "equity" and "fairness."

In the attainment of these goals, in the United States and many other market economies, the preferences of society favor use of the market mechanism over governmental conduct of activity except in those situations in which governmental intervention has specific justification in terms of attainment of other goals. This bias in favor of private enterprise over government is a product of attachment to the status quo and dislike of change; of fear of the loss of personal freedom in an economy dominated by government; of conviction that private enterprise, spurred by the profit motive, is more effective in satisfaction of wants.

The undertaking of economic activity by government therefore reflects the belief of society that in certain respects the market economy fails to attain the top-priority preferred goals as fully as possible; accordingly governmental intervention is accepted. Specific governmental activities must be evaluated, therefore, in terms of the attitudes of society toward the goals and relative fulfillment of them by private sector and governmental activities. Thus activities of government that affect the allocation of resources, that is, the relative outputs of various goods, must be judged on the basis of the importance attached by society to the goal of optimal patterns of output, relative preferences for the goods affected by the allocational activities, and relative effectiveness of governments in insuring fulfillment of the preferences. Governmental activities that affect the pattern of distribution of income must be evaluated on the basis of the attitudes of society about the fairness of various patterns and relative preferences for equity and other goals.

An Alternative Approach—Maximization of Satisfaction

Were it possible to compare satisfactions of individuals, more precise definition of the goals of society and determination of optimal programs of governmental activity would be possible, employing the rule of maximization of total satisfaction in society, that is, the attainment of maximum total utility. The criterion for governmental activities would be maximization of satisfaction: the adjustment of all activities to the levels at which marginal satisfactions from the last units of expenditure on all goods and services provided by private or governmental sectors were equal. Tax structures would be designed to minimize aggregate sacrifice by attaining equimarginal sacrifice by all persons; the sacrifice from the last dollar of taxes paid by all persons would be equal. Optimal redistributional activities would be defined as those that produced a pattern of real income distribution that allowed maximum total satisfaction; transfer of income would be carried to the point at which no further transfer would increase the satisfaction of the recipient more than it reduced the satisfaction of the person from whom the money was taken.

Unfortunately, interpersonal utility comparisons are not possible; there is no way of comparing satisfactions received by various individuals, and therefore the concept of an optimum based upon equimarginal satisfaction and sacrifice is meaningless. The satisfaction gained by a welfare recipient from an additional dollar cannot be compared with the sacrifice by the millionaire who paid the dollar in taxes. Even the Law of Diminishing Marginal Utility does not necessarily apply to income as a whole in the fashion that it applies to waffles or refrigerators; as incomes rise, desires may rise in equal degree.

The Pareto Criterion

Since interpersonal utility comparisons are impossible, the only meaningful statement that can be made about the effect of changes upon total satisfaction is that any change that benefits one person without injuring anyone increases total satisfaction. Thus an optimum is reached when no further changes of this type are possible. The term "Pareto criterion" is given to this rule in recognition of the work of the economist Vilfredo Pareto, who first developed it. Such an optimal position is, however, only one of many possible such optima; there is no way of defining the "best" optimum on the basis of relative satisfaction. The Pareto analysis merely defines a number of possible situations in which the requirements are met, and not the particular one that is best.

In terms of the Pareto criterion, governmental activity is justifiable only in very restrictive circumstances, namely, when it will benefit at least one person without injuring anyone. Strictly interpreted, this situation is virtually never encountered; even the elimination of monopoly, for example, injures the monopolist. Recognition of the possibility of bargaining and of compensation broadens the possibilities of change to a limited extent. For example, A might be willing to accept a change that he does not like in order to get B to accept a change which B dislikes but which A wants very much. Or, if the person benefiting would be willing to compensate the person injured adequately to induce the latter to withdraw his objection, the change may be regarded as justifiable.[1]

Even with these qualifications, the Pareto approach to the definition of optimum governmental activity would be very restrictive and would prevent any redistributive activity, which by its nature benefits some persons at the expense of others. Accordingly, the preferences of society as a whole would not be fulfilled. The criterion for determining governmental activities, therefore, can be expressed only in terms of the preferences of society, as consolidated into the *social welfare function*—the function expressing the composite relative preference

---

[1] The literature on the Pareto criterion and the principle of compensation is extensive; see J. G. Head, "The Welfare Foundations of Public Finance Theory," *Revista di Diritto Finanziero e Scienza delle Finanze*, Vol. XIX (May, 1965), pp. 5–15. There are a number of difficulties with the compensation principle, the basic one being that it is based on an implicit assumption of equal marginal utility of income to the two persons. Without this assumption, willingness of one to pay adequate compensation to the other would not demonstrate an increase in total satisfaction.

schedules for various patterns of resource allocation and income distribution.

THE DESIRE FOR GOVERNMENTAL ACTIVITIES

Over the centuries governmental activities have continued to expand; the exact scope varies with the country, but the general trend has been universal. Given the bias in the Western world in favor of private-sector activity over government, the rising governmental activity can be attributed primarily to greater recognition of the inadequacies of the market mechanism in meeting the preferences of society. The deficiences and the consequent governmental programs can be grouped into four major classes, relating, respectively, to allocation of resources, to efficiency in the use of resources, to economic stability and growth, and to redistribution of income.

Allocational Activities

The allocational activities arise out of the failure of the market mechanism to adjust the outputs of various goods in accordance with the preferences of society, in light of the goal of maximizing per capita real income. Optimal adjustment, given the pattern of income distribution, can be attained in a market economy only under the following conditions:

1. Absence of *externalities* in production and consumption; that is, in the utilization of resources in production and the utilization of goods to satisfy wants, there are no interdependencies among producers or among consumers. Use of resources in production by one firm does not affect the costs or outputs of another firm, and all costs to society from production of the goods appear as costs to the producers. All benefits from particular goods accrue individually and separately to the purchasers of the goods rather than indivisibly to society as a whole, and consumption of these goods by one person does not create either benefits or costs for other persons.

2. Prices of all commodities at levels that reflect relative real costs of production. Thus prices equal marginal costs, and factor prices equate factor supply and demand.

These conditions would be attained with perfect competition in all factor and commodity markets and full employment of resources, and adjustment of activities in conformance with the maximization assumption by factor owners, business firms, and households.

In a number of respects these conditions for optimal adjustment of resource allocation in terms of consumer preferences are not attained, and recognition of this failure leads to support for activity by governments to eliminate the deficiencies, in light of the goal of optimization of real per capita income.

Collective or Public Goods. Basic traditional governmental activity, still a major segment in the overall picture, is attributable to the collective or public nature of certain goods and thus to the absence of the condition that goods solely convey benefits directly to individuals with no interdependence in consumption. Public goods are jointly supplied to the community as a whole in the sense that benefits accrue collectively to society. They are not appropriable by individuals, that is, they are not divisible into units that can be sold separately. Consumption by one person does not reduce the amount available to others. No one can be excluded from the benefits either in any fashion, or in a fashion tolerable to society.

By their nature, these goods cannot be produced by private enterprise; in a sense governments developed initially because of the recognition that persons desired certain goods that could be provided only through an organization representing society as a whole and having powers of coercion. Private enterprise cannot produce the goods because it cannot sell them to individuals; if the goods are produced, no one can be denied benefits from them. No individual is willing to pay for the services because he knows that his willingness to pay will not result in the services being produced if other persons are not willing to pay, and if the services are provided he will benefit from them whether he pays or not.

In a few instances voluntary cooperation may bring about production of public goods. If the number of persons is small, some take the initiative to get the activity under way, preferences are similar, and all persons seek to avoid the ill will of their fellows that will result if they do not cooperate, the results may be attained without the intervention of government. Some early road improvements were made in this way; sidewalks are sometimes financed by cooperative action of all persons in a block; early-day fire protection was provided by volunteer companies, individuals lured in part by the glamour of fighting fire and the praise from fellow citizens whose property was saved. The basic obstacle to voluntary action is the difficulty in getting all or most persons to cooperate; anyone who does not will still enjoy the benefits without making a contribution. If a sidewalk is to be useful it must run the whole length of the block—and persons not contributing cannot feasibly be barred from walking on it. Provision of such services is usually possible only if government undertakes them and finances them on a compulsory basis.

National defense is the best example of a public good; benefits in the form of protection from foreign invasion, seizure of foreign territory, or prevention of invasion of friendly countries accrue indivisibly to the entire community, and no one can be prevented from benefiting. Private production is therefore impossible. Many regulatory activities of government are similar in nature; all persons benefit from pure food and drug laws and their enforcement, for example, and the benefits cannot be withheld from any individuals.

Partial Externalities in Consumption. Some goods that are divisible and salable, yielding certain benefits directly and separately to individuals, with the possibility of excluding other persons from the benefits, offer significant externalities of consumption, in the sense that use of them by some persons creates benefits for others for which the initial users cannot obtain compensation. Optimal resource allocation is not attained, since an individual adjusts his purchases according to the direct benefits he receives. Education is the classic example; the recipients benefit economically and culturally while other persons gain as well. Additional education results in improved efficiency in management and in more rapid technological and organizational change and thus more rapid economic growth and higher per capita real incomes. These benefits accrue to all persons as consumers, not merely to those gaining the higher incomes. High levels of education also permit more effective and stable democracy and higher levels of cultural enjoyment; not only does an individual who gains greater training in art or drama benefit, but those who view his paintings or performances do so as well.

Public health measures have obvious external benefits; vaccination against smallpox not only protects the person vaccinated but others who might have been infected by him as well. Persons benefiting from certain governmental services lessen their use of a substitute and make it more readily available for others. For example, provision of rapid transit and commuter service will lessen traffic congestion on the highways and benefit those who continue to use the roads.

Goods yielding externalities of consumption will be produced by private enterprise but in quantities less than the optimum, since private producers cannot realize on the externality or indirect gain. The amounts purchasers are willing to buy are determined by the direct benefits, and therefore do not reflect the gains to society from the externalities. In the major field of education additional interference with optimization arises because the parents may pay the costs, while the children ultimately benefit through higher income. In view of these indirect gains, governments must increase the quantity produced beyond the amounts that would be provided by private enterprise if optimal allocation of resources in terms of preferences of society is to be attained. In a sense the consumers of these goods are being encouraged or required to acquire more units than they would if they had to pay the full cost because of the external benefits. Musgrave calls these "merit goods."

Externalities in Production. Less significant are externalities in production, in the sense of interdependence of outputs of particular firms on the cost schedules of others. The traditional example is the decreasing cost industry; as total output of the mines in an area increases, a point is reached at which a railroad can economically be built, thus lowering transport costs of all firms. Thus the total cost of an increase in output by any one firm is less than the cost to the firm because of the effect in lowering the cost schedules of other firms. A similar example is provided by the interdependency in the pumping of water from adjacent mines; the more pumped by one mine, the less water the others must pump. Fire protection measures taken by one timber company will benefit nearby property owners by lessening the risk of fire spreading to their land. Since the firm cannot charge for the benefits of these externalities, the total amount of the activity will be less than optimal.

External Diseconomies of Consumption and Production. In the reverse situation, the production or consumption of a good gives rise to costs to others, who cannot obtain compensation to cover them. A neighbor's dog ruins a person's flowers, bites his children, runs away his friends and clients. Cigar smoke nauseates a person in the adjacent seat on a bus. Wild parties keep the neighbors awake. Excessive use of liquor results in property damage, motor vehicle accidents, and financial and emotional injury to other members of the family. In the production sector, methods used by some firms may raise costs for other firms or for consumers, through air or water pollution, for example. The more planes using an airport beyond a certain traffic limit, the greater the delays, costs, and accident hazards for the other airlines. In an increasing cost industry, as one firm expands, the costs of the other firms rise; the increase in cost to the economy is greater than the increase in cost to the individual firm.

Relationship between Price and Marginal Cost. Conditions approaching perfect competition, necessary for optimal price relationships, are found in only a small sector of the economy, and various forms of imperfect competition are widespread. In nonperfectly competitive markets price will exceed marginal revenue and thus marginal cost, since maximization of profit requires that MR = MC. Imperfect competition is in part a product of increasing returns to scale. In some industries the economies of scale are so significant, relative to the market potential, that only one firm can operate, and marginal cost is less than average cost at the level of optimal operation. Thus, if price were to equal marginal cost it could not cover average cost; accordingly private enterprise could not operate. In other instances, while several firms may be able to operate profitably, the number is so small as to create price interdependencies; at the optimal profit point price is well above marginal cost (which must equal marginal revenue for maximum profit). In many industries differentiation of product breaks the market into segments and results in deviation between price and marginal cost.

Likewise factor prices do not always equate factor supply and demand, because of imperfections in the factor markets or inadequacy of aggregate demand in the economy.

Operational Efficiency in Resource Use

Maximum efficiency in the use of resources requires the attainment of three conditions:

1. Attainment by all producers of least cost combinations, that is, the best combinations of factors, given their prices and the technological constraints. At the least cost combination, the marginal rates of substitution between each set of factors will equal the ratios of the prices of the factors.

2. Operation of the firms at the lowest long-run average cost.

3. Provision of maximum incentive for developing and introducing new techniques.

While the private sector is presumed to be less deficient, on the whole, in attaining optimal efficiency than in attaining optimal allocation of resources, nevertheless in several situations governments may be more effective.

Avoidance of Collection Costs. Private enterprise must collect prices from the purchasers of the goods. While typically these costs are minor elements in overall costs, they may be substantial, as, for example, the costs of collecting tolls for use of roads or admission charges for parks; costs may not only be high relative to potential revenues but may also be a source of delay and nuisance to the users.

Governments have the alternative of financing by taxes, which are typically cheaper to collect than tolls or charges.

Long-Range Capital Investment. For some types of production, very long-term capital investment may allow greater efficiency in resource use, yet, because of risk considerations, may extend beyond the horizon that private enterprise regards as feasible. Long-range projects may be subject to risk of several years of losses immediately after construction. Risk to society is frequently less than risk to individuals. Revenues are available from other sources to avoid bankruptcy in periods of loss; time horizons are not limited to the prospective lifetimes of particular persons; governments can take measures to avoid loss of business if necessary to protect the return on the investment. Examples of long-range investments potentially appropriate for government include hydroelectric power and irrigation projects, urban water supplies, and transport facilities. Several of these services offer partial externalities (indirect benefits) as well, to provide further justification for governmental activity.

Organization of Production. While the profit motive gives strong incentive to maximize efficiency, it may not be fully effective. Particular firms in monopoly or semimonopoly situations may fall into routine patterns, failing to make most efficient use of resources, and, particularly, failing to introduce new methods and techniques. In developing economies, entrepreneurship is often inadequate; despite good opportunities for profit, no one takes advantage of them. Under such circumstances governments may provide initiative and improved organization of factor use.

The requirement for maximum efficiency of operation at lowest average cost may not be attained when entry is relatively free into an industry and too many firms enter to allow any to operate at the point of lowest cost.[2] In some industries individual firms may be so small that organized research activity is impossible and technological developments lag.[3]

Full Employment and Economic Growth

Failure to obtain full utilization of factor units obviously reduces total output below potential levels and accordingly lowers per capita real income and the path of actual economic growth. At the same time, by altering relative factor prices, unemployment distorts resource

---

[2]Garbage collection in some cities is an example.

[3]Thus the federal government undertook research in agriculture because individual farm operations were too small to make research possible or directly advantageous.

allocation and reduces efficiency in factor combinations. Finally, unemployment of factor units alters distributional patterns from those regarded as acceptable, as the unemployed suffer drastic reductions in living standards.

Unemployment may be general (often called "Keynesian") or structural. The former is a reflection of inadequate total demand in the economy; total spending lags behind total output at full employment and the economy therefore stabilizes at less than full employment. While, theoretically, adequate wage and other factor price reductions should restore full employment, institutional restrictions often prevent changes of the magnitudes that would be required. Structural unemployment, on the other hand, reflects imperfect adaptation of labor of various types to needs; certain skills are no longer required, and persons lack the means or the initiative to train for other occupations or to move to other areas. The wage level that would be necessary to allow reemployment in jobs requiring little or no skill would be so low as to be intolerable to the persons and to society.

With unemployment, the real cost to the economy of additional economic activity is less than that to the firm undertaking it, since the factor units would otherwise be idle. The provision of employment not only removes from society the need for supporting the unemployed by relief or other means but also, by increasing aggregate demand, leads to still further increases in output and employment. The business firm, however, cannot realize financially from these benefits, which are essentially externalities. Governments therefore undertake measures to eliminate unemployment and realize for society the externality benefits.

Given full employment and the available resources and population, the rate of economic growth is dependent upon the rate of capital formation, introduction of new technology, and improvements in the levels of education. Capital formation is limited by the amount of savings at full employment. While the optimum rate of economic growth cannot be defined objectively, a society may regard the current rate as inadequate—perhaps by comparison with other countries—and seek deliberately to increase it. In allocating their incomes between consumption and savings, persons are influenced by their own immediate situation, with uncertainty about the future and the horizon of a limited lifetime. As a consequence, the total rate of savings may restrict the rate of growth more than persons would prefer in terms of their concern for future levels of total output and the interests of future generations. Yet no one person by his own action can increase the overall rate of capital formation; in this instance again, externalities are significant.

Therefore persons will support action by society to increase overall savings and capital formation. Governments may also seek to speed growth by other means, such as by preventing labor unions or other groups from restricting the introduction of new techniques, by providing assistance for research, and by increasing expenditures on education over the levels that might otherwise be regarded as optimal.

The Pattern of Income Distribution

The pattern of income distribution that develops in a market economy, dependent upon the prices paid for the various types of factors and the relative amounts of factor units owned by various families, may be regarded by society as inequitable. There is no scientific way of defining an "optimal" income distribution since the question is an ethical one, involving value judgments about what is "fair" and "just." Even if an economy were characterized by completely perfect competition in all respects, the resulting pattern of income distribution would not necessarily be judged optimal. Optimality can be defined only in terms of consensus in a particular society. There appears to be widespread acceptance of the view that the market economy produces a degree of inequality of income that is excessive, a few persons having far more income and wealth than are required for any reasonable living standard while others are at bare starvation levels.

In summary, governmental activities are conveniently grouped into four classes:

1. Allocational: ones that increase or decrease the allocation of resources to the production of various goods, particularly public goods and ones offering major externalities. These activities alter the overall mix of gross national product.

2. Efficiency: those increasing total output from given resources by more efficient use.

3. Stabilization and growth: those reducing economic instability and unemployment and increasing the potential and actual rates of economic growth.

4. Distributional: those altering the pattern of distribution of real income.

NATURE OF GOVERNMENTAL ACTIVITY

Intervention of government in the economy takes a number of forms. The government may undertake the conduct of production, either of the final product alone or of intermediate goods as well. Alternatively, governments may influence private economic activity by subsidies or taxes, or they may exercise direct control over behavior in the private sector. Governments may deliberately alter their total spending and taxation to influence the level of national income. Finally, governments may transfer purchasing power from some persons to others.

Governmental Conduct of Production

If public goods such as national defense are to be provided, they must be supplied by government, since by their inherent character they cannot be produced and sold on a profit-making basis by private enterprise. The governmental participation may vary in depth. A government can simply contract with a business firm to produce a service and provide it free of charge to the public, but this is virtually never done; mercenary armies and "farming out" of tax collections in past centuries are the closest examples. Requirement of close adaptation of the nature of the service to the wishes of society necessitates actual conduct of production by governmental units. On the other hand, the government does not usually produce the intermediate goods—the planes and tanks and supplies, for example, that are used in the provision of the services. Many of these are bought from firms also producing for the private sector; they can produce the goods more economically than the government.

Governments may also undertake the production of goods with significant externalities in order to adapt the service to the preferences of society, although other alternatives are feasible. Note education as an example. By subsidies to private firms and grants to lower income families, governments could bring about an increase in the amount produced without actually operating schools. But in order to adapt the nature and quality of education to meet community goals, governments produce the services directly, although allowing private enterprise to provide them as well for persons who prefer the private product. Governments may likewise undertake production when other devices to avoid evils of monopoly prove unsatisfactory.

Governmental conduct of production may also be undertaken for efficiency reasons: to avoid collection costs, to obtain advantages of longer term investments, or to attain economies of large scale operation.

The Subsidy Approach

An alternative to governmental production is subsidization of private producers to induce them to increase output or to undertake investments that they would not otherwise make. Thus private schools could be subsidized to provide additional education at prices less than those equal to marginal cost; private power companies could be subsidized to compensate for the additional risk of long-range investments; early railroad building in the United States was fostered by grants of land. Subsidies might also be used to increase investment to lessen unemployment or to lower output when carried beyond the optimal figure.

While acceptable in certain instances, the subsidy approach brings inevitable conflict of interest between the government on the one hand and the firm and consumers on the other because of the differences in their goals. Close supervision is required to insure that the subsidies are having the desired effect,[4] and the firms might have undertaken the action without compensation. Outright bribery may be difficult to prevent.

The Control Approach

For some purposes, direct control of private sector activity, with no governmental production except the limited amount involved in administration of the regulatory rules, is a satisfactory solution. Activity that gives rise to significant external costs, such as river pollution, may be subjected to controls, such as requirements for adequate waste disposal. Zoning ordinances are designed to prevent external diseconomies arising from adverse effects upon owners of surrounding property of the location of certain activities: a pulp and paper mill in a residential area, for example. Monopoly may be broken up by antitrust legislation, or monopoly firms may be subjected to detailed regulation of rates and service. This form of regulation creates a continuous clash of interest between government and the firms.

Conversely when an activity gives rise to external diseconomies to society, that is, costs that the producers do not pay, a tax on the output of the firms reflecting the external costs may be an effective means of reducing output to optimal levels. This technique is used with liquor.

Aggregate Spending

Prevention of unemployment and attainment of the potential rate of economic growth or prevention of inflation may require fiscal and monetary policy that influence aggregate demand in the economy.

[4] The subsidies provided under the federal agricultural price support program illustrate the problems.

To eliminate unemployment the government may raise its level of spending and the scope of its activities beyond levels warranted by other considerations or may reduce taxes below otherwise optimal levels. The additional spending may involve more production activity or increased welfare payments designed to raise aggregate demand by increasing the spending of the recipients.

Transfer Payments

In part governments seek to bring the pattern of real income distribution more closely in line with that desired by contemporary society by providing goods and services, such as education and parks, free of charge, and by various types of transfer payments. These may be granted for specific uses, as, for example, scholarships to universities. Primarily, however, general transfer payments are made without specification of use, on the basis of the income status of the recipients in conjunction with various criteria of needs. Examples include old-age pensions, aid for dependent children, direct relief, or negative income tax, that is, payment of cash amounts to persons with incomes less than the income tax exemption figures. This method gives the recipients maximum freedom and simplifies the tasks of the government, but it does not insure use of the money for purposes that will lessen the future dependence of the recipients upon transfer payments. While insistence that aid be used for retraining instead of buying liquor may interfere with freedom of choice of the lower income groups, the latter use is unlikely to enable the persons to become self-supporting.

Governments also influence the patterns of distribution of income by the nature of the tax structure; the more progressive the structure, that is, the greater the increase in tax liability as income or wealth increases, the more equal will be the after-tax distribution.

CHARACTERISTICS OF THE GOVERNMENTAL SECTOR

Governmental conduct of economic activity differs from private enterprise in several major ways. First, the price mechanism, the guiding force in the private sector, cannot be used by governments as a guide for most of their activities and is not necessarily used even when it can be. Public goods cannot be sold; stabilization and distributional activities create no "product"; goods yielding externalities cannot be sold for prices covering all costs or the benefits of governmental production will be lost; goods produced by government to avoid collection costs cannot be sold. Thus prices can be used as the complete source of financing only for those goods whose production has been taken over for efficiency reasons other than avoiding collection costs. They can be used as partial sources for goods yielding both direct benefits and externalities.

Restrictions on the use of the price mechanism bars from governmental use, for most activities, the automatic guide to output and investment that operates in the private sector of the economy. With the price mechanism, output can be adjusted to the amount customers are buying at the existing price. Governments must find a substitute in the form of collective decision making based upon community preferences; that is, they must develop some means of estimating society's preferences for public goods for those goods yielding partial externalities and for others that are not sold.

Inability to use the price mechanism, coupled with the lack of competition and the absence of the profit motive, removes a major pressure toward attainment of optimal efficiency that influences private business firms. Other pressures give some incentive toward efficiency, particularly the desire to hold taxes as low as possible for a given level of governmental services. Nevertheless, ascertainment of optimum efficiency is more difficult without the automatic guide of the marketplace.

Governments differ in one other major respect: their ability to use coercion to attain their goals, a privilege that private enterprise lacks. Coercion is an inevitable concomitant of governmental activity: the power to require persons to change their behavior, to make contributions toward the support of governmental activities, and even in some instances to provide factor units, either without full compensation (the draft) or with it (condemnation of land). Wishes of society imply various rules relating to coercive power for equity reasons; thus taxes are established on the basis of standards that appear to be equitable, and, in a democracy, maintenance of as much individual freedom as possible and minimization of direct restraint are regarded as important goals in themselves.

Governments also have one other power that the private sector lacks: the ability to create money to meet expenses. In this instance also, preferences of society dictate restrictions on the use of the power.

POTENTIALITIES AND REALITIES

Governments can bring the functioning of the economy more closely into conformity with the wishes of society if certain conditions are met.

First, the government must be able to ascertain the preference schedules and to reconcile individual differences by use of criteria that society sanctions. In other words, the government must know what society wants.

Second, various elements in the preferences of society must be mutually consistent. If society seeks (1) full employment and (2) a balanced budget at all times, government may not be able to provide both; full employment may be attainable only if the government operates at a deficit. Inconsistency in objectives is often a product of inadequate knowledge.

Third, governments must be able to ascertain and employ those policies that will allow closest fulfillment of the overall preferences of society and society must permit the government to do so. This condition requires adequate knowledge on the part of the government of the effects of various alternative policies: the relative effects upon labor supply or investment, for example, of income and sales taxes. The condition also requires that the government implement the policy with maximum efficiency.

These conditions are never fulfilled in their entirety. Complete knowledge of preference schedules is impossible, and technical difficulties noted in Chapter 2 affect their summation. Power groups may gain sufficient influence to prevent governments from following policies that maximize attainment of the goals. Key officials may determine policies in terms of their own attitudes without regard to the interests of society, even if this proves to be suicidal politically.

Society may demand fulfillment of inconsistent goals or require the use of methods that will not permit attainment of the goals. The effects of many policies are not fully known (For example, do income taxes reduce incentives significantly?) Ascertainment of optimal policies may be particularly difficult when human reactions are involved, especially the reactions of persons in other countries. A country may seek to defeat a hostile country without bringing into the conflict other and more powerful countries. In order to attain victory it may blockade the coast of the enemy with the assumption that other countries will not enter the fight—but this proves to be wrong.

A basic problem of governmental intervention in economic activity is the danger that when the economy suffers from a number of deviations from the optimum and various constraints prevent the elimination of all of them, elimination of some may result in a shift away from, rather than toward, the optimal situation. This possibility is an application of the Theory of the Second Best.[5] For example, suppose that a country is using several excise taxes that are having distorting effects on the economy. Replacement by a general sales tax or general income tax would avoid these distorting effects. But replacement of some of the excises by an income tax while others are retained—necessary, perhaps, because of the impossibility of administering high-rate sales or income taxes—could easily aggravate the situation; adding additional excises and moving closer to a general tax might be preferable to partial elimination. Determination of the best adjustments under such circumstances is particularly difficult, since necessary empirical data to permit ascertainment of the best kinds of changes are frequently lacking.

As a consequence of these various problems and dangers, governmental activity is not likely to bring about optimal fulfillment of preferences; it might even move the economy farther away from fulfillment. Governments offer opportunities for better attainment of the goals of society, but they are also capable of doing great harm.

Two major questions relating to the determination of optimal programs of governmental activity must next be explored. The first includes the nature of individual preferences for the output of the governmental sector, the way in which these preferences are ascertained by governments, and the problem of reconciliation of conflicting desires. The second relates to the procedures used by governments in determining actual levels of expenditures for various activities, and particularly the measurement of benefits and costs.

REFERENCES

BAUMOL, W. J. *Welfare Economics and the Theory of the State*. 2d ed. Cambridge, Mass.: Harvard University Press, 1965.
   A review of recent welfare theory as it affects the theory of government activity, and detailed analysis of externalities.

HEAD, J. G. "The Welfare Foundations of Public Finance." *Revista di Diritto Finanziario e Scienza delle Finanze*, Vol. XIX (May, 1965), pp. 3–52.

MCKEAN, ROLAND N. *Public Spending*, chap. v. New York: McGraw-Hill, 1968.

MUSGRAVE, R. A. *The Theory of Public Finance*, chaps. i, iii. New York: McGraw-Hill, 1959.

PIGOU, A. C. *A Study in Public Finance*, Part I. 3d ed. London: Macmillan, 1947.
   The neoclassical statement of government activities.

[5] R. G. Lipsey and K. Lancaster, "The General Theory of Second Best," *Review of Economic Studies*, Vol. XXIV, No. 1 (1956), pp. 11–32.

SAMUELSON, PAUL M. "The Pure Theory of Public Expenditure," *Review of Economics and Statistics,* Vol. XXXVI (November, 1954), pp. 387–89.
The basis of the contemporary approach to expenditure theory.
———. "Aspects of Public Expenditure Theories," *Review of Economics and Statistics,* Vol. XL (November, 1958), pp. 332–38.

| *Chapter* | INDIVIDUAL PREFERENCES |
| 2 | AND PUBLIC GOODS[1] |

The justification for governmental provision of goods and governmental redistributive activities is, in a democratic society, the desire of individuals for such goods and activities, rather than an authoritarian determination that such action is desirable in the interests of society. While individual preferences for public goods are greatly influenced by government as an organization of society, they constitute the ultimate source of justification for governmental activities. Accordingly, the basic decisions concerning production of public goods and output levels must reflect, in a democratic society, the preference patterns of the people of the society, if the goals in such a society are to be fulfilled.

Decision making in the governmental sector differs significantly from decision making for private-sector output, since collectively produced goods are not produced with a profit-making motive nor are they sold in a market to individuals "buying" particular quantities for their own exclusive use. Collective decision making gives rise to three major questions:

1. How does the individual arrive at his opinions about governmentally produced goods, and governmental action to redistribute income?

2. What system is accepted for reconciling the conflicting desires of various individuals in the society?

3. How effectively are the desires of individuals reflected in governmental decision making?

We shall assume that individuals as citizen-voters, as representatives of voters, as government executives, as "bureaucrats" are motivated by the desire to fulfill optimally their own preference schedules. These reflect self-interest in large measure, but also concern for the welfare of others, for particular activities of government per se, and

[1]This chapter has been influenced by the work of J. M. Buchanan and Anthony Downs. Many of the conclusions, however, differ.

for society. This behavioral assumption would appear more realistic than the alternate, that all persons in their capacities relating to government are motivated by the interests of society as a whole, whereas in other aspects of their life they are primarily motivated strictly by self-interest. Individuals in the governmental sector, while seeking to satisfy their own preferences, are subject to serious constraints by the need to bargain with others and the desire to obtain the favor of superiors, retain their positions, or be reelected. Thus their ability to act as they wish is greatly restricted.

INDIVIDUAL EVALUATION IN THE REALM OF PUBLIC GOODS[2]

An individual is confronted with a range of possible public programs, with various possible levels of activity and various possible "prices" in the form of taxes that he must pay if the respective programs and levels are provided. The quantity that he prefers to have supplied depends on several elements: his preference schedules, his income, and the "prices," in the form of higher taxes, that he must pay for public services. Before these determinants are analyzed, reference to the differences between consumer decision making in the public and private sectors is necessary.

Differences from Consumer Decision Making for Private-Sector Output

Individual decision making for public-sector output differs in several significant ways from decision making for private-sector output:

Inability To Control the Amount Purchased. A person decides upon the amount of a private good he wishes at the prevailing price and buys it. This he cannot do with a public good. The output of a public good and the tax price of this output are decided by government on the basis of overall preferences.

Nature and Knowledge of Benefits. Individual goods can be "wrapped up and taken home"; they are consumed individually and exclusively by an individual, who therefore is aware of the strength of his preference. Strictly public goods are consumed collectively; the benefits, indivisible in nature, accrue to persons of the community as a group. Accordingly the individual may not realize that he benefits at

---

[2]One of the few studies of this question is that of J. M. Buchanan, *Public Finance in Democratic Process* (Chapel Hill, N.C.: University of North Carolina Press, 1966). See also Roland McKean, *Government Spending* (New York: McGraw-Hill, 1968).

all, yet if the activity were not carried on, he might be worse off (or better off). A person may be unaware of public health measures designed to eliminate malaria, yet if the activity were not undertaken he and his family would be ill.

Uncertainty. There is an unusually high degree of uncertainty associated with public goods. A person may be highly uncertain about their benefits—the gain from additional spending on national defense, for example. He is also uncertain about the consequences of his own action for the actual determination of the level of government activity, and about the actual tax price he will pay, that is, his share of the cost of the additional activities. Will taxes be raised or not? If so, what form will the increase take? Even if the answers to these questions are known, the person is often uncertain about his share of particular taxes, particularly with the corporate income tax (the distributional effects of which are not clear even to experts in the field) and progressive income taxes.

Finally, a person is uncertain about his ability to escape the tax by altering his activities (earning less or altering consumption patterns, for example) and the extent to which the "tax price" will be affected by the changes in activity by other persons. If a tax is levied on a certain commodity and purchases decline by 50 percent, a given level of government spending will require a doubling of the tax rate (which in turn will curtail purchases still more).

Community Interest Motivation. The self-interest assumption does not preclude consideration of the interests of others either in the purchase of individual goods or in decision making for public goods. In the former, people do consider to some extent the welfare of others: they are encouraged to paint their houses because the neighbors appreciate it, and they contribute to private charity. In decision making relating to public goods, broader motives have greater significance. Individuals become concerned about the welfare of Indians or the preservation of forests, although they have no expectation of seeing an Indian or enjoying the forest preserves. Many attach substantial weight to the interests of future generations.

Mixture of Allocation and Distributional Activities. The provision of most governmental services of an allocational nature, those that increase outputs of certain goods relative to others, has distributional implications as well; given the nature of the tax structure, a net redistribution of real income results. Education, which conveys direct benefits to the recipients as well as "public" benefits to society as a whole, conveys particular benefits to lower income families but may be financed primarily by higher income groups. Thus individual preference schedules for the service are influenced by attitudes toward the redistributional consequences.

Individual Preferences for Public Goods

Individual preferences for public goods are influenced by a number of forces:

Tastes. Individual preference schedules for public goods are influenced in part by the same forces that affect the demand for private goods. Individual preferences vary; to some persons education is important, to others, resource conservation. Since many public goods convey some direct benefit to individuals as well as indivisible public benefit, those persons receiving the greatest direct gains will have greater preferences, other things equal. Thus families with several children to educate in public schools will have greater preference for education expenditures than childless couples or those preferring to send their children to private school. Some persons have high preference for paying taxes to maintain national parks, while others prefer spending their incomes at luxurious Caribbean resorts.

Information. Since the benefits do not accrue separately to individuals, externally obtained information is necessary if the individuals are to have meaningful preference schedules. If the person has no knowledge whatever of the benefits of a particular government service, he can scarcely have a demand for it, and he will therefore take no action on the proposal or will oppose any change because he knows nothing of the situation. For rational action he must have information about costs and their distribution. For most persons optimal allocation of time and money dictates against scientific endeavor to obtain information necessary for a rational position on many issues relating to governmental activities. To the extent that the person does reach a position, he usually relies upon information readily available from the newspapers and similar sources, which may be neither accurate nor unbiased and will almost certainly flow in part from governmental news releases. A government inevitably seeks to defend the position it wishes to take and to provide information that will support the position.

There are several consequences of this information gap. Individuals frequently do not have opinions on various issues of governmental activity, and therefore the small group that does is in a position to dominate policy making. Secondly, persons in higher income groups are in a better position to gain information and are likely to have more influence on governmental policy than those in lower income groups. Thirdly, many opinions are formed upon meager and biased information: a chance newspaper headline, a comment made by a person who knows even less about the activity.

Degree of Uncertainty. Preferences are affected by the certainty of the consequences of governmental activities on both benefit and cost sides. All the information a person can gather may not lead to a conclusion to which he attaches a high degree of certainty. National defense provides an excellent example, since optimal policies depend upon unpredictable actions of other countries. Similarly a person may be uncertain about distribution of burden of a particular tax and thus his own share of the costs of the governmental services. A person's share of any tax will depend in part upon the reactions of other persons to the tax; if they reduce their own tax liability by altering their behavior, the person will bear more of the cost. These reactions may be difficult to predict.

In general, the more certain a person is about the attainment of benefits from government, the greater will be his preference at any particular tax price. His preference, however, is also affected by his estimates of the relative possibilities of the benefits being more or less than anticipated. With national defense the possibility that the benefits may be much greater than expected (in the event of attack which, while not expected, may occur), leads persons to favor higher levels of the service than otherwise.

Uncertainty about tax prices has similar effects. If a person fears that there is greater chance that the tax cost to him will exceed the anticipated figure than be lower, he will prefer less of the service than he otherwise would.

Philosophy of Government. Many persons have strong biases in favor of or against governmental activity generally; in terms of Gilbert and Sullivan, everyone is born a little liberal or a little conservative. More seriously, many persons develop "liberal" or "conservative" biases as a result of environmental influences. One is inherently biased in favor of governmental activity of any kind, the other against it.[3] There is a correlation between income, wealth, and occupational activity and bias; conservatism is typically found in higher income business and

---

[3] With the exception, in some countries, including the United States that the persons generally unsympathetic to governmental activity favor high defense spending, and the ones sympathetic to government prefer lower levels of defense activity. There are, of course, exceptions. The wealthy are in a sense seeking to insure preservation of their wealth.

professional groups. There are of course exceptions, and many persons in these groups strongly favor certain specific governmental activities.

Emotional Reactions. Persons are conscious of the reactions of others to their attitudes on certain types of governmental activities and their decision making relative to these activities is influenced thereby. National defense provides the most significant example. Few persons like to feel that they are open to the charge of neglecting national security, of failing to support their country, of appearing to be cowards—even if they do not reveal their preferences to others. Thus they can easily be led to support governmental activities that on the basis of more logical reasoning they might oppose. The argument that any difference of opinion favors the "enemy" and the charges of appeasement play a significant role in individual decision making in this sphere.

Another example relates to morality; no politician likes to appear to be on the side of sin and against home, motherhood, and thrift. Thus measures to enforce customary standards of morality may enjoy more support than measures to promote the use of birth control among lower income families, even though the need for the latter is widely recognized and the former are not taken very seriously. A well-organized group may succeed in carrying through a program that a majority of the persons actually do not support but are reluctant to oppose publicly. The establishment of prohibition in the United States was an example.

Income Elasticity of Demand for Public Goods

Income elasticity of demand for public goods, that is, the relationship between persons' incomes and their demands for public goods, may be positive or negative. As incomes rise, many persons will feel that they can afford more governmental services just as they can afford more consumer durables and expensive steaks and they may wish higher standards of such services—better schools, varied curricula. For public goods regarded as inferior the reverse will be true; as incomes rise, some persons will shift from public schools to private, from public parks to expensive resorts. Many persons become increasingly less sympathetic toward growth in governmental activity generally as they move into higher income levels, the "conservative bias" of the wealthy exercising greater influence on their behavior and reducing income elasticity of demand.

Closely related is the interdependence of demand for private and public goods. Relationships may be complementary; as more families have cars, their relative preferences for highways and national parks will increase. Others are of a substitute nature, particularly demands for governmental services that convey individual as well as community benefits. Thus increased availability or lower charges for private swimming pools will lessen preference for public pools.

The Relationship of the Cost of the Services and Quantity Demanded

Given a person's preference schedules, income, and the prices of other goods, the amount of the particular service that he wishes produced is a function of the "tax price" that he must pay for it; the lower the tax price, the greater the quantity he will prefer. This conclusion follows, as with private-sector output, from the assumptions of (1) the Law of Diminishing Marginal Rate of Substitution, (2) given incomes,[4] (3) goal of maximizing satisfaction from income, (4) ability of a person to rank various forms of public goods and levels of output on the basis of his preference. Under these assumptions, at each tax price for each public good the person will seek the provision of the quantity such that marginal net gain is zero; output of the service is extended to the level at which marginal gains and marginal costs (in the form of additional taxes) are equal.

The actual "tax price," given the tax structure, is affected by the ability of the person to escape the tax, legally or illegally. For example, if a person is willing to stop purchasing the article that is taxed to finance the service or does not use it at all, his demand for the service will be greater than if he is not able or willing to avoid the tax. Similarly the convenience of the tax and the person's attitude toward its desirability, or toward the tax system as a whole if the service is not related to a particular tax, influence his demand.

Another significant aspect is the question of financing from a new tax or a tax increase, from growing revenue from existing levies, or from curtailment of other spending. Persons are much more willing, on the average—as borne out by empirical evidence—to support additional activities that can be financed without tax increases than ones requiring increases, even though, with the former, if the service were not increased, they could benefit from tax reduction or increases in other services. This is an aspect of the "threshold" or "displacement" phenomenon in taxation.[5] Persons become accustomed to certain tax levels

---

[4] The possibility that public spending may increase income is considered elsewhere.
[5] See A. T. Peacock and J. Wiseman, *The Growth of Public Expenditures in the United Kingdom* (Princeton, N.J.: Princeton University Press, 1961).

and will oppose increases in governmental services that require passage across the threshold. Only when shocked by some drastic event such as a major war or a severe and prolonged financial crisis will a country be able to pass the tax threshold. But once it has done so, a new tax plateau is reached, persons become accustomed to a higher level, and there is little pressure to move back below the original threshold. Thus World War II brought drastic changes in United States federal income tax rates and exemptions that would have been inconceivable before; the new threshold was obviously much higher after the war than before. The financial emergencies of the depression years of the thirties were responsible for establishing the sales tax in state finance in the United States and raising the tax potential significantly.

A final consideration is the taxpayers' attitude toward a balanced budget, when the alternative to a tax increase to finance additional services is governmental borrowing or money creation. Persons wish governmental services and dislike taxes. If there is widespread acceptance of the doctrine that expenditures can be increased freely without taxation, the quantity of governmental services sought will be greater. With full employment the governmental services will be responsible for costs in the sense of reduction in the quantity of resources available for private-sector output, whether taxes are used or not. If persons do not realize this and have no aversion to borrowing or money creation, the quantity of governmental services demanded will be greater than otherwise. In this situation there is a substantial difference between the actual cost of the services and the one anticipated. The principle of the balanced budget is widely ingrained, partly for good reason based on experience of the past, partly by analogy from individual to government, partly by sheer dogma. This attitude serves as a strong restraining influence on pressures for governmental services.

Some Consequences of the Nature of Public Goods Decision Making

The peculiarities of individual decision making relative to public goods and the influences on such decision making have several major consequences that affect allocation of resources to the public sector.

Lack of a Clearly Defined Demand Schedule. The demand schedules for private-sector outputs and for governmentally produced goods sold to the users are clearly defined and directly affect the decisions about output of the goods. Since persons do not buy and privately consume public goods, their demand schedules for them are not so clearly defined and some means must be found to ascertain them and to resolve conflicts. Varying desires for individual goods require no reconciliation; individuals adjust their purchases to the quantities they desire and production adjusts accordingly. But since public goods output must be determined in a single decision with a single quantity made available to society, conflicting desires among individuals must be resolved.

Inability of Individuals to Reach an Optimal Position. Since public goods are indivisible, individuals cannot obtain an optimal adjustment unless their particular preferences are identical with the collective decisions. An individual expresses his demand in accordance with his preference and the tax cost, but this may differ from the overall decision. If his preference does not agree with the collective decision, there is no adjustment that he can make that will improve his position. A person seeks, for example, zero spending on national defense and conservation of natural resources, regardless of the tax price. The community as a whole desires a substantial amount of each and these amounts are produced. The person's preference is not fulfilled and he cannot adjust to reach his optimum. By the indivisible nature of governmental services, amounts cannot be adjusted to each individual's wants, as can the production of bread. Nor can the government bargain individually with each person to determine the amount he wishes and is willing to pay for. Not only would this task require excessive time and resources but individuals would not reveal their actual preferences if their tax payments depended upon them.[6]

Tendency to Let Others Make Decisions. An individual typically realizes that his participation in the decision-making process is not likely to influence the outcome, and that decisions will be made about public goods whether he acts or not. Participation requires time and effort. There is therefore a tendency to take no part in collective decision making. Persons prefer to delegate the task of decision making to others, and many even abstain from voting to choose the representatives who will make the decisions. Or, if they do participate, partly because of a feeling of obligation to make democracy function and partly because of pressures applied on them (it is your patriotic duty to vote), they do so in only a perfunctory fashion, choosing among candidates on the basis of general ideology rather than on any real understanding of the issues. One consequence is that small interested groups exercise primary influence in decision making.

Attempts to Influence Preferences. A closely related consequence

---

[6]This approach is the basis of Lindahl's theory of government decision making.

is the effort exerted by interest groups or by those to whom decision making is delegated to influence the preferences of the minimal-interest public. Governments do so to justify the policies they are carrying out or for which they seek approval—policies which the government officials either believe will best serve their own interests or which they sincerely believe will benefit society as a whole and would be supported by individuals if they had adequate information.

Relative Attractiveness of Individual and Public Goods. Certain general biases may favor private over public goods. First, as noted, public goods cannot be taken home and the benefits enjoyed separately and directly; many people undoubtedly tend to favor those that can. Second, the greater uncertainty that characterizes both the anticipated benefits from public goods and the distribution of their costs is a discouraging factor. Third, the extensive advertising of private-sector output in the modern economy may reduce relative preferences for public goods; certainly in dollar magnitude private-sector advertising exceeds propagandizing in support of governmental activities.[7]

On the other hand, distributional considerations are never entirely absent with public goods; persons will favor production of public goods expected to benefit themselves while other persons pay for them.

Disproportionate Influence of the Higher Income Groups. While in theory all persons are equal in a democracy for purposes of collective decision making, in practice their influence is not equal, the higher income groups exercising a disproportionate share. There are at least three reasons. The wealthy are in a much better position to acquire information about governmental activities and to participate in government. Secondly, because of their knowledge and stake in the protection of property, they are likely to have stronger desires for certain types of governmental services, and their biases toward governmental activity generally, although often adverse, may be stronger. Thirdly, they are in a position to buy influence; while votes cannot legally be bought and sold, persons contributing substantial amounts of money to political groups are in a position to receive favors in return.

RECONCILIATION OF CONFLICTING PREFERENCES

In the market sector of the economy, no problem of reconciliation of varying preferences arises; effective demands are summed by the market and production adjusts accordingly. With public goods, sum-

---

[7]This is the basic element in J. K. Galbraith's argument that governments spend too little. See *The Affluent Society* (Boston: Houghton Mifflin, 1960).

mation does not occur automatically since the amounts to be produced must be determined in a single nonmarket decision. So long as preference patterns are identical, there is no difficulty. If everyone in the community believes that at given costs the city should have five fire engines, the appropriate decision is obvious. But if some believe that the city should have two and others believe it should have ten, resolution of the conflict is necessary, because a single decision about the number must be made: the city cannot have two for the persons who prefer only two, and ten for the persons who prefer ten. Various techniques may be employed.

The Unanimity Rule

At one extreme, the unanimity or complete consensus rule could be employed: only those actions relating to output of public goods on which there is complete agreement can justifiably be undertaken. This rule is closely related to the Pareto criterion of economic welfare explained in Chapter 1: a change increases economic welfare only if one person is benefited without anyone suffering loss. Given rational behavior, any change in the output of public goods benefiting one or more persons and injuring no one will receive unanimous support, whereas changes not meeting this requirement will not. This rule, first developed and defended by the Swedish economist Wicksell,[8] avoids what may be called the "external cost" of change, that is, injury to persons who do not wish the change, and provides maximum protection of minority interests.

The proposal is not so rigid and extreme as it may appear, since various persons with divergent views will seek to compromise to obtain a solution acceptable to all. Since the group is confronted with a variety of issues relating to governmental activities, vote trading and compromise are feasible. Some persons will concede on certain issues to obtain approval of other persons on measures that they favor. Committees and small groups, so long as they are not segmented along ideological or representative-party lines, reach unanimity on most issues, even if there are substantial differences in preferences.[9]

---

[8]See Knut Wicksell, "A New Principle of Just Taxation," in R. A. Musgrave and A. T. Peacock (eds.), *Classics in the Theory of Public Finance,* (London: Macmillan, 1958), pp. 72–118 (article originally published in German in 1896).

[9]Even though members may have differing preferences, committees frequently reach unanimous decisions. In addition to the implicit "logrolling" consideration, committee members also seek to minimize the amount of time spent in reaching decisions and to present a united front to the larger group or higher authority, to increase the likelihood of acceptance of their decisions.

As a general rule for decision making on governmental activities, however, the unanimity rule is unacceptable, and in fact is never employed for this purpose. With modern complex governments involved in a wide range of activites, the time and effort that would be required to obtain unanimity through compromise and bargaining would be intolerable, even if actual decisions were made by a small representative group.

The unanimity rule gives small minority groups tremendous bargaining power to block change unless they receive concessions that are intolerable to the majority. Thus inertia—doing nothing, changing nothing—is tremendously favored. If literally complete unanimity is required, one person could block the change—and there exists in any society a fringe of fanatics whose behavior, in terms of the desires of society as a whole, is irrational. A government wishes to build a dam yielding great benefits to large numbers of persons, but requiring one hermit to move out of his shack. Uninterested in money, he will not move if he is offered $10 million for property worth $100 in the market. Under the unanimity doctrine and the strict Pareto rule the government is not justified in proceeding with the dam. Clearly, society will not tolerate such dictatorship by the minority; the unanimity rule must give way.

Finally, the rule is unworkable for purely distributional (welfare) functions of government, since these, by their nature, involve transfer of wealth from some persons to others.

Majority Decision Making

Modern democratic society accepts the rule that conflicting preferences must be resolved by the rule of majority vote, with each adult vote counted equally. Acceptance of this rule involves, of course, a value judgment, but a judgment that is accepted in most societies in the world today. The rule is workable and does not favor inertia or block the interests of the many to protect the few. It presumably serves the interests of the largest number in society, but the claim cannot be made that it maximizes economic welfare, since benefits received and injuries suffered by various individuals cannot be compared.

The majority rule is not, however, so simple in its operation or so obviously desirable in its results as may first appear. There are several limitations.

1. Order of Presentation. Where several choices are possible, as is true for levels of various government activities, the sequence of presentation of alternatives is significant for the outcome. If persons

are asked to select from a wide range, no figure will obtain a majority if preferences are widely dispersed. If under these conditions persons are asked to act on successive alternatives, a majority may be obtained for one even though another alternative would have received still stronger support. But practical considerations prevent the presentation of all possible alternatives, and the order of presentation determines the alternative that will first attain a majority support.

2. The Arrow Problem. The work of Kenneth Arrow[10] has called attention to a phenomenon now known as the Arrow problem; when persons are confronted with several alternatives and their preferences are not ranked in the same order, there may be no rational majority position. To any alternative policy, there are other alternatives that are preferred by a majority. Let us consider a simple example. There are three voters, A, B, and C. Their preference schedules for the number of fire engines the town should acquire are as follows:

| Choice | Voter | | |
	A	B	C
First..................	1	2	3
Second.................	2	3	1
Third..................	3	1	2

Examination of the table indicates that there is no majority choice; there is a majority against each of the three. If the three are voted on in pairs, (1) will win over (2), (2) will win over (3), and (3) will win over (1) even though (1) is preferred to (2) and (2) is preferred to (3). No rational ordering is possible. If the voters decide that some decision must be made, and that the winner of the last pair of alternatives presented shall be chosen, the outcome will depend on the sequence of presentation. If (1) and (2) are voted on first, (1) will win; if the winner, (1), is then voted on against (3), (3) will win. But if (2) and (3) are voted on first, (2) will win, and the vote between (2) and (1) will be carried by (1). The result is purely arbitrary. The source of the trouble is voter C: he regards three fire engines as imperative; if the town is not to buy them it is wasting its money buying any because it will be destroyed by fire anyway—so the less money spent on fire engines the better. This is not irrational reasoning. There is simply no majority position; the actual decision will depend upon the procedure and sequence of voting.

If the pattern of preferences follows the same sequence, this difficulty will not arise:

[10]See K. J. Arrow, *Social Choice and Individual Values* (New York: Wiley, 1951).

	Voter		
Choice	*A*	*B*	*C*
First...............	1	2	3
Second..............	2	3	2
Third...............	3	1	1

As in the previous example, if each alternative is voted on separately, no one will receive a majority, since only one prefers each; preferences are diverse. But in this instance, if the alternatives are voted on in pairs, (2) will be the choice regardless of the order of presentation, because two voters prefer (2) to either of the alternatives.

Where consensus is greater, one alternative will receive a clear majority when each is voted on separately:

	Voter		
Choice	*A*	*B*	*C*
First...............	1	2	1
Second..............	2	3	2
Third...............	3	1	3

Alternative (1) will receive a clear majority no matter how the voting is conducted.

The actual significance of the Arrow problem is not easily assessed. As shown by Coleman, the problem vanishes if voters can express intensity of preference, or if a number of decisions are involved, thus allowing bargaining.[11] Since most decisions are made without endless delay, either the problem is not significant for this or other reasons, or persons are willing to tolerate decisions reached under the procedural rules adopted (even though they frequently prefer a different choice) in order to minimize time spent on decision making.

3. *Varying Intensity of Preferences.* While there is no way of comparing intensity of relative preferences of various persons for governmental services, commonsense observations suggest that there are significant variations. Many persons have little interest in particular governmental services, and while they may express preference (with some inclination to react negatively) they are essentially indifferent. Other persons have very strong desires for the service. Many public goods convey individual benefits as well, for which no charges are made. Those persons particularly benefiting—those with children in school, for example—will have strong preferences. Even for purely public goods, preferences vary; to some persons national defense is all-important; to others, of minor concern. The majority rule ignores these intensities of preferences and thus almost certainly prevents the

---

[11] J. S. Coleman, "The Possibility of a Social Welfare Function," *American Economic Review*, Vol. LVI (December, 1966), pp. 1105–22.

attainment of what might be defined as an optimal adjustment of total levels of various activities. Public goods urgently desired by minority groups willing to pay for them may not be produced because the majority is not interested.

4. Exploitation of Minorities and Disregard for Minority Preferences. Closely related to the question of varying intensities of preferences is the danger that the majority will deliberately undertake programs that will benefit it at the expense of the minority. Fear of such exploitation was the prime source of the unanimity doctrine and its acceptance by many present-day conservatives. For example, suppose a particular society is characterized by a large number of relatively low-income families who benefit greatly from public education. The low-income majority could be expected to propose high levels of spending on education to be financed by the higher income groups, who may send their own children to private schools. Such tendencies are primarily products of the redistributional features of the activities and are likely to be most important with purely distributional activities (welfare), discussed later in the chapter.

The significance of these considerations is lessened by the ability of minority groups with strong preferences to unite together against the relatively indifferent majority, particularly with representative government. By vote trading and logrolling one minority will support another and policies will reflect preference intensities. Logrolling may go so far as to bring an overall level of government activities in excess of majority preferences, but it allows greater recognition of legitimate interests of minorities. Such behavior is possible only if the various minority groups consist, at least in part, of different people; otherwise joining forces could not produce a majority.

Alternative procedures for voting are sometimes suggested as a more direct means of recognizing the varying intensities of preferences. Plurality voting allows ranking of the various choices and determination of the outcome on the basis of the total score of the rankings, obtained by aggregating the rankings.[12] The closely related point score system allows each voter a certain number of total points that he may allocate as he wishes, all to his first choice, for example, or distributed among various choices.[13] While both systems offer the advantage of recognizing the voters' degree of preference, they encourage strategic

---

[12]A person may cast three votes for his first choice, two for his second, one for his third. These are totaled and the choice receiving the largest number is the winner.

[13]A person is allocated, for example, six points; he may cast them all for his first choice and none for the others if he wishes, or divide them among the choices.

moves: a person may not reveal his actual preferences but vote in such a way as to assure avoidance of an undesired result. His voting is greatly influenced by his estimates of what other voters will do and the actual outcome may reflect preferences less adequately than majority voting.[14] The process of voting is likewise made much more complex.

Another alternative, favored by Buchanan to lessen the danger of deliberate exploitation of minorities by majorities, is the separation of allocational and distributional considerations by constitutional means; tax patterns would be determined by constitution, the allocational decisions by current action of the voters.[15] The tax patterns could not easily be altered to facilitate exploitation, while in making decisions on constitutional questions persons would be influenced to a greater extent by long-run considerations—and many persons do not expect to remain poor indefinitely. Uncertain about their future position in the income scale, persons will be reluctant to favor constitutional provisions that may trap them at a later date.

In practice, constitutional provisions in the states, such as those requiring more than a majority vote to approve changes in the basic tax structures, serve this purpose to some extent. In part, however, constitutional restrictions on tax and expenditure programs have been designed to restrict the powers of the legislature, a safeguard on the part of voters to insure that their representatives will not act contrary to their wishes on major issues.

REVEALING OF PREFERENCES

Individuals do not automatically reveal their preferences for public goods as they do for private-sector output. Some system must be developed to ascertain the preference schedules. First, however, let us consider the basic question: will individuals reveal their preferences at all? The answer is that they will so long as they know that their tax burden is not dependent upon the preferences that they indicate. The refusal to reveal preferences if their tax payments depend upon them requires that governments, rather than voluntary organizations,

---

[14]This issue is discussed at length in R. A. Musgrave, *The Theory of Public Finance* (New York: McGraw-Hill, 1959), chap. vi.

[15]Buchanan goes so far as to suggest that a person should have only one opportunity in his lifetime to vote on constitutional matters; he will vote when he is young and expects to be rich in the future. Elderly poor people know that they have no chance to become wealthy and are particularly inclined to favor exploitation measures. See Buchanan, *op. cit.,* chap. xv.

provide public goods, and makes it impossible for governments to negotiate "purchase" of public goods by individuals on the basis of their preferences. So long as the person knows that the tax structure through which payments will be collected is not dependent upon his preference for expenditure levels, he has no reason to conceal his actual preferences. Even if his tax was affected he would still be willing to reveal his relative preferences among various kinds of expenditures at a given tax level.

What techniques may be employed to ascertain preferences? In a small community group, such as the New England and Swiss town meetings, individual voting on various measures is possible. Larger units of government may submit a few major issues to the voters on written ballots or utilize public opinion polls. This technique, however, is clearly not feasible for use on any scale. In the first place, in the modern complex society, far too much time and effort would be required to utilize the referendum technique on all issues, particularly because of the number of alternatives frequently available for possible levels of government spending.

Secondly, most individuals lack adequate information for reaching a decision about the various programs. Voting on the basis of complete lack of information cannot give results that reflect significant preferences. There is an observed tendency for persons to vote against any change on which they lack information, and thus there is a built-in bias against a shift from present levels of activity.

Thirdly, individual voters, either because of a lack of information or because they realize that their action will have little influence upon the overall outcome, may act irresponsibly, voting to increase expenditures and disapproving all proposals for financing them, for example. Finally, voting by all individuals on proposed measures makes the logrolling necessary for recognition of the interests of minorities virtually impossible.

To meet these problems, institutions have developed through which individual preferences are ascertained and coordinated for the making of expenditure decisions.

Representatives

Typically, the voters choose legislators who will reflect their preferences in collective-goods decision making. Each person running for such an office will, under the assumption that he wishes to attain and retain office, seek to estimate the preferences of his constituents for various levels of governmental activities (as well as other governmental policies) and establish a platform that in his belief most closely coincides with the preferences of the majority. The person elected is the one who most successfully estimates preferences, and once elected presumably he will follow policies that reflect his estimate of the wishes of his constituents, under the assumption that he seeks reelection of himself or, if he is ineligible, a person with similar views. Primary opportunity for logrolling and vote trading arises in the work of the legislative bodies, an activity that may bring the program of governmental activities more closely in line with individual preferences.

The representative system, while in a rough way bringing about policies that coincide with the preference schedules of the individuals in society, suffers from obvious limitations, arising primarily out of imperfect information. First, the candidates may seriously err in their estimates of individual preferences, and the voters may have little real choice; none of the candidates may take an overall position which coincides with majority preferences. Voters are also concerned with questions other than those involving the level of government activities, such as civil rights, and may cast their votes entirely on the basis of these other considerations. Many voters lack information about the positions of candidates, and do not trouble themselves to obtain it. Their votes, if cast at all, are based upon misinformation, or upon purely extraneous considerations such as the candidate's name. An Olsen has an inherent advantage over a Smith in Minnesota, and a candidate named Piggpenn starts the race with a serious handicap. Once elected, legislators may make little effort to ascertain the preferences of their constituents and may have great difficulty in doing so if they try. But imperfect as the system is, there is no feasible alternative in a democratic society.

Political Parties

At the national and state level, and to some extent at the local level, political parties play a major role in the decision-making process.[16] The party may be defined as a group of men with like interests seeking control of government. The goal of the party leaders is assumed to be the maximization of votes in order to gain and retain office. Accordingly, they seek to frame party platforms that most closely coincide with the preference of the voters as a whole. Since voters regard additional governmental spending as favorable and taxes as

---

[16]See Anthony Downs, *An Economic Theory of Democracy* (New York: Harper & Row, 1957), for an analysis of the role of parties in decision making on governmental activities.

unfavorable, the party will, in designing its program, attempt to expand each activity to the level at which the marginal gain from the activity is exactly equal to the marginal adverse response to the concomitant taxation. People will presumably vote for the party that they regard as maximizing their gain. Thus the parties serve as intermediaries, facilitating the functioning of the representative system by providing individual candidates of the party with a more or less common set of proposals and simplifying voting as particular parties come to stand for certain general positions, that is, to represent a particular ideology. The effectiveness of the system is higher to the extent that general consensus in society prevails on major issues. In fact, under these conditions, the positions of the two parties become very similar, as each seeks to reach as closely as possible the median consensus position. While the voters have little choice, this is not significant because of the high degree of consensus. If on the other hand there are several sharply divergent points of view on major issues, a multiparty system develops. Since no one party is likely to gain a majority, the consequence is instability of power and difficulty in deciding on and carrying through any consistent set of policies.

Even with general consensus and a two-party system neither party can usually remain in power for long periods, as the opposition has certain inherent advantages. First, it can obtain support of strong minorities whose policies are not acceptable to the majority; by bringing together minorities with intense preferences on various subjects, the opposition may bring about the downfall of the governing party. The latter's policy of seeking to follow majority preferences on all issues leaves in its wake a number of dissatisfied minorities, which may be united into a majority. This can be avoided only if the governing party is sufficiently successful in horse-trading with the minorities. Second, the government may encounter Arrow-type problems, issues on which there is no majority position. Since the government must indicate its position first, it is vulnerable to defeat, for a majority will oppose any policy that it adopts. Finally, voters appear to tire of the party in power, seeking change per se, even if the other party offers little prospect of meeting preferences more satisfactorily. How prevalent these problems are and how successful the opposition will be in utilizing them in elections determine their significance for stability in government.

The parties may not estimate correctly the preference schedules of the majority of voters on all issues of governmental activities. This is inherently an extremely difficult task, and any high degree of perfection is impossible. Accordingly, party leaders may substitute their own judgments for those of the community and seek to obtain popular support for them. Such a policy may cause parties to mislead their constituents about the merits of certain policies or the effectiveness of those carried out.

THE DECISION-MAKING ROLE OF EXECUTIVE AND BUREAUCRACY

The chief executive in government is the leader of the governing party and as such has primary responsibility for interpreting the wishes of the public and developing, subject to legislative approval, and executing policies to meet the wishes of society. A capable executive can do far more than this, however; through his position he can exercise great influence in molding public opinion, and thus in shaping the nature of individual preference schedules for public goods. This influence is made possible by the lack of information on the part of voters and thus their uncertainty about the outcomes of various policies. The net result is a complex interplay of executive and legislative interpretations of the preferences of individuals and executives' and legislators' own attitudes toward various governmental activities.

Great influence is likewise exercised over governmental programs by the administrative organization—the bureaucracy of government, the term not being used in any derogatory sense. The administrative organization not only influences the overall program of government but also, since it has responsibility for execution of the program, determines in large measure the manner in which it is carried out. At best the voters can influence only the general nature of an activity, while the bureaucracy determines the details. The public may favor a policy of victory in a war but cannot choose techniques for accomplishing this goal, except on a few major questions on which many persons have strong feelings—use of atomic weapons, bombing of cities, and the like.

What may be assumed about motivation of bureaucrats? The answer is not simple. As suggested by Downs,[17] no single motive can appropriately be assumed, since both purely personal motives as well as those relating to furtherance of the activity influence behavior. A reasonable assumption for strictly personal motivation is the desire to

[17]See Anthony Downs, "A Theory of Bureaucracy," *Proceedings of American Economic Association for 1964*, pp. 439–46; and his *Inside Bureaucracy* (Boston: Little, Brown, 1967).

maintain position and gain promotion. Some persons seek to attain this goal primarily by performing their tasks with as little change as possible, aiming never to incur the enmity of anyone and to avoid policies that might fail and thus discredit them and their superiors. Others—the climbers, in Downs' terminology—emphasize the innovational role, seeking change and improvement to demonstrate their capacities to their superiors. This group is willing to take more risk, and thus may move up very rapidly, on the one hand, or fail completely on the other. Both motives provide incentives toward efficiency and toward implementing as effectively as possible policies determined at higher levels. Unfortunately, they sometimes also lead to empire building: the attempt to secure as many subordinates as possible in the belief that the larger the empire, the higher the salary and the greater the chances for promotion.

The most casual observation of the functioning of governmental units (as well as those in larger businesses) suggests that other motives are frequently significant. Many persons become zealots for the activity with which they are associated. Preservation of wildlife or forests, strengthening of the Navy, eradication of termites, building of more and better highways, improved standards of education become highly important goals to the persons.[18] This phenomenon appears to be a basic characteristic of human nature, one that furthers efficient operation of particular governmental units on the one hand but which can lead to expansion of activities beyond society's preferences, on the other. Without question, also, most persons in higher administrative tasks do become concerned with the interests of society as a whole and not alone with their immediate personal interests. Most persons have some concern for society; those who find themselves in responsible government positions not infrequently feel that attainment of such positions carries even greater responsibility for consideration of the interests of society. Any economic analysis of government that fails to recognize this attitude will lead to inadequate and perhaps erroneous results. There are, of course, exceptions: mercenaries, for instance, who will work for anyone.

With this dual motivation—the exact importance of each segment varying with the individual—the bureaucracy not only influences the manner in which governmental activities are carried out but also exercises influence upon the scope of various government programs. The chief executive and the legislators must rely heavily upon the bureau-

---

[18]See A Wildavsky, *The Politics of the Budgetary Process* (Boston: Little, Brown, 1964), pp. 160–67.

crats for advice concerning benefits from expansion or contraction of each function, since they have on-the-spot knowledge of benefits and needs. Unfortunately both personal and activity motivation lead bureaucrats to favor continually higher levels of activity, which they seek to justify. The bureaucrats benefit, both personally and in terms of broader interests, from expansion of their activities but bear little of the additional costs. Thus legislative bodies must exercise independent judgment on their recommendations in terms of their estimates of the preference of individuals, considering both benefits and costs. The attitudes of those who bear costs as well as gain benefits must play a part in the decision-picture.

REDISTRIBUTIVE FUNCTIONS

Not only do most governmental activities incidentally result in redistribution of real income, but a significant portion of governmental activity is deliberately aimed at redistribution. The basic assumption of self-interest would suggest that each person would always prefer any program that benefits him and is paid for by others, and that the majority would always favor programs that benefit them and are paid for by the minority. If a majority of the population is relatively poor, they could be expected to introduce programs that would transfer income from the smaller wealthy group to themselves. Undoubtedly there is some tendency in this direction, as evidenced by the relative growth in the welfare activities of government, although it must be noted that these programs are often favored by some persons in the higher income groups.

Several explanations of the failure of the poorer majority to exploit the richer minority—a phenomenon long feared by the rich—can be offered. First, the majority, in terms of income groups, may consist of neither rich nor poor, but of a large "middle-income" class, one that realizes that the potentiality of gain at the expense of the relatively small high-income group is not great. There is not enough total income in this group to raise substantially the levels of other groups. Second, some persons, especially legislators and senior bureaucrats, recognize that drastic reduction in the income of the higher income groups would reduce incentives and retard economic development. Third, especially in a mobile society such as the United States, few in the lower income groups, particularly the large numbers of young persons, expect to stay poor. Many hope to rise to higher income levels and thus will not favor programs that exploit the rich in favor of the poor. Finally, the rich have disproportionate political strength relative to their numbers, because of their greater information and interest in programs and their ability to influence governmental action by their wealth. Persons chosen as legislators, especially at the national level, typically come from higher income groups, since education and wealth are important in gaining strategic party postions and victory in elections, and thus they are biased against share-the-wealth programs.

The opposite question warrants attention: why do many persons in middle- and high-income levels support programs that will primarily aid the minority low-income group? Why will the voters as a whole show preference for aid to dependent children, direct relief, and old-age pension programs? One explanation is that most persons dislike fighting off beggars and seeing bad slum conditions.[19] They may also fear that the very poor are the potential source of mass crime and political instability. Beyond these purely personal self-interest factors, persons surely are motivated by humanitarian considerations. Just as they will give to private charity, so will they support governmental programs that will aid the very poor. Partly the attitude is one to which persons are indoctrinated from childhood, an attitude encouraged by religious groups.

Several empirical studies have been made of the relative support by the rich and poor of various types of governmental activities. The most significant conclusion is that programs of extension of governmental activities are typically favored by the higher and lower income groups and opposed by the middle-income ranges.[20] Whether a particular measure receives majority support depends upon the relative size of the low-, middle-, and high-income groups and the size and attitude of the majority in each group. The poor tend to support activities because they estimate that benefits to themselves will exceed the taxes they will pay to finance them, the rich because of a high elasticity of demand for government services and greater recognition of indirect benefits to the community as a whole from the governmental activities.

CONCLUSION

In a democratic society, governmental activities and expenditures, as well as the tax structure, are based upon the preference schedules

---

[19]The beggar phenomenon characteristic of cities with large numbers of persons at bare subsistence levels and no welfare aid comes as a great shock to persons from high-income countries when they first visit such cities.

[20]See J. O. Wilson and E. C. Banfield, "Public Regardingness as a Value Premise

of individuals for the particular activities. These preference schedules reflect a mixture of direct personal self-interest and social considerations, which may be interpreted as an element in a broader context of personal preferences. If there is almost universal consensus on certain issues— as there appears to be—determination of the level of the activities is clearly defined and the same results will be attained regardless of the exact technique used to ascertain preferences.

On most issues, however, and even on the levels of activities for which there is strong general support (the year-to-year decisions are in fact marginal ones, involving change from existing levels, not the review of the whole program), most persons apparently have no clearly defined preference schedules, in part because they lack information on which to base a decision and do not find it worth their while to obtain it, in part because they may have no personal interest in the activity whatever.

As a consequence of the large numbers of issues and lack of clearly defined preference schedules, actual decision making is delegated by the people to representatives, typically elected on a party basis. Persons seeking election attempt to prepare a program that will coincide with the desires of the majority of the voters and if elected will presumably seek to implement the program. On many issues, however, they must use their own judgment since so little information is availabe about voter preferences.

The principle that majority will shall prevail is typically accepted in a democracy. On many issues, however, most persons have so little interest that the will of a small interest group prevails, or the status quo is favored as persons vote no on issues on which they lack information. Other issues encounter Arrow problems—the absence of a definable majority position. Furthermore, majority rule suffers from the basic limitation that the relative intensities of preferences are ignored and a lukewarm majority can overwhelm a minority with intense preferences. The alternative—the requirement of unanimity or near-unanimity—while preventing any change that does not meet the Pareto criterion, would in fact paralyze action and necessitate intolerable expenditure of time and effort in individual bargaining. So

in Voting Behavior," *American Political Science Review,* Vol. LVIII (December, 1964), pp. 876-87. See also W. C. Birdsall, "A Study of the Demand for Public Goods," in R. A. Musgrave (ed.), *Essays in Fiscal Federalism* (Washington, D.C.: Brookings Institution, 1965), pp. 235–94. A major conclusion of this empirical study is that voting in the lower income levels is based primarily upon vague attitudes rather than on calculation of benefits and costs.

the majority rule in fact prevails and is made tolerable by two considerations: vote trading—logrolling—among various intense-feeling minority groups that frequently enables each to get that it wants, and the "social responsibility" element that enters into the preference schedules of many persons and thus lessens deliberate efforts to exploit minorities. Logrolling is more effective in legislative bodies than with individual voters.

Lack of information on the part of both individuals and legislators results in the exercise of substantial power over the level of governmental activities by the executive and the bureaucracy, partly through dissemination of information to the public and the legislative body about governmental activities, partly because of the attention that is paid in budget determination to the recommendations of the executive, which in turn are based largely upon those of the top levels of the bureaucracy. While such influence is inevitable, it suffers from one unfortunate bias: persons in the bureaucracy have a tendency, following both self-interest and activity-interest motives, to seek continuous expansion of their own functions without regard to the relative merits of other activities or the attitudes toward further increases in taxes.

Thus in a democracy, expenditure (and tax) decision making reflects a complex blend of considerations based upon the preference schedules of individuals (themselves influenced by governmentally supplied information), interpretations by the legislative body of these preference schedules, and the interests and attitudes of the "government" itself in the sense of the executive and administrative personnel.

REFERENCES

BUCHANAN, J. M. *Public Finance in Democratic Process.* Chapel Hill, N.C.: University of North Carolina Press, 1966.

   The most detailed analysis of individual decision making relating to governmental activities.

BUCHANAN, J. M., AND TULLOCK, G. *The Calculus of Consent.* Ann Arbor, Mich.: University of Michigan Press, 1962.

   Considerations relating to constitutional rules for decision making.

DOWNS, ANTHONY. *An Economic Theory of Democracy.* New York: Harper & Row, 1957.

   Analysis of the role of the political party in decision making.

DOWNS, ANTHONY. *Inside Bureaucracy.* Boston: Little, Brown, 1967.

   Decision making within the administrative organization.

MCKEAN, ROLAND. *Public Spending.* New York: McGraw-Hill, 1968.

MUSGRAVE, R. A. *The Theory of Public Finance,* chap. vi. New York: McGraw-Hill, 1959.

Alternative approaches to voting rules.

TULLOCK, G. *The Politics of Bureaucracy.* Washington, D.C.: Public Affairs Press, 1965.

The nature of bureaucracy and its role in decision making.

Chapter | BUDGET SYSTEMS AND

3 | COST BENEFIT ANALYSIS

We assume that governments in a democratic society seek to meet the preferences of society to the maximum extent possible, granting that in the process they exert substantial pressure upon the nature of these preferences. Given the lack of precise, clearly defined preference schedules and the difficulties of ascertaining the schedules, governments must themselves determine the levels of various activities and the exact amounts to be spent on each activity. The basic power over expenditures rests with the legislative body as representative of the voters but of necessity the chief executive and the administration exercise great influence. Furthermore, the government—in practice primarily the executive and the administrative organization—selects the methods to be used to attain the goals of society, as, for example, the types of missiles to be developed or the mode of transport to handle mail.

The year-to-year decisions are incremental decisions; no government reconsiders each year whether or not to continue its basic programs, just as a family does not review annually its basic expenditure patterns.

To facilitate annual (or, in many states, biennial) decision making on expenditures, governments have developed budget systems, which provide for systematic presentation of recommendations for expenditures by the executive to the legislative branch of government and, through appropriations legislation and control of expenditures, also provide a basis for insuring that actual expenditures conform with the law. A budget may therefore be defined as a financial plan that serves as the basis for expenditure decision making and for subsequent control.

Contents and Types of Budgets

Budgets contain, usually, financial data for the previous year (or years), estimated figures for the current year, and recommended figures for the coming year, for both expenditures and revenues. Most of the space in the budget, however, is allocated to expenditures.

Several questions arise about the exact coverage of a budget and differences in approaches to them led for a time to three separate budget totals for the federal government. One major set of issues relates to trust funds to which certain revenues are allocated and from which certain specified expenditures are made; to federal lending operations; and to the use of cash versus accrual accounting. At the federal level the two major trust funds are those for social security and highway purposes. Since the expenditures from the funds are determined by substantive legislation and are not subject to normal review each year, the funds were omitted from the federal *administrative* budget, which traditionally served as the basis for consideration of appropriations legislation. Federal loans granted, however, were included in the totals, and the cash basis was used. The totals in this budget were stressed, prior to 1967, in the discussion of magnitudes of governmental activity and deficits or surpluses.

The administrative budget understated the total magnitude of the governmental activities and their potential impact on the economy, and thus the trust funds were included in the *cash* budget, which was developed to show the total inflows and outflows of cash between the government and the private sector. This budget gave a much more realistic picture of the overall magnitudes and potential economic effects. In the mid-sixties the deficit of the cash budget was much less than that of the administrative budget because the trust funds experienced surpluses.

TABLE 3–1

ALTERNATIVE FEDERAL BUDGET TOTALS, UNITED STATES, 1967–68 (ESTIMATES)

(In Billions of Dollars)

Budget	Receipts	Expenditures	Deficit
Administrative.....................	118.6	137.2	18.6
Cash............................	158.8	176.0	17.2
National income accounts...........	161.1	171.1	10.0
New unified (without lending)			
operations.......................	155.8	169.9	14.0
Adjustment for net lending.........		5.8	19.8

SOURCE: U.S. Bureau of the Budget, *The Budget in Brief*, 1968–1969.

Both the administrative and cash budgets treated loans made by the Federal government as expenditures, and both were on a cash rather than accrual basis. Accordingly the magnitudes differed from figures employed in the national income accounts. Therefore in the 'sixties a *national income accounts* federal budget was developed, which included the trust funds but excluded federal lending operations and placed the figures on an accrual rather than cash basis, with expenditures on a goods-delivery rather than payment basis.

In 1968, following the recommendations of the President's Commission on Budget Concepts, a single unified budget was established. This budget includes trust funds and separates spending and governmental lending, showing the surplus or deficit with and without lending activities. Temporarily the cash basis is used, but the plan is to shift ultimately to the accrual basis.

Totals of the four approaches are compared in Table 3–1 for 1967–68 (estimated figures).

Another question of coverage relates to governmental activities of essentially commercial nature with large revenues from the sale of services, such as TVA and the post office. The typical practice is to include only the net earnings or deficit figure and capital expenditures, rather than the gross expenditures and revenues. This same rule was extended in the unified budget of 1968–69 to include additional market-oriented activities such as sales of timber from national forests. These receipts are deducted from the expenditure figures of the respective agencies and only the net is shown. At the municipal level similar practices are usually followed. To include the gross figure gives a misleading picture of governmental activity and is less useful for purposes of decision making relative to governmental activities, since the revenues of the governmental commercial projects serve primarily to cover the expenses of operation.

The Budget Cycle

The budgetary process in larger governmental units involves four steps: preparation of the budget and submission to the legislative body, enactment of appropriations legislation on the basis of the proposals, execution of the appropriations legislation, and audit. Responsibility for preparation of the budget usually rests with the executive branch of government; a special budgetary agency is established in larger governments to handle the work of preparation, under the jurisdiction of the chief executive. In the United States the Bureau of the Budget, an independent agency (independent, that is, of any department), has the responsibility.

The United States federal budget cycle is outlined briefly below:

A. Preparation.

1. Preparatory work for the budget is commenced about 18 months before the beginning of the fiscal year involved; that is, for the fiscal year 1968–69 work began in January, 1967. At the agency

level, preliminary estimates are made of needs for the year. At the same time, officials of the Bureau of the Budget, the Treasury, and the Council of Economic Advisers prepare tentative budget guidelines and in April or May discuss these with the President.

2. Following the establishment of the guidelines, the Bureau of the Budget (hereafter referred to as the Bureau) requests preliminary estimates from the agencies; these are developed within each department, discussed with the Bureau, and revised to conform with the guidelines established.

3. In late Spring (often June) the Director of the Bureau of the Budget discusses the proposed figures with the President, who may require changes upward or downward in conformity with his general plans for governmental activities and fiscal policy.

4. The Bureau of the Budget then requests the formal detailed estimates from all departments. These are worked up in the period July–September, in conformity with ceilings and other guidelines established at the earlier stages.

5. The requests are then submitted to the Bureau and studied intensively by the Bureau's examiners, with discussion with personnel of the agencies involved.

6. The recommendations of the examiners are then discussed with the Director of the Bureau of the Budget, and the final figures then reviewed with the President.

7. Agencies are notified of the amounts to be recommended for them and they prepare statements to justify these amounts.

8. The budget document itself is then prepared and in early January is presented by the President to Congress with the Budget Message, summarizing the proposed changes.

B. Enactment.

1. By tradition all appropriations measures originate in the House and are initially considered by the House Appropriations Committee. This committee is divided into 12 subcommittees organized on functional lines (national defense, agriculture, and so on). The subcommittees review the recommendations carefully, with hearings in which officials of the agencies testify, and may change items upward or downward. The recommendations of each subcommittee are considered and merged by the Appropriations Committee, frequently with little change. The appropriations measures—usually 12—are then voted on by the House (usually with little change) and sent to the Senate.

2. The Senate follows a similar but less lengthy and detailed review.

3. Differences are ironed out by a Conference Committee and the bill sent to the President. He can only sign or veto it; he cannot change particular items. The appropriations measures authorize the expenditures of certain amounts; the authorizations may extend beyond the current year. Frequently congressional action is not completed by July 1, and expenditures on the basis of the previous year's appropriations are extended on a temporary basis.

C. Execution.

1. The funds authorized are released to the agencies by the Bureau of the Budget, usually with allotments by quarter of the year.

2. Expenditures are made by the agencies in conformity with the authorizing legislation. The appropriations are allotted by agency, but with considerable flexibility in the use of the funds.

3. Checks are written by the disbursing officer of the agency, and payment made through the Treasury.

D. Audit.

Post audit is made by the General Accounting Office to insure that funds are spent in conformity with the law. The Comptroller General, who heads the GAO, is appointed by and responsible only to Congress.

Operation of the Budgetary Process

A budget is designed to improve adjustment of governmental activities in terms of the preferences of society by facilitating the comparison of conflicting programs and methods in the attainment of the goals as defined by preferences and to facilitate attainment of greater efficiency in the use of governmental resources. This task, especially for the federal government, is an extremely complex one—particularly in establishing priorities for competing goals. How are the relative priorities for defense and the elimination of poverty to be established— even if the relative preference schedules of society for the attainment of these goals were known? How are the relative advantages of deterrent atomic power versus larger armies, and of various equal opportunity programs, to be compared as relative means of attaining the objectives? The task is extremely complex, even with the aid of the most modern systems analysis and computers. The task for a state or a city may be somewhat simpler, but the complexities and need for value judgments remain.

As a consequence of these complexities, the operation of the budgetary process has inevitably developed many shortcuts in order to be workable—just as business firms develop shortcuts to pricing since calculation of marginal revenues and marginal costs for all products is neither economical nor feasible. These take several forms:

1. *Specialization.* The various agencies play a key role in determination of actual expenditure levels; each is concerned only with its own specialized work, with which its officials are familiar. In the Bureau of the Budget detailed examination of requests is made by examiners specialized by type of work. The appropriations subcommittees, which play the dominant role in congressional action, are likewise specialized by type of work. Furthermore, each of these groups believes that it must consider only the direct needs of the particular activity, since other groups are considering other activities.

2. *Fragmentation.* The overall budget is fragmented into small pieces for most of the work, both at the level of preparation and at the congressional committee level—and even at the level of overall action by Congress, since there are a number of appropriations bills rather than one.

3. *Incremental Nature of Action.* Existing programs are not reviewed in detail each year. No one considers each year the questions: Are we to continue antitrust regulation? Is the post office to continue to operate? Are we to maintain consulates and embassies abroad? The presumption is that existing activities will continue unless there is strong evdience that their existence should be reconsidered, and the principle that new appropriations should be similar to the existing ones is accepted with little question. If the Indian Service spends $50 million one year, no thought is given to the possibility of its spending $5 million or $500 million next year. Consideration is given only to incremental changes from the present figure—and usually of course upward changes. Consideration is likewise sequential; if this year's figure turns out to be undesirable in terms of the goals, correction can be made next year, or even in a supplemental appropriation this year.

Thus the budgetary process becomes manageable. But is there any coordination or central review at all? What prevents rapid expansion of some agencies, far exceeding any reasonable level of expenditures in terms of the goals, while others, lacking dynamic leadership, wither? What prevents agencies whose work has become obsolete from continuing forever?

The basic coordination is provided by the competition of the various programs for funds in face of strong legislative resistance to continuous increases in taxes—the struggling of various agencies for money. The department head—the Secretary—exercises some restraining influence over the divisions, so that the overall requests of the department will not appear completely unreasonable. The Bureau of the Budget, as representative of the Chief Executive, seeks to hold down overall spending, and the congressional committees do likewise. Without any direct, centralized decision making about the relative activities, there is downward pressure on all—and particularly on those that appear to conform least with estimates of society's preferences. Each unit, each subcommittee of appropriations, is well aware of the overall constraints and makes its own decisions in light of them. The chief pressure to eliminate obsolete activity is the desire of the agency or department to use the funds for expansion of other activities.

Roles

Each element in the expenditure decision-making process comes to exercise a certain primary role—a role to which there are exceptions, of course.

The agencies are the *advocates* of additional activity, seeking virtually always to expand their activities, the strength of their pressure to do so depending upon their estimates of needs and the attitudes of the agency heads. As specialists in their fields, they are most familiar with the contributions that the activities make; and they are inevitably enthusiastic about their activities, as explained in the previous chapter. The agency head may also be influenced by the more direct considerations of pure and simple empire building. Expansion typically conveys benefits to the agency heads without direct costs to them; the pressure is always toward more, never toward less.

The question of how much to ask for is answered partly by the belief of the agency head about the need for the activity, and in part by considerations of strategy. The tendency is always to ask for more than is expected, partly because the heads believe in the activities, partly because they expect to be cut, in the face of the general constraints against all increases and the competition of other agencies, partly because they think that higher authority believes they pad their requests. In a sense padding strengthens the hand of the Bureau of the Budget and Congress, which can point to the reductions they have made in the requests as evidence of their drive for economy. To pad too much, however, is to generate loss of confidence.

There are several techniques that agencies use in their efforts to get higher figures.[1] One is to cultivate a clientele—farmers, truck operators, chambers of commerce, clergymen—any group that will bring pressure on the administration and Congress to provide additional funds.

[1] See Aaron Wildavsky, *The Politics of the Budgetary Process* (Boston: Little, Brown, 1964), chap. iii.

The agencies that suffer are those that lack an organized clientele. A second is to build confidence by all means possible with higher echelons and with congressional subcommittees—a long-range subtle endeavor. Closely related is the technique of seizing every opportunity to propagandize the activity; if current attention is centered on elimination of poverty in urban centers, all agencies will seek to relate their work to this activity—even if this work is education of the Navajos.

When agencies fail to obtain approval of the desired amounts from their department or the Bureau of the Budget, they may seek to influence the appropriations subcommittee that deals with their activity. Many attempts have been made by the Executive to prevent this run-around, but doing so is difficult. Officials of the agency may develop close personal relationships with subcommittee members, who are themselves sympathetic to the activity and not infrequently will heed the pleas of the agency.

The role of the Bureau of the Budget is that of the *President's representative,* one that reviews the requests in light of the overall preferences of the President for expansion or contraction of certain activities, and for general expenditure-level trends. The Bureau inevitably has a bias toward cutting requests, because of the advocacy nature of the agencies themselves and their well-known tendency to pad demand figures—in face of the usual desire of the President to hold down overall expenditure and tax levels. The Bureau cannot make a careful review of benefits and costs of all budget requests; it can merely give them a broad review in terms of apparent merits—given the estimates of what society wants and in light of its estimates of congressional attitudes—and look for excessive padding. The Bureau is reluctant to come up with a total 20 percent higher than last year when it knows that Congress is seeking to hold the line at existing figures, or to approve a large increase for a certain activity to which it knows Congress to be most unsympathetic. The Bureau's actions are based on political considerations as much as or more than on economic considerations, as well they should be in view of the goal of adjusting expenditures in light of community preferences.

The House Appropriations Committee and its subcommittees play the primary role of *guardian of the Treasury,* reflecting the common desire of society to hold taxes down. The Committee therefore has a strong bias in favor of cutting requests, and in fact cuts far more than it increases.[2] There are exceptions, in which the subcommittee supports the agency and overrules the Bureau of the Budget, or may even raise

---

[2]One extensive study showed that of 443 measures over a 12-year period, the Appropriations Committee left 74 unchanged, cut 342, raised 27. See Wildavsky, *op. cit.,* p. 41.

the figure over the agency request. But these represent a minority of cases.

The Senate, particularly the Senate Appropriations Committee, serves primarily as a *court of appeal* from reductions made by the House. Traditionally the Senate tends to be more liberal, raising many House-approved figures, the final figures therefore being compromises between the two.

Proposals for Greater Coordination and Broader Evaluation

Many studies have been made of federal budgetary procedure over the years and most have called for the same general type of reform: more effective overall review of expenditures for various purposes, that is, for lessened emphasis on the shortcuts noted earlier in the chapter. The existing system has been criticized for unnecessary fragmentation, especially at the congressional level. Each expenditure is considered independently, with little or no attempt—either by the Bureau of the Budget or Congress—to weigh relative merits of various activities against one another, except in the crudest fashion. Thus argument has been made for a single appropriations bill instead of several, for establishment by the Senate and the House of a joint committee to determine overall budgetary policy, for increased technical staffs for Congress to review budget requests in greater detail. The first two proposals were attempted in 1946 and failed miserably, while the third has been tried on a small scale. The attempt to use a single bill proved unworkable because of sheer complexity, and the joint committees found agreement on totals without knowledge of details to be impossible.

The impossibility of such an approach has been accepted increasingly in recent years; the expenditure program of the federal government is so complex that no person or group can make the necessary overall comparison—to do so is beyond the capacity of the human brain. The task is rendered even more difficult by the lack of clearly defined goals (society's relative preferences for various objectives) and the high degree of uncertainty about the outcome of various policies (how effective will increased defense spending be in deterring attack?).

As stressed by Wildavsky, the present decentralization of expenditure decision making is a reflection of the nature of the political process in the United States; no group has the political power to make all of the basic decisions about expenditures. The system is inherently one of checks and balances, and the distribution of political power has been such that no group can completely dominate. In a country with the parliamentary form of government, domination by the majority party, and strict adherance to party policy much greater centralization in decision making is possible. But the United States situation is not of this character, and no change in budgetary processes can make it so.

The present fragmented structure, it is true, may not make overall review and balancing of relative needs of various activities completely effective. Those activities having strong clienteles—pressure groups— behind them may succeed in pushing their activities beyond what might be regarded as reasonable. Inertia may restrict readjustment of activities for long periods and preserve obsolete activities. But the system is workable; it insures pressure to expand useful activities on the one hand, and provides general constraint on the other. It may not be ideal, and, as subsequently noted, improvements in budget structure and better evaluation of benefits are possible. But the overall system is much better than its critics have made it out to be.

State and Local Budget Systems

While the discussion has centered on the federal budgetary process, much is applicable to state and local activities. On the whole the processes are simpler and the benefits of many of the activities are easier to measure. In most states the governor has responsibility for preparation of the budget, with an agency to assist him. The legislature, in enacting appropriations measures, makes less detailed inquiry into the activities than does the House Appropriations Committee. Many of the activities are less controversial and less complex, and programs change less frequently. On the other hand, budget restraints are sometimes more severe because of the lesser scope of potential tax resources and constitutional restrictions on borrowing. Local budget systems differ in one major respect: typically legislative and executive branches are not sharply distinguished, and thus responsibility for both preparation and enactment rests upon the legislative agency (city council, school district trustees, and so forth).

Earmarking and Expenditure Determination

The federal government has never allocated particular taxes to specific functions—a practice called earmarking—by constitutional provision; by congressional action, certain taxes have been allocated to the trust funds. In a number of states, however, the revenues from various taxes are specifically allocated by constitution to certain functions. The gasoline tax is the most common example, but some states have carried earmarking much farther. At the local level, the same effect as earmarking is produced by the formation of special districts with the taxes imposed by these districts allocated to the specific activities of the districts (schools, mosquito control, and so on).

Earmarking reflects in part the desire to make a particular tax more palatable to the public by allocating its revenues to a purpose for which there is strong popular support; motorists may support a gasoline tax used solely for road purposes but may oppose one if it may be used for general state activity. A sales tax proposal may gain organized support if it is to be used solely to finance education. Some persons argue that it is easier to undertake and expand an activity having strong support by this means than by incorporating it in the general budget. Buchanan has argued that earmarking gives the individual voter and representative greater choice in expressing his attitudes about various forms of government spending.[3]

The primary objection to earmarking is the reduction in budgetary flexibility that results; the hands of the legislative body are tied so far as the earmarked funds are concerned, and relative allocation may differ sharply from present legislative preferences. Long delays in making constitutional changes may perpetuate arrangements that have become obsolete as a result of changes in circumstances. To the extent that representatives have an opportunity to express preferences on various segments of a budget, earmarking gives them no greater choice and in fact lessens their freedom. The best case for earmarking is that for highway financing with taxes justified as user charges. These taxes have, by usual standards, little justification as sources of general governmental revenue.

PROGRAM BUDGETS

A primary function of the budget system is to facilitate evaluation of proposals and to compare the relative merits of various requests. Unfortunately the traditional presentation of material in budget documents has not facilitated the fulfillment of this task.

First, the usual budget is organized on the basis of agencies, without regard to interdependencies among various agencies or the conduct of closely related work by other agencies. As a consequence, all costs of particular activities are frequently not revealed and estimate of benefits is made difficult. Second, the budgets are organized in such

---

[3] J. M. Buchanan, "The Economics of Earmarked Taxes," *Journal of Political Economy,* Vol. LXXI (October, 1963), pp. 457–69.

a fashion as to stress inputs—purchases of various types of items, hiring of various classes of personnel (typists, filing clerks, and so forth)—without reference to the programs or outputs produced with them. Accordingly relationships between inputs and accomplishments are not established, and no basis is provided for comparing the relative effectiveness of programs from year to year or between jurisdictions, or of various alternative means to attain the same end products. Such comparisons are presumably made within the agency in developing its work program and its budget requests, but the information does not show up in the budget. Not infrequently there is no reference to end product at all.

Finally, the typical budget is on a strictly one-year (or, with the states, two-year) basis, without regard to future prospects or commitments arising out of the proposals included in this year's budget.

These deficiencies have been recognized for decades, and many suggestions have been made for remedying them, as well as some attempts to do so. The principal approach, in terms of budget structure, is the replacement of the traditional agency and input emphasis by the performance or program budget (the former name, at first widely used, has been replaced by the latter). The local governments and to some extent the states have also been introducing program features into their budget systems.

The program approach stresses the end product, such as eliminating poverty in urban core areas or providing a retaliatory striking force of a certain magnitude, relative to the goals of governmental activity, rather than the inputs of various types of materials and manpower. The approach is designed to consider the pursuit of policy objectives of government in light of all economic costs of the programs.

Secondly, program budgeting stresses the relationship between various outputs or programs and the inputs necessary to produce them, facilitating the use of techniques to analyze alternative programs that will attain the goals and various alternative means of implementing them. Thirdly, the approach seeks to be all-inclusive, recognizing all contributions that the activity makes and all costs incurred, regardless of the organizational structure.

The primary advantage of the program budget structure is obvious from its nature: it provides a more useful basis for evaluation of agency requests by department, Bureau of the Budget, and Congress by concentrating on end products instead of inputs and by providing better information on costs and all benefits. Use of this structure forces the agencies, in preparing budget requests, to stress product and input-to-output relationships and to give attention to a wider range of benefits and costs. The main limitation to the program form of budgets is the difficulty of defining output of many activities. Foreign policy is an extreme example, but even such activities as police protection give rise to difficulties. The aim, after all, is not to arrest as many persons as possible, but to deter crime; this is hard to measure. With many activities the final product is not definable in a meaningful way and thus a secondary "output" must be used: strategic striking power in the case of national defense, for example. This is no argument against program budgeting, where it can be used.

PLANNING-PROGRAMMING-BUDGETING SYSTEMS (PPBS)

The program budget, per se, is merely a form of budgetary presentation—a particular type of budget document. Accompanying its introduction has been growing use of Planning-Programming-Budgeting Systems (PPBS). These systems seek to integrate long-range planning of governmental activities and programming of specific activities with annual budgeting, making use of the program-budget structure and of various quantitative techniques in the evaluation of proposals. Systems analysis and cost-benefit techniques are employed, with quantification of costs and benefits to aid in the selection of the best alternatives. This approach seeks to aid in defining the goals and in choosing among the goals, in specifying alternative programs to attain the goals, in choosing the best alternatives, and, subsequently, in measuring performance. Planning is extended forward for several years, rather than focusing attention on the current year, with reconsideration of the overall plan at frequent intervals as the specific budget for each year is developed. Programming involves the statement of the relationship of inputs and outputs, under various alternatives, to accomplish the desired objectives.

Extensive use of PPBS was introduced into the Defense Department in the early sixties and its extension to all federal agencies was established by Presidential order in 1965.

Merits. The potential advantages of the PPBS system are much broader than those of program budgeting. PPBS is primarily a tool of management, facilitating better utilization of governmental resources in the attainment of the objectives. Stress is placed upon quantification and upon consideration of trade-offs between alternatives, that is, the use of given resources in different ways. Because of the long-range approach, advance planning is possible, and a better picture is given of all costs and benefits over a period of several years. Accordingly, the foot-in-the-door technique on the part of subordinate agencies—starting a program with a small sum of money without calling attention to the large sums that will eventually be necessary to complete it—is made more difficult.

Limitations. The limitations and objections to PPBS are in part related to the basic weakness of the program budget. In many fields ultimate objectives are not clearly definable, and priority of goals cannot be determined except on the basis of value judgments. Comparison is primarily made between various alternative subordinate programs— various ways of accomplishing secondary objectives. Even for these, consideration of all alternatives—all possible trade-offs—is impossible, and the exact structure of the budget determines which ones will be stressed and which largely ignored. Actual costs are often difficult to ascertain even with the best methods and involve arbitrary allocations of overhead or common costs. Even more fundamental, PPBS is unable to estimate benefits from various activities in the face of uncertainty— of particular importance in the national defense and foreign policy fields. In other words, program budgeting is not capable of solving many of the basic issues of determining optimal government activities; it merely facilitates decision making.

A more positive criticism is the charge that PPBS tends to centralize decision making in government, thereby lessening innovation and concentrating power. To some observers the promoters of the overall PPB system seek to eliminate political review from decision making as much as possible, with decision making on grounds of economic efficiency alone and the ultimate aim that decisions be made by computers! Only political review can insure consideration of the relationship of the various programs to community preferences—which cannot be defined in such a way that they can be programmed for computers. Significant value judgments must be made. Admiral H. C. Rickover has become the best known opponent of the use of PPB systems in the national defense field.[4]

Another obstacle to effective PPBS is the lack of adjustment to the existing administrative organization. While the approach seeks to take into consideration elements in programs in a number of administrative agencies, implementation of the programs may be seriously restricted by the structure of the administrative organization—yet change in the

---

[4]See H. C. Rickover, "Cost-Effectiveness Studies", in *Planning-Programming-Budgeting,* (Committee on Government Operations, U.S. Senate, 1967), pp. 35–43.

organization may be strongly resisted. Furthermore, given the interdependencies of modern governmental activity no particular organizational structure may be ideal for implementation of all activities.

On the whole, program budgeting and PPBS may make very significant contributions to rational decision making about governmental expenditures, but they cannot solve all problems; they do little to define objectives in light of preferences of society for various public goods, or to lessen the uncertainties about the benefits from many governmental activities.

COST-BENEFIT ANALYSIS

Governments presumably consider both the benefits and the costs of programs. But this consideration has often been haphazard, with little serious effort to quantify benefits or to include all costs and benefits. Governmental decision making is sometimes dominated by the "absolute needs" approach: a certain expenditure is imperative and must be undertaken regardless of cost; sometimes by the "money first" approach: only a certain amount of revenue is available for the purpose and expenditures are therefore confined to this amount. In recent decades, to some extent concurrently with the development of program budgeting and PPBS activities, systematic analysis of benefits and costs, with maximum quantification, has increased in importance. The first major applications were in the field of water resources, characterized by long-term investments and strong pressure groups, but more recently the analysis has been extended to other fields. Increased stress on cost-benefit analysis has been due partly to rising scope of governmental activities and increased interest in more scientific budgeting, partly to the development of improved techniques and computers that allow more thorough analysis.

More specifically, cost-benefit analysis can be defined as a systematic examination of the benefits and costs of a particular governmental program, setting out the factors that should enter into the evaluation of the desirability of the program and frequently analyzing several alternatives for the attainment of the objective. Cost-benefit analysis is designed to determine whether or not a particular program or proposal is justified, to ascertain the optimal alternative for the attainment of the desired goals, and to rank other alternatives. In contrast to usual evaluations, cost-benefit analysis seeks to take both a long range view of benefits and costs and a broad view, considering, so far as possible, all benefits and costs, direct and indirect, rather than merely the direct, obvious benefits alone.

The Elements in a Cost-Benefit Study[5]

Cost-benefit studies are typically undertaken within a particular government department as a preliminary to budget preparations, or as a continuing program to ascertain optimal expenditure patterns and budget recommendations. Or, they may be undertaken by persons outside government, such as the pioneering work of Otto Eckstein in the water resources field.[6] A study involves several major steps.

Statement of Objectives. Obviously, the goals of the particular programs must be defined; what does the activity seek to attain? The goal may be very specific, such as that of an irrigation project, with the immediate objective of bringing 2,000 acres under cultivation by providing adequate water. The longer range objective, to increase the country's potential food supply, may be much less well defined, especially in a situation of crop surpluses. Other projects have multiple goals; dams may have flood control, irrigation, navigation, and recreational objectives. Others may have goals much more difficult to define specifically, such as in the area of foreign policy. The more sharply the goal can be defined, the greater the contribution that cost-benefit analysis can make to decision making. The significance to be attached to a goal is not a question for cost-benefit analysis to answer, but one of general governmental decision making relating to priority of goals.

Statement of Alternatives. With many types of activities, there are various alternative ways of attaining the goals: different locations for irrigation facilities, different timing for parts of the project (one large dam now versus many small dams built successively over a period of time), different methods of construction. Cost-benefit analysis seeks to ascertain relative benefits and costs of the major alternatives. Obviously all possible alternatives (such as building irrigation canals by pick and shovel or dams of brick) are not considered, since many are so clearly inferior that they do not warrant attention. Cost-benefit analysis is itself costly, and the number of alternatives considered must be held to a tolerable number. The alternatives are sometimes referred to as systems if they are highly complex (such as different programs for

---

[5]See Roland M. McKean, *Public Spending* (New York: McGraw-Hill, 1968), chap. viii.

[6]Otto Eckstein, *Water Resource Development* (Cambridge, Mass.: Harvard University Press, 1958).

defense of the country against military attack), and the consequent analysis designated as systems analysis, an approach now widely used in large-scale-business decision making.

Analysis of Benefits. With the objectives defined and alternatives established, analysis proceeds to a consideration of the benefits. With many activities, this analysis involves determination of the physical units of "output" from the activity and valuation of these units. Thus a dam will provide a certain amount of water, which will allow cultivation of a given number of acres of land; output of the most profitable crops can be estimated and valued at expected prices. Other costs are then subtracted to ascertain the benefit from the provision of the irrigation water. If it were possible to value the water directly on the basis of amounts farmers would be willing to pay for it, the calculation of benefits would be far easier, but this is often not feasible. For a power project, a city water system, or a railway, the expected revenues do provide a measure of the direct benefit but not necessarily of all benefits.

Unfortunately, precise measurement of benefit is often impossible. Basic difficulty arises with collective goods, which cannot be sold to the public, and any valuation must be based upon an estimate of preferences of the persons in society as a whole for the goods. As a consequence, with truly collective goods, cost-benefit analysis is relegated to a comparison of alternative methods; it can throw very little light on the question of whether or not the particular project or program is justified.

Even with activities that provide more direct benefits, valuation of output often gives rise to serious questions. The output is frequently not sold and a constructive valuation is required. An example is recreational activity; how does one measure the value of a day spent by a person fishing on a lake created by a dam, or camping in a forest preserve? Attempts are made to provide such valuation, but they are highly arbitrary. Even ascertainment of the appropriate physical output figure may be complicated. The number of users of a recreational project can be counted once the project is in operation, and advance prediction may be feasible. But if users are not charged for the service, the number using the facilities free of charge may be far greater than the number who would use it if they had to pay for usage. To employ the former figure overstates the benefits from the project.

Another valuation problem arises from the lack of perfect competition in the market for the activity, or in the markets for the products produced as a result of the program. If the government charges for the service and prices on a monopoly basis, total revenues and thus the measure of benefit will differ from the competitive market figure. Or, if the benefits are measured indirectly on the basis of the revenue from the sale of the products produced with the aid of the governmental activity (farm produce grown on the irrigated land), the sales may not be made in perfectly competitive markets, or, in the case of farm products, may be made at prices held artificially high by government support programs. Or alternatively, particularly with major projects in developing economies, the government project may have such great impact upon the whole price structure that valuation of benefits at either old or new prices gives a misleading picture of the actual benefits.

Apart from valuation difficulties, estimation of benefits is always colored by uncertainties about future conditions. This is particularly true with many collective goods, but it is also true of those goods that yield more measurable gains. Benefits from irrigation facilities will depend upon future trends in population and farm output; if we are to have many decades of farm surpluses, the gains from additional irrigation facilities are much less than they would be if in a few years surpluses will be exhausted and farm product prices will rise. The uncertainties with some activities are so great that any precise conclusions are impossible.

Another major issue is the question of the extent to which indirect benefits should be taken into consideration, and which indirect benefits are relevant. The answer to the former question is that precise evaluation of the undertaking requires that all appropriate indirect benefits be considered; in practice the inclusion must be restricted to major categories. The answer to the second aspect of the question is more complex. In general, benefits in the form of lower costs or increased business arising through the use of the service are not indirect benefits or externalities and should not be measured and included. The values involved are derived from the direct benefits and are reflected in their values. For example, the building of a rapid transit system may increase the business of stores located near transit terminals and the value of property in these areas, but these are not true externalities; they are a by-product of the use of the subway. Lower production costs due to better highways are not indirect benefits to be calculated separately, as the benefits are reflected in highway usage. With irrigation facilities, the additional revenues and profits received by the firms purchasing and shipping the farm produce, the railroads and trucklines from hauling it, or the farm equipment companies selling more equipment to the farmers should not be counted in indirect benefits, as the values involved are reflected in the values of the farm produce itself.

On the other hand, if the building of an irrigation dam reduces flooding or provides more pleasant scenery for tourists driving past the lake created by the dam, these indirect benefits should be included in the picture, although some are very difficult to measure. The building of a subway, by lessening the traffic on expressways, saves time for persons continuing to use their cars, reduces accidents, and lessens the funds that the government must invest in more expressways; these are all external or indirect benefits that should be included in the overall benefits from the activity. In other words, those benefits that alter the *physical* conditions of production or consumption for persons or businesses other than those directly using the activities should be included; those that reflect changes in prices and incomes arising out of the use of the activities should not be included, or double counting will result. Precise delineation, however, may be difficult.

Costs. Analysis of cost involves the same type of problem as that of benefits, although costs are more easily calculable. The direct costs include both capital costs and operating costs over the years. Indirect costs include those created for other governmental agencies (for example, more manpower for the Bureau of the Budget, if the program is a major one), and overall costs to society not directly borne by the government. These are in a sense negative benefits. Additional expressways in urban areas will increase air pollution by increasing motor traffic; they may aggravate traffic congestion in downtown areas and increase delays and accidents in these areas; they make the continuation of public transportation more difficult and necessitate subsidies to insure its continued operation or losses to persons who would prefer to have it continued. Without cost-benefit analysis indirect costs are often not taken into consideration. There are obviously measurement and valuation difficulties, just as there are with benefits. Air pollution provides an excellent example.

The Interest Rate. With many governmental programs, especially those of types that lend themselves to cost-benefit analysis such as water and transport development, the benefits will be obtained over a period of years. Likewise some of the costs will be incurred at the time the program is undertaken while others will be incurred in subsequent years. But a dollar of benefits now is worth more than a dollar of benefits 10 years from now because of the interest phenomenon. In order to evaluate a particular project and to compare alternatives, therefore, an interest factor must be used to determine the present value of future benefits and costs; in other words the stream of consumption benefits and the stream of costs must be discounted back to the present for a comparison to be made.

The major issue is the rate of interest or discount to be employed.[7] There are several alternatives:

1. Government Borrowing Rate. A simple alternative is the rate at which the government can borrow, or, alternatively, the borrowing rate of independent government corporations, such as TVA. These figures indicate the direct, immediate cost to the government, but they may differ because of imperfections in capital markets from the potential earnings of the funds in the best alternative investment, and they involve essentially no element for risk.

2. Marginal Productivity of Capital in Private Investment. If the opportunity cost is regarded as the amount that the funds would earn from investment in private enterprise, the appropriate rate is the typical earnings rate of new investment in private business. But the risk element is much greater in the private sector, because the risks confronting the owners of the business are substantially greater than those confronting the government. The owners may lose their entire investment and control of the firm; the government—and thus the members of society—face no equivalent danger. Thus private enterprise cannot advantageously extend investment as far as government can. The projects, however, involve some risk of failure to attain objectives and thus of waste of resources. Accordingly, the appropriate interest figure is one in excess of the pure rate as indicated by the interest the government must pay, but less than that of private enterprise.

3. Social Rate of Return. Another alternative approach is the use of the "social rate of return," the figure that represents society's relative preferences between present and future consumption. This figure would be equal to marginal productivity of capital and the borrowing rate (with risk adjustments) if capital markets were perfect. As they are not, there may be substantial differences. One method of ascertaining society's current preference between present and future consumption is to consider how a tax reduction of magnitude equal to the cost of the governmental program would be divided between

[7]S. A. Marglin, "The Social Rate of Discount and Optimal Rate of Investment," and "The Opportunity Costs of Public Investment," *Quarterly Journal of Economics,* Vol. LXXVII (February and May, 1963), pp. 95–111 and 274–89; and M. S. Feldstein, "Net Social Benefit Calculation and the Public Investment Decision," *Oxford Economic Papers,* Vol. XVI (March, 1964), pp. 114–31; E. J. Mishan, "Criteria for Public Investment: Some Simplifying Assumptions," *Journal of Political Economy,* Vol. 75 (April, 1967), pp. 139–46.

savings and consumption. This return figure, which may be regarded as the optimal one, is difficult to ascertain in practice.

The argument is also advanced that the time preference of individuals excessively favors the present over the future compared to the interests of society as a whole; thus the government should employ a lower interest rate than the social rate of return figure. According to this point of view individuals give inadequate attention to the interests of future generations, while society as a whole has responsibility for the future as well as the present. This general argument, however, is not consistent with democratic principles of individual choice—except to the extent that each person would wish to save more provided everyone else did so in the interests of economic growth. Otherwise there is no scientific basis for the argument that society's rate of time preference differs from that of individuals as a whole.

In summary: selection of the appropriate discount rate, given the imperfections of the capital markets, must be somewhat arbitrary. In light of the practical impossibility of ascertaining the social rate of return, the government borrowing rate, adjusted upward in terms of the risk element, is the most suitable figure.

The Criteria for Judgment. With estimates of benefits and costs discounted back to present value, the final question in cost-benefit analysis is the selection and use of criteria for evaluation; which programs should have priority? Which are justified? Which alternatives best fulfill the goals? The basic comparison is between two streams: those of benefits and those of costs (in other words, other benefits foregone), both discounted back to the present. The alternative that provides the maximum excess of benefits over costs may be regarded as the optimal one, and any particular project that is the best for attainment of the goals and has discounted present value of benefits equal to the discounted present value of costs is warranted. In other words: in the selection among alternatives for the same purpose, the program that offers the maximum excess of gain over cost is the preferred one. In evaluation of various programs, all those with benefits at least equal to cost are warranted if funds are available for all of them; if not, priority goes to those with the greatest excess of benefits over costs, given equal priority of goals.

Merits and Limitations of Cost-Benefit Analysis

There are several limitations to the effectiveness of cost-benefit analysis; like PPBS it does not solve all problems of determination of governmental expenditures. In evaluating programs of relatively broad scope and in comparing programs with different objectives, cost-benefit analysis is of limited usefulness. It does not assist in the establishment of priorities for various goals (national defenes versus education, for example). The problems of measurement of benefits and the uncertainties are so great with many of the programs that quantification is almost impossible. This is particularly true with public goods, but the problem of complex interrelationships is encountered with other activities as well. Many of the programs have redistributive effects, benefiting some persons at the expense of others, and cost-benefit analysis makes no contribution toward the establishment of the social welfare function that provides society's answer about the relative desirability of various patterns of income distribution.[8]

The greatest specific usefulness is found at lower levels of the governmental decision-making process, in selection among alternative means of accomplishing given ends, and with activities such that quantification of benefits is possible on some reasonable basis. With clearly defined objectives and measurable benefits and costs, the analysis gives specific assistance in ascertaining the decisions that are most advantageous in terms of the objectives accepted. Even with the broader questions, however, the cost-benefit approach stresses the importance of quantification whenever possible, of making implicit judgments more explicit, of lessening the influence of bias, and of at least eliminating the worst projects. As long as too much is not expected of cost-benefit analysis, it can make, and is making, significant contributions toward governmental decision making.

REFERENCES

General Studies of Budgeting:

BURKHEAD, J. *Government Budgeting.* New York: Wiley, 1957.
A detailed examination of budget systems and practice.

SMITHIES, A. *The Budgetary Process in the United States.* New York: McGraw-Hill, 1955.
A detailed study of the federal budget system, with proposals for reform.

Recent Developments in Governmental Decision Making:

CHASE, SAM B., JR. (ed.). *Problems in Public Expenditure Analysis,* Washington, D.C.: Brookings Institution, 1968.

---

[8]Solutions to this problem are discussed in A. M. Freeman, "Income Distribution and Planning for Public Investment," *American Economic Review,* Vol. 57 (June, 1967), pp. 495–508, and B. A. Weisbrod, "Income Redistribution Effects and Benefit-Cost Analysis," in S. B. Chase, ed., *Problems in Public Expenditure Analysis* (Washington, D.C.: Brookings Institution, 1968), 177–223.

DORFMAN, R. (ed.). *Measuring Benefits of Government Investments.* Washington, D.C.: Brookings Institution, 1965.
Case studies of benefits and costs of governmental activities in several fields.

HITCH, C., AND MCKEAN, R. N. *The Economics of Defense in the Nuclear Age.* Cambridge, Mass.: Harvard University Press, 1965.
An analysis of governmental decision making in the national defense area.

MCKEAN, R. N. *Public Spending.* New York: McGraw-Hill, 1968.
A study of governmental decision making.

NATIONAL BUREAU OF ECONOMIC RESEARCH. *Public Finances: Needs, Sources, and Utilization.* Princeton, N.J.: Princeton University Press, 1961.
A series of papers on budgeting and decision making.

NOVICK, D. *Program Budgeting.* Washington, D.C.: U.S. Government Printing Office, 1965.
A RAND study of program budgeting and related activities.

PREST, A. R., AND TURVEY, R. "Cost Benefit Analysis: A Survey," *Economic Journal,* Vol. LXXV (December, 1965), pp. 683–735.
A survey of the literature in the field, with an extensive bibliography.

U.S. SENATE COMMITTEE ON GOVERNMENTAL OPERATION. *Programming-Planning-Budgeting, Selected Comment; Official Documents; Initial Memorandum.* Washington, D.C.: U.S. Government Printing Office, 1967.
Three documents on program budgeting and PPBS.

WILDAVSKY, AARON. *The Politics of the Budgetary Process.* Boston: Little, Brown, 1964.
A study of budgetary processes and influences.

| Chapter 4 | REVENUE STRUCTURE DECISION MAKING AND FORMS OF TAXATION |

Governments must acquire command of resources if they are to carry on their activities. These may be seized, as in early days of civilization, particularly from conquered subjects; they may be commandeered under legal procedures, as by selective service; they may be purchased with money, as is typical in modern society. This money, in turn, may be created by government; it may be borrowed; it may be obtained from charges for services; it may be raised through taxation—the usual contemporary source.

In a democratic society the structure of revenue sources presumably reflects the consensus of attitudes in society about various objectives and the effectiveness of various revenue measures for the attainment of these objectives. The revenue structures are designed primarily by the legislative bodies, with some direct participation of the voters through constitutional provisions and (at the state-local level) voting on revenue proposals. The chief executive and the administrative organization exercise influence through their recommendations and their activity to gain popular support for or against various proposals. In the development of the revenue programs, legislators and executives presumably seek to adjust the structures in line with popular preferences in view of their desire to retain office. Since, however, preference schedules for particular measures are ill-defined, the views of legislators and executives exercise substantial influence on the actual structure, particularly the details. These persons in turn are subject to influence by two outside sources: pressure groups that seek changes to benefit their members and experts who are called on for their advice or who offer it.

Revenue versus Expenditure Decision Making

While expenditure programs and revenue sources are developed in similar fashion, there are substantial differences. In the first place, individuals have much greater distrust of legislative bodies in the revenue field than they do in the expenditure field. Therefore they seek to restrict their action by constitutional provisions that can be changed only by direct voter action, often requiring more than a bare majority. Or, alternatively, certain types of action, such as the issuance of bonds, require popular vote. This distrust in part reflects the popular fear that the "power to tax is the power to destroy." Governmental expenditures provide benefits for society; while one person might prefer more of one type and less of another, the imbalance does him little direct harm. Revenue measures, and particularly taxation, on the other hand, can directly reduce his wealth. Conservatives—those who ideologically dislike expansion of governmental activity, both of allocational and redistributional natures—tend to favor restrictions on legislative taxing powers, partly to prevent the placing of heavy taxes upon themselves, partly to dampen the expansion of governmental activity.

The restrictions in the United States and to some extent in other countries take three principal forms:

1. *Constitutional Restrictions on Taxing Powers.* The federal Constitution directly restricts congressional taxing powers in three ways: (1) direct taxes (except, by terms of the 16th Amendment, the income tax) must be allocated among the states according to population, (2) indirect taxes must be uniform throughout the country, and (3) export duties are prohibited. These restrictions barred the use of an income tax for a number of years but otherwise are not important in practice. The federal Constitution restricts the states from taxing imports, exports, or ships calling at their ports, and, through interpretation, restricts their power over interstate commerce, federal instrumentalities, and in other ways—as noted in detail in Appendix I. In part these rules are designed to protect the federal governmental structure and freedom of trade within the country, rather than being restrictive of legislative action in the usual sense.

Many states severely restrict the taxing powers of their own legislative bodies, with a wide variety of patterns. In some states even the rates are set in the constitution. Appendix I gives greater detail.

2. *Restrictions on Borrowing.* While there are no constitutional restrictions on federal borrowing, Congress restricts the powers of the executive by setting a debt ceiling. The state constitutions sharply restrict state borrowing power, and constitutional provisions and state legislation restrict local borrowing, approval of the voters usually being required.

3. *Referendum Provisions.* In a number of states the voters have an opportunity to override legislative action by referendum, and to

initiate proposals that are placed on the ballot without legislative approval.

A second major difference is the greater relative role of the legislative body. Legislative action is obviously influenced by the executive and the administrative organization, but by and large the influence is less than on activities and expenditures. Revenue issues are less complex than the annual budget-making process; legislatures feel that they have greater competence in this area, and they are subject to greater pressure by the voters. Few individuals are concerned about precise federal or state expenditures for many purposes, but they are concerned about tax legislation because it affects them directly.

A final difference is the relative role of the judiciary. The courts play a much more significant role than with expenditures. The direct adverse impact of the taxes upon individuals encourages litigation, and the greater importance of constitutional restrictions provides a basis for legal action. Expenditures benefit; taxes injure. The traditional position of the courts that they will not entertain suits over the legitimacy of particular expenditures on the grounds that no taxpayer has sufficient personal interest to allow him to bring legal action lessens still more any resort to the courts on expenditure questions. As a result of the common appeal to the courts on tax matters, the exact meaning and coverage of tax legislation is greatly influenced by the attitudes of the courts.

THE CHOICE OF MONEY CREATION, BORROWING, OR TAXATION

Governments have four major potential sources of revenue:

1. *Charges.* Certain types of services are sold to the users, the charges covering all or part of the costs of providing them. This source, considered in Chapter 13, cannot be used for public goods because they cannot be divided and sold separately to individuals. Use of charges with many other services is considered to be objectionable on grounds of equity or efficiency in resource utilization. Charges do not constitute a significant source of revenue for noncommercial governmental activities.

2. *Taxes, the Primary Revenue Source.* Taxes, which by their nature are mandatory, represent payments by the community as a whole for governmental services. But the amounts paid by individuals bear no necessary relationship to the amounts of governmental activities they have received, which are often unmeasurable.

3. *Borrowing.* Money is obtained currently through loans, with subsequent payment of interest and principal from taxes or other sources.

4. *Money Creation.* This alternative is open only to national governments.

How are the choices made between money creation and borrowing and between each of these and taxation? Both individual and governmental preferences on these questions require attention.

Money Creation

National governments, by virtue of their sovereign powers over the monetary system, may meet their expenses by the creation of money. Money creation takes two forms: issuance of paper money and borrowing from the central banking system. The first form requires no elaboration; the government prints paper money and pays its bills therewith. With the second, credit is granted to the government by the central bank in exchange for government bonds. The government then draws checks on this credit in payment of bills and meets its expenditures without directly reducing personal wealth of anyone.[1] The purchasing power has simply been created. There is no necessity for payment of interest on these loans; even if it is nominally paid but the earnings of the central bank over and above expenses (plus in the United States, a specified return to the member banks) are returned to the Treasury, there is no net interest burden.

While sale of government bonds to the central banking system constitutes money creation at the time of sale, differences may arise over a period of time between this form of money creation and the issuance of currency; in fact, many persons regard sale of bonds to the central bank as borrowing, not as money creation. If the central bank ultimately sells the bonds to the public, for example, government debt rises. With identity of governmental and central bank policy, however, the central bank will not sell bonds to the public unless the government deliberately seeks to replace money creation by borrowing; when the central bank sells the bonds, it substitutes loans for money.

Preference for Money Creation. How does an individual evaluate the use of money creation as a source of revenue? Would he not consider it to be the most attractive of all revenue sources, since the costs of governmental activities can be covered without the imposition

---

[1] In addition the reserves of the commercial banks are increased, and banks may expand the money supply still further by extending additional private loans. This extension can, however, be prevented by central bank action.

of taxes or creation of debt? Most persons learn at an early age that one rarely gets something for nothing and specifically that paying of bills by issuance of paper money produces a train of undesirable consequences. The most obvious one is inflation; with full employment the financing of governmental activity by money creation will raise the general price level and distribute costs of governmental activities on the basis of holdings of fixed-money-value assets (bonds, mortgages, bank deposits, and so forth) and the extent of the lag of persons' incomes behind increases in the price level. Persons who hold no fixed-price assets and whose incomes rise at the same rate as the general price level escape all costs of governmental activities. Such a pattern of distribution is usually regarded as less equitable than tax methods of financing, and the dislike for it is increased by the uncertainty about precise burden distribution. Inflation is almost universally regarded as undesirable for other reasons as well: the labor strife that it generates, the lessened willingness to buy bonds, the disorganization introduced into the economy, the uncertainty created. Persons whose decisions are made on a somewhat higher plane of sophistication realize that universal acceptance of the money-creation approach would lead to higher levels of governmental activity. If money creation were regarded as painless, the offset against the preference of persons for additional governmental activities reflecting their real costs to society would be removed.

As a consequence of these reactions plus practical experience of various countries in the past with money creation for revenue purposes (including the Confederacy during the Civil War) most persons accept the principle that financing by money creation is inherently objectionable and irresponsible. This extreme position overlooks the merit of the use of money creation in certain circumstances. When a government seeks to increase the level of economic activity from less than full-employment levels, its primary task is to increase total spending in the economy. The most efficient means to do so is to substitute money creation for taxes (or borrowing) to finance existing or increased activities. With this method the maximum expansionary effect is attained per dollar of budget deficit, and interest burdens are avoided. Taxes curtail consumption and investment spending, and borrowing, unless offset by central bank action, will restrict investment (and possibly consumption). Unfortunately the bias against money creation, which has become accepted to the point of dogma, interferes with the use of this method of financing when it is warranted. Central bank borrowing, however, is typically not regarded as money creation, and thus governments are relatively free to use it without popular disapproval.[2] Misunderstanding in this instance may be regarded as a virtue.

The Choice of Borrowing

Governments, like individuals and business firms, may obtain revenue by borrowing, through the issuance of bonds and other securities. Such borrowing may be internal, the funds being obtained from domestic sources without effect upon the total supply of real resources available to the economy, or external, the funds coming from foreign sources, with consequent increased availability of resources.

Individual Evaluation of Borrowing versus Taxation. What determines the preferences of individuals between taxation and borrowing as revenue sources, when money creation is ruled out?

The borrowing alternative offers the advantage of allowing each person greater freedom in choice of time for downward adjustment of private-sector consumption. With taxation he must make the adjustment immediately; with borrowing, he may make it now if he wishes (using the funds to purchase bonds and thus offset his liability for public debt) or he may postpone the adjustment to a later period. If he follows the former alternative, borrowing offers no advantage. But the borrowing technique alone gives him the alternative of postponement. Theoretically, if capital markets were perfect and risks uniform, the person could accomplish the same result by borrowing privately to meet his tax liability and curtailing consumption at some date in the future. In practice, the government can borrow more cheaply than individuals (some of whom would find it impossible to borrow at all) and governmental borrowing allows all persons access to the government's ability to borrow freely and cheaply.

At the same time, use of the borrowing alternative introduces a much greater degree of uncertainty about each person's ultimate tax liability, which the person cannot ascertain precisely. If the current tax approach is used, uncertainty is lessened but not entirely removed. The significance for his decision will depend upon his estimates of future tax liabilities. If he believes that he is likely to pay less in the

[2]In the United States, the government was long prohibited by law from selling bonds to the Federal Reserve. This source of funds was drastically restricted in the depression of the thirties and unnecessary debt and interest obligations to the public created. During World War II sale of bonds to the Federal Reserve became necessary; until the law was changed this had to be accomplished by selling bonds to the public simultaneously with Federal Reserve purchase of bonds. This was a clumsy roundabout device to accomplish what could have been done much more simply.

future than he would pay now, he will have greater preference for borrowing. This attitude may be found on the part of persons close to retirement age. On the other hand, if a person expects his tax liability to rise, as would younger persons expecting increases in their income, he will be less sympathetic toward borrowing. Buchanan argues that a prime reason persons oppose borrowing is their fear that other persons will not prepare themselves for payment of their share of the debt, and thus one who succeeds will bear a disproportionate amount.[3] Accordingly they prefer taxes, which others cannot escape.

Borrowing involves not only delay in payment of tax but also the possibility of shifting the burden from the present group of taxpayers to other persons. Particularly in urban areas, geographic shifts in population may be significant. A substantially different (and larger) group may be living in the city a decade from now, and, by the use of borrowing, a portion of the burden can be transferred to them. There is also always the possibility of shifting burdens to persons not yet born or of taxpaying age, that is, to future generations. The possibility of actual shifting of burden forward is considered in Chapter 11; certainly voters typically regard forward shifting as possible. To what extent do persons regard such shifting to others as desirable? On a narrow self-interest basis, they would always prefer that others bear the burden. But persons presumably do not necessarily think in such narrow terms; while concepts of intergeneration equity vary, many persons do not regard transfers to others as universally desirable. First, to the extent to which persons regard their heirs as extensions of their own lives, they will consider the interests of their heirs as well as their own. To many persons the shifting of burden of current governmental activity to future generations is inherently unfair. Second, attitudes are influenced by the expected time distribution of benefits. If benefits will be spread over a number of years, persons will regard the use of borrowing to spread burdens forward as justifiable. The obvious activity of this type is nonrecurrent expenditure on major capital improvements that will last for a number of years. Long life of a particular item of capital equipment does not in itself make borrowing desirable; if a large city spends $1 million each year on schools and is expected to do so in the future, there is no long-range gain from borrowing, as the annual amortization payments will soon equal the annual expenditures, even though each school building will last for a long period. The nonrecurrent char-

---

[3]J. M. Buchanan, *Public Finance in Democratic Process* (Chapel Hill, N.C.: University of North Carolina Press, 1966), chap. xvii.

acter of expenditures makes borrowing attractive as a means of spreading costs forward.[4] Other nonrecurring expenditures yielding benefits over a period of years include those for "crash" programs to raise standards of education or public health and for conduct of major wars. With all these activities, widely accepted philosophy holds that since the activities convey benefits to persons in the future, the present generation is justified in passing a portion of the burden forward.

A final influence that affects the choice between borrowing and taxation is the concern that many persons have for the interest burden created by the borrowing and the significance of both the interest and the debt for the functioning of the economy.

The interest is an obvious phenomenon; borrowing adds to the total cost of governmental activities. While any individual may escape the interest cost by reducing his consumption immediately—as he would do if he were taxed—and buying bonds, most persons appear not to consider this alternative. The more sophisticated citizen is also aware that a debt may have adverse consequences for economic development. Taxes necessary to pay interest charges may retard investment; fear of the debt per se may be a confidence-reducing influence on the economy. At the subordinate levels of government, persons may fear that a heavy outstanding debt may deter establishment of new industry. Finally, many persons, reasoning by analogy with the individual, regard borrowing as inherently undesirable if it can be avoided.

In summary: persons will be most inclined to favor borrowing in preference to taxation:

1. When financing by taxation would require a sharp temporary curtailment in their consumption.

2. When they expect their own tax liabilities to be less in the future than at present.

3. When they feel that shifting of burden to future generations is desirable, either as a simple device to escape tax, or because the expenditures will yield benefits in the future and thus intergeneration equity requires forward shifting.

Their preference for borrowing will be greater:

1. The lower the interest rate level and thus the interest burden.

2. The less the fear that borrowing and the debt will have undesirable consequences for the economy.

3. The weaker their emotional bias against debt.

---

[4]Persons may err about the nonrecurrent nature of expediture programs. In the 1920's building of a major state highway network was regarded as a nonrecurrent expenditure.

Government versus Individuals. While we assume that democratic governments seek to follow the wishes of the people and that their decisions relative to borrowing reflect the preferences of the majority of the voters, as on all questions governments exercise considerable influence over voter choices. In what major respects may governments, per se, take different attitudes toward the desirability of borrowing than the typical voter and thus disregard or seek to alter voter preferences? First, there is presumably some disposition on the part of legislatures and administrations in an unsophisticated society to have stronger preferences than voters for borrowing, since by this means they can provide services (which voters like) without taxes (which they dislike). The provision of governmental services becomes very painless—so long as no thought is given to the future. This attitude was common on the part of local governments in the United States in the last century. Today the typical voter has learned to consider the future as well as the present and borrowing thus has somewhat less appeal to government.

Second, governments, with their expert advisers, are in a better position to estimate the effects of borrowing upon the functioning of the economy than is the typical voter. As a consequence under some circumstances the government may be less favorably inclined toward borrowing than the typical voter. On the other hand, recognition of the evils of borrowing may become so strongly accepted by the voters that governments will find it necessary to persuade the public that borrowing is not actually irresponsible but desirable in the interests of economic stability—as in depressions if money creation is ruled out.

TAX STRUCTURE DECISION MAKING

Just as with the broader issue of selection of taxes or other revenues, decisions about the tax structure made by the legislative body presumably reflect overall community preferences—or at least the legislators' interpretation of these. As with expenditures, decision making in the taxation field is incremental, changes being made periodically from the existing tax structure. Frequently the changes under consideration involve only minor adjustments in rates or structure; occasionally they involve the establishment of a new tax. In rare instances drastic overhaul of the entire tax structure is considered. Partly because of reliance on incremental, piecemeal types of change, occasionally governments will establish tax study committees, common in the states, or, in the Commonwealth countries, Royal Commissions, to review the overall tax structure. Seldom do these commissions propose complete change—and when they do, rarely are drastic changes actually made.

Individual Attitudes toward Tax Structures

To most persons taxes are necessary evils that they accept in order that governments may provide the services they desire and avoid the use of less acceptable methods of financing. While no one likes taxes that he must pay, most persons are resigned to their necessity. The average person also feels that as an individual he can exercise little or no influence over the framing of the tax structure, but he is probably more willing to take the trouble to express himself than he is on expenditure proposals, other than those in which he has a direct, vital interest.

Secondly, a person—under the usual maximization assumption—prefers taxes that primarily burden other persons rather than himself.[5] In fact, under a very narrow self-interest assumption, the majority group in the society would favor the enactment of taxes that placed the entire burden on the minority—a consequence that the wealthy minority sometimes fears. Actually, this is far too narrow an interpretation of motivation; a better interpretation is that persons favor those taxes that will place upon themselves no more burden than they regard as essential, consistent with the attainment of the objective, namely, the financing of the services. In other words, persons recognize that they cannot expect to escape payment if the governmental services are to be provided and financed; they recognize that placing all the burden on a small minority is impossible, and thus they must make some contribution themselves. They are also influenced by concepts of fairness; few persons in this world seek to place upon others all of the costs of services from which they benefit. Persons will oppose taxes that they feel strike them "unfairly" and allow others to escape a "reasonable" burden, and they will favor taxes they expect to concentrate on others, especially when the "others" are nonhuman persons such as corporations—thus the popularity of the corporate income tax—but they do not seriously hope to avoid all payment.

Attitudes are also greatly influenced by generally accepted criteria in a particular society. In Western countries the traditions that equity

[5]Note the study by Elizabeth Likert David, "Public Preferences and State-Local Taxes," in H. E. Brazer (ed.), *Essays in State and Local Finance* (Ann Arbor, Mich.: University of Michigan Institute of Public Administration, 1967), pp. 74–106. Mrs. David concludes that self-interest considerations explain most of the variation in individual attitudes toward alternative tax measures.

requires taxation on the basis of ability to pay, that ability is best measured by income, and that progression is justifiable are widely accepted, and lead many persons to favor tax proposals that they might otherwise oppose because of the tax they would pay. The governments themselves exert substantial influence on attitudes, particularly through the use of propaganda in support of a tax increase or tax change. There is also a strong bias in favor of existing taxes unless they grossly violate accepted standards; uncertainty is minimized, as well as the need for decision making about new proposals. Any change offers the danger of heavier burden. Persons may accept existing levels of taxes with little opposition, or may tolerate small annual increases, but they strongly resist changes that sharply increase annual payments—the "threshold effect." Only a severe financial emergency will jolt persons into accepting a drastic change, such as the great increase in income taxes at the beginning of World War II. Such rates would have been unthinkable before the war but there was little pressure to return to the lower rates after the war.

Ideological biases play a more significant role in taxation compared to those for most specific governmental expenditure programs. Certain organizations come to support certain taxes or tax features and fight others, without reconsideration of changing conditions, and partisans of these groups accept the position without serious evaluation. They fear approbation of fellow members if they do not and they accept the group position as a shortcut to decision making. Labor unions typically oppose sales taxes and favor income taxes, although many of their members may pay more under the latter than under the former. Political parties become committed in like fashion. There are curious instances of strong biases about particular taxes built up in a large part of the population of a state without any obvious reason—the strong bias in Illinois against income taxation (to the point at times that a person supporting the tax was regarded as a dangerous radical), and the bias in Oregon for so many years against sales taxation.

Certain specific conditions obviously influence preferences. A person's preference for a tax is increased if the tax—or an increase in it—is tied directly to expenditures that he strongly favors. Many persons would approve a property tax increase to allow elimination of overcrowding of schools but oppose one for a general increase in local government spending. The gasoline tax has always been one of the least unpopular taxes because it is so closely tied to the financing of highways. Secondly, a person looks more favorably upon a tax that he regards as basically fair. Thirdly, the actual and expected effectiveness of enforcement plays a role; persons generally will be less favorable toward taxes they believe to be poorly administered—at least unless they themselves expect to be able to escape. Overall attitudes toward taxes and tax increases are influenced by attitudes toward the general desirability of the governmental expenditure programs and toward the government itself. Persons opposed to expansion of activities will fight tax increases or the use of new taxes that will increase revenues and facilitate growth of spending; persons unsympathetic to the administration will be less inclined to support proposed tax changes.

Attitudes of Governments

Governments—we assume—seek to frame tax policy in terms of the overall preferences of society. The problems of doing so are similar to those encountered in developing expenditure programs. Preferences are not well defined and not easily ascertained, and there may be no majority position. Preferences may even be contradictory; majority support may be obtained for a balanced budget but not for any combination of taxes that will permit it. Not infrequently, as happened in 1966 in Nebraska, voters will turn down all alternative tax measures offered. The preferences relate to overall objectives and types of taxes, not to detail.

Accordingly, society gives to governments the responsibility for devising means to carry out the major objectives and to develop the precise tax structure that will best fulfill the preferences. Society in turn is typically willing to accept the structures unless they appear to be highly objectionable; if they do, the government may be defeated in its attempt to gain reelection. But too many issues enter into the voters' decisions for tax considerations alone to control the outcome. Thus governments have broad discretion in fulfilling this responsibility. As a consequence the views of persons in the executive and legislative branches responsible for determination of tax legislation play a major role in framing the tax structure.

Governments sometimes have an unfortunate tendency to devise tax structures that conceal the actual tax burden from the public. This policy has been less popular in the United States than elsewhere, but even in this country it plays a part in the strong support in the administration and Congress for the corporation income tax, the burden of which is well hidden from consumers, stockholders, and others who experience reduction in real incomes. Support for the manufacturers' sales tax in Canada rests primarily upon concealment from the public, whereas the principal alternative, the retail sales tax, is clearly evident to the customer. Some European countries prohibit vendors from showing sales taxes separately from prices in order to keep the public unaware of the actual burden. Such a policy, while understandable, can be criticized on the grounds of making reasonable appraisal of the tax structure by the voters more difficult.

Governments, and particularly legislative bodies, not only give some attention to preferences of the public about particular taxes but also are subject to strong pressure groups. Tax policy is not made in a vacuum, but by human beings in the context of a particular situation. Powerful truck lobbies, not adverse, it is rumored, to sharp threats, have substantial influence over tax legislation affecting their members. Groups not infrequently warn of dire consequences if certain tax legislation is passed, including threats of firms to close down and move out of the state if tax rates are increased. Farm groups, chambers of commerce, educational associations, labor unions often have substantial influence on legislatures, and to some extent on Congress, although the latter is less easily subjected to pressure and threats. But organizations that develop doctrinaire positions often lose most of their influence; the otherwise powerful National Association of Manufacturers in the United States, for example, has little influence on tax legislation because of its rigid positions.

In the framing of legislation, there is always danger that small groups with unusually strong bargaining power may distort tax structures to their own benefit, contrary to the interests of society as a whole. The unusually favorable treatment of oil producers through liberal depletion allowances under the federal income tax is an example. As with other legislation, the higher income groups have disproportionate influence on tax structures compared to their numerical importance, for reasons noted in Chapter 2. In the United States, actual progression is very much less than it appears to be on the basis of rate tables because disproportionate political strength of the higher income groups prevents adequate taxation of capital gains.

THE PROCESS OF ENACTMENT OF TAX LEGISLATION

In the United States, as in many countries, the route of revenue legislation is different from that of expenditure legislation. The budget document itself contains only a summary of revenue forecasts with existing taxes, prepared for the Bureau of the Budget by the Treasury; it does not contain detailed plans for changes in taxation.

Preparation of Recommendations[6]

Primary responsibility for preparation of the recommendations on taxation rests with the Treasury. On major issues of policy, however, and particularly on those relating to the level of taxation compared to expenditures (the deficit or surplus position), the responsibility is shared with the Bureau of the Budget and the Council of Economic Advisers. The President and his economic advisers may also play a major role in the decisions. The Treasury has a permanent staff with the primary task of making continuous studies of the tax structure and considering objections to features of taxes raised by taxpayer groups or others, or noted by the Internal Revenue Service in the administration of the tax laws. If the Treasury is convinced that major reform measures are needed, the Secretary will consult with the President on the possibility of a tax measure; if he obtains approval, the details of the proposal will be developed by the Treasury staff. At the later stages of preparation the proposals will be discussed with the Bureau of the Budget, the Council of Economic Advisers, and the President. On matters of fiscal policy such as a general increase in taxes to lessen inflationary pressures, the initiative for the proposal may come from the Council or from the President himself, but the Treasury will undertake the task of preparing the specific recommendations. With agreement on the proposals, the President may make some general reference to them in his State of the Union message, and again, in more detail, in the budget message; if the proposed changes are significant, he may present a separate tax message to Congress following the transmission of the budget, outlining the proposals and the justification for them in detail.

Congressional Consideration

By constitutional requirement, all revenue measures must originate in the House. The proposals go to the Ways and Means Committee, the most powerful committee of the House, for hearings. The Secretary of the Treasury presents a detailed statement of the proposals to the committee accompanied by substantial supporting evidence, and is subjected to questioning. The committee over the next several months receives statements from numerous groups and individuals favoring or opposing particular changes. After the hearings, the committee reviews the evidence and statements, obtains assistance from the staff of

[6]See J. A. Pechman, *Federal Tax Reform* (Washington, D.C.: Brookings Institution, 1966), chap. iii.

the Joint Committee on Internal Revenue Taxation[7] and from the Treasury, reaches a position on the various major issues, and produces a tax bill. While voting on some issues tends to be along party lines, on many issues substantial consensus is reached. The measure is sent to the House and debated under rules limiting debate, with amendments usually barred, and the committee's proposal is almost always approved.

The bill next goes to the Senate and is first considered by the Senate Finance Committee, with procedure comparable to that of the Ways and Means Committee, but briefer. The committee then considers the various provisions in the measure and almost always makes some changes from the House version. Debate is unrestricted on the Senate floor, and amendments to the committee proposal are frequently approved.

Since the House and Senate versions inevitably differ, a Conference Committee works out a compromise and the amended version is almost automatically approved by each house. The measure then goes to the President for signing. On a few occasions the measure has been so distorted from the original proposals that the President vetoed it. At least six months typically elapse from the President's message until the measure is signed. Needless to say, the administration seeks through its key supporters on the two committees and in the Senate to obtain approval of the provisions it regards as important, and to keep out undesirable ones, but it is not always successful; the final bill always differs substantially from the original proposal.

A few incidental features of the process should be noted. In recent years the Ways and Means Committee has conducted extensive review of the major features of the tax structure by requesting experts in various fields to prepare papers and present them to the committee. After publication the papers served as the basis for hearings and provided background for subsequent action. For example, the repeal of most federal excise taxes in 1965 grew out of hearings on the taxes held by the committee in 1964. This procedure has helped to lessen the long-standing criticism that the committee listens only to biased evidence from interested groups and not to persons who are experts in the field and consider the issues more objectively. Secondly, while appropriations measures must be enacted annually, general revenue measures are considered at less frequent intervals; there were 10 between 1948 and 1966, and not all these were major. Thirdly, while

[7]The Joint Committee is made up of members of the Ways and Means Committee and the Senate Finance Committee, and has a permanent staff of experts.

individual members of Congress may introduce tax measures, virtually never do the bills get out of committee, or even receive committee attention. The Ways and Means Committee has tremendous power, subject to potential overrule by action of the House, to prevent action on tax proposals, and, in turn, the chairman has great influence over committee action. No one person in the United States has more influence over tax legislation than the Chairman of the Ways and Means Committee.

Thus the process of development of tax legislation involves a combination of influences: taxation experts, especially on more technical aspects of the law; the economists of the Council of Economic Advisers, the Bureau of the Budget, the Treasury, including outside consultants of these agencies, especially on questions of fiscal policy (deficits and surpluses); the President; and members of Congress, particularly of the two key committees. Both administration and Congress are subject to substantial pressure by interested groups; presumably Congress is somewhat more directly responsive to attitudes of the public than are the technical experts of the administration. Perhaps the most serious criticism that can be advanced against the procedure is the excessive influence on the tax structure of a relatively few persons in key positions, whose attitudes may not reflect more widely accepted ones. Small pressure groups may likewise exercise disproportionate influence.

Another issue is the separation of consideration of expenditures and revenue measures, which are handled by separate committees, with the measures voted on at different times. As a consequence, inadequate specific consideration may be given to the relationship of the totals of the two magnitudes, and thus to the deficit or surplus. Obviously the President considers this relationship in his recommendations, and neither set of congressional committees completely diregards the other side of the picture. But better consideration of the relationship might be developed.

State Tax Measures

The enactment of tax legislation at the state level is similar but much simpler. Initial recommendations usually come from the governor, who may get them from a variety of sources. Only a few states have agencies that give continuing study to tax questions. Some major proposals are products of the work of state tax study commissions noted above. The legislative committees give much briefer attention; their members are typically much less expert in the taxation field than members of the congressional committees and the influence of outside pressure groups is likely to be stronger. The legislative committees may follow the recommendations of the governor rather closely, or they may deviate sharply from them. Several states have encountered serious financial crises because of inability of the legislature and the governor or of both houses of the legislature to compromise on a mutually accepted tax program.

Since local governments rely primarily on the property tax, they make no continuing review of the tax structure, but occasionally consider new tax sources.

THE APPROACHES TO TAXATION

While numerous forms of taxes have developed over the centuries, they can be classed into a relatively small number of groups:

1. Taxes related to income:
   a) Personal.
   b) Corporate.
   c) Payroll taxes.
2. Taxes relating to consumption spending:
   a) The expenditure tax, collected in the same fashion as an income tax on reported spending.
   b) Customs duties and sales and excise taxes, levied upon importers or sellers but regarded as consumption-related taxes under the assumption that they are shifted forward.
3. Taxes related to ownership or transfer of wealth:
   a) Taxes on the net wealth of individuals.
   b) Taxes on gross value of property owned.
   c) Site value and land taxes.
   d) Capital levies.
   e) Taxes on the transfer of property at death or through gift.
4. Taxes directly related to business activity per se, imposed on gross receipts, capital stock, or some other measure, or on specific forms of business activity.
5. Taxes on exports.[8]

The term "direct tax" has been used traditionally to refer to taxes collected from the persons expected to bear the budren: income, expenditure, and property taxes. Indirect taxes are those presumably shifted forward from the taxpayer to someone else: sales, customs, and excise taxes. In practice this classification is not precise or too useful.

---

[8]Barred in the United States by constitutional provision.

The ultimate distribution of burden is not always clear; for example, the corporation income tax may not rest on the owners of the corporation, and a portion of the property tax almost certainly shifts from property owners. Most of the personal income tax is actually collected from employers via withholding.

1. Income Taxation

Direct taxation of income is employed in most countries of the world; it is the most important element in the overall tax structure of the United States, and a major element in the tax structures of most developed economies. The income tax can be regarded as an outgrowth of the poll tax, a levy of a flat amount per person, and one of the earliest forms of taxation.[9] The obvious inequity of such a tax, by usual standards, led to its replacement by one related to income. In some countries, particularly in tropical Africa, the immediate successor of the poll tax was the graduated personal levy, which provides for grouping of persons into a small number of rate classes on the basis of income or some measure of probable income, uniform taxation of all persons within each group, and higher rates for successively higher income groups.

a) Personal Income Taxes. The modern income tax applies percentage rates to taxable incomes, the rate structure usually being progressive relative to income. The intent is to tax "net income," that is, gross income less expenses of earning it. Thus persons operating businesses are allowed to deduct all business expenses to ascertain taxable income. While a country may tax net income without allowing further adjustments, most allow two types of deductions: certain expenditures, such as medical expenses and contributions, which are presumed to reduce taxpaying ability or which the government wishes to encourage, and an allowance for the taxpayer and his dependents, designed to free the lowest income groups from the tax and to adjust tax liability according to the size of the family.

Income taxes may be global in nature, as in the United States, applying to the lump sum of all income except that specifically excluded or specially treated; or schedular, each type of income (salaries, rent, profits, and so on), being taxed separately, often with a variety of rates, as has been characteristic of the Latin countries. A global surtax may be superimposed upon the schedular taxes.

Income tax may be collected from individuals on the basis of an-

---

[9]In the United States, the poll tax was continued in some states until recent years primarily for the purpose of restricting voting, for which payment of the tax was a prerequisite.

nual returns or by withholding[10] from wages and other incomes for which this technique is feasible, with reconciliation at the end of the year.

b) *Corporations.* Countries differ widely in the relationship established between personal and corporate income taxes. At the one extreme, in the United Kingdom and many Commonwealth countries, the corporate tax was initially regarded merely as a device for collecting the personal income tax on income earned through the corporation. Stockholders were given full credit against their personal income tax liability for tax paid at the corporate level on their dividend income, and the corporate tax in effect applied only to the undistributed profits of the corporation, with no double taxation of corporate income.[11] By contrast, the policy in many countries (including, in most of the years of the tax, the United States) has been to regard the corporate tax as a completely distinct levy, corporate income being fully taxed as well as the dividend element in personal income, thus producing double taxation of dividend income to the extent that the corporate tax reduces funds available for payment as dividends (rather than being shifted forward).

A variant of the corporate income tax is the excess profits tax, imposed upon profits in excess of an amount defined to be "normal," typically at high rates. Firms have been given the choice of two methods of calculating normal profits: actual profits in the years immediately preceding the imposition of the tax, or a specified return on investment. Were the tax used as a permanent revenue measure, only the latter alternative would be possible. As used in the United States, the tax has been employed only as a temporary wartime measure, with both options allowed.[12] Unlike the corporate income tax, the excess profits tax requires a valuation of the company's property to ascertain the base for calculating normal return.

c) *Payroll Taxes.* Levies on wages and salaries only, on the employer, employee, or both, are widely used to finance social security programs. Rates are usually proportional.

2. Consumption Taxation

Whereas income taxes apply to all income less deductions, without regard to use for consumption or saving, the consumption approach

---

[10]Called PAYE in most British Commonwealth countries.
[11]This is no longer true in the United Kingdom and many other countries that once followed this policy.
[12]The excess profits tax was used in the United States during World Wars I and II and the Korean War period.

taxes only the portion spent on consumption, either in total or for certain purposes. Alternatively, a tax could be applied only to the portion of income saved, but no such tax is in use.

a) *The Expenditure or Spendings Tax.*[13] The expenditure tax is collected directly from individual taxpayers through returns comparable to those used for income taxes; in fact the two taxes could be collected on a single return. Tax liability is determined by deducting net increase in savings during the period from total income. Thus if a person had income of $7,000 and showed a net increase in savings of $2,000, his taxable consumption expenditure would be $5,000. Similar deductions and personal allowances could be provided as those of the personal income tax, and some additional types of expenditures, such as ones for education, might be made deductible. The tax rate could be made progressive, and in fact very steeply so if the government wished to discourage spending in an inflationary period. This is one of the few levies that can employ a rate in excess of 100 percent. The expenditure tax has been widely proposed as an anti-inflationary measure and as a means of lessening undesirable economic consequences of the income tax, but its use has been confined to brief periods in India and Ceylon.[14]

b) *The Indirect Approach.* Consumption taxes in practice take the indirect form, being collected from importers or vendors, with the assumption that the tax is reflected in higher prices to the purchasers, distributing the burden in relation to consumer spending. Since the number of importers and vendors is very much smaller than the number of families, these taxes have always offered the advantage of relative ease of administration.

(*1*) *Custom Duties* are the oldest of these indirect consumption taxes and continue to play a major role in the tax structures of less developed economies, although unimportant, revenuewise, in the United States. They may be levied on either specific (fixed rate per physical unit) or ad valorem (percentage of value) bases. The former is simpler since no valuation is necessary, but the latter is more closely related to consumer expenditures. To the extent to which customs duties are reflected in higher domestic prices they are borne in relation to consumer spending on the taxed items. Typically articles regarded as luxuries are taxed more heavily than those regarded as necessary items,

---

[13]The term "expenditure tax" is used in Great Britain, "spendings tax" in the United States.

[14]The chief exponent of the tax for some years has been the English economist Nicholas Kaldor; see *An Expenditure Tax* (London: Allen and Unwin, 1955).

and basic necessities may be exempted. High rates are also applied when protection rather than revenue is the goal. The greater the extent to which customs duties provide effective protection for domestic industry, the less revenue they produce.

(2) *Sales Taxes,* levies on the sale of all commodities, are distributed in relation to total consumption, under the assumption that they are reflected in higher commodity prices relative to factor prices. Since sales taxes are collected from the vendors, they are enforced more easily than a direct expenditure tax. Technically, they may be imposed upon the sale or transaction per se,[15] upon the vendor on the basis of his sales or gross receipts,[16] or, as in the Canadian provinces, upon the customer, the vendor being a collecting agent of the government. The precise legal form has little or no significance for the distributional effects.

While sales taxation dates back to the *alcavala* of medieval Spain, in modern form it is of relatively recent origin, having been introduced in Europe and Canada at the end of World War I, and in the states of the United States during the depression years of the thirties. In addition to the states, it is now employed by all countries of Western Europe except Spain, by India and Pakistan, by Brazil, Chile, Argentina, Mexico, and several other Latin-American countries, and in Canada (dominion and provincial). It is not usually employed in less developed economies.

The sales tax takes several major forms:

1. The multiple stage or turnover taxes, applying to all or most transactions through which a commodity passes on the way from initial production of materials to final sale to the consumer. This is the type represented by the German *umsatzsteuer* (replaced January 1, 1968 by a value-added tax), and used in the other European Common Market countries except France, and in Chile, India, and some other countries.

2. The single-stage taxes, applying only once to each commodity as it passes through production and distribution channels. There are three possible levels:

    a) The manufacturers sales tax, applied at the manufacturing level; either to final products only, as in Canada, or to all sales of manufactured goods, with credit given at one stage

---

[15]For example, the Belgian transactions tax, the earlier French sales taxes, and the sales taxes of a number of states.

[16]The German turnover taxes and other levies modeled after it, and the sales taxes of some states.

for tax previously paid on parts and materials purchased from an earlier stage in production.

b) The wholesale sales tax, applied to the sale to retailers, whether by manufacturers, wholesalers, or importers, as used in Switzerland, Australia, and New Zealand.

c) The retail sales tax, applying to the final retail sale to the consumer, as in states of the United States and the Canadian provinces, and Norway.

Several countries have developed hybrid forms. Finland applies sales tax to the last wholesale sale and to the gross margin (value added) of the retailers, and Honduras collects the tax on the sales of the larger retailers and on the purchases of the smaller ones, via their suppliers, to minimize enforcement problems.

3. The value-added tax, applying at all production and distribution stages, but to value added only, that is sales less cost of goods which were taxed when purchased by the firm. This tax is used in France and Germany and is scheduled to replace turnover taxes in the other ECM countries.

The precise coverage and rate structure are largely independent of the type of sales tax used. At the one extreme some jurisdictions provide no exemptions for consumption goods (although in practice most tax only a small range of services) and thus reach all consumption expenditures on commodities. Many jurisdictions, however, exempt items regarded as basic necessities. Some vary the rate, with higher figures on goods regarded as luxuries, but a uniform rate is more common.

Tax treatment of capital goods varies substantially with the single-stage taxes (they are fully taxable under multiple-stage taxes). Policies vary all the way from complete or almost complete exclusion of capital goods from tax (the French value added tax and the sales taxes of a few states) to one of taxing all capital goods except those that actually become physical ingredients of taxable products.

(3) *Excise Taxes*[17] are those taxes imposed upon the production or sale of particular commodities or group of commodities. Virtually all governments make use of excises; in some (for example, Spain) the coverage is so great that the system is comparable to a sales tax. More commonly, however, excises are concentrated on three groups of commodities:

[17]Historically the term "excise" referred to taxes on production only. Usage has gradually broadened. Occasionally a sales tax at the manufacturing level is referred to as a general excise tax.

1. Liquor and tobacco, singled out for centuries for heavy taxation. These levies are often referred to as sumptuary taxes, because in part they were designed to regulate consumption.
2. Motor fuel, in the United States specifically allocated to highway finance on the benefit principle.
3. Items regarded as luxuries, such as motor vehicles, jewelry, furs, electrical appliances.

Excises, like customs, may have specific or ad valorem rates.

Closely related to excises, although not falling within the usual definition, are annual taxes on the use of particular kinds of property. The principal examples are motor vehicle license "fees," which are taxes rather than fees since they greatly exceed costs of licensing.

3. Taxation Related to Wealth

The third major type of taxation is related to wealth and thus to a stock rather than to a flow of income or consumption. There are several major types:

a) *Net Wealth Tax.* A tax on net wealth is a levy against individuals, based upon their net personal wealth of all kinds, including both real property (land and improvements), tangible personal property (movable property having intrinsic value, such as motor vehicles or jewelry), and intangible personal property (claims against or evidence of ownership in other property, such as bonds, mortgages, and stocks, plus money and bank deposits). From the gross value of the person's property is subtracted all claims outstanding against the property to arrive at the net value. Corporations, per se, are not subjected to the tax; the value of corporate property is reached via the bond and stock holdings of the investors. Net wealth taxes are common in northern Europe.

b) *Property Tax.* A major element in the tax structures of English-speaking countries is the property tax, the mainstay of local government revenue in the United States and in Canada, Great Britain (where the term *rate* is employed), and other Commonwealth countries. The tax is an *in rem* levy, imposed against property as such rather than the owners, and thus constituting a legal claim against the property. The tax is imposed upon the gross value of the property without regard to personal or corporate ownership, the personal circumstances of the owners, or liabilities outstanding. The rate is usually proportional.

More commonly, the tax applies to real property alone (characteristic of the British Commonwealth countries and some states, including New York), or real property plus some forms of tangible personal property, intangibles being exempt in practice (because of the difficulty of finding them) or by law.

c) Site Value and Land Taxes. A major variant of the property tax is the site value tax (sometimes called the single tax[18]), applying only to land values, with improvements excluded. In complete or partial form (lower rate on improvements than on land) this tax is used in parts of Canada, Australia, and Commonwealth countries of east and central Africa. Graduated taxes on land values have been widely discussed in Latin America to aid agrarian reform and used to a limited extent.

d) Capital Levy. Unlike net wealth and property taxes, which are annually recurrent levies, a capital levy is a once-and-for-all tax imposed upon persons upon the basis of their wealth, at rates much higher than those of the typical wealth or property taxes. They have been used in only a few instances, primarily to reduce the burden of debt in the period following a major war.

e) Death and Gift Taxes (Usually Called Death Duties). Taxes upon transfer of property at the time of death are regarded as taxes upon property, although technically these levies are imposed upon the transfer. Inheritance is not, however, a regular flow for any one taxpayer, and since the transaction is not a commercial one, constructive valuation is required. Death taxes take three principal forms:

1. The estate tax, as used by the U.S. federal government, is imposed upon the entire estate, less deductions, without regard to the number of heirs or the relationship of the heir to the decedent.[19] The rate is progressive according to the size of the entire estate.

2. The inheritance tax, as used by most states, is imposed upon the individual shares going to various beneficiaries, the exemptions and rates varying with the relationship of the beneficiary to the decedent, with lower rates and higher exemptions for direct heirs than for others. The progression operates separately on each individual bequest.[20]

3. Accessions taxes, not used but long suggested; liability would

[18]This name originated from the work of Henry George, who proposed that governments employ as their only tax a levy on land value, to recover for society the unearned increment arising out of population growth and economic development. The single-tax proposal gained considerable political strength around the turn of the century.

[19]In the United States special treatment is accorded the surviving spouse, to whom up to one half the estate may be left tax-free.

[20]The successions tax, as used in Canada, is a hybrid of estate and inheritance taxes, the rates based partly on the shares to the particular heirs (and thus influenced by relationship), partly upon the size of the entire estate.

be placed upon the recipient, on the basis of the cumulated totals of amounts received from various donors.

Gift taxes, although imposed upon gifts among living persons, are regarded as a part of the death tax structure, since they are imposed to prevent avoidance of death duties by gifts of property prior to death, and the rates are closely related. Smaller gifts are exempt. The taxes are imposed upon the donor, not upon the recipient, and the amounts received are excluded from income tax.

4. Business Taxes

Most taxes fall clearly into one of the major categories noted. The only significant exception consists of levies labeled "business taxes," ones imposed on business firms as such under the context of a charge for the privilege of doing business. Many of these are imposed only upon corporations, although some apply to noncorporate businesses as well. Little thought is given, in imposing these taxes, to their final distributional effects. The corporation income tax can be regarded as a type of business tax, particularly at the state level. National corporate income taxes, however, are usually considered to be portions of the income tax structure. Other business taxes include levies on gross receipts, capital stock, corporate excess (excess of "going concern" value over assessed value of property for property tax purposes) plus flat rate occupational taxes, frequently used by local governments.

5. Export Taxes

Taxes upon exports are used extensively in developing economies, imposed upon the export of primary agricultural, mineral, or forest products. Rates may be uniform or may be progressive according to the market prices of the products. These taxes may produce the same distributional pattern as an income tax on the producers by reducing their net income.

APPENDIX I—CONSTITUTIONAL TAXING POWERS: UNITED STATES

THE FEDERAL GOVERNMENT[21]

Section 8 of Article I of the Constitution gives Congress specific power to levy taxes: "The Congress shall have Power to lay and collect

---

[21]See S. Ratner, *American Taxation* (New York: Norten, 1942) for an historical review.

Taxes, Duties, Imposts, and Excises, to pay the Debts and provide for the common Defense and general Welfare of the United States . . . ." This power is subjected, however, to certain limitations, some by specific provisions of the Constitution, others by court interpretation of other sections of the Constitution.

Specific Limitations

1. *The Uniformity Clause.* Section 8 concludes with the statement: "but all Duties, Imposts and Excises shall be uniform throughout the United States." This section has been interpreted to mean that any federal tax regarded by the courts as an indirect tax shall be levied at a geographically uniform rate, the rate being the same in all states. In earlier years the use of progressive rates was contested as a violation of the uniformity clause, but this argument was overruled by the Supreme Court when it upheld the use of exemptions and progressive rates with the inheritance tax. The term *excise* has never been clearly defined by the courts. Taxes on sale of commodities, plus death taxes and the original corporation income tax, have been held to be excises. The personal income tax has been held to be a direct tax.

2. *The Apportionment Clause.* Section 9 of Article I states: "No capitation, or other direct Tax shall be laid, unless in Proportion to the Census or Enumeration herein before directed to be taken." Under the terms of this provision the amounts to be collected from any tax interpreted to be direct would have to be apportioned among the states according to population rather than be collected at a uniform rate throughout the country. Thus, if $10 billion were to be collected from a property tax and 6 percent of the population of the United States were in Illinois, the federal property tax rate in Illinois would be set at such a level that the amount collected in the state would equal 6 percent of $10 billion, or $600 million. Thus the federal tax rate would be high in states with low per capita wealth and low in states with high per capita wealth. Because of the inequity of this rule, any tax interpreted to be a direct tax is effectively barred from federal use.

A major issue was encountered with the attempt of the federal government to levy an income tax, namely, whether, at law, the income tax was direct or indirect. In 1872 the Civil War income tax was held to be indirect and thus valid. But portions of the income tax of 1894 were held to be direct and therefore unconstitutional because the tax was not apportioned among the states according to population. As a consequence, the 16th Amendment was enacted (1913), providing that "the Congress shall have power to lay and collect taxes on incomes, from whatever source derived, without apportionment among the several states, and without regard to any census or enumeration."

Implied Restrictions

1. *The Welfare Limitation.* If a tax is interpreted by the courts to be levied for purposes other than the general welfare, it may be held invalid. In a very few instances, taxes were interpreted to be regulatory rather than revenue measures: the special tax on industries using child labor and the processing tax of the Agricultural Adjustment Act. However, other taxes imposed with the primary aim of regulation have been upheld.

2. *The "State Instrumentalities" Doctrine.* The Supreme Court has held that the basic division of power between federal and state governments requires that each level of government be prevented from taxing the "instrumentalities"—the property, securities, and activities—of the other, to insure that the taxing power would not be used to weaken the powers of the other level of government. Thus the federal government has been denied the right to tax interest on state and local bonds and sales to the states under federal excises. The attitude of the courts has shifted somewhat on the interpretation of this doctrine over the years, and the Supreme Court might uphold taxation of state and local bond interest, were Congress to change the law to make such interest taxable.

3. *The Due Process Requirement.* The federal government is prohibited from depriving persons of "life, liberty or property without due process of law." This provision prevents completely arbitrary classification for tax purposes and retroactive (past the current year) imposition of taxation and insures the right of appeal to the courts from the decisions of tax administering agencies.

THE TAXING POWERS OF THE STATES

The states, with residual sovereign powers, possess full powers of taxation without specific designation by the federal Constitution. However, the Constitution does specifically restrict their taxing powers, and other limitations have arisen out of the interpretation of provisions of the Constitution not directly relating to taxation. In addition, the states have imposed limitations in their own constitutions on the taxing powers of their legislatures.

Specific Federal Restrictions

The federal Constitution specifically prohibits use by the states of three types of taxes: (1) import duties, (2) export duties, and (3) tonnage duties (levies upon ships for the privilege of entering or leaving a port). These restrictions were designed to insure for the federal government complete power over foreign commerce.

Implied Restrictions

1. *Federal Instrumentalities.* In order to protect the powers of the federal government, the states (and their subdivisions) are denied the right to tax federal instrumentalities. Thus, property taxes may not be applied to federally owned property or federal securities, and sales to the federal government may not be taxed under states sales and excise taxes, at least if tax liability is on the purchaser.

2. *The Due Process and Equal Protection Clauses.* The states, by provision of the 14th Amendment, are prohibited from depriving persons of life, liberty, or property without due process of law. This prohibition insures the taxpayer the right of appeal to the courts from the action of tax administration agencies and protects against arbitrary procedures. In addition, it has been interpreted to mean that a state may apply a tax only within its territorial jurisdiction. In very rare instances the courts have held taxes to violate due process on the ground that they were confiscatory but usually the courts have taken the position that the question of the height of a tax is one within the discretion of the legislative body.

The 14th Amendment also requires that no state shall "deny to any person within its jurisdiction the equal protection of the laws." This clause has been interpreted by the courts in such a manner as to invalidate some state taxes, such as certain ones on chain stores, on the basis of arbitrary classification and thus denial of equal protection. In practice, however, the courts will not interfere with classification unless it is extremely arbitrary.

3. *Discrimination against Citizens of Other States.* Closely related is the prohibition of discrimination against citizens of other states; residents and nonresidents must be treated equally. Thus, property owned by nonresidents cannot be taxed at a higher rate than that owned by residents. This provision applies only to citizens, not to corpora-

tions, and thus a state may apply heavier taxes to businesses incorporated outside the state than to those incorporated in the state.

4. *Interstate Commerce.*[22] Some of the most significant restrictions on state taxing powers arise out of interpretation of the clause of the Constitution that gives control over interstate commerce to the federal government. States cannot levy discriminatory taxes against goods brought into the state from other states and cannot directly tax interstate sales as such under sales or excise taxes, although they may apply use taxes to goods bought outside the state and brought in. Businesses engaged in interstate commerce can be taxed on their gross receipts or net profits only if the totals are allocated on a reasonable basis. Taxation of railroads is complicated by their interstate character. The powers of the states to tax interstate motor carriers are considerably broader because of the states' proprietary interest in the highways. Legislation currently under consideration in Congress would significantly curtail the taxing powers of the states over interstate commerce.

5. *Miscellaneous Restrictions.* State taxation must not violate treaties made with other countries by the federal government. The states may not tax in such a manner as to impair contracts. For example, interest on bonds issued free from state income tax cannot subsequently be taxed.

Restrictions Imposed by State Constitutions

The state legislatures are subject to restrictions imposed by the state constitutions as well as by those of the federal Constitution. The exact degree of restriction varies widely. In a few states, legislatures have complete freedom. In others, they may levy any type of tax they wish subject to certain general requirements, such as uniformity of treatment. These uniformity clauses have been interpreted differently in various states, sometimes to prevent the use of progressive taxation. Other legislatures are permitted to levy only certain specified types of taxes, and in a few states, such as Louisiana, virtually the whole tax structure is prescribed directly by the state constitution.

The significance of these restrictions depends to a great extent upon the ease of amending the constitution. If amendment is relatively

---

[22]An exhaustive study of this question is to be found in the October, 1960, issue of the *Virginia Law Review*, "A Symposium on State Taxation of Interstate Commerce," and in *State Taxation of Interstate Commerce,* Report of the Special Subcommittee on State Taxation of Interstate Commerce of the House Judiciary Committee, 3 vols. Washington, D.C.: US Government Printing Office, 1964.

simple, as in California, the restrictions do not prevent readjustment in the tax structure. If amending is very difficult, as in Illinois, the tax structure may be essentially frozen for long periods.

THE TAXING POWERS OF THE LOCAL GOVERNMENTS

The local governments, as creations of the states, are subject to the same restrictions imposed by the federal Constitution as are the states themselves. Furthermore, they can levy only those taxes that are specifically authorized for them by the states, since they have no inherent taxing powers of their own.

The taxing powers of the localities may be established by provisions of the state constitution or, more commonly, by general state law, and by provisions of municipal charters. Virtually all local governments are given the right to levy property taxes. Many, such as school districts and townships, have no other taxing powers. Cities are frequently given powers to impose various forms of license taxes and, in some cases, sales, excise, and income taxes.

APPENDIX II—CONSTITUTIONAL TAXING POWERS: CANADA[23]

Under the British North America Act, which is the Canadian Constitution, the provinces have only those powers specifically authorized, while the Dominion retains the residual powers. This is the reverse of the United States situation.

Federal Taxing Powers. The Dominion government is given unlimited taxing powers, being authorized to make laws relating to "the raising of money by any mode or system of taxation." The primary restriction prohibits taxing provincial lands and property, interpreted to mean also purchases by a province for governmental use. Otherwise, there is no provincial instrumentalities doctrine, and interest on provincial bonds may be taxed. If a tax is levied for attainment of *ultra vires* purposes rather than for revenue, it may be held invalid.

The Provincial Powers. The powers of the provinces are more

[23]See G. V. La Forest, *The Allocation of Taxing Power under the Canadian Constitution* (Toronto: Canadian Tax Foundation, 1967); V. C. MacDonald, "Taxation Powers in Canada," *Canadian Bar Review,* Vol. XXVII (October, 1941), pp. 75–95; J. H. Perry, *Taxation in Canada* (3rd ed.; Toronto: University of Toronto Press, 1961), chap. viii.

limited than those of the states. The provinces are given the right to levy only direct taxes, and the taxes must be levied for the purpose of "raising a revenue for provincial purposes."

Substantial difficulty arose over the meaning of the term *indirect taxes,* particularly when the provinces required gasoline and sales tax revenue. In their usual form, these taxes are indirect, in terms of the definition formulated by John Stuart Mill and generally accepted by the Canadian courts, since they are ordinarily shifted from the taxpayer to the purchaser. By the guise of imposing these taxes on the consumer, the vendor being required to collect and remit the taxes as an agent of the province, the provinces have succeeded in making them acceptable as direct taxes in the eyes of the courts.

The taxing clause limits taxation to persons or property within the province. This clause has been interpreted very broadly; a resident may be taxed on his entire income, for example, even though it is earned outside the province. Dominion companies, however, may be taxed only in a fashion nondiscriminatory as compared to other corporations. Only property with situs in the province may be taxed.

Taxes must be levied for the purpose of raising revenue, being invalid if levied in order to gain control over activities that are not within provincial jurisdiction.

In addition to the power to levy direct taxes, the provinces are authorized to impose "shop, saloon, tavern, auctioneer, and other licenses in order to the raising of revenue for provincial, local or municipal purposes." Only limited use is made of this power.

The provinces are not subject to a federal instrumentalities doctrine comparable to that in the United States, although they are not permitted to tax federal property or direct purchases by the federal government. Likewise, they are not subject to restrictions on taxation comparable to those arising out of the interstate commerce clause in the United States except insofar as they are prohibited from levying duties on the importation of goods from other provinces. They can, for example, tax an out-of-province purchaser on an article bought in the province for out-of-province delivery. Their power to compel out-of-province vendors to collect sales taxes for them is less than the power of the states in the United States.

Local Governments. Local governments have no inherent taxing powers, but only those which the provinces give them by terms of general laws or charters. The provinces may delegate to them any taxing powers which they themselves possess.

APPENDIX III—TAX LEGISLATION IN CANADA AND OTHER COMMONWEALTH COUNTRIES

Countries such as Canada with the parliamentary form of government have somewhat different procedures for the enactment of tax legislation, because of the lack of a sharp distinction between executive and legislative branches of government. Proposals for tax changes are developed by the Cabinet on the basis of recommendations of the Department (Ministry) of Finance, which prepares the detailed recommendations. The Cabinet will debate the proposals, obviously taking into consideration attitudes of the public in light of the desire of the party to gain reelection. Once the Cabinet reaches agreement, the proposal is presented to Parliament, having been kept secret up to this point. Extensive debate ensues, with opposition members attacking the proposals and government members defending them. There are no committee hearings. The Cabinet will sometimes modify the proposals as a result of debate. At the conclusion of discussion, enactment is almost automatic, since party discipline is strong and failure of the House of Commons to approve the tax measure would result in fall of the government and a new election.[24] Action by the Senate is a formality, as is approval of the Governor General; there is no executive veto power, by the nature of the parliamentary form of government. Many of the proposals will have become effective the day of their presentation to parliament, subject to subsequent ratification.

Use is also made of the government-appointed Tax Committees or Royal Commissions on Taxation. The group, made up of persons familiar with the field, assembles a staff for detailed study and prepares a report. The recent Royal Commission on Taxation in Canada, appointed in 1961, carried on an extensive study of the Canadian tax structure a a whole, and prepared a six-volume report, issued in 1966, calling for drastic changes in the tax structure.[25] Whether these will be made remain to be seen. Similar studies have recently been made in most of the provinces.[26] Traditionally governments pay substantial at-

---

[24]In February 1968 a bill in Canada to apply a 5 percent income tax surcharge was defeated in the House of Commons by two votes, with a large number of absentees. The government would have fallen had it not succeeded in winning a subsequent vote of confidence. A modified version of the proposal was then enacted.

[25]See *Report of the Royal Commission on Taxation* (6 vols.; Ottawa: Queens Printer, 1966).

[26]See for example *Ontario Committee on Taxation Report* (Toronto: Queens Printer, 1967); *Rapport de la Commission royale d'enquête sur la fiscalité, Gouvernement du Quebec* (Quebec City, 1965).

tention to the recommendations of these commissions, but they are not necessarily accepted if the government is convinced that there is strong popular opposition to them, or that the proposals are unwise.

REFERENCES

BLOUGH, ROY. *The Federal Taxing Process.* New York, Prentice-Hall, 1950.
Out of date, but one of the few general studies of the question.

BUCHANAN, J. M. *Public Finance in Democratic Process.* Chapel Hill, N.C.: University of North Carolina Press, 1967.

PECHMAN, JOSEPH A. *Federal Tax Policy,* especially chap. iii. Washington, D.C.: Brookings Institution, 1966.

| Chapter 5 | GOVERNMENTAL EXPENDITURE AND REVENUE STRUCTURES |

Patterns of governmental expenditures and revenues develop over the years as successive incremental decisions are made on expenditure and tax changes. Many of the annual changes are minor, and the relative importance of major activities and major taxes does not shift greatly from year to year except at rare intervals, prompted by a war or depression, the introduction of a new tax, the establishment of a new program. This chapter reviews the expenditures and revenue patterns of the United States for the fiscal year 1966, the last year for which complete data are available, with reference to federal 1968–69 budget recommendations. In view of the slow pace of change, however, the relationships shown are significant far beyond the particular year. A summary of the Canadian picture appears in Appendix I to the chapter.

MAJOR ACTIVITIES AND EXPENDITURES

Figure 5–1 shows the relative expenditures by major type of activity for the three levels of government in the United States for 1966. For the federal government and for all levels combined, national defense is by far the most significant activity. Various forms of welfare, including those of the social security program and public health, constitute the next major segment both in terms of federal and total. Education, while unimportant at the federal level but dominant at the local and significant at the state levels, is the third most significant category. The other major sector consists of a group of semicommercial activities: highways and other transport facilities, the postal service, sewerage and sanitation, parks and recreation, and other resource development, such as dams and irrigation facilities. The highway item is significant at all levels, while the relative emphasis on the others differs among the levels of government. This general pattern is found in most federal countries: the national government concentrates on national defense but with growing welfare activities; education is primarily a local function but with substantial financing from above; all governments participate in welfare activities, and all levels undertake some functions of a semicommercial nature. Interest, the final major cate-

FIGURE 5-1

RELATIVE EXPENDITURES BY MAJOR FUNCTION, UNITED STATES, 1966 FISCAL YEAR
Including Trust Fund Expenditures

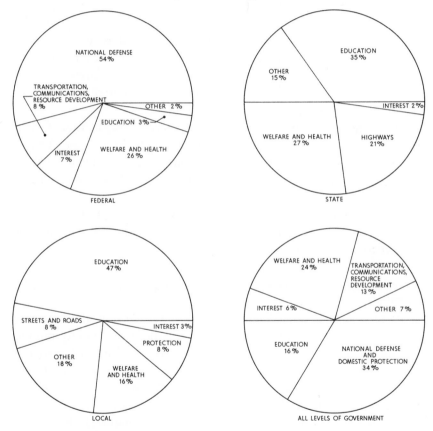

SOURCE: U.S. Department of Commerce, Bureau of the Census, *Governmental Finances in 1965–66.*

gory, is a derivative of the others, arising out of loans made to conduct the various activities. The costs of regulation, control, financial and general administration are a surprisingly small portion of the total: 1 percent at the federal level, 2 percent for all levels.

National Defense and Related Activities[1]

FEDERAL DEFENSE EXPENDITURES

Billions of Dollars

	1969 Budget Estimate	1966
Armed forces, including atomic energy research	79.8	$56.0
Space	4.6	5.9
Foreign affairs and foreign aid	5.2	4.9
Veterans' assistance	7.1	6.7
	96.7	$73.5

Federal expenditures for national defense and related items for 1966 and the budget projections for the 1968–69 year totaled $74 billion and $97 billion respectively, constituting in the former year 64 percent of the administrative budget and 54 percent of total federal expenditures; 53 percent of the total in 1968–69.

In addition, a large portion of the interest cost, a total of $9.6 billion in 1966, is attributable to wars and high defense spending; if 90 percent of this, a rough approximation of the part attributable to defense, were added, the overall total for 1966 would be $82 billion, and $110 for 1969, or about 60 percent in each year of total federal spending, and about 11 percent of gross national product. This is by far the largest item of governmental spending, as it has been in most of the years of the history of the country.

National defense activity is the classic example of a public good: one yielding indivisible benefits to the community as a whole, and thus of necessity a governmental activity. While the space program is not wholly national defense related, it is usually classified as an element in the overall defense picture. Similarly foreign aid is not wholly military in character, but a major motive was the strengthening of actual or potential allies of the United States. The substantial item of aid to veterans includes hospital and other medical care and veterans' pensions. This assistance is directly related to past defense activity.

Only pacifists question the desirability of national defense activity. There is widespread dispute, however, over the optimal magnitude and nature of the programs, over manpower supply, and over some of the related activities. The high degree of uncertainty about the need for various levels of defense activity and the interdependence between our own spending on national defense and that of other countries complicate the task of attaining agreement on appropriate levels. The military inevitably stresses the need for high levels of spending. The

[1]See Stephen Enke (ed.), *Defense Management* (Englewood Cliffs, N.J.: Prentice-Hall, 1967) for a discussion of major defense issues.

complexity of the operation of the armed forces and the need for secrecy in certain aspects of operation make independent evaluation difficult; it is sometimes said that whereas doctors bury their mistakes, the armed forces classify theirs as secret, thus barring investigation. The Defense Department in recent years has stressed the need for more efficient determination of expenditure levels and programs and has pioneered in the use of PPBS and systems analysis. The tasks of determination of optimal levels and optimal use of the funds are nevertheless very serious ones.

Several of the major issues of recent years in the national defense area can be summarized briefly (apart from the Vietnam war):

1. *Relative Emphasis upon Nuclear Deterrents and Forces to Fight More Limited Traditional Warfare.* For a time primary emphasis was placed on the former, but changing conditions led to renewed attention to more traditional means.

2. *The Development of a Protective Network against Missiles.* This could become an expensive undertaking, and opponents fear that construction would merely stimulate other countries to do the same.

3. *Manpower Supply and Selective Service.* In a period of all-out war, the principle of drafting men to provide necessary personnel, requiring persons to serve in the armed forces and paying them much less than civilian earnings, has been widely accepted in all countries. Likewise the principle that all persons (or at least all males) should gain some military training and contribute time to defense activity, as is the practice in such countries as Switzerland and Israel, has widespread support, although not regarded as feasible in the United States. In recent years, however, and particularly during the Vietnam war, the United States has been drafting only a small percentage of men in the age groups involved. This system has led to widespread criticism. First, the system amounts to an inequitably distributed tax. Persons are required to serve when they prefer not to; they are paid less than they would earn in civilian employment, and still less than the amount necessary to get them to serve voluntarily in the armed forces. No matter what system of selection is used, the burden concentrates on a relatively few persons and thus is contrary to usual standards of equity; proposed employment of a lottery for selection is equivalent to the use of a lottery to determine which persons must pay income tax.

Second, the system creates great uncertainty for persons about their likelihood of being drafted and causes some to change their activity in such a way as to escape—to attend college when they would not otherwise do so, or even flee to Canada. Third, the system produces armed forces that consist primarily of persons who do not want to serve, with a heavy rate of turnover. The patriotism that a country can generate in time of major war is very different from that which can be cultivated in peace-time or in conduct of a highly unpopular smaller scale war.

The alternative is the use of a pay scale sufficiently high to induce adequate numbers of persons to serve without coercion—the same procedure followed for other governmental acquisition of goods and services. Thus the present "tax" on those drafted would be replaced by higher general levies distributed on a more equitable basis. This procedure would eliminate complaints about equity, the uncertainty, and the great disutility inflicted on persons who do not want to serve, and produce much less turnover and a more competent army.[2] The only serious objection is the added cost, estimated at $4 billion or more per year.[3] The government refuses to consider this alternative seriously, preferring to follow the cheaper traditional method and seeking to rationalize it on grounds of obligation to serve the country, an argument of questionable acceptability when only a small sector of the population is required to fulfill the obligation.

4. *Foreign Aid.* The foreign aid (AID) programs have never been highly popular in Congress and differences in opinion are found within the administration and outside about their effectiveness. The programs take several forms: shipments of U.S. farm surpluses to countries in dire need of food; development loans to aid growth in less developed countries; funds to aid development of schools and other activities in Latin America; technical assistance in many fields, including tax administration; and the Peace Corps. These reflect increased interest in the last two decades in the less developed economies, the competition of East and West for support of these countries and the desire to strengthen existing regimes against communism, and some purely humanitarian concern. Congress views these programs with the inevitable doubt that arises over any expenditure whose benefits are not clearly apparent to the voters of the country. Questions are raised about the conduct and effectiveness of the activities, which at times involve attempts to export American methods and standards into situations for which they are not well suited and in which they may have political overtones. A large portion of the money goes into administration.

5. *Space Exploration, Now Costing Some $5 Billion a Year.* This is related to national defense and international prestige considerations;

---

[2] One has only to compare the morale and attitudes of Marine Corps units (made up primarily of volunteers) and many Army units (mostly draftees) during World War II to note the difference.

[3] W. Y. Oi, "The Economic Cost of the Draft," *Proceedings of the American Economic Association* for 1967, pp. 39–62.

questions are raised about the potential benefits from this activity compared to the solution of some pressing problems on the earth.

Police and Fire Protection and Correction

EXPENDITURES
Billions of Dollars

	1966
Federal	$0.3
State	1.0
Local	4.1
Total	$5.4

The protection of life and property, the domestic counterpart of national defense, is primarily a local government function. These governments spend over $4 billion annually for this activity, the states $1 billion, and the federal government, for corrections, $.3 billion. Federal protective activity (primarily Secret Service and FBI) is included in the general control function. While direct benefits to individuals are important, the uncertain incidence of the benefits and the externalities preclude provision by private enterprise. Since a fire in one house may spread to all property in the city, extinguishing the first fire conveys important externalities to other residents of the city. Adequate police protection is important to all persons but there is no effective way in which it can be sold separately to individuals.

The Welfare and Public Health Programs[4]

EXPENDITURES
Billions of Dollars

	1969 Federal Budget Estimate	1966 Federal	State	Local	Total*
Public welfare (direct relief), old-age pensions, aid to dependent children, etc.	$ 3.6	$ 3.8	$ 6.0	$3.7	$ 7.0
Social Security Trust Fund expenditures (old-age annuities, unemployment compensation)	33.7	23.3	4.0	0.8	28.1
Economic Opportunity programs	2.0	—	—	—	—
Housing and urban renewal	1.4	1.6	0.1	1.4	2.4
Public health, medicare, and medical research	10.7	1.5	3.0	2.9	7.4
Farm aid	4.1	4.3	—	—	4.3
Other	2.0	0.6	0.5	—	0.9
Totals	$57.5	$35.1	$13.6	$8.8	$50.1

*Excluding double counting arising from intergovernmental grants.

[4]The various welfare programs are discussed in O. Eckstein (ed.), *Studies in the Economics of Income Maintenance* (Washington, D.C.: Brookings Institution, 1967).

The welfare programs cover a wide range of activities, all designed to increase the incomes of various groups in the economy, primarily those in the lowest levels. The programs are selective, each dealing with the problems of certain groups, rather than all persons with low incomes. Governments have for centuries taken some steps to aid the very poor, at least to the extent of providing subsistence on poor farms and in old people's homes, as reflected in the old line, "over the hill to the poorhouse." For years the care was minimal, primary responsibility for the poor resting in the hands of private charity. Gradually attitudes of society changed to accept greater responsibility—a change facilitated by rising incomes. In the United States the depression of the thirties, by accentuating the problems of the poor, led to the introduction of many new permanent programs. In the last five years greater awareness of poverty in the slum areas of large cities, coupled with riots and other violence, has increased concern with the problem. In other countries fear of revolution and increased political power for the lower income groups have led to greater attention to poverty.

All of the programs rest for their justification upon the attitude of society that financial assistance should be given to certain income groups. Since there is no scientific basis for determining programs and amounts, endless disagreement ensues over magnitudes and exact programs, and the economic effects of present programs are not at all clear. The major programs and key issues will be noted briefly.

Public Welfare. Welfare payments are financed by all three levels of government. The federal government gives substantial sums for specific categories: aid for dependent children, aid for the blind, old-age assistance (as distinguished from old-age annuities noted below) and other purposes. These grants are matched (under various formulas) by state and local funds. Direct relief to other needy (mostly the unemployed) is a state-local responsibility, the sharing between state and local varying with the state. These amounts are given only on a means-test basis with proof of need and are accompanied by investigation and assistance by social workers. The payments are limited in amount to little more than bare subsistence.

Social Security Trust Fund Payments. In dollar magnitude, the social security payments are now the largest of the welfare activities. The largest element is the old-age annuity program, exclusively a federal system. The fund is financed by payroll taxes on employer and employee and taxes on the earnings of self-employed. Payments are based upon the years the person has been covered and the wages earned. The recipient is limited as to the amount he can earn in covered employment and still draw benefits. This is a semi-insurance system, but with no close linkage between amounts paid in and benefits ultimately received.

Unemployment compensation systems, also financed by payroll taxes, are state operated, with the aid of grants from the federal government for administration. Amounts paid are based upon the wage and are limited in duration. The systems are designed to care for temporary unemployment, not that of a long-continuing nature.

Economic Opportunity Programs. In the last five years stress has been placed on meeting the problems of poverty in the core areas of metropolitan regions and in certain declining rural areas, such as Appalachia. The problem of urban poverty, which involves a whole complex of economic, educational, and cultural elements, tends to be self-perpetuating. Originating out of the flow of poorly educated families from rural areas and from Puerto Rico, the combination of poverty and social disorganization has trapped many persons and their children in a vicious circle from which escape is difficult and has led to degeneration of educational facilities, riots and racial strife, and other difficulties. Several programs, under the direction of the Office of Economic Opportunity, have been established, including Project Head Start to aid education of underprivileged children, the Job Corps program, and other activities. Urban renewal, noted below, is related.

This type of poverty is particularly intractable, requiring a complex of education, financial, and other activities, and so far the results have not been encouraging. There is widespread acceptance of the need for eliminating these large pockets of poverty in an otherwise prosperous economy, but the most effective methods for doing so are by no means obvious.

Housing and Urban Renewal.[5] The federal government has played an increasingly important role in seeking to improve the living conditions of persons in urban poverty areas, by providing grants for low-rent housing construction and for other forms of redevelopment of blighted areas. Many of the earlier programs have been sharply criticized for eliminating old housing without providing adequate new housing, and the newer programs stress rehabilitation of housing and view the urban renewal activities in a broader fashion, considering transport facilities, parks, and other elements in urban living. Programs for subsidization of rental payments of low-income families have also been extensively debated.

[5]A survey and evaluation is to be found in the book by Jerome Rothenberg, *Economic Evaluation of Urban Renewal* (Washington, D.C.: Brookings Institution, 1967).

The federal government has long assisted in the financing of purchase and construction of homes by persons in all income levels through FHA (Federal Housing Administration) guarantee of mortgages on home loans.

Medicine and Health. Traditionally public health activity in the United States consisted primarily of care of the mentally ill in state institutions and the provision of hospital care for the indigent by the local governments. This type of activity is still important. It was motivated primarily by distributional considerations: the desire to insure at least minimal care for ill persons unable to finance hospital care.

Two other types of health activity have grown in importance. The first is medical research, an activity of limited direct profitability for private enterprise but a source of significant externalities. A cancer preventative will be of tremendous benefit to society, far more in dollar terms than a private enterprise developer could, as a practical matter, gain in profit. Accordingly, about $1 billion per year is provided by the federal government for research in the medical area, much of it utilized at universities.

The other major activity has been the establishment of Medicare, to insure more adequate health protection for elderly persons above the poverty level and not eligible for free services under welfare programs. Medicare was integrated with social security and financed by an addition to the payroll taxes. In addition, other federal aid for improved medical services to the poor (Medicaid) has been increased in recent years. This policy reflects partial acceptance of the view that society should insure basic medical care to all. A problem, as encountered in other countries, is to prevent unnecessary drain on medical facilities (such as overstay in hospitals) and to insure adequate expansion in hospital and medical facilities. Providing funds to pay for these services is to little avail if hospital beds are not available.

Other aspects of public health now receiving greater attention are those of air and water pollution. Significant external diseconomies of particular activities (with air pollution, primarily motor vehicle use) are creating increasingly serious costs for society not borne by the individual users or producers.[6]

Farm Price Stabilization Programs. While the various farm aid programs are not usually classified as a type of welfare activity, they

---

[6]See R. G. Ridker, *Economic Costs of Air Polution* (New York: Praeger, 1967); and H. Wolozin (ed.), *The Economics of Air Pollution* (New York: Norton, 1966).

are essentially of this character because their principal goal is to increase the income position of farmers. The basic programs, designed to reduce crop surpluses, were introduced in the depression years of the thirties.

Mere palliatives rather than solutions to the problem of crop surpluses, they have perpetuated and to some extent aggravated the problems. Few federal programs have been less efficient in solving the problems they were designed to meet.

Criticisms of the Various Welfare Programs. No elements in the governmental expenditure programs have been subject to more criticism than the welfare activities. In brief, these include:

1. The complexity of the old-age annuity system, with its hybrid insurance-transfer-payment characteristics. An extensive administrative organization is required, at substantial cost to employers, to operate the individual account system, yet the payments received by individuals are not closely related to the payments into their accounts. The present system was designed partly to avoid any "welfare" connotations, partly to lessen the pressure by recipients for larger payments. But frequent deviations from the insurance principle have prevented the attainment of this original objective. A much simpler system could have been devised without the need for individual accounts.

Likewise the financing by payroll taxes is open to objection, since these taxes are regressive and give employers incentive to replace labor by capital.

2. Incentives. Certain features in both the social security and welfare programs lessen incentives unnecessarily. The former limits the income a person may receive and still draw benefits (despite the semi-insurance characteristics) and various welfare programs discourage persons from seeking to earn income, because every dollar they earn reduces their benefits by a dollar.

3. Outright abuse, particularly in the aid to dependent childern (ADC) program, and to some extent with unemployment compensation. The former program has proven particularly difficult to control and encourages husbands to "disappear" so that the families can draw benefits. Controversy arises over benefits for children born out of wedlock and over attempts to encourage birth control by welfare recipients.

4. The very extensive administrative organization necessary for the operation of the various programs. The comment is sometimes made that the gain from the equal opportunity programs is primarily in the creation of administrative positions for persons from the underprivileged groups.

5. The piecemeal nature of the activities. There is no overall program benefiting all persons at poverty levels.

6. Stigma. Many of the programs have means tests and other features that place a stigma upon the recipients and make some persons reluctant to take advantage of the benefits.

The Negative Income Tax Alternative.[7] An alternative approach to the attainment of redistributional goals of contemporary society is the negative income tax. While this plan takes various forms, basically it involves the payment by government of a sum equal to a certain percentage, perhaps 50 percent, of the difference between a family's actual income and a minimum income requirement figure. One form would use the present income tax exemption figure for the minimum. Thus a family of five earning $2,000 a year would receive a payment from the government of 50 percent of the excess of $3,000 (5 × $600) over $2,000 or $500. The system would in effect guarantee an income equal to one half of the sum of the exemption.

As originally suggested by Milton Friedman,[8] this plan would replace other welfare (but not, presumably, health) programs, providing a much simpler approach that would avoid the extensive administrative costs of the present system, the use of means tests, and the investigation by social workers, at the same time lessening the adverse incentive effects. Under the present systems a person frequently loses $1 in aid for every additional dollar he earns and has no incentive to earn more. With the negative income tax and a 50 percent rate, he would keep half of additional earnings. Others have suggested the system as a supplement to existing programs, to provide assistance to the substantial number of low-income families not covered by the present specialized programs (for example, a family with an employed husband and total income above the figure for direct relief but inadequate for a minimum standard of living). Greater freedom in the use of the payments and lesser use of means tests are advantages in terms of individual freedom.

In summary, while presumably the system could not replace all of the present programs, it could replace several and provide greater equity. The exact cost would depend upon the figures and rates employed; estimates range from $3 billion to $8 billion. Since certain types

---

[7]See Christopher Green, *Negative Taxes and the Poverty Program* (Washington, D.C.: Brookings Institution, 1967).

[8]Milton Friedman, *Capitalism and Freedom* (Chicago: University of Chicago Press, 1962).

of hard-core poverty cannot be solved with cash payments alone, the program could not dispense with social work but could reduce the necessary amount.

The universality of the program, in contrast to the present programs that cover only certain categories of the poor, would aid in the attainment of the goals. The adverse effect on work incentives would be less than that of the present programs. Less stigma would be attached to receipt, since the payments would be automatic, given the income. Less discretion would be involved, with much lower administrative costs. A major problem is the difficulty of reconciling the aims of guaranteeing a minimum income with the need for only a partial reduction of payments as the persons' incomes rise to minimize adverse effects on incentive.

There are numerous technical issues to be resolved in devising a system to accomplish the desired results.[9] Problems of definition of taxpaying unit and control of accuracy of reported income figures would be comparable to similar problems in income taxation. Resolution of major issues in the selection of the base would be necessary.

Education

	EXPENDITURES			
	Billions of Dollars			
1969				
Federal		*1966*		
Budget				
Estimate	*Federal*	*State*	*Local*	*Total*
$4.4	$4.6	$17.7	$25.8	$34.0

Educational activities have for a century constituted the major function of local governments and at present account for over 40 percent of all local government spending. In the form of grants to public schools and support of state institutions of higher education, educational activities have also become the largest single element in state spending. The federal government was slow to enter the field in light of the long tradition of local autonomy in the educational field and the opposition to federal intervention in educational policies. While federal expenditures still remain small they have been expanding rapidly, primarily in the form of grants to poorer school districts and aid for school construction and teacher education.

[9]See Martin David and Jane Leuthold, *Formulas for Income Maintenance* (Madison, Wis.: Institute for Research on Poverty, 1967).

Education became a governmental function for two reasons: recognition of the significant external benefits of all children receiving a certain minimum level of education; and distributional considerations—the desire to insure better economic opportunities for children of families in the lower income levels. The major problem in recent years was the rapid increase in the number of children of school age due to the jump in the birth rate in the 1940's, plus the increase in the percentage of children attending high school.[10] With the more recent drop in the birth rate, the problem of growth at the lower levels has come to an end except in rapidly growing areas, and the total number of children entering primary grades will fall in the next several years. The increasing percentage seeking to enter college, however, creates need for expanding facilities and faculty at this level and has revived old controversies over the desirability of making recipients pay a larger portion of the costs of higher education—an issue not easily resolved.

The current problem facing the school system as a whole is the restoration of quality education in the low-income areas of the large cities, an aspect of the broader core city problem noted above. As poorly educated low-income families poured into the old city areas, the original inhabitants moved to the suburbs, and the urban ghetto developed, with heavy concentrations of minority groups. The result was a decline in the quality of education and difficulty in retaining qualified teachers, partly because of discipline problems. Unfortunately most cities did little to stop the vicious circle until race riots and other violence led to renewed attention to the problem. Even when the problem is recognized, however, the solutions are not simple. For a time stress was placed on integration of the low-income-area school pupils with those of higher income areas, and this has proved successful in a few places. But in others the policy requires substantial cross-busing, which is often vigorously opposed by the higher income-area parents. In cities with a predominantly low-income population integration becomes impossible; if it is pushed, more and more above-poverty-level families move to the suburbs or send their children to private schools, and there is no one left in the public schools except the low-income children.[11] To merge the large city and suburban schools into integrated schools serving the entire area is an expensive undertaking, and one beset by strong opposition and political boundary difficulties. The best solution probably lies in concentrating attention on raising the standards

---

[10]Total school enrollment rose from 28 million in 1940 to 50.7 million in 1967.
[11]Washington, D.C., is the extreme example.

of education in the ghetto schools by use of more qualified teachers, a much lower pupil-teacher ratio, and new buildings, in order to provide the same quality education as that of the high-income areas. Financial aid from state and federal sources is imperative.

Transportation, Communications, Resource Development and other Semicommercial Activities

EXPENDITURES

Billions of Dollars

	1969 Federal Budget Estimate	1966			
		Federal	State	Local	Total
Highways and streets.........	$ 4.4	$ 4.1	$10.3	$4.2	$12.9
Air and water transportation..	2.3	2.2	0.2	0.5	2.9
Postal service deficit..........	0.8	0.8*	—	—	0.8
Sewerage and sanitation......	—	—	—	2.6	2.6
Parks and recreation.........	0.5	0.5	0.3	1.2	2.0
Other resource development†..	3.4	3.5	1.2	0.5	5.2
Total	$11.4	$11.1	$12.0	$9.0	$26.4

*1966 total expenditure $5.7 billion.
†Primarily water and power development.

The fourth major category of governmental activities consists of a group of functions of a semicommercial nature, that is, ones providing services yielding direct benefits, so that they could be produced by private enterprise and governmental agencies can use charges to finance them. One motive for governmental conduct of these activities has been greater operational efficiency through the avoidance of the need for collecting charges. Another is the avoidance of the undesirable feature of private monopoly. A third basis is the importance of externalities of several of the activities.

Highways. Governments have traditionally played a role in the provision of roads, at least of city streets, but the coming of the motor vehicle greatly increased the activities and expenditures. The alternative of private toll roads would be less efficient in resource use, and the companies would be less concerned about adaptation to public needs than their own profits. Initially provision of roads was a strictly local function except for federal aid to a few major roads in the pre-railroad era, and this category is still an important one at the local level. With the development of the motor vehicle, however, the states took over a large part of the activity in developing state highway systems and providing grants for local roads. The federal government entered the field with grants for the federal highway network in 1914 and greatly increased expenditures with the establishment of the interstate highway program in 1956. The question of highway financing is discussed in Chapter 13.

The principal issue in domestic ground transportation development today is the relative emphasis to be given expressways and rapid transit facilities in urban areas. While a few cities undertook development of rapid transit facilities at an early date, primarily public transport has been provided by private companies—local transit systems and commuter railroads. Thus public funds concentrated entirely on expressways while public transport deteriorated. This trend in turn increased still more the demand for expressway construction. The lag in expressway construction behind needs, its tremendous expense, its external diseconomies in terms of carving up cities and adding to noise and air pollution finally brought renewed interest in improvement and extension of rapid transit facilities, including commuter railroad operation. Moving persons in congested areas by rapid transit is far more economical and less expensive than continued expansion of expressways, and limited federal aid is now being provided for the purpose. Rarely can these facilities be operated profitably, but the external benefits in the form of lessened need for expenditures on expressways and lessened congestion on streets warrant operation of them at charges less than full cost. Unfortunately certain interested groups, particularly automobile associations, have resisted expansion of these transit facilities—probably shortsigthedly so—and a few transportation experts have also questioned the ability of rapid transit to pull persons from the highways. One aspect of urban development has admittedly made the task of providing rapid transit more difficult: the tendency toward decentralization in urban areas, which disperses traffic flows. Los Angeles is the extreme example. But with growth in metropolitan area traffic there may nevertheless be many instances in which the volume of traffic will be adequate to make rapid transit advantageous. The field of urban transit has provided probably the worst instance of misallocation of resources attributable to the location of one form of transportation in private hands, the other (highways) in public hands.

Water Transportation. Traditionally, in the United States, the federal government has undertaken improvements in navigable waterways. Many of these have been essential for important transport routes. Others, unfortunately, have taken the form of "pork barrel" expenditures benefiting limited areas at substantial cost to society. Few areas of governmental activity have come under greater fire over the years. The problem is compounded by the failure to charge the firms using

improved waterways for any portion of the costs. More recently substantial subsidies have been paid to the owners of the American mer-
chant fleet to keep the vessels in operation in competition with lower
cost foreign vessels. Needless to say, questions have been raised about
the desirability of this policy, which can be defended only on grounds
of international prestige and national defense.

Air Transportation. In recent decades the federal government
has provided funds to develop airport facilities in conjunction with municipal governments. The air transport firms are charged for use but
often in insufficient amounts to cover all costs. In addition, the federal government subsidized the air transport industry to enable it to
get started. The trunk carriers have in recent years been able to operate profitably without aid, but the secondary carriers still receive
subsidy—a questionable policy if continued indefinitely. Subsidization
of one form of transport when others are not can lead to distortion of
resource use and indirectly benefits users who are in no need of financial assistance.

The most pressing problem facing air transport is the growing
congestion of air space in and around metropolitan airports, a natural
facility that cannot be expanded. The consequence has been increasing
delays and costs of operation, and accident hazards. Construction of more
airports does not increase air space unless they are well separated from
the old airports; if they are, the other problem of air transport, the
long period required to get from terminal to the downtown area, is
aggravated. Improvement of connecting ground transport has long
been neglected. The air congestion and the airport-to-downtown problem have revived interest in better and faster rail passenger service
between major cities under 200 miles apart. For these distances the
overall time saving for air travel is small, and if much of this travel
can be returned to rail transport, the air congestion problem can be significantly reduced. But rail pasenger transport is rarely profitable and
governmental participation in financing is imperative—justified by the
externality of lessened air space congestion.

The Postal System. Total expenditures on the operation of the
post office were $5.7 billion in 1966, and an estimated $7.3 billion for
1969. Most of the revenue, however, comes from the charges for the
services, leaving a deficit of $0.8 billion in 1966, and an estimated
$0.8 billion for 1969. Governmental operation of the postal system,
a universal practice throughout the world, reflects the importance attached by governments to effective communication between all parts
of the country. Private operation would give rise to evils of monopoly

in a type of activity in which adaptation of service to the interests of society is particularly important.

Unfortunately the postal system, considered in somewhat greater detail in Chapter 13, is not one of the showpieces of effectiveness of governmental conduct of economic activity. While service in some ways may be excellent, in other respects it leaves much to be desired, particularly in the extremely irregular handling of nonfirst-class mail. The postal rate structure, set by Congress, results in a deficit of substantial magnitude because of the low rates on the least essential type of mail— the bulk advertising, which many persons would be quite happy to do without.

Parks and Recreation. While recreational activities are provided primarily by the private sector, certain forms of unique resources have been taken over by governments to insure their preservation and availability to the public. These include public beaches, mountain areas, and historic spots. To turn over Yellowstone, Yosemite, and similar natural beauty areas to private enterprise is contrary, under usual standards, to the best interests of society as a whole, since they are unique and nonreproducible. Parks in metropolitan areas provide both recreational facilities and open space, to relieve the monotony of the asphalt jungle. With many parks, costs of collection of admissions would be highly expensive relative to total costs. In terms of dollars spent, parks and recreation are primarily local activities, although the federal government and the states have played some role.

Sanitation and Sewerage Facilities. Because of externalities and the importance of making the services available to all families, municipal governments have taken over the tasks of providing sewerage facilities in virtually all urban areas and sanitation facilities in many. Specific charges may be made (often, with sewerage, related to the water bill), or the services may be financed from taxation.

Other Public Utilities. To insure adequate service and avoid the problems of regulation of monopoly, many municipal governments have undertaken the operation of water, power, and transit systems. The gross expenditures are excluded from the budgets and only the deficit or surplus included in budget totals. Capital outlays are usually shown separately in the budget.

The states have undertaken very little activity of this type. The federal government operates several services, including the Tennessee Valley Authority and the Alaska Railroad, but these comprise a relatively small segment of the overall governmental sphere, particularly by comparison with other countries.

Other Resource Development Activities. In addition to construction of highways, the federal government has for years played a role in natural resource development. Irrigation and other water use activity has been significant in many parts of the West since 1900. Attempts by private enterprise or local governmental units to provide irrigation facilities were often unsuccessful, primarily because the charges that could be obtained for the water would not cover all costs. The local or private enterprises were unable to realize on the external benefits (such as lessened flood danger) of the facilities.

The conversion to national forests of a large portion of the timberland that remained in private hands by 1910 has proven to be of great value in preserving these resources. The typical private operator— except the very large ones—finds it most profitable to strip the land of all timber and abandon the land instead of cutting on a sustaining yield basis and keeping the land permanently in use—yet society obviously benefits from the latter policy.

General and Financial Administration

EXPENDITURES

Billions of Dollars

1969 Federal Budget Estimate	1966			
	Federal	State	Local	Total
$2.8	$2.3	$1.0	$1.9	$5.2

The general routine operations of government account for a relatively small portion of the total expenditures. These include the costs of regulatory activity of all types, the courts, the legislative bodies, revenue and financial administration, personnel and property management, auditing, and other activities.

Interest

EXPENDITURES

Billions of Dollars

1969 Federal Budget Estimate	1966			
	Federal	State	Local	Total
$14.4	$9.6	$0.9	$2.3	$12.8

Payment of interest on borrowed money does not represent a separate form of governmental activity, being attributable to specific activities (for example, borrowing to build highways) or governmental activity as a whole (to meet deficits arising from inadequacy of tax revenue). Most of the federal debt is attributable to World Wars I and II, the Korean and Vietnam wars, and high levels of defense spending in other periods. Of the remainder, perhaps $30 billion dates back to the deficit financing of the depression. State and local borrowing is undertaken almost solely for particular capital undertakings and is allocable to specific activities.

In summary: a relatively few functions—national defense and domestic protection, welfare, education, and various semicommercial activities such as highways—account for a large portion of total government spending. The routine costs of governmental operation are minor elements in the overall picture. As a corollary, significant reduction in government spending can occur only if some of the major items can be cut.

Trends in Government Spending

Figure 5–2 shows the growth in governmental spending in the United States in absolute dollars from 1916 to 1966. These figures give a misleading picture of the actual growth of the governmental sector, as shown in Table 5–1. More than half of the overall increase since the 1920's is attributable to the increase in the general price level. If governments conducted no more activities today than they did in 1929, they would nevertheless be spending over twice as much money. Secondly, the population of the country approximately doubled between 1916 and 1966. While not all governmental activities are directly related to population, some of the major ones, such as education and highways, are. Placed on a per capita basis in constant dollars, the increase from 1929 to 1966 is reduced from a twenty-fold change (unadjusted figures) to a sixfold increase. Finally, GNP has grown very rapidly during the period; in other words the size of the private sector has greatly increased. The best measure of trends in the size of the governmental sector is the ratio of governmental spending to GNP. On this basis, the increase has been very moderate, from 10 percent in 1929 and 19 percent in 1933 to 22 percent in 1946, 27 percent in 1960, and 28 percent in 1966.

Much of the growth in the governmental sector can be explained by two forces: the unsettled international conditions over recent decades, which have necessitated a much higher level of defense spending than would otherwise be required, and increased welfare activity.

FIGURE 5-2. TOTAL GOVERNMENT EXPENDITURES BY LEVEL OF GOVERNMENT,
UNITED STATES, 1916-66

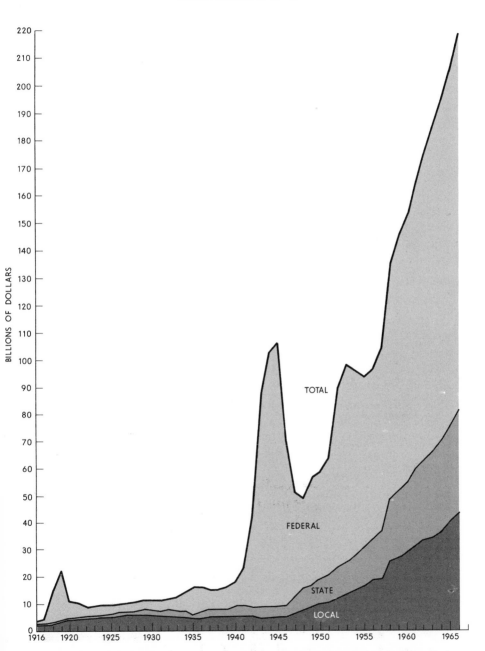

Expenditures from grants-in-aid included in figure of grantor government only. Thus, total
expenditures of states and localities as shown are less than actual dollar expenditures of these units.
    SOURCE: National Industrial Conference Board, *Economic Almanac;* Tax Foundation, *Facts
and Figures on Government Finance;* publications of U.S. Department of Commerce, Bureau of the
Census.

The principle that society has significant responsibility toward the lower income groups through various forms of assistance and medical care has become much more widely accepted. In addition, increase in the birth rate in the forties caused a sudden rise in the need for school facilities. Finally, growth in use of the motor vehicle, partly a product of higher incomes, led to large increases in expenditures for this purpose.

TABLE 5–1

GOVERNMENT EXPENDITURES FOR ALL LEVELS OF GOVERNMENT, ADJUSTED FOR PRICE LEVEL AND POPULATION CHANGES, SELECTED YEARS 1914–66, UNITED STATES

Calendar Year	Total Expenditures (Billions of Dollars)	Total Expenditures in 1926 Dollars (Billions of Dollars)	Per Capita Expenditures in 1926 Dollars
1914.............	$ 3.1	$ 4.4	$ 44.6
1919.............	22.1	16.0	152.0
1924.............	9.7	9.9	87.2
1929.............	11.3	11.9	98.0
1934.............	14.6	19.5	153.9
1939.............	17.0	22.0	168.1
1944.............	103.1	99.2	718.0
1949.............	59.7	38.5	262.6
1952.............	94.4	53.0	337.8
1957.............	124.4	66.2	389.4
1961.............	164.2	89.2	490.1
1966.............	$209.9	$115.3	$586.7

SOURCE: *Survey of Current Business*, various years; National Industrial Conference Board, *Economic Almanac*.

Other elements played a part as well: increased urbanization has required governments to provide services that individuals could provide for themselves in rural areas (water, sewerage, sanitation) and has created the urban core city problem. Higher levels of income have led persons to seek better quality governmental services. Awareness of the external benefits of some activities (for example, rapid transit) has increased.

Alternative Measures of the Size of the Governmental Sector

As noted above, the ratio of governmental expenditures to GNP provides a useful measure of trends in the relative size of the governmental sector over the years and is the best indicator of the overall impact of government upon total spending and resource allocation.

This ratio, however, is misleading as a measure of the actual size of the governmental sector in the economy. Government expenditure figures include transfer items whereas GNP totals do not; these activities affect the distribution of income but they do not in themselves reflect governmental conduct of economic activity. This problem can be avoided by use of the ratio of the value of governmental services to GNP (21 percent in 1966). This measure eliminates the element of transfer payments and compares final-product production in the two spheres.

This second measure, like the first, suffers from the limitation that governments produce few of the intermediate goods that they employ in providing their services—the patrol cars, the buildings, the radios, the uniforms used by the police force. A measure based on final product, therefore, overstates the relative sphere of governmental activity in the economy. A measure that adjusts for this difference is the ratio of value added in the governmental sector, or the equivalent, income originating in the governmental sector, to total national income. For highways, for example, value added is the difference between total expenditures on highways and amounts paid for materials, equipment, and other goods purchased. In 1966 13 percent of all income in the United States originated in the governmental sector.

Influences Affecting Expenditure Patterns

Several attempts have been made to isolate influences responsible for variations in per capita expenditures among the states and local governments in the United States. The pioneer work of Solomon Fabricant showed that three factors, per capita income, population density, and percentage of the total population in urban areas, accounted for most of the variation, the first factor being the dominant one.[12] In other words, the income elasticity of demand is positive, persons seeking more governmental activities as their incomes rise. There are, however, a number of exceptions, some of the high-income states spending relatively small amounts. The relationship between population density and per capita state expenditures is negative, reflecting the high cost of providing services in thinly populated areas. High urbanization necessitates additional activities not required in rural area.

A 1961 study by Glenn Fisher showed similar results, but less of the variation was explained by these three factors.[13] A second Fisher

[12]S. Fabricant, *The Trend of Governmental Activity in the United States Since 1900* (New York: National Bureau of Economic Research, 1952).

[13]Glenn Fisher, "Determinants of State and Local Government Expenditures," *National Tax Journal*, Vol. XIV (December, 1961), pp. 349–55.

study, published in 1964, added additional factors and analyzed the variations by major functions.[14] He found that seven variables explained most of the variations (except in the welfare field):

1. Percentage of families with incomes under $1,000.
2. Potential yield of a representative tax system, found to be a better variable than per capita income, upon which it depends in substantial part.
3. Population density.
4. Percent of population in urban areas.
5. Percent increase in population, 1950–60.
6. Index of two-party (political) competition.
7. Percentage of population over 25 with less than five years' schooling.

Items (3) and (4) are the same as two of the Fabricant items, and (2) is a closely related substitute; the others are added. The study showed several other results as well. The percent of families with low incomes was highly correlated (negatively) with per capita expenditures, a result suggesting that low-income families resist increases in government spending. Highway expenditures are found to decrease as the percentage of urbanization increases, while other expenditures rise.

A study by Seymour Sacks and Robert Harris showed the three Fabricant variables to be even less significant, and a high degree of correlation was found between per capita expenditures and another variable: federal grants to the states and state grants to the local governments.[15] A study by R. W. Bahl and R. J. Saunders, emphasizing changes in the Fabricant determinants, in grants-in-aid, and in public school enrollment, also concluded that grants-in-aid were a major determinant.[16] Analysis of the 15 high-income, high-density states showed grants to be much less significant and the three Fabricant determinants to be of primary importance in explaining differences. Unfortunately, discovery of the importance of the federal aid influence throws little additional light on expenditure decision-making processes; inevitably states getting greater federal aid spend more—except to the extent that they curtail expenditures from their own funds, and the nature of the

[14]Glenn Fisher, "Interstate Variation in State and Local Government Expenditures," *National Tax Journal,* Vol. XVII (March, 1964), pp. 57–64.

[15]Seymour Sacks and Robert Harris, "The Determinants of State and Local Government Expenditures and Intergovernmental Flows of Funds," *National Tax Journal,* Vol. XVII (March, 1964), pp. 75–85.

[16]R. W. Bahl and R. J. Saunders, "Determinants of Change in State and Local Government Expenditures," *National Tax Journal,* Vol. XVIII (March, 1965), pp. 50–57.

grant systems makes this difficult. A study by Ira Sharkansky[17] revealed that when state expenditures alone are considered, per capita income or an equivalent variable explains much less of the variation; low per capita incomes constrain the local governments much more than the states. Secondly, he showed the great significance of the level of previous expenditures upon current expenditures; the totals do not vary much from year to year, and thus this year's variation is in large measure a reflection of differences in previous years. This is scarcely a surprising result, but it does warn of the need for considering historical developments. Attempts to explain the source of sharp deviations from the past pattern were not successful.

The most recent study, by Robert F. Adams, considers variations in municipal expenditures for various functions, using 11 variables.[18] Expenditures on police protection were found to vary primarily with density of population and degree of urbanization, as well as size of transient population. To a lesser degree variations in fire protection are primarily explained by the same elements. Sanitation is primarily dependent on population density; recreation varies with transient population, population density, and percentage of foreign-born. Variations in general control, on the other hand, are not explained significantly by any of the variables. While these studies are of interest, they have thus far not thrown much light on expenditure decision making. As a basis for prediction they suffer from their cross-sectional nature; a time series approach would produce more useful results but is more difficult to make. In all these studies exceptions are numerous, to be explained only in terms of such factors as attitudes of local political leadership.

THE OVERALL REVENUE PICTURE

Governments in the United States in 1966 received $225 billion in current revenues, and net debt increased by $10 billion. Of the $225 billion, 71 percent came directly from general taxes and 14 percent from insurance trust fund levies, 9 percent from current charges, 2 percent from municipal utilities, 1 percent from liquor stores, and 3 percent from other sources. Data for the three levels of government are shown in Table 5–2.

[17]Ira Sharkansky, "Some More Thoughts About the Determinants of Government Expenditure," *National Tax Journal*, Vol. XX (June, 1967), pp. 171–79.

[18]Robert F. Adams, "On the Variation in the Consumption of Public Services," in Harvey Brazer (ed.), *Essays in State and Local Finance* (Ann Arbor, Mich.: Institute of Public Adminstration, University of Michigan, 1967).

TABLE 5-2

SOURCES OF CURRENT REVENUE, 1966 FISCAL YEAR, BY LEVEL OF GOVERNMENT
Percent of Total

	Federal	State	Local	Total*
General taxes.............	74	53	46	71
Trust fund taxes..........	16	13	1	14
Charges..................	7	7	10	9
Utility revenue...........	—	—	9	2
Liquor store revenue......	0	2	0	1
Other sources.............	3	3	4	3
Intergovernmental........	—	22	30	—

*Intergovernmental grants are excluded in calculating the total to avoid
double counting
SOURCE: U.S. Bureau of the Census, *Governmental Finances in 1965–66.*

FIGURE 5-3

TAX REVENUES BY TYPE OF TAX, UNITED STATES, FISCAL YEAR 1966
Including Social Security Payroll Taxes

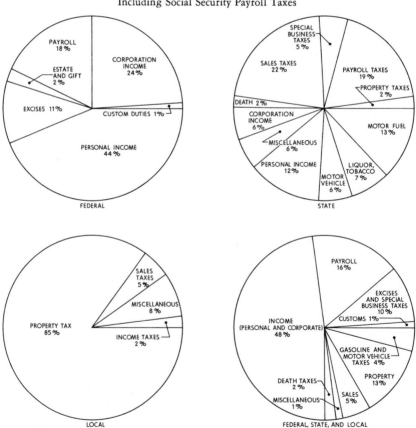

SOURCE: U.S. Bureau of the Census, *Summary of Government Finances in 1965–66.*

The relationships do not shift significantly from year to year and thus the figures are relevant beyond the particular year. Tax structures change even more slowly than expenditure patterns. Most of the items in the table are self-explanatory. The trust fund taxes are the payroll taxes used to finance the old-age annuity (federal) and unemployment compensation (state) programs. Revenues allocated to the federal highway trust funds are included in the category of general taxes. The principal charges at the federal level are those for the postal services and natural resources use, such as sale of timber and grazing rights. Tuition and fees for institutions of higher education are the principal state charges, and those for school lunches and hospital service the major ones at the local level.

Figure 5–3 surveys the revenues from taxes, excluding those allocated to the Social Security Trust Funds, at the three levels of government, and overall. The income tax, which yields 68 percent of the total tax revenue of the federal government and 48 percent in the overall tax structure, is by far the most important single source of revenue. The payroll taxes and the property tax, the chief source of local tax revenue (85 percent) are the next in importance, followed by the excise taxes (including liquor, tobacco, motor fuel, and other federal excises), 10 percent, and sales taxes, the chief single source of state tax revenue, 5 percent (22 percent of state revenue).

The structure of each of the major types of taxes will be summarized briefly: analysis of the problems involved in framing an optimal structure of each type of tax will appear in Chapters 14–16.

Federal Taxes

As of early 1968, the United States federal tax structure consisted of three major budgetary revenue sources, plus the payroll taxes of the Social Security program. These elements are:

1. *The income taxes,* consisting of the personal income tax, with yield of $63 billion, and the corporate income tax, with yield of $34 billion (1967 fiscal year). These yield 51 and 28 percent respectively of the federal nontrust tax revenue, and 44 and 23 percent of total tax revenue, including the receipts of the trust funds.

   The personal income tax is imposed on taxable income at rates ranging from 14 to 70 percent. Tax is determined as follows:

   A. All income is totaled to ascertain *gross income,* with the exception of the following excluded items:

 1. Casualty insurance proceeds and most life insurance proceeds.
 2. Gifts and bequests received.
 3. Certain military and veterans' allowances.
 4. Unemployment compensation and social security benefits.
 5. Interest on state and local bonds.
 6. Fellowship grants.

 Capital gains—realized increases in the value of assets held—receive special treatment; on assets held over six months the taxpayer has the option of including half of the gain in regular income, or applying a flat rate of 25 percent to the amount of the gain. Gains on owner-occupied residences receive more favorable treatment.

B. From gross income is deducted expenses of gaining the income to ascertain *adjusted gross income.* For a business, including farming and the professions, all ordinary business expenses are deductible. Persons working for wages and salaries are restricted to a few items, including costs of work-related travel away from home and a limited range of educational expenses necessary to maintain qualifications for a position.

C. From adjusted gross income the taxpayer is allowed two sets of adjustments:

 1. Personal deductions: expenditures of specified types that are assumed to reduce taxpaying capacity, or that the government wishes to encourage. The principal items include:

 a) Medical expenses, with specified minima and maxima.
 b) Contributions to charitable, educational, and religious organizations, subject to a maximum.
 c) Interest on personal loans.
 d) Most state and local taxes paid.
 e) Casualty losses, in excess of a specified figure.
 f) Alimony.
 g) A few miscellaneous items related to employment, such as union dues.

 Alternatively, the taxpayer may use the standard or optional deduction, equal to 10 percent of adjusted gross income to a maximum of $1,000, with a minimum of $200 plus $100 per dependent.

 2. Exemptions (credits for dependents): An allowance of

$600 for the taxpayer and for each dependent, defined in terms of relationship to the taxpayer, portion of support supplied (in excess of half), and income earned (under $600, with exceptions).

The tax is then calculated from the tax rate table provided or the schedule of rates, for 1967 as follows (married couple):

Taxable Income		Tax	
Not over $1,000		14%	
Over—	But not over—		of excess over—
$1,000	— $2,000	$140, plus 15%	— $1,000
$2,000	— $3,000	$290, plus 16%	— $2,000
$3,000	— $4,000	$450, plus 17%	— $3,000
$4,000	— $8,000	$620, plus 19%	— $4,000
$8,000	— $12,000	$1,380, plus 22%	— $8,000
$12,000	— $16,000	$2,260, plus 25%	— $12,000
$16,000	— $20,000	$3,260, plus 28%	— $16,000
$20,000	— $24,000	$4,380, plus 32%	— $20,000
$24,000	— $28,000	$5,660, plus 36%	— $24,000
$28,000	— $32,000	$7,100, plus 39%	— $28,000
$32,000	— $36,000	$8,660, plus 42%	— $32,000
$36,000	— $40,000	$10,340, plus 45%	— $36,000
$40,000	— $44,000	$12,140, plus 48%	— $40,000
$44,000	— $52,000	$14,060, plus 50%	— $44,000
$52,000	— $64,000	$18,060, plus 53%	— $52,000
$64,000	— $76,000	$24,420, plus 55%	— $64,000
$76,000	— $88,000	$31,020, plus 58%	— $76,000
$88,000	— $100,000	$37,980, plus 60%	— $88,000
$100,000	— $120,000	$45,180, plus 62%	— $100,000
$120,000	— $140,000	$57,580, plus 64%	— $120,000
$140,000	— $160,000	$70,380, plus 66%	— $140,000
$160,000	— $180,000	$83,580, plus 68%	— $160,000
$180,000	— $200,000	$97,180, plus 69%	— $180,000
$200,000	. . . .	$110,980, plus 70%	— $200,000

Single taxpayers are subjected to substantially higher rates, since the income of a couple is in effect divided equally between the two persons in the establishment of the rates.

From the tax thus calculated is subtracted the amount withheld by the employer from pay during the year plus that paid on declarations of estimated income. In addition the taxpayer is allowed a *credit* for certain foreign taxes paid, a portion of retirement income, and minor items.

The corporation income tax applies to taxable income of corporations, determined by subtracting expenses of gaining the income and a few other items (for example, contributions to charitable organizations). The

1967 tax rate was 48 percent, with a reduced rate of 22 percent on the first $25,000 of taxable income, a concession designed to lessen the adverse effect of the tax on the growth of small businesses. Firms are allowed credit against tax of 8 percent of the cost of new capital investment.

2. *The excise taxes,* limited, since 1965, to levies on liquor, tobacco, motor fuel, sales of motor vehicles, telephone service, and a few minor items. The excises, basic rates, and 1967 revenue are shown in Table 5–3. The excises yield about 11 percent of total tax revenue. Prior to 1965, there was a lengthy list of excises on goods regarded as luxuries, such as jewelry, cosmetics, furs, electric appliances, and radios, many of them introduced during World War II as anti-inflationary measures.

TABLE 5–3

MAJOR FEDERAL EXCISE TAXES, 1967 FISCAL YEAR

Excise	Rate	Yield (millions of dollars)
Liquor.................	Various*	$4,076
Cigarettes and tobacco...	8c per package (cigarettes)†	2,080
Motor fuel..............	4c per gallon	2,933
Other highway levies.....	Various	1,138
Motor vehicles...........	7% of manufacturer's price (buses and trucks 10%)	1,138
Telephone service........	10% of charge	1,077
Other.................		1,672

*Distilled spirits $10.50 per gal. (proof); wines 17c to $2.50 per gallon according to alcoholic content; beer $9 per barrel.
†Various rates on other products.

3. *Other Nontrust Levies.* The other general fund federal taxes are of minor revenue importance:

A. Estate and gift taxes, levied upon estates at the time of death, in excess of $60,000, at rates ranging from 3 to 77 percent. A marital deduction allows the bequest of up to half the estate to the surviving spouse tax-free. The taxable estate includes proceeds of insurance policies as well as the estate itself. Costs of transfer and bequests to charity are deducted. Heirs may be given up to 10 years to complete payment to avoid forced liquidation of the estate.

The gift taxes applied to the donor at rates three fourths of the estate tax rates, on gifts among living persons. Tax applies only to gifts in excess of $3,000 per year per recipient ($6,000 for a married couple), and then only when the life-time excess over $3,000 per year cumulates beyond $30,000 ($60,000 for a couple).

The yield of the estate tax was $3.1 billion in 1967, or 3 percent of the federal revenues. Judicious arrangement of a person's estate and the liberal allowances of the gift tax allow extensive avoidance.

B. Customs duties, yielding $1.8 billion.

4. *Payroll Taxes.* The payroll taxes of the social security system, although sometimes regarded as insurance premium payments and excluded from the administrative budget, are very significant revenue-wise, yielding, in 1967, $27 billion, or 18 percent of the total tax revenue. Rates in 1967 were 4.2 percent on the employer and on the employee, and 6.1 percent on self-employed, up to maximum taxable earnings of $6,600. The rate has been steadily raised over the years to produce additional revenue for social security purposes.

The States

The tax patterns of the states vary substantially; a few major levies produce most of the revenue:

1. *Sales Taxes.* Retail sales taxes, now employed in 44 states, yielded, in 1967, $8.9 billion, or 22 percent of state tax revenue. The taxes range in rate from 2 to 6 percent, 3 percent being the median figure. With minor exceptions these are retail sales taxes, applying only to the sale to the final consumer. Fourteen states exempt food and a number exempt medicine, but otherwise most of the taxes have very broad coverage. Several of the taxes levied in the last five years provide a broader scope of exemptions, including such articles as clothing. Treatment of capital goods varies; many states apply tax to business purchases other than items becoming physical ingredients of taxable goods, whereas others exclude industrial and farm machinery and other producers' goods in an effort to confine the tax so far as possible to purchases for personal consumption.

2. *Income Taxes.* As of January 1968, 37 states employed personal income taxes, and 40 states the corporation income tax; the two taxes yielded, respectively, 12 and 6 percent of total state tax revenue in 1967. The rates of the personal taxes are progressive to a limited degree, with rates very much lower than the federal rates. A schedule from 1 to 6 percent is typical; the highest figure is 14.6 percent. Some states allow deduction of federal income taxes; others do not. The corporate rates are usually proportional, with 5 or 6 percent as the typical figure and a range from 1.75 to 9.4 percent.

3. *Motor Fuel Taxes and Motor Vehicle License Taxes.* All states

tax motor fuel, with a yield of $4.8 billion or 13 percent of total state tax revenue in 1967. Likewise all states employ motor vehicle license taxes, yielding 6 percent of total tax revenue. These taxes are regarded primarily as sources of funds for highway finance.

4. Payroll taxes, to finance unemployment compensation, plus other insurance trust revenue, 19 percent.

5. *Other Excises.* All states tax liquor and all except one tax cigarettes; the two taxes together yield 7 percent of the total. Most states employ no other excises.

6. *Other.* The other levies are of minor importance in the overall picture but some are significant in particular states (figures in parentheses indicate percentage of total state tax revenue):

A. Special levies on insurance companies, usually based upon gross premiums (2 percent).

B. Levies on public utilities (2 percent).

C. General corporation taxes other than the corporate income taxes, on gross receipts, capital stock, or other bases, regarded as "business taxes" per se (2 percent).

D. Death and gift taxes, in 15 states taking the estate tax form and modeled after the federal tax, in the others the inheritance tax form (2 percent). The rate and exemptions vary with the relationship of the heirs to the decedent. Only Nevada does not use this form of tax.

E. State property taxes, confined to a small number of states, usually applied to types of property not easily assessed under the local property levies (2 percent).

F. Severance taxes, levied on the output of mineral products and petroleum, of major revenue importance in a few states (2 percent).

G. Other (3 percent).

The relative percentage figures vary among states; there are the three principal patterns:

1. States depending primarily upon the sales tax, such as Illinois and Washington, in which the tax yields about half of total tax revenue.

2. The states relying primarily on the income tax, such as Oregon and, in the past, Wisconsin and New York. In Oregon, the personal income tax yields 55 percent of state tax revenue.

3. Those relying on both taxes. This now includes most states.

No state now has neither income nor sales tax, although the New Hampshire income tax is of limited scope.

Local Government Tax Sources

The chief revenue source of the local governments is the property tax. This is a levy on the gross value, without adjustment for debt or other obligations, of real property (land and improvements), and, in many states, tangible personal property, that is, movable property that has intrinsic value, such as motor vehicles, furniture, livestock, and inventories of business firms. Several states exempt all or most tangible personal property, and most exempt, by law or practice, intangible personal property, that is, money and claims against or titles to property, such as bank deposits, mortgages, notes, bonds and stocks. A few states still nominally include intangibles, but few are reported for taxation. This is an *in rem* levy, imposed against property per se, rather than against the owners; it constitutes a lien against the property and passes to a new owner. Failure to pay results in sale of the property at public auction. Rates, universally proportional in the United States, are determined each year by each local governmental unit employing the tax by dividing the amount to be raised from the tax by the total assessed valuation of the taxing unit. This rate is then enacted by the local legislative body, subject to the requirement that the figure not exceed the maximum established by state law.

The local governments in recent years have commenced to make some use of nonproperty taxes. Local sales taxes, some locally administered but most collected by the states as supplements to their sales taxes, are used in several states, including California, Illinois, and New York. Local income taxes, most of them confined to wage and salary earnings, are employed in several states. Local cigarette and motor fuel taxes are used in a few states. Other local taxation consists of various license taxes on business firms.

APPENDIX I—CANADIAN GOVERNMENTAL EXPENDITURES AND REVENUES

Figure 5A–1 shows the major categories of governmental expenditures in Canada for the federal government for 1968 (budget estimates), the provinces for 1967, and for the municipalities and the overall picture for 1964, the latest year for which data are available.[19]

The primary federal functions, as in the United States, consist of national defense, welfare and health, and transportation and other re-

[19]See Canadian Tax Foundation, *The National Finances 1967–68* and *Provincial Finances, 1967,* for details.

source development. The relative expenditures on national defense, however, are substantially less than in the United States (including veterans' aid, 20 percent instead of 54 percent of the total), a reflection of the different role that Canada plays in the international picture. Canada has assumed a significant role as a mediator and as a supplier of troops for the United Nations rather than as an independent military

FIGURE 5A-1

EXPENDITURES BY MAJOR FUNCTION, BY LEVEL OF GOVERNMENT, CANADA

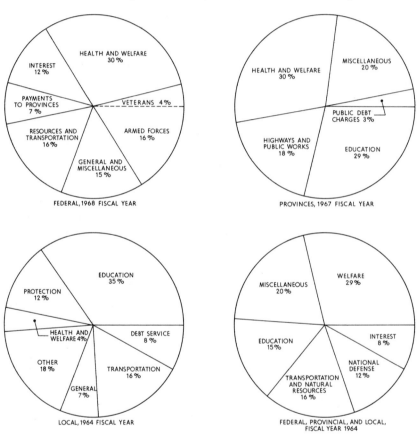

SOURCE: Canadian Tax Foundation, *National Finances*, 1967-68; *Provincial Finances*, 1967.

power. Armed forces manpower is not drafted, partly because of long-standing hostility to the draft in Quebec. Welfare and health activities are more important, relatively, than in the United States. The federal government has several major programs.[20] A universal system of old-

[20]The welfare programs are summarized in I. J. Goffman, *Some Fiscal Aspects of Public Welfare in Canada* (Toronto: Canadian Tax Foundation, 1965).

age pensions is provided, the funds raised by supplements to the personal and corporate income tax and the sales tax, and pensions paid to all persons over the age of 70 at a uniform rate (in recent years, $75 per month). In 1965 a supplementary system based on employee and employer contributions was established. A universal family allowance system grants to all families $6 per month for each child under 10 years and $8 for each child from 10 to 15. Other welfare programs provide assistance to the blind, disabled, and others.

The federal government has not developed a system of highway grants comparable to that in the United States except for the trans-Canada highway system. On the other hand, the government has operated one of the two major railway systems since the early twenties (and portions from the last century).

The provincial expenditure picture is comparable to that in the United States. Welfare and health programs and education are of equal importance, each accounting for about 30 percent of the total, and highways constitute the third major element, about 20 percent. As in the United States, but to a slightly lesser degree, education dominates the local expenditure picture, with about 35 percent of the total.

For governments as a whole, the primary difference from the United States is the somewhat greater importance of welfare and

FIGURE 5A–2

RATIO OF GOVERNMENT EXPENDITURES TO GROSS NATIONAL PRODUCT, CANADA, SELECTED YEARS, 1929–65

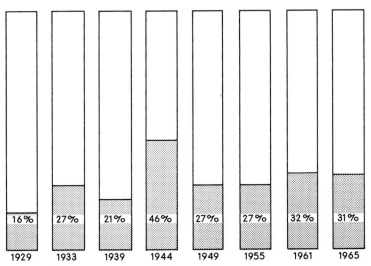

SOURCE: Canada, *National Accounts: Income and Expenditures,* various years.

FIGURE 5A-3

GOVERNMENTAL REVENUES BY MAJOR SOURCE, CANADA

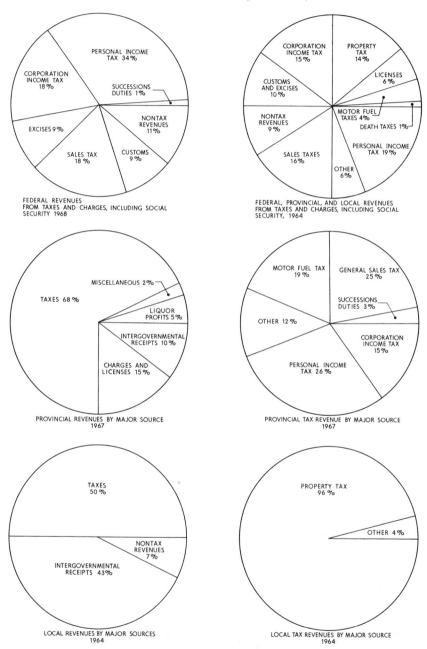

FEDERAL REVENUES
FROM TAXES AND CHARGES, INCLUDING SOCIAL
SECURITY 1968

FEDERAL, PROVINCIAL, AND LOCAL REVENUES
FROM TAXES AND CHARGES, INCLUDING SOCIAL
SECURITY, 1964

PROVINCIAL REVENUES BY MAJOR SOURCE
1967

PROVINCIAL TAX REVENUE BY MAJOR SOURCE
1967

LOCAL REVENUES BY MAJOR SOURCES
1964

LOCAL TAX REVENUES BY MAJOR SOURCE
1964

SOURCE: Canadian Tax Foundation, *National Finances*, 1967–68; *Provincial Finances*, 1967.

health activities and lesser importance of national defense; otherwise the activities are comparable. Figure 5A–2 shows the growth of governmental expenditures in Canada as a percentage of gross national product.

Revenues. Figure 5A–3 shows the major revenue sources by level of government in Canada. While the sources are similar to those in the United States, there are some significant differences. The primary one is the greater reliance on indirect taxes; the sales tax, customs duties, and excises together yield about 36 percent of the federal governmental revenue, compared to 10 percent in the United States. The yield of the income tax is, accordingly, relatively less. There is less significant difference at the provincial and municipal level; thus the overall picture is characterized by greater reliance on indirect taxation.

APPENDIX II—SUMMARY OF THE CANADIAN TAX STRUCTURE

The Canadian tax structure is complicated by the various abatements of provincial taxes against federal tax.

Federal Taxation

The personal income tax with a yield in 1967–68 of $3.6 billion, or 34 percent of budgetary and social security revenue, is comparable in many ways to that of the United States. The major difference is the exclusion from tax of all capital gains (although the category is more narrowly defined in Canada than in the United States, and thus some income receiving favorable tax treatment in the U.S. is taxed at regular rates in Canada). Other exclusions are more restricted; family allowances, unemployment benefits, and veterans' pensions are the most significant. Provincial and municipal bond interest is taxable.

Other deductions are restricted to contributions and medical expenses, certain payments to registered pension and retirement savings programs, union dues, and student fees. Taxes are not deductible. An optional deduction of $100 is allowed in lieu of the medical and contributions items.

Personal exemptions, as of 1968, are $1,000 for the taxpayer and $1,000 for his wife, $300 for children eligible for family allowance, and $550 for other dependents as defined. For certain classes of dependents the deduction is defined as the amount spent in support up to the specified maximum, rather than the latter figure as such.

Tax Rates. The rates range from 11 to 80 percent (1967), thus starting slightly lower but rising to higher figures than in the U.S.[21] From these figures are allowed abatements (28 percent in 1967) for provincial income taxes paid; thus the effective federal rate ranges from 5.72 to 57.6 percent in 1967, but in all provinces the overall combined rate is brought to the maximum of the abatement (8.8 to 80 percent),[22] and in Manitoba and Saskatchewan the rate goes beyond to bring the combined figure to a range of 9.35 to 84 percent.

Corporation Income Tax. This levy applies to the total net income of all corporations, yielding (1967–68) $1.7 billion, or 18 percent of the tax-combined revenues. Including the social security supplement, the rate is 50 percent on income in excess of $35,000, 21 percent on income less than this figure. An abatement of 10 percent is allowed for provincial corporate income taxes, and thus the Dominion rate is, in effect, 40 percent on income above $35,000, and 12 percent below.[23]

Sales Tax. The Dominion government has employed a general sales tax since 1920, with the single-stage manufacturers tax form since 1923. The tax applies to all finished products manufactured in or imported into Canada, at the rate of 12 percent on the manufacturer's selling price (three percentage points being earmarked for old-age security). Exemptions are limited to food, certain basic medicines, specified farm supplies and equipment, and, commencing in 1968, all production equipment and machinery (which had long been exempted, but made taxable again in 1964). The tax yields about $2.2 billion, 18 percent of the total.

Excise Taxes and Duties. Excise taxes are imposed at 15 percent rates on television sets, phonographs, and cigars, and at 10 percent on jewelry, cosmetics, watches, and a few other items. These are levies on the manufacturer's selling prices and collected in conjunction with the sales tax. Specific-rate excise taxes are imposed on cigarettes, wines, and a few minor items. Excise *duties* are levied, at specific rates, on liquor and tobacco products. The excise taxes yielded revenue of $340 million (3 percent), excise duties $495 million (5 percent).

Customs. Duties on imports are far more significant, revenuewise, than they are in the United States, yielding, in 1968, $815 million, or 9 percent of the total tax revenue. Iron, steel, and textile products yield a large portion of the total.

Estate Tax. The tax applies to the net estate, with deduction of

---

[21]A temporary surcharge added late in 1967 was replaced by a 3 percent surcharge in March 1968 following defeat of the legislation for the former.

[22]For Quebec the abatement (1967) is 50 percent because Quebec chose not to participate in certain federal grant programs.

[23]Plus a 3 percent surcharge effective March 1968.

$40,000 ($60,000 if there is a surviving wife) and $10,000 for each dependent child. Rates range from 10 to 54 percent. Seventy-five percent of the revenue is allocated to the provinces. Gifts in excess of $4,000 are subject to a gift tax ranging from 10 to 28 percent.

The estate and gift taxes yield about $110 million, or 1 percent of total tax revenue.

Provincial and Municipal Revenue

The revenue structures of the provinces are basically very similar, except for the absence of a sales tax in Alberta.

Income Taxes. All provinces employ both personal and corporate income taxes, adjusted to at least equal the federal abatement figure. The personal tax rates range from 5.5 to 40 percent in Quebec, 3.63 to 26.40 percent in Manitoba and Saskatchewan, and 3.08 to 22.40 percent in the other provinces. The combined rates, federal and provincial, are thus higher in Manitoba and Saskatchewan than elsewhere. The base is identical to that of the Dominion tax, and all taxes are collected by the Dominion in conjunction with the Dominion tax except in Quebec. Allocation is based upon residence of the taxpayer.

The corporate income tax rates range from 9 percent (the amount of the federal abatement) to 12 percent. The taxes are collected by the Dominion government except in Ontario and Quebec. The base of the tax is identical to the federal tax; allocation is prescribed by Dominion legislation.

Retail Sales Taxes. All of the provinces except Alberta impose retail sales taxes, technically levied upon the customer, the vendor being an agent of the province for purposes of collection and remittance of tax. The rates range from 3 to 8 percent (Quebec), 5 percent being the median. Exemptions are more extensive than in the United States; food, prescription drugs, various items for farm use, and school books are exempt in all provinces and children's clothing in all except two. Except in Ontario and Quebec, the taxes are not designated as sales taxes, but on the basis of the use of the revenues (for example, hospital tax).

Motor Fuel. All provinces tax motor fuel, at rates ranging from 12 to 20 cents per imperial gallon, with the tax on diesel fuel from 14 to 27 cents. There is less tendency to earmark the revenue specifically for highway use than in the United States, but nevertheless the levies are regarded as benefit-based.

Other Excises. Seven provinces tax admissions, six tax tobacco products, and all gain revenue from liquor sales via markup in provincial stores or tax.

Successions Duties. Three provinces, Ontario, Quebec, and British Columbia, levy successions duties, with exemptions and rates varying with the relationship of the heir to the decedent, the rate also dependent upon the size of the total estate. The exemptions are relatively high for direct heirs, being comparable to the Dominion estate tax exemptions. The other seven provinces receive a portion of the federal estate tax instead.

For the provinces as a whole, in 1967, the retail sales tax yielded 25 percent of total tax revenue, motor fuel taxes 19 percent, personal income taxes 26 percent, corporate income taxes 15 percent, successions duties 3 percent; others, 12 percent.

Local Taxes. To a greater extent than in the United States, the municipal governments rely on the property tax as the primary source of tax revenue. The taxes are levied upon real property only, except for a limited amount of personal property in the three maritime provinces and Manitoba. In the western provinces, typically land is taxed at a higher rate than improvements, in conformity with the single-tax philosophy. Property is assessed by local officials, with substantial provincial assistance in several provinces.

The property taxes are supplemented in most provinces by occupancy taxes on business firms, based upon the value of the property occupied, collected from the tenant. Rental value, floor space, and sales are employed in ascertaining taxable value for this purpose.

REFERENCES

United States

GOODE, RICHARD. *The Individual Income Tax.* Washington, D.C.: Brookings Institution, 1964.

MAXWELL, J. A. *Financing State and Local Government.* Washington, D.C.: Brookings Institution, 1965.

PECHMAN, J. A. *Federal Tax Policy.* Washington, D.C.: Brookings Institution, 1966.

U.S. BUREAU OF THE BUDGET. *The Budget in Brief.* Annual.

U.S. TREASURY, INTERNAL REVENUE SERVICE. *Your Federal Income Tax.* Annual.

Canada

CANADIAN TAX FOUNDATION. *The National Finances.* Annual; and *Provincial Finances.* Annual.

PERRY, J. H. *Taxation in Canada.* 3rd ed. Toronto: University of Toronto Press, 1961.

Report of the Royal Commission on Taxation. 6 vols. Ottawa: Queens Printer, 1967.

PART II

*Economic Effects of Governmental
Expenditures and Revenues*

Chapter 6

ALLOCATIONAL AND EFFICIENCY EFFECTS OF GOVERNMENTAL EXPENDITURES AND REVENUES

The conduct of economic activity by governments and the transfer by governments of purchasing power from some persons to others have potentially significant effects upon the private sector of the economy:

1. *Allocational and Efficiency Effects.* Governments deliberately reallocate resources from some goods to others by the production of public goods and ones with some external benefits, and their transfer activities alter resource allocation because the donors and recipients of the money will have different expenditure patterns. Taxes used to finance the activities may result in reallocation of consumer expenditures and therefore of resources.

Governments may affect the operational efficiency in the conduct of economic activity, altering the amount of output obtained from a given quantity of resources through their conduct of economic activity and through the effects of taxes used to finance the programs.

2. *Factor-Supply Effects.* Governments may affect the level of real GNP by altering the supplies of various factors available for use in production, both by expenditure programs, such as those for education, and by financing programs, which may alter the willingness of factor owners to supply factor units.

3. *Distributional Effects.* Governments affect the pattern of real income distribution through the provision of benefits on the one hand and reduction of private-sector real income on the other, resulting in an overall pattern different from the one otherwise prevailing.

4. *Stabilization and Growth (Fiscal) Effects.* Expenditure and financing programs will affect the extent to which full employment of resources is attained by altering aggregate spending in the economy and thus the level of GNP and may affect the rate of economic growth.

Allocational and efficiency effects will be considered in this chapter, the others in succeeding chapters.

ALLOCATIONAL EFFECTS

Governmental activity affects the allocation of resources and thus the relative outputs of various goods—the overall product mix—in several ways.

Public Goods and Transfer Activities

First, the conduct of most governmental activities results in an increase in output of the governmental services and thus a reduction, given the overall level of national income, in private-sector output. Public goods, by their inherent character, would not be produced at all by the private sector, and goods with some direct benefits but governmentally produced because of externalities, such as education, would be produced in much smaller quantities. Accordingly, GNP consists of more national defense activity (which now accounts for more than 10 percent of total GNP) and education and protection and health, and less of automobiles and other private-sector goods. Even the outputs of commercial activities of government, such as water and postal service, will be altered if governments follow different pricing policies than the private firms. These alterations in resource allocation are deliberate and reflect the desire of society to benefit from additional output of public and semipublic goods.

The transfer activities of government likewise result in resource reallocation since the recipients typically have different consumption patterns than the taxpayers. Most distributional programs shift purchasing power from the higher income to the lower income groups, and thus the output of cheaper cars will be greater and that of expensive cars less, for example. Some programs (such as old-age annuities) shift wealth from the young to the old, thus lessening the purchase of household furniture and increasing that of round-the-world cruises. These changes are inherent consequences of the transfer activities.

Effects of Taxes

While the allocational effects of governmental expenditures are obvious and deliberate, those of taxes usually are not. Nevertheless they may be very significant. First, any tax that alters the relative prices of various goods will cause a reallocation of consumer expenditures, under the assumptions that consumers have limited incomes, seek to maximize satisfaction, and have preference schedules such that commodities are substitutable. Prior to the levying of such a tax, consumers will have sought to extend purchases of all commodities to the levels at which the marginal rates of substitution are equal to the ratios of the prices of the commodities—under the assumption that they seek to maximize satisfaction. When a tax raises the price of one commodity relative to that of another, the consumer will reduce the relative purchases of the more expensive commodity and increase that of the other commodities. Accordingly, production will be altered, with increased output of the commodity that has fallen in price and a decrease in the one that has increased in price. The reaction is the same as that which follows from governmental pricing of commercial services at figures different from those private producers would have set.

This effect will not be encountered with a universal sales tax applying to all consumption, nor with an income tax applying to all income uniformly, regardless of use, except indirectly through effects on factor supplies. The reaction will occur with excise taxes reflected in higher prices of taxed items relative to those for untaxed items, with sales taxes with exemptions or rate differentiation, with corporate income taxes that result in price increases that do not bear a uniform relationship to pretax prices, and with property taxes when the ratios of taxable property to prices of the commodities are not uniform. Goods produced with real-property-intensive methods, such as railroad service, will rise in price relative to those utilizing less-property-intensive methods, and less of the former will be produced. The significance of this reallocative effect, which is often called consumer excess burden, will be discussed in Chapter 16.

When the production of particular commodities is favored by tax laws, the relative outputs of the products will be greater. The chief example in the United States is the production of petroleum, and to a lesser extent mineral products, as a result of the very favorable depletion allowances. Since income tax is less on income earned in these industries than in others, production of additional output is encouraged. Conversely, when taxes are heavier on the production of certain products than others, their relative outputs will be less. For example, a tax on the export of specific products, as found in many developing countries, will cause producers to shift away from these products to nontaxed ones.

Allocational effects will also result from personal income taxes of such nature that tax liability is affected by consumption patterns. When the value of self-produced goods is not taxed, as is usual, a person is given incentive to consume more of goods that he himself can produce such as vegetables of a type that he can grow, or housing that he can provide by owning his own home, and therefore less of goods that he would otherwise buy with income earned. More significantly, with present income taxes, a person is encouraged to spend more on items that may be claimed as business expenses and thus deducted from taxable income. Entertainment of customers, acquisition of books and magazines remotely related to one's work, are examples, available only for persons gaining income from sources other than wages and salaries.

All personal deductions encourage reallocation of expenditures. Some of these are deliberate. Thus persons are encouraged to give more to charity or to provide additional support for parents or children to insure that they are classified as dependents, or to obtain more adequate medical care. Property taxes may have comparable but unintended effects. Where the tax applies to durable consumer goods, persons are given some incentive to buy fewer durables, since other purchases do not give rise to property tax liability. The heavy impact of the property tax on housing probably reduces the total amount spent for this purpose and may deter improvements to housing if they increase tax liability.

Changes in relative factor supplies, discussed in Chapter 8, will also affect resource allocation by altering the relative costs of goods; those produced with factors whose supply is reduced will rise relative to those of other goods.

EFFECTS UPON OPERATIONAL EFFICIENCY

Operational efficiency, in the sense of the ratio of output to given inputs, is affected by governmental activities and revenue systems in a number of ways: through the utilization of resources in the conduct of governmental activity, through collection of taxes and other revenues, and through the effects of the revenue and expenditure systems upon private-sector factor combinations.

Efficiency in Use of Resources by Government

Generalizations about relative efficiency of governmental and private-sector use of resources are difficult. Traditional folklore of the United States and many other countries assumes that governments inherently use resources less efficiently than private enterprise, with less output per unit of input. In the private sector, the price system and the forces of competition aid in ensuring efficiency. The higher costs per unit of output of a less efficient firm will stimulate it to eliminate inefficiency. In a higher competitive market maximum efficiency is required or the firm will be forced out of business. Governments have no equivalent test since, with rare exceptions, they do not produce goods sold in competitive markets. Furthermore, the profit motive leads a firm to seek maximum efficiency in production even if it is not subject to competition, since profit maximization is possible only with maximum output per unit of input, given the constraints of skill and technology. Governments are affected neither by the profit motive nor the danger of bankruptcy.

Pressures toward Governmental Efficiency. This argument is not conclusive. Governments are subject to other forms of pressure toward efficiency—strong pressures. At the higher echelons, the government per se, in the sense of the executive and legislature, seeks—we assume—to retain power, and therefore to maximize services, which persons want, and to minimize taxes, which they do not want. The more efficiently a government operates, the greater the services that can be provided with given revenues and the more popular the government will be. This is not to argue that governments actually attain maximum efficiency; apart from the restrictions noted below, the elimination of inefficiency is in itself costly, and a point is ultimately reached at which further effort to find inefficiency would cost as much as the gain. Business firms are confronted with exactly the same problem; they may not actually attain maximum efficiency any more frequently than governments.

There is no way of comparing the relative strength of the market price, profit-motive pressures to efficiency with that of the desire of governments to provide maximum service at minimum cost in order to remain in power. There is no evidence, however, that one is weaker than the other. Some indication of the interest in gaining efficiency in government in the United States is offered by the extensive review of operations of governmental agencies by the General Accounting Office and by congressional committees, and by the pioneering work of various governmental units, federal and state, in the introduction of computer equipment and development of operations research.

The desire on the part of high echelons of governments to maximize efficiency is reflected in part in the motivation of personnel in the lower administrative levels. Subordinate administrative personnel in government, as in business, presumably seek to obtain favor of their superiors by implementing the policies developed in the higher echelons, since salary and promotion and even retention of position depend upon such favor. Even more significant is the desire to avoid danger of an investigation that may discover inefficiencies. Likewise, subordinate bureaucrats are also interested in output—in product—and the more efficiently the agency operates, the greater is the output possible with a given budget. They likewise frequently accept the goal of efficiency as important in itself.[1] Pride in effectiveness and efficiency of operation—in doing a job well—is a strong motive in human behavior that has too often been ignored.

In at least two respects governmental units have advantages over private-sector units. First, they operate in a goldfish bowl; details of their operations are available to legislative bodies, to newspaper reporters, to members of opposition parties, all frequently interested in uncovering and publicizing inefficiency. Private enterprise operations permit a greater veil of secrecy. Even the stockholders of corporations may be denied access to details of operations, and except in the rare event of a fight for control, there are no outsiders watching for inefficiency that they can publicize to their own advantage. Second, governmental units are much more inclined to exchange information with each other, since they are not in any sense competitive. One state tax administrator will share his techniques and improvement with an administrator from another state, whereas a businessman is not interested in aiding his competitors.

Restrictions on Efficiency—Higher Echelons. There are, however, various restrictions on the attainment of efficiency, some of which are more significant with governmental units than with private firms, although many are experienced in common by both.

The first set relates to top echelons of government. Policies that restrict efficiency will sometimes appear to be more effective means of gaining votes than those that maximize efficiency. The patronage system was the classic example, providing government jobs for political supporters, so that they would work hard in elections to gain and retain their jobs. While a patronage employee may be highly efficient, he is likely to be less qualified for the job than other persons, and administrative efficiency will be reduced. While the United States has moved a long way from the patronage rule that was once dominant, vestiges remain. The Commonwealth countries developed a tradition of a nonpolitical civil service at a much earlier date.

---

[1]This statement is certainly true, for example, of state tax administrations, with which I have had substantial contact over the last decade. There are a few exceptions, but most administrators in this field constantly seek to improve efficiency of operations, to introduce new techniques as they become available, to study and utilize methods employed in other jurisdictions.

Other activities are affected by strong political pressures that small groups are able to exert, often through logrolling in its undesirable manifestations. Attempts to close an obsolete and inefficient military base will encounter strong political opposition from local interests. Transfer of the Forest Service from the Department of Agriculture to the Department of the Interior has been blocked by farm groups who prefer it in a department more favorably inclined toward the interests of ranchers seeking to graze cattle on forest land, although the transfer would presumably increase efficiency.

Governments, particularly at the national level, develop rigid rules of operation, designed primarily to prevent misuse of funds and to standardize policy, which may interfere with efficiency and adaptation to new conditions. One of the most serious consequences is the prevention of reprogramming—making of changes in procedures as conditions change. Rules to prevent firing of employees for political reasons may make discharge for inefficiency virtually impossible. The magnitudes of operations of larger units of government—the national defense forces, for example—increase the need for standard rules and complicate the attainment of efficiency. In the context of a somewhat broader concept of efficiency: governments may be less concerned about adapting their services to the needs of the users,[2] despite the overall desire to retain office.

Restrictions on Efficiency within the Bureaucracy. There are likewise significant restrictions on the attainment of maximum efficiency within the bureaucracy itself. One is the importance of the "satisficing" motive: placing of emphasis upon attaining satisfactory rather than optimal performance. In view of the costs of gaining information about the consequences of change and the uncertainty about results even with the best attainable information, governmental agencies, just as units within large-scale business firms, will stop short—and do so quite rationally—of the level of minimizing costs. In government particularly, responsible officials may stand to gain very little if a change is successful and may be in serious difficulty if it is not. Thus, granted the uncertainty, they will favor the status quo—leave matters alone so long as performance is reasonably satisfactory. If their rewards from successful changes were greater, as they are to the proprietor of a small business, the desire to maintain status quo would be less.

---

[2]The U.S. Post Office provides some excellent examples, as for example the failure to adapt post office hours to the desires of the customers, and the failure to provide mail delivery on certain days (e.g., Veterans' Day and Washington's Birthday) that are not holidays for business firms.

Beyond this consideration is the vested interest that persons develop in existing agencies and procedures. Agency heads and subordinate personnel strenuously resist efforts to reduce the scope of their activities and the size of their staffs and efficiency in the use of resources is reduced. This resistance reflects partly fear of loss of employment or transfer to a less satisfactory job, and partly reluctance to admit a decline in importance of the activity. As stated by Anthony Downs, government agencies never retire and virtually never die.[3]

Another phenomenon is empire building: the desire to expand the number of personnel even if the agency is not producing greater output. This is a manifestation of what may be called "Parkinson's Law," for the British historian who first publicized the idea. Partly it is a result of the tendency to judge prestige and adjust rank and salary on the basis of the number of subordinates.

A final consideration is the inherent difficulty in any bureaucracy of substantial size in insuring that information passed up the chain of command and instructions passed down are not altered along the way, either accidentally or deliberately. Actions at the higher levels must be based on information that comes up from below. Persons inevitably dislike painting a black picture of themselves or providing information that they know will lead to policies that they oppose. They will likewise interpret instructions in the preferred direction and delay action on undesired ones.[4]

Subordinate personnel can disregard "customer" interests just as can higher authority, particularly if the person regards his position as secure. The relationship between his treatment of persons with whom he deals and his own success in his occupation may appear so remote that he ignores it. This is not the typical pattern, but it occurs. Clerks and other persons dealing with the public can be abrupt and discourteous and unhelpful; most of us have had experience with government employees who have behaved in this fashion, and the treatment given to "outsiders" is often particularly bad because there is no fear of complaints: the tourist in a small town traffic court, the bewildered emigrant to the United States.

Granted these restrictions, there is little doubt that governments typically do not maximize efficiency. Most of these restrictions are not characteristic of governments alone, but either of large-scale operations, private or public, or of all operations, large or small. In any

---

[3]See Anthony Downs, "A Theory of Bureaucracy," *Proceedings of the American Economic Association for 1965,* pp. 439–46.
[4]Anthony Downs, *Inside Bureaucracy* (Boston: Little, Brown, 1967), chap. x.

large-scale organization, the interests of particular individuals may not coincide with those of the organization. Satisficing is common, partly because of the uncertainty and cost-of-information problems, partly because any change from the status quo may offer little benefit to the individuals if successful but may be fatal if the change does not succeed. Empire building, Parkinson's Law, and the resistance to contraction of agencies whose activities have declined must be fought by large-scale business as well as government. Arbitrary rules are as prevalent in business as in government. Businesses may not always adapt their operations to the desires of their customers, partly because of the complications of size and the need for rules of procedure, and employees may be as obnoxious as those of governmental agencies.[5] Smaller businesses may be less bureaucratic, but they are more likely to lack knowledge adequate to obtain maximum efficiency, as anyone who has dealt with small repair firms and contractors knows only too well.

Use of Resources for Tax Administration and Compliance

Collection of tax or other revenues requires the use of resources on the part of both the government and the taxpayer that do not produce a product that satisfies wants. The activity is comparable to that of business firms in collecting prices from customers. The quantity of resources used for the purpose depends upon the rule governments follow about optimal levels of enforcement activity.

A government presumably seeks to minimize expenditures for tax collection by obtaining maximum efficiency in use of resources for collection purposes. But the direct correlation between amounts spent on collection (if they are used with maximum efficiency) and the effectiveness of collection complicates the statement of the optimum. Clearly the objective is not to spend as little as possible, because the loss in revenues from evasion could be very substantial. Increases in expenditures up to a certain point will increase revenues by amounts greater than the additional expenditures; beyond a certain point the revenue will be less. One approach to the optimal point, therefore, is in terms of costs and additional revenue directly gained. The point at which marginal cost and marginal direct gain are equal, however, is not necessarily optimal because improvements in enforcement lead to better voluntary compliance on the part of taxpayers. As some taxpayers are checked carefully this year, they will be more careful next year, as will

---

[5]Store clerks and ticket agents can be as uncivil as government employees, and negotiations with large publishing firms over subscription errors or with the telephone companies can be as frustrating as any negotiation with government agencies.

other persons who hear about the experience. Accordingly, the optimal point may be defined in terms of these indirect increases in revenue as well as the direct ones, but the indirect ones are difficult to calculate. Alternatively, some governments accept the philosophy that any evasion of tax is intolerable in the interests of equity and respect for law and seek complete enforcement. Rarely is this result obtained, however.

The ratios of costs of collection to revenue are surprisingly uniform for major taxes. Netzer, in a recent study, concludes that the property tax collection costs in larger cities average from 1 to 1.5 percent of revenue.[6] State sales taxes typically cost from 1 to 1.5 percent of the revenue; the costs for federal income tax are 0.6 percent of revenue. Cost for a few levies, such as the excise on telephone service, is very much lower.

Collection costs, and thus resource use, are a function not only of the thoroughness of enforcement but also of the tax rate, the number of individual taxpayers relative to revenue, the complexity of the tax, and the ease with which the tax base is calculated. The higher the tax rate, the lower is the administrative cost per dollar received, other factors given. Taxes with large numbers of taxpayers, each owing a small amount of tax, are more expensive to collect than those with a few large taxpayers. Similarly the literacy of the taxpayers, the nature of record systems, and general attitudes toward taxation all play a part.[7] Simplicity in taxation lessens the cost of effective administration; exemptions are frequently a prime source of difficulty. Taxes on easily ascertainable figures (for example, gallons of gasoline sold) are easier to administer than those for which constructive value figures must be ascertained (taxes on value of property; ad valorem customs duties).

Resources are used not only in administration but in compliance as well. Individuals must allocate time that they would prefer to use for other pursuits to fill out tax returns or must hire experts to do this work. Substantial skilled manpower devoted to the work of devising means for the higher income groups to reduce income and estate liability is not available for other purposes. Inconvenient timing for paying tax may require persons to borrow money to meet tax obligations.

Business firms, which in a sense serve as tax collecting agents for the government for income tax withholding, payroll tax deduction, and

[6]D. Netzer, *Economics of the Property Tax* (Washington, D.C.: Brookings Institution, 1966), pp. 174-75.

[7]Attitudes, although unmeasurable, rather obviously vary widely. Evasion is regarded as a legitimate game in many Latin and Arab countries, while frowned upon in northern Europe.

sales tax collection, incur considerable cost in so doing.[8] The argument is sometimes advanced that business firms should be compensated for their work as tax collectors, and a number of states and the Canadian provinces do provide an allowance (a specified percentage of total tax due) to retailers as compensation for their work in collecting and remitting tax. Since resources are employed and costs incurred, payment is not without merit. Unfortunately, however, governments cannot ascertain the actual cost of compliance and the formulas used are highly arbitrary. Greater equity is gained automatically over time if the compliance costs enter into the prices of the products.

The administrative and compliance costs do not represent a net loss of output to society, since, without government, the private sector would incur costs to collect prices from their customers, in the form of clerk time, costs of cash registers and other collection equipment, and collection of delinquent accounts. There is no way of ascertaining the magnitude of these costs relative to those of tax administration and compliance.

Taxation and Operational Efficiency

Taxation will alter choice of factor combinations and methods of organization of production and physical distribution if the amount of tax liability is affected by factor combinations or production methods employed.

Factor Combinations. Optimal factor combinations will be altered whenever a tax leads to change in relative factor supplies, or when the tax liability is affected by the factor combination chosen. Changes in relative factor supplies, discussed in Chapter 8, will alter relative factor prices. If labor supply is reduced by the tax structure relative to land and capital, firms will find less-labor-intensive production methods more advantageous. Any tax applied to payments to particular factors will alter the optimal combination. The payroll taxes of the social security program, with their relatively high rates, have potentially great effects; by raising the cost of using labor they encourage the replacement of labor by capital. Application of sales taxes to capital goods makes capital relatively more expensive compared to labor, leads to use of less-capital-intensive methods, and delays the replacement of old capital equipment by new. A real property tax raises

---

[8]Various estimates of cost of compliance have been made; see particularly M. H. Bryden, *The Costs of Tax Compliance* (Toronto: Canadian Tax Foundation, 1961); and J. C. Yokum, *Retailers' Cost of Sales Tax Collection in Ohio* (Columbus: Ohio State University Bureau of Business Research, 1961).

the relative cost of production methods using extensive land and durable capital goods subject to tax. On the other hand, liberal depreciation deductions and tax credits on new equipment reduce the relative cost of factor combinations employing it. Conversely, if depreciation on new equipment is not permitted, as has been the policy at times in some countries, the relative cost of using capital increases.

Methods of Production. Taxes may affect the selection of methods of production, financing, and organization whenever the tax liability is greater with one method than with another.

Income tax structures frequently affect the choice between corporate and noncorporate forms of organization. If the earnings of the corporation are taxed and dividends are fully taxable at the personal income level, the owners of smaller businesses are given incentive not to incorporate if they expect to pay out most of their earnings to themselves. On the other hand, if the corporate rate is less than the personal rate for higher bracket taxpayers and capital gains receive favorable treatment, the owners have incentive to incorporate if they plan to retain earnings in the business and ultimately benefit via capital gains. The lower tax rate on corporations with profits under $25,000 encourages a corporation to split into several, all owned by the same persons, to take advantage of the lower tax rate. Sales taxes that exempt small firms, as they do in some countries, favor the small firm over the large. Ability of small firms to evade tax will produce the same result. Death taxes encourage mergers, to insure that one's heirs are not forced to sell the business to pay taxes. Methods of financing may be affected; the deductibility of bond interest and the nondeductibility of dividends paid on stock encourages relatively greater use of debt.

Taxes on commodities and services or business gross receipts frequently alter the relative advantages of various methods of organizing and conducting business. If a sales tax applies to all sales transactions through which commodities pass, as does the turnover type of tax, incentive is given for firms to integrate both forward into distribution channels and backward to the production of parts and materials in order to minimize the number of taxable transactions. If production of materials, semifinished goods, and finished products and wholesaling and retailing of a product are carried on by separate firms, the tax will apply five times; if one firm carries on all this activity, the tax applies only once. In the countries that have used this type of tax, the complaints against the integrative effects have universally been strong.

If a sales tax is imposed at a level prior to the final sale to the consumer, firms are given incentive to shift production and distribution activity, and thus cost elements subject to tax, forward beyond the point of impact of the tax. Thus the manufacturers' sales tax encourages firms to avoid integration forward; if they undertake wholesaling or retailing activities, the taxable price will be higher. Retailers are encouraged to integrate backward, particularly through the use of private brands. Since the producer provides only the basic manufacturing activity, the taxable price is relatively low compared to those of manufacturers undertaking extensive advertising and distributing activities. These problems have long plagued the Canadian government in the operation of its manufacturers' sales tax; while adjustments in taxable price have been allowed for integrated manufacturers, complete uniformity has not been attained and the operation of the tax has been complicated. In fields in which costs of packaging are significant (for example, cosmetics), the packaging is likely to be taken over by wholesalers or retailers rather than by the manufacturer.

When the tax is placed on the wholesale level, that is, the purchase by the retailer, the retailer is given strong incentive to integrate backward, undertaking wholesale and even manufacturing functions, so that his purchase price is low compared to the figure paid by non-integrated firms. This tendency led the United Kingdom to apply uplift under the purchase tax, whereby the taxable price was increased on purchases by integrated retailers. Such instances are difficult to isolate and the degree of integration varies widely.

If a sales tax were imposed at the final retail level on all consumption purchases—goods and services—shift in methods of operation would be minimized. No sales taxes, however, are so inclusive. For example, most services are not included when rendered separately, while a single charge covering both sales and services is fully taxable. Thus firms are given incentive to exclude service elements such as installation, delivery, freight, and interest from the price wherever possible, even though efficiency may call for their inclusion. Since real-property-contract labor is usually not taxable, incentive is given with certain types of work, such as steel fabrication and installation of heating and air conditioning systems, to maximize the amount of fabrication performed on the site and minimize prefabrication, although the latter may be more efficient. Charges for printing are often not taxable. If a person buys printed materials, he pays tax on the entire cost; if he buys materials and has them printed on a custom basis, only the purchase price of the unprinted materials is usually taxable.

An excise on one particular form of transportation, with other types free of tax, will alter the choice of transport methods. This was true of the federal excise tax on freight, which applied to freight charges by public carriers but not to the cost of carrying freight in trucks owned by the shipper.

Locational Effects. Another source of loss of efficiency is the effect on location of geographical rate differentials, which are substantial between and within states. For example, the property tax burden in Oregon, relative to value of property, is nearly twice that in Washington.[9] Within states, rates are often substantially higher within metropolitan areas than in smaller towns or rural areas, and they are typically, but not always, higher in the central city than in the suburbs. While property taxes may have little effect on the choice of the general geographic area by manufacturers or wholesale distributors, they may have significant influence on the decision about the exact site within a metropolitan area, unless offset by other elements, such as differences in governmental services or nontax factors.

Differences in property tax coverage and assessment policy may also influence location. Failure by some jurisdictions to tax personal property such as inventory of materials and finished products is significant for some types of business. Netzer and others have concluded that the tax on personal property of businesses is more significant for location decisions than that on real property.[10] Assessments for property taxes relative to sale value are highly uneven. Thus an extraneous element is introduced into the competitive picture; success of a firm depends not only upon efficiency of operation, but also upon its treatment by the tax assessor or, in some instances, on its willingness to bribe the assessor.

Timing Influences. A tax may alter the conduct of activity timewise and thus affect efficiency in the utilization of resources. One example is the anticipatory effect of changes in sales or excise tax rates, which may cause temporal changes in purchasing patterns, particularly if the tax rate is high. If consumers believe that an excise tax will be removed or reduced, they will curtail buying, to the detriment of efficiency in production and distribution channels. Expectation of an increase will encourage persons to buy sooner than otherwise. Tax anticipation has been a major problem with the high-rate British purchase tax and has been the subject of attention when revision of excise taxes has been contemplated in the United States.

A property tax on timberland may cause the timber company to

---

[9]See Netzer, *op. cit.*, chap. v.
[10]*Ibid.*, p. 163.

log the land completely and abandon it, instead of logging selectively and keeping the land permanently productive. As a consequence of this phenomenon, lumber-producing states have found modification of the application of the property tax to timberland essential, the annual tax being related to yield instead of to current sale value.

Incentives to Maximize Efficiency. A final question is the potential effect of a tax upon the extent to which a firm strives to attain maximum efficiency. A tax based on net income results in the sharing by the government of higher costs due to failure to attain full efficiency. If the firm is earning more than the rate of profit it regards as satisfactory, the tax may reduce its concern about eliminating inefficiency, since a portion of the "loss" is borne by the government. If, however, before the tax it is making only a rate of profit regarded as satisfactory, the tax will cause it to seek to lessen inefficiency in an effort to restore pretax profits to the satisfactory figure. A tax on net profit encourages firms to increase expenditures on activities with uncertain benefits to the firm, such as advertising—provided that the overall profit is satisfactory—because the government bears a portion of the costs. A very high-rate excess profits tax will almost certainly lessen pressure toward efficiency and increase advertising and other marginal expenditures, since the firm gains so little—10 percent in World War II—from reductions in efficiency or curtailment of outlays. Taxes have similar effects on business "luxury" spending—the type that yields primary benefits to top management—luxurious offices, cars for executives, and so on, since the tax reduces the cost to the firm of these amenities.

On the other hand, taxes that are not directly related to profits may provide strong encouragement to seek to gain greater efficiency. A lump sum tax or a tax based on an estimate of what profits should be will encourage the firm to seek greater efficiency, since the earnings of the firm do not increase tax liability, whereas the tax reduces the current net profit figure. A tax on land based upon its value or income in the most productive use may force the landowner to make more effective use of it, rather than holding it idle in hope of an increase in value or using it for submarginal purposes such as cattle grazing.

Other Effects on Behavior and Conduct of Economic Activity. Taxation may affect economic behavior in other ways as well. For example, income taxation of the usual type leads households to seek to convert real income from taxable to nontaxable form, under the assumption that they seek to minimize taxes. The most significant effect is the incentive given to purchase homes rather than rent, given the structure of the income tax in the United States and most countries.

The income value of the home is not included in income, whereas the return from an equivalent sum placed in money-income-yielding investments by a person preferring to rent is taxable. In the United States the distortion is compounded because property taxes and interest on money borrowed to buy homes is deductible, whereas the tenant is allowed no similar deduction of an element of the rent which he pays.

Similarly, persons are given incentive to produce goods and services instead of gaining additional money income and buying the goods; home-grown fruit and other produce and home repair are examples. While the value of some items, such as produce, theoretically might be included in income, practical difficulties are serious, and the value of repair and other services could not possibly be included. Likewise, wives are given incentive to do their own housework instead of seeking employment and hiring their housework done, since the value of the former is not taxable and could not feasibly be made so.

Households also prefer employers to increase noncash fringe benefit forms of compensation in lieu of cash income: health insurance, medical care, free parking, use of company cars, recreation facilities.

Relative treatment of the income of husband and wife under income taxes may affect marriage patterns. The income splitting in the United States, which sharply reduces the tax liability of a couple compared to a single person with the same income, may be regarded as a stimulus for marriage. On the other hand, with the reverse policy of requiring husband and wife to combine their incomes at the same tax rates applied to single persons, marriage increases the tax liability for a couple making comparable incomes and may encourage persons to live together without benefit of a marriage license. Exact neutrality of treatment is difficult in this field.

MAGNITUDES AND EVALUATION OF ALLOCATIONAL AND EFFICIENCY EFFECTS

Evaluation of the effects of government upon resource allocation and efficiency depends in part on the magnitude of the effects. These cannot be determined by analysis, but only by empirical studies, and few have been made. Attempts to measure the magnitude of cost to the economy of distortions caused by the favorable treatment of owner-occupied homes under the federal income tax structure indicate an annual figure of cost from $.5 billion to $1.0 billion.[11] This estimate did not

[11]See A. Harberger, "Taxation Resource Allocation and Welfare," in *The Role of Direct and Indirect Taxes in the Federal Revenue System* (Princeton, N.J.: Princeton University Press, 1964), p. 62.

consider the adverse effects of the property tax on home ownership. The reallocation in the direction of additional housing may be justified on the grounds of general social policy—that good housing offers significant external benefits to society. The distortion arising out of depletion allowances, estimated to be of comparable magnitude, may be regarded as much less justifiable.

Locational effects of governmental activities have been the subject of a number of empirical studies. Many of these have sought to ascertain the effects of state tax structures upon the industrial development of the state. Some have correlated rates of growth with tax structures and levels, but have found no significant correlation. Several have used the interview approach to ascertain factors influencing industry location, while others have examined tax differentials in various states compared to other cost differentials and the importance of taxation in overall business costs. The principal conclusion has been that taxation is not a major factor influencing location, although it may be the determining influence in some instances, especially in the selection of a specific site within a metropolitan area. Tax structures also play a role in development of the "general business climate" of the state as viewed by business groups, which has some influence on location decision making.[12]

Several studies have been made of the influence of sales taxes upon loss of business to other states. An analysis by H. G. McAllister, based on expenditure patterns and interviews, indicated that border communities in Washington lost substantial sales to merchants in Oregon and Idaho, neither of which had a sales tax.[13] A quantitative study by William Hamovitch showed that New York City, surrounded at the time by nonsales tax areas, lost substantial sales volume (about 6 percent) to the neighboring states, whereas increases in the Alabama tax had no noticeable effect on sales in the state; few shoppers had access to tax-free shopping area.[14] A study of Kentucky's unique tax on production of distilled spirits indicated that the tax had caused substantial relocation outside of Kentucky of production of distilled spirits

[12]Summarized in J. F. Due, "Studies of State-Local Tax Influences on Location of Industry," *National Tax Journal,* Vol. XIV (June, 1961), pp. 163–73. An article by R. K. Struyk, "An Analysis of Tax Structures, Public Service Levels, and Regional Economic Growth", *Journal of Regional Science,* Vol. VII (Winter 1967), pp. 175–87, shows some inverse correlation between tax levels and rates of growth for cities of certain population levels.

[13]H. G. McAllister, "The Border Tax Problem in Washington," *National Tax Journal,* Vol. XIV (December, 1961), pp. 362–74.

[14]William Hamovitch, "Sales Taxation: An Analysis of the Effects of Rate Increases in Two Contrasting Cases," *National Tax Journal,* Vol. XIX (December, 1966), pp. 411–20.

other than whiskey. Production of whiskey remained in the state because of the importance of the Kentucky location for prestige of the product.[15] Kentucky later repealed the tax.

In recent decades a number of state and local governments, particularly in the South, have sought deliberately to lure industry by various forms of inducements, including tax concessions, making of loans or guarantee of loans, often at low interest rates, and leasing buildings financed by tax-free bonds at low cost to industrial users. Studies of the effectiveness of these programs suggest that they have not been great, the financial inducements being a secondary location factor even within a region. In some instances, however, location is undoubtedly affected, particularly in the selection of a site within a particular region. The only possible justification for such programs from a national point of view is the better adaptation of industry location to surplus labor that may result, although there are other better means of meeting this problem. For the most part the concessions become competitive, primarily benefiting the firms that get them with little gain to anyone else.[16]

Evaluation

In a perfect world, in which optimal allocation of resources and optimal efficiency in the use of resources were attained, thus providing maximum economic welfare—given the pattern of income distribution—any change in resource allocation or in factor combinations or methods of organization of product would be undesirable. The world is, unfortunately, not perfect. Some of the changes, such as those arising from governmental production of public goods, are deliberately designed to bring closer attainment of the goals of society. Taxes that discourage the use of a commodity with important external costs (liquor) are justified because of this effect. Measures that stimulate business firms to seek greater efficiency in production are regarded as desirable. Furthermore, since we know that the world is not perfect, no expenditure or tax measure can be conclusively condemned because it alters behavior. Thus, for example, an excise that increases the price of one commodity and decreases its use may merely be redressing an imbalance caused by greater deviation of price from marginal cost in some industries than in others due to differences in competitive condi-

---

[15]Charles Gamson and Don M. Soule, "Economic Effects of Kentucky's Distilled Spirits Production Tax," *National Tax Journal*, Vol. XX (March, 1967), pp. 20–28.

[16]See Ben Bridges, Jr., "State and Local Inducements to Industry," *National Tax Journal*, Vol. XVIII (March and June, 1965), pp. 1–14; 175–92.

tions. Or, effects regarded as objectionable from an allocational point of view may be desirable in terms of distributional considerations when the existing pattern of income distribution is not regarded as acceptable. A tax on luxuries, while distorting consumption choices may be preferred on distributional grounds to a universal sales tax that has no allocational effects but concentrates its burden more heavily on the poor. As shown by the Theory of the Second Best, with some imperfections in the economy, alteration of behavior that is undesirable in a perfect society may bring the economy closer to an optimal position.

Even in an imperfect world, however, there is an a priori or presumptive case against tax- or expenditure-induced changes in allocation and resource use. There is no assurance whatever that the changes will be in the desired direction. By usual opinion, the private sector does a tolerable job of resource allocation and attainment of efficiency, even though it does not do a perfect job. Accordingly, any change from that produced by the private sector may be reasonably assumed to be disadvantageous in the eyes of society, except when there is evidence to the contrary. Firms clearly do not always attain maximum efficiency, but the profit motive and competition encourage them toward it; there is, therefore, an a priori argument against a tax measure that leads to a change—except in the specific cases where the opposite is demonstrated. In other words, granted the imperfectness of the operation of the private sector, the case against distortion is not a conclusive one, but it is a reasonable a priori one.

REFERENCES

DOWNS, ANTHONY. *Inside Bureaucracy*. Boston: Little, Brown, 1967.

FISHER, J. E. "Efficiency in Business and Government," *Quarterly Review of Economics and Business,* Vol. II (August, 1962), pp. 35–47.

JOINT ECONOMIC COMMITTEE, U.S. CONGRESS. *Economy in Government.* Washington, D.C.: U.S. Government Printing Office, 1967.

TULLOCK, GORDON. *The Politics of Bureaucracy.* Washington, D.C.: Public Affairs Press, 1965.

Chapter : EFFECTS UPON
7 : FACTOR SUPPLIES

Governmental expenditure and revenue systems may alter the supplies of various types of factors. In so doing, they affect the total level of output at full employment and the potential rate of economic growth; the ability to attain full employment and the potential growth rate; the allocation of resources to the production of various goods through changing relative factor and commodity prices; and the pattern of distribution of real income among various families in society. They will have no effect only if the supplies of various types of factors are absolutely fixed and perfectly inelastic; otherwise, both governmental expenditures and taxes will affect the quantities offered by their owners by altering the gains from supplying factor units. They may also affect the potential number of units available. Analysis cannot provide answers about actual effects of present systems, but it can suggest likely directions of change; only empirical studies can give definitive answers. Few of these have been made and the results are not by any means conclusive.

As suggested above, the effects upon the potential factor supplies must be distinguished from those upon the amounts made available to prospective users at various prices. Thus expenditures and taxes may affect the numbers of skilled workers available in a society at a particular time; they may also affect the willingness of skilled workers to make their labor services available and the numbers of hours they are willing to work. Effects on three major factor groups—labor, risk-taking, and land—will be reviewed. Effects upon the total amount of savings in the economy will be analyzed in Chapter 9.

LABOR

Given the population, age distribution, and available skills, at any one time a certain quantity of labor is potentially available to the economy. The initial question to be considered is the effect of taxes and governmental expenditure programs upon the willingness of persons to supply these potential labor hours for use in production. The question of possible effects upon potential supply will be considered later in the chapter.

The Basic Model

Workers presumably seek to adjust the number of hours that they work in light of their relative preferences for income and leisure, given the wage rate, which measures the gain in income from substitution of work for leisure. On Figure 7–1, curve AA indicates a worker's preference schedule; he is indifferent among the various combinations of income and leisure shown on the curve. The curve flattens out toward each end. Beyond a certain point additional leisure cannot be substituted for work (one does not enjoy leisure as one starves to death) and satisfaction maintained. At the other extreme, additional work

FIGURE 7–1

INCOME-LEISURE EQUILIBRIUM

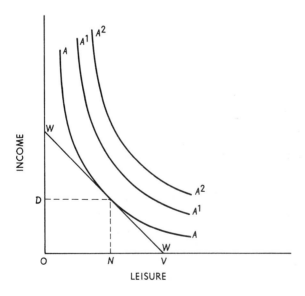

will not be substituted for leisure, since one must have time to eat and sleep. The former rule is not relevant for a person with nonlabor sources of support. The work-leisure preference curves appear to vary among individuals; to some, additional income beyond a certain level has little attraction; to others the marginal rate of substitution between income and leisure falls very slowly. Successive AA curves show work-leisure combinations with higher levels of satisfaction.

Line *WW* indicates the wage rate, the gain from substitution of additional units of work for units of leisure. With the wage rate independent of the amount worked, *WW* is a straight line. The point of tangency of *WW* with a work-leisure preference curve is the goal the worker pursues, under the assumption that he is seeking to maximize satisfaction. On Figure 7–1, income is *OD,* leisure *ON,* work *NV.* Institutional considerations may prevent a worker from attaining the optimum by denying him control over the hours worked. A worker on an automobile assembly line that functions seven hours a day has little control, for example. But we assume that he seeks to attain this point as closely as possible.

FIGURE 7–2A

REACTION TO A WAGE INCREASE,
INCOME EFFECT DOMINANT

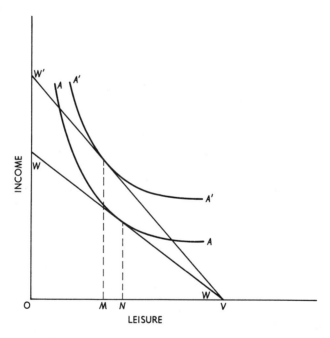

The net effect of a change in the wage rate—the income gain from sacrificing leisure for work—depends upon the relative strength of two considerations. If wages rise, the *substitution* effect encourages the person to substitute additional work for leisure, since the relative gain from doing so is higher, as indicated by the shifting of the tangency of the wage line with the work-leisure line *(AA)* in the direction of more work. On the other hand, the *income* effect of the wage increase, which places the person upon a higher AA curve in the sense of a higher level of satisfaction, encourages him to enjoy more leisure, since he can gain a given income with fewer hours of work. Leisure is in a sense a good which a person buys by working less; unless it is an inferior good, a person will seek to buy more as his income rises.

FIGURE 7–2B

REACTION TO A WAGE INCREASE,
INCOME EFFECT DOMINANT

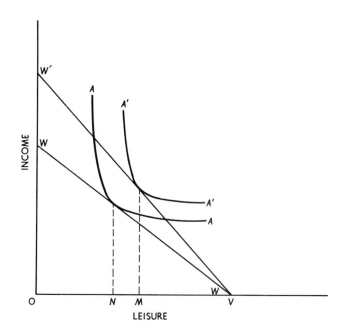

The net effect is determined by the curvature of the AA line. If the person has relatively high preference for additional income and relatively little dislike of sacrificing leisure, extensive substitution will occur and outweigh the income effect. On Figure 7–2A as the wage rises to W', leisure falls from ON to OM, and thus the hours worked rise, from VN to VM. If he is more concerned with maintaining a given level of income than gaining additional income, the income effect of the wage increase will outweigh the substitution effect and the person will work less as the wage rate rises, as shown in Figure 7–2B. On the diagram, the income effect is shown by the shifting of the WW curve to a higher level and thus can be isolated by a line drawn parallel to WW and tangent to $A'A'$; the substitution effect is shown by the change in slope of the *WW* curve. The same influences apply to the number of hours a person is willing to work and the willingness of a person to work at all. As the wage level rises some persons—those with supplementary income earners in the family—may drop out of the labor market entirely as the income of the main wage earner becomes adequate to maintain the desired living standard. Those for whom additional income has relatively great utility but who depend upon others when wages are low will be lured into the labor market if the wage is sufficiently high.

Governmental Expenditures and Total Labor Supply

The effects upon labor supply of governmental activities and the expenditures for them depend upon the nature of the services and expenditures and their relation to the recipients' income:

1. Transfer payments positively correlated with income. Transfer payments bearing a direct positive relation to income produce conflicting income and substitution effects, in the same fashion as a wage increase. By making work more rewarding the payment encourages the substitution of work for leisure, while the income effect encourages the person to work less. The net effect depends upon the nature of the work-leisure relationship, as explained in greater detail in the discussion of effects of income taxation.

2. Transfer payments declining as income rises, typical of certain relief programs and part of the social security system, and of negative income tax proposals. These are more likely to reduce the quantity of labor.[1] If an additional dollar of income costs the person a dollar in transfer payments, the program will certainly reduce the quantity of labor available, since the marginal gain from additional work is nil. This rule will not be valid if persons prefer earned income to relief, as many undoubtedly do. Negative income tax proposals usually provide for only partial (perhaps 50 percent) loss of benefit as earned income rises to minimize this effect. Even more serious effects result if a person loses all benefit when his income exceeds a certain figure with full benefits up to that figure.

3. Transfer payments not related to current income, such as lump sum veterans' bonuses and family allowances. These produce a negative income effect and no substitution effect and thus reduce the labor supply currently available.

4. Governmental services financed by taxation. Governmental

---

[1]The *WW* curve becomes more nearly horizontal.

services have a variety of possible effects. As a general principle, the provision of governmental services increases the real incomes of the recipients and thus can be expected, through the income effect, to decrease total labor supply, provided the recipients regard the services as making them "better off." The services most likely to do so are those conveying important individual benefits, such as education and recreational facilities that are direct substitutes for privately produced alternatives. For example, the provision of public education free of charge lessens the necessity for earning additional income to finance education of one's children at private schools. The negative effect will be particularly strong if the goods are complementary to leisure: recreational facilities, or highways to reach them. If the services are complementary to work—free commuter transportation, for example— the effect is not so obvious since both real income and marginal gains from work are increased.

As noted later, these services may increase total labor supply over a period of time although reducing it at a particular time.

Taxation and Total Labor Supply

The basic reaction to taxation is the reverse of that to governmental expenditures: taxes reduce disposable real income and as a consequence, apart from exceptions noted below, have effects comparable to those of a money wage reduction. The effect on total labor supply, therefore, depends upon the relative influence of the income and substitution effects. The net influence is likely to be different if the tax is related to income than if it is not.

Proportional Income Tax. A proportional income tax without exemptions is identical to a proportional reduction in money wages, giving rise to both substitution and income effects. If, therefore, the income effect is dominant, the total supply of labor will rise, as shown in Figure 7–2B. As the after-tax wage falls from W' to W, leisure falls from OM to ON. Families seek to maintain their old income levels—by lessening absenteeism, seeking additional overtime and moonlighting, and sending wives and children to work. Persons living on nonlabor income will enter the labor market to supplement their incomes. These are the groups that regard the maintenance of a given income level as paramount and have a low substitutability of leisure for income when the marginal gains from income are reduced. Persons at a bare minimum income level, those barely attaining the income they regard as imperative, and persons subject to heavy fixed commitments are the ones most likely to react in this fashion.

The tax will reduce the labor hours supplied when the substitution effect outweighs the income effect, as illustrated on Figure 7–2A. Leisure rises from *OM* to *ON*. These persons have a high elasticity of substitution between work and leisure at the margin. After the tax increase they will not find it worthwhile to work as many hours as before, preferring additional leisure now that it is less costly, and their wives and children will quit working. They either have no concern about a minimum income level or are currently well above this level. The strength of the substitution effect is increased if additional work requires expenses that are not tax deductible: expenses of housework if the wife works, for example, or of driving to and from a moonlighting job.

Several other considerations influence the net result:

1. Limited Individual Control over Work. The individual frequently lacks significant discretionary control over time worked. In many lines of economic activity, he must work the standard work period if he is to hold the job and has little opportunity for overtime. Some flexibility is introduced through availability of part-time work and varying absenteeism, but for many persons the discretion is not substantial.

2. The Importance of Nonpecuniary Motives. Persons are influenced not only by money income and leisure but also by such goals as satisfaction arising from accomplishing the task, power and prestige, and diversity in life and freedom from boredom that work may provide. Many wives who work do so to escape the monotony of housework and women's clubs, not because they are greatly concerned about the money. The importance of these goals lessens the significance of the tax upon labor supply.

3. "Spite" and "Purchase" Effects of Taxes. Persons may react differently to taxes than to wage changes. They may so dislike the notion of being taxed that they react strongly out of spite, perhaps significantly reducing their work and incomes. General attitudes toward the government and the use of tax revenues are significant for spite effects, as is awareness and direct payment of the tax. Withholding, for example, resembles pay reduction much more than does direct payment of tax, but it is a current continuing occurrence rather than an annual event.

On the other hand, persons may regard a tax as the price they are paying for governmental services rather than as a wage reduction. While this reaction is likely to be more common with benefit-related levies such as the motor fuel tax than it is with the income tax, taxpayers are less inclined to reduce labor in response to income taxation if they are thoroughly indoctrinated with the importance of the governmental expenditures, as, for example, during a war.

Progression. From the standpoint of a particular individual paying a given sum of taxes, a tax with a relatively high marginal rate and low basic rate is more likely to lead to a reduction in labor hours supplied than a tax with a proportional rate, as illustrated on Figure 7–3. The line showing net income after tax with a progressive rate,

FIGURE 7–3

REACTION TO A PROGRESSIVE INCOME TAX

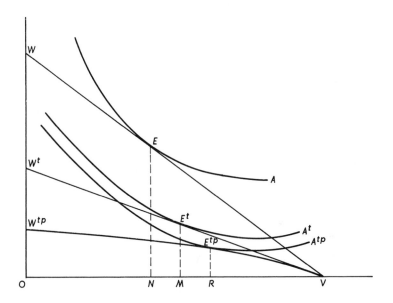

W^{tp}, is less steep than W^t (proportional rate) because the tax rate rises as the income rises, and the point of tangency with the work-leisure curve is farther to the right (OR instead of OM). Thus the person works less than with a proportional tax (but not necessarily less than with no tax at all). A high marginal rate increases the significance of the substitution effect, since the net loss from gaining additional leisure is reduced. A 100 percent marginal rate would lead to complete replacement of work by leisure once the person reached this level, apart from the influence of nonpecuniary motives. Why work, if the government takes all the additional gain?

What is true for individuals subjected to progressive rates, however, is not necessarily valid for labor supply as a whole, when alternate income tax structures are considered. Persons in the lower income brackets will be subject to lower average and marginal rates and those in middle brackets to lower average rates but higher marginal rates than they would be with a proportional rate income tax yielding the same revenue. Thus their reaction will be different and not necessarily in the direction of less work. The overall influence depends upon the relative reactions of the different income groups to changes in average and marginal rates.

Taxes not Directly Related to Income. As a general rule, when taxes are not directly related to income, the importance of the substitution effect is reduced, since additional earnings do not necessarily increase tax liability, while the income effect remains significant. These taxes, therefore, are more likely to result in greater total labor supply than that available with an income tax, particularly of a highly progressive nature.

1. Lump Sum Taxes. A poll tax has only an income effect, with no impact on the substitution of work for leisure, and the persons are therefore given incentive to increase their incomes. Poll taxes were introduced in colonial areas for the deliberate purpose of inducing persons to enter the labor market. Taxes based upon potential income rather than actual income may have even stronger effects, unless they are so heavy that they cause the person to cease attempting to earn an income at all.

2. Consumption-Based Taxes. The difference in effects of taxes on consumption from those on income is controlled by the nature of the preference schedules for taxable consumption and nontaxable uses of income, particularly savings, as well as expectations about ultimate disposition of the amounts saved. If income is desired solely for purposes of consumption—as may well be true of the typical family in developing economies and many persons in other countries—a tax proportionately related to consumption will produce the same effect as one related to income, except for possible influence of the money illusion noted below. Income and consumption are identical if persons do not consider savings as an alternative. If the elasticity of substitution between savings or other nontaxable uses of income and expenditures for taxable purposes is significant, the direct relationship between income and consumption is lost, and the consumption-related taxes will have weaker substitution effects. One must also keep in mind, however, the influence that a high degree of elasticity of substitution has upon the tax rate necessary to reduce private-sector spending by a given amount. If substitution of savings for consumption is extensive, less

tax revenues are required to prevent inflation. The more limited the scope of a consumption tax, the weaker is the effect upon work effort, because of the greater possibility of substitution of nontaxable for taxable uses of income.

Reaction to a consumption-related tax is also influenced by expectations about future use of savings and permanency of the tax. If savings are made this year to buy taxable goods in the next few years while the tax is expected to be in operation, tax liability is merely deferred. If, however, the taxpayer does not contemplate spending the amounts on taxable goods or believes that the tax will be temporary, the effect on work effort will be reduced.

The reactions of the taxpayer to consumption levies may be different from those to income taxes reducing real income by the same amount because of differences in the manner of collection and the money illusion. The typical consumption tax is collected from the vendor and paid by the customer at the time of purchase, often in small amounts. The spite effect may be less, per dollar of revenue, than it is with the income tax, particularly if the tax is hidden in the price of the product. The reverse may be true, however.

Whether separately stated or not, consumption taxes strike the taxpayer in the form of higher consumer goods prices rather than lower money wages. Accordingly, he is likely to react much less than he would to an income tax reducing his real income by the same amount because of the money illusion: the greater emphasis placed upon changes in money wages relative to that on changes in the cost of living. One evidence of the money illusion is the much greater tendency for workers to strike in response to a cut in money wages than to a rise in the cost of living that reduces real income by the same amount.

Another major source of difference in practice between the effects of income and consumption taxes is the typically greater progression of the former. Accordingly, the quantity of labor available is likely to be somewhat greater with a sales tax than with an income tax. But this result is not a product of differences in the inherent character of the two forms of tax.

3. Taxation of Wealth. If additional income earned is to be used for purposes other than purchase of goods that will be subject to a wealth tax, such a levy will have only an income effect and will tend to increase labor supply. Family income is reduced but marginal use of income is not affected. If the additional income is to be saved and placed in goods subject to wealth tax, however, the substitution effect

is relevant and the net relative effect of wealth and income taxes is not predictable. Negative effect on labor supply will be less likely if the taxable durable goods to be acquired are supplementary to leisure—homes, power boats, summer cottages.

The Longer Period Supply of Workers

Some governmental activities affect the total number of workers in the economy, either directly or over a period of time. Compulsory education systems reduce total labor supply by taking teen-agers out of the labor market, and a social security system that supplies substantial pensions provided the person retires from work reduces the number of older persons in the labor market. On the other hand, public health and welfare programs reduce infant mortality and chronic illness and lengthen the life span, and thus increase the number of workers in the economy. Rehabilitation of the disabled has the same effect, and education increases the number of workers with skills useful in modern society. Even the birth rate may be affected by governmental activities; welfare programs may lead families to feel that they can afford to have larger families, and family allowances (grants of specified amounts per child) lessen the costs of having more children; on the other hand, provision of free contraceptives would lower the birth rate.

The tax system may also affect the number of potential workers. While decisions to marry and decisions about family size are influenced primarily by motives not affected by taxes, the tax structure may have some influence on such decisions. The relative tax treatment of married and single persons may affect the decision to marry, and high exemptions for dependents may encourage persons to have larger families. Heavy income or sales taxes on the lower middle income groups may lead families to curtail family size to maintain a given level of living.

Supply of Particular Types of Labor

Governmental activities have greater potential effects upon the relative supplies of various types of labor than upon the total supply; the elasticity of supply of each type is greater than that of the total, since workers can shift from one occupation to another.

Expenditure programs influence the availability of various types of labor. Education increases the supply of workers in occupations requiring high levels of education and reduces the supply of unskilled workers. By the adjustment of the nature of education provided, a government can influence trends in the supply of particular types of labor, an effect of crucial importance in a developing economy. Relative emphasis upon trade schools as compared to college preparatory education, for example, is highly significant for the relative supplies of craftsmen and professional personnel.

Taxes can be expected, in a general way, to have the opposite effect, since they reduce the monetary differential between highly trained and unskilled workers and lessen the incentive to gain the skill and training necessary for the former. The income effect is still relevant as well as the substitution effect, but the latter is more significant for the overall supply of labor because of the greater tendency to shift among occupations than into and out of the labor force. Nonpecuniary motives, however, play an important role in occupational decision making. To many persons the primary attractions of higher paid occupations are prestige, more favorable working conditions, greater stability of income, and other advantages that are not affected by a tax.

Closely related is the possible effect of the tax in causing persons to refuse to accept more responsible positions for which they have the qualifications because the tax will reduce the net monetary gain. The greatest effect is likely to be found at high salary levels with a progressive tax. Again, other considerations play a major role in these decisions. Prestige and power are significant motives, and social and traditional business pressures and mores strongly influence behavior. A vice president offered the presidency of a company does not usually refuse it merely because taxes reduce the net gain. There are undoubtedly exceptions, especially if living expenses will increase materially as a result of the change. But given the importance most persons attach to the nonpecuniary advantages, they are likely to be rare.

These effects are most significant with income taxes, and particularly progressive income taxes. They will not be entirely absent, however, with consumption-related taxes if elasticity of substitution of consumption and savings is low.

Additional influences on relative labor supplies are produced by differentials in the tax treatment of various forms of income under income tax laws. Tax structures frequently penalize irregular incomes and reduce the relative supplies of labor available for these occupations. Any occupation with a relatively high nonmonetary gain becomes more attractive relative to those with strictly monetary rewards. The most significant example is housework. If the wife works and hires the housework done, she must pay tax on her income and cannot deduct the housework expenses; if she does the housework herself, the gain from it is not, and could not feasibly be made taxable. University teaching, with its flexible schedules, long vacation periods, and other nonmonetary rewards, is made relatively more attractive compared to other occupations. Finally, the flow of labor will be increased into those occupations in which enforcement of tax is more difficult— those not subject to income tax withholding or effective audit.

Empirical Studies

Economic analysis outlines possible reactions and avenues for empirical study, but can provide no answers about the actual direction or magnitude of effects of present taxes upon factor supplies. Several empirical studies of rather limited scope have been made in recent years. The only approach thus far found feasible utilizes interviews to ascertain the significance of taxes for work-leisure, choice of occupation, and related decisions.

1. On the whole, the studies show very low sensitivity of quantity of labor available to changes in wage rates, whether due to taxes or other forces. Thus without exception they conclude that present taxes are not having significant effects upon the overall supply of labor or the supply of executive and professional man-hours available to society.

a) The most recent and significant survey of the effects on the higher income groups is a study made for Brookings Institution by R. Barlow *et al.*[2] The conclusions are based upon interviews with a selected sample of 957 persons with incomes in the upper levels. Only 12 percent of the sample indicated that taxes had any effect upon their incentives to work, and even these were, from all indications, working hard despite the taxes. The group as a whole averaged a 48-hour workweek, 50 weeks a year. The study concluded: "The implication of these findings is that the loss of annual output due to work disincentives caused by the progressive income tax is of negligible proportions."[3] The small group reporting adverse tax effects were not usually in the highest marginal rate bracket, but in those from 50 to 59 percent; this range may be the peak of the spite effect.

b) An extensive survey of wage earners in 1962, with interviews with 2,997 families, showed a negative relationship between the wage

---

[2]R. Barlow, H. E. Brazer, and J. N. Morgan, *Economic Behavior of the Affluent* (Washington, D.C.: Brookings Institution, 1966).

[3]*Ibid.*, p. 3.

rate and hours worked; an income or consumption tax would, therefore, increase the number of labor hours available.[4]

c) An earlier study by Sanders of executive behavior, with interviews of 160 executives, concluded that there was no significant influence of the tax upon the supply of executive talent, although behavior was affected in some respects.[5] A few executives reported that the taxes caused them to work harder; a few, to work less hard.

d) Break's study of 306 solicitors and accountants in Great Britain in 1956—a group having more control over hours worked than many—showed that over half reported no tax influence whatever; of the remainder some reported working more, some working less. Break concluded that he could not ascertain the magnitude of influence or even net direction of change, but indications were strong that the overall effects were not great.[6]

e) A Social Survey study for the Royal Commission on the Taxation of Profits and Income in Great Britain, concentrating on workers who had some discretion over their hours of work, showed no evidence of significant influence of the tax, some persons reporting positive effects, some negative.[7]

2. Very limited evidence has been found of refusal of executives to transfer to other jobs when the shift involved considerable expense and little gain in net remuneration.[8] The general conclusion is that the consequences for job transfers are not significant, although occurring in isolated cases.

3. While Sanders found some evidence that the tax caused workers to postpone retirement, similar effects were not encountered in the Brookings study.

4. One of the few positive results found in any study is that the income tax apparently causes physicians to take longer vacations in conjunction with attendance at medical conventions.[9]

These empirical studies, while of limited scope, suggest that present income taxes in the United States are not having significant effects

---

[4]J. N. Morgan, M. H. David, W. J. Cohen, and H. E. Brazer, *Income and Wealth in the United States* (New York: McGraw-Hill, 1962), pp. 76-77.

[5]T. H. Sanders, *Effects of Taxation on Executives* (Boston: Graduate School of Business Administration, Harvard University, 1951).

[6]George Break, "Income Taxes, Wage Rates and the Incentive to Supply Labor Services," *National Tax Journal,* Vol. VI (December, 1953), pp. 333-52.

[7]*Second Report,* CMD 9105 (London: 1954), Appendix I, pp. 91-124.

[8]Sanders, *op. cit.*.

[9]R. Davidson, "Income Taxes and Incentive," *National Tax Journal,* Vol. VI (September, 1953) pp. 293-97.

on labor supply. No empirical studies have been attempted of the effects of other taxes on labor supply. The results of interview surveys are always subject to the limitations that persons may not be fully aware of the effects taxes actually have on their behavior or they may give answers that they feel place them in a favorable light or that may influence subsequent tax legislation.

RISK-TAKING

Analysis of the effects of taxation and government expenditures upon the willingness to undertake risk, in the sense of supplying money capital for and in real investment, is much more complex than that of the effects upon labor supply, and the conclusions are even less positive. The analysis is based upon the assumption of a given volume of savings and level of employment; the effects upon the propensity to save and the ability to maintain full employment will be considered in Chapter 9. We are therefore concerned with the effects of governmental expenditures and alternate tax measures upon the willingness of persons with liquid wealth to take the risk of supplying money capital for use in production and the willingness of business firms to undertake real investment with funds available. The former may be designated as financial investment, the latter as entrepreneurial or real investment. These effects have significant implications for the maintenance of full employment and for the level of output and the rate of growth at full employment. If for example a tax reduces the willingness of persons to take risks of financial and entrepreneurial investment, the rate of increase in real output will be reduced.

Taxation Effects—The Basic Model

A holder of personal wealth has a number of alternative ways of investing it, ranging from cash on the one hand through highly liquid safe loans and relatively secure equity investments to extremely speculative investments at the other extreme. He may have choice only among various financial investments, or he may combine financial and real investment by expanding his own business. Or he may use funds of other persons to make real investments. These alternatives provide a spectrum of combinations of risk and yield, as shown by the *RY* curve on Figure 7–4. With the assumption that prices are not expected to change, holding of cash provides zero risk and zero yield. With successive alternatives, investors expect higher yield and a higher degree of risk, based upon probability estimates. Initially the curve rises slowly, the risk being limited as funds are placed in savings accounts and similar outlets. Ultimately the curve rises rapidly as potential high rate returns are accompanied by very high chance of loss.

Persons have relative preference schedules for yield and risk-avoidance. These schedules presumably vary widely on the basis of their financial resources and their general attitude toward risks of the individual. A typical pattern is shown by curve *PP* on Figure 7–4. This

FIGURE 7–4

YIELD-RISK EQUILIBRIUM

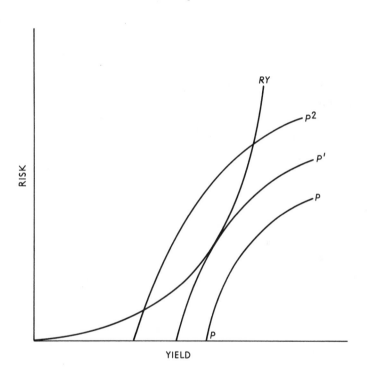

curve shows various combinations of potential yield and risk which are equally satisfactory to the person. Under the assumption of the operation of the Law of Diminishing Marginal Utility relative to income, the curve flattens out to the right; at higher yields, the gain from additional income is progressively less significant relative to the increased risk of loss. A person has a pattern of preference curves (*P, P′, P²*) with different levels of satisfaction.

The investor seeks, we assume, to obtain the optimum yield-risk combination, as indicated by the tangency of a *P* curve *(P′)* with the

RY curve, since this point represents the highest preference curve that he can attain, given the sum he has to invest.

This analysis involves oversimplification. In the first place, the person may have varying expectations about the certainty of attainment of the various probabilities. Some may be much more certain of attainment than others, and the likelihood of the extent of complete versus partial loss may not be uniform. Risk, which is based upon probability considerations—must be distinguished from uncertainty, attributable to nonpredictability. With many types of investments, uncertainty is highly significant and influences the investor's decision making, but generalization about the effects is impossible.

Secondly, expectations of possible price level changes complicate the picture. If inflation is anticipated, holding of cash is not riskless, and the whole pattern of yield-risk relationships is altered. Fixed-dollar securities and cash are replaced as minimum risk investments by ones whose value will rise with the general price level.

In a formal sense the analysis is not altered by these two considerations, but they complicate the analysis and in practice may be significant for investment behavior.

Income Taxation

Let us now introduce a proportional-rate income tax into the picture, initially with the assumption that loss offsets (deduction of losses from other income) are not permitted. The effect of the tax is to reduce the yield without reducing the risk; the risk-yield alternatives curve steepens, as shown on Figure 7–5 *(RYᵗ)*. As with labor, both income and substitution effects are encountered. The reduction in income leads the person to take more risk to restore his income, while the reduction in the marginal gain from substitution of yield for risk encourages him to lessen the total amount of risk. The net effect is not predictable, with this exception: as the tax increases to high levels, the substitution effect is almost certain to become dominant, because the gain from additional risk-taking becomes so small. With a 100 percent tax rate obviously the income effect ceases to have significance, since the yield after tax is zero. If this rate applied to all investment income the person would select his investment solely on a security basis, holding cash if he had no expectation of a price level increase.

If loss offsets—the privilege of deducting the losses from other income—are provided, as they typically are, at least partially, the reactions are altered. No longer does the government share in the gains but not in the losses, but equally in both, with full offset and a proportional tax rate. With a 25 percent income tax rate, for example, the yield is reduced by 25 percent, but so is the potential loss—the amount being risked—since any loss can be deducted against other taxable income. Accordingly, a tax gives rise only to an income effect. Yield and risk are reduced equally and there is no substitution effect, provided that the taxpayer recognizes the significance of loss offset.

FIGURE 7-5

YIELD-RISK RESPONSE TO A PROPORTIONAL INCOME TAX

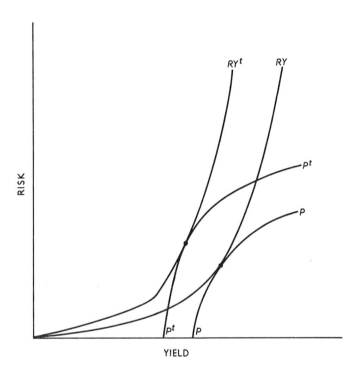

Risk-taking will be greater than it would be with a similar tax with no loss offset, and possibly greater than with no tax at all. For society as a whole, total risk-taking will increase. Total yield to society (private and governmental sectors) and total risk are not altered by the tax. Since individuals will seek to offset some of the risk removed from them by the tax by seeking additional yield and thus undertaking additional risk, there will be an overall net increase.[10] This is the

[10]This rule was first developed by E. D. Domar and R. A. Musgrave, "Proportional Income Taxation and Risk Taking," *Quarterly Journal of Economics*, Vol LVIII (May, 1948), pp. 388–422.

reverse of the usual conclusion that income taxes necessarily reduce risk-taking.

In practice several elements reduce the tendency toward additional risk-taking. First, loss offsets are not necessarily complete. In the United States and elsewhere, business losses are deductible from other income, but income may not be adequate to cover them and the power to carry losses to past or future years may be restricted (three and five, respectively, in the U.S.). If the loss is capital rather than business in nature, as is typical for the individual investor, deductibility is not permitted in many countries and severely restricted in the United States.[11]

Second, many investors are eternal optimists; they give little heed to the possibility of loss and therefore pay little attention to the loss offset possibilities. This attitude may result in greater pretax investment, but it also increases the likelihood that the tax will reduce total risk taking.

Third, certain forms of investment have important nonmonetary advantages that are not reduced by the tax. Diamonds, expensive paintings, and the like are examples. The loss offset does not eliminate the influence of the tax in encouraging persons to shift to this type of investment.

Investment Decisions by Management. Substantial financial investment and an even greater portion of real investment decision making is undertaken by hired management rather than by the owners of the money capital. This is true of financial investment by banks and insurance companies, for example, and of real investment by firms characterized by separation of ownership and management. One major difference is the altered significance of the income effect; success of the investment does not automatically increase the incomes of the decision makers (although indirectly they may be increased), whereas failure of the investment may endanger their positions and thus their incomes. Thus without loss offsets total risk-taking is likely to be less than it would be if all the decisions were made by the owners of the wealth. However, with partial loss offset, the result is not so obvious; the ability to deduct losses is in fact much greater in a larger business than it is for individuals, since the firm is more likely to have adequate income to allow attainment of full offset. If an individual loses more than his total income he cannot deduct the difference; for a large business, no one investment is likely to be great enough to exceed the profits earned from other activities of the business.

---

[11]Deduction is permitted against capital gains and against other income to the extent of $1,000 a year, with unlimited carry-forward.

Furthermore, while the income effect does not operate, a somewhat similar influence arises from the desire of management of many firms to earn a given dollar volume of profits; if the tax reduces the earnings below this figure the firm may take additional risk in an effort to restore it.

Depreciation Rules. The significance of income taxation for willingness to undertake investment is also dependent upon rules relating to depreciation deduction. In general, the more rapid the rate of write-off allowed, the less adverse effects the tax will have upon the willingness to undertake real investment and, indirectly, financial investment. One major reason is the reduced net cost of the investment; the sooner that the capital cost can be recovered via tax deduction, the sooner the firm has the money for reinvestment, or, in different terminology, the present value of the tax savings is greater the earlier the date at which deduction is permitted. Consider the extreme case in which firms may charge off capital immediately in full at the time of purchase. The government is providing an interest-free loan; the interest gain will equal the tax paid over the years, and the firm is in effect completely free of the tax;[12] the government, on the other hand, gains nothing from the tax. Rapid write-off also restores the liquid funds of the firm more quickly and increases the real value of the write-off in periods in which inflation is expected. Finally, the rapid write-off lessens uncertainty; there is less danger that income will fall so much before the investment is fully recovered that full tax deduction is not possible.

As suggested by the extreme example of immediate tax write-off, the more accelerated the depreciation allowance, the lower will be the governmental tax revenues. Quite apart from the direct and immediate interest consideration, in a growing economy the government's tax revenue will be lower, year by year, the more rapid the write-off allowed. Accordingly, if a tax is to raise a given sum of money, the rate must be higher with rapid write-off and part of the reduced impact on risk-taking is lost.

The Significance of Progression. The discussion thus far assumes proportional rates. If rates are progressive, the additional tax on gains from high-risk investments is greater than the tax saving from loss offsets from unsuccessful investments. The size of the person's total investment and the degree of progression determine the difference in amounts between gains and losses. As shown in Figure 7–6, the *RY*

---

[12]This is feasible only if the firm can immediately reinvest the original sum in additional equipment, obtain another tax credit, reinvest it, and so on.

curve steepens more sharply, thus moving the point of tangency with the preference curve to a point of lower risk. The importance of the substitution effect is increased relative to that of the income effect. Theoretically the net effect with full loss offset could still be one of increased risk, but the possibility is much less.

FIGURE 7-6

YIELD-RISK RESPONSE TO A PROGRESSIVE INCOME TAX

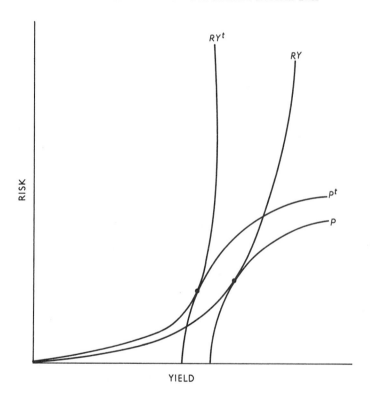

Differential Treatment of Various Kinds of Income. Favorable or unfavorable differential treatment of particular types of income may have net effect upon the overall willingness to undertake risk:

1. Taxation of Corporate Income. Under the usual nonintegrated system of taxing corporate income, as found in the United States and elsewhere, income is taxed directly at the corporate level, and dividends received are fully taxable at the personal level. Under the assumption that the tax is not shifted forward, the combined tax on dividend income is higher than that on other income, while the tax on undistributed profits may be higher or lower than the amount that would

be paid on this income by individual owners of the business. There are several possible effects. First, the application of the tax at the corporate level is likely to result in greater effects on real investment decisions than would application of the tax only to the income of the corporate owners, since there is a direct impact on the yield from such investment, the element of primary concern to management. Second, collection of substantial tax at the corporate level reduces the amount of money capital directly available for investment; corporate management may regard the risk of expansion with retained earnings as much less than that of expansion with money acquired from other sources. On the other hand, the more favorable treatment given undistributed profits relative to the tax applicable to owners in high tax brackets encourages retention of earnings and increases the sum available for direct real investment, compared to that with a completely integrated income tax. Finally, the greater combined burden on dividend income—assuming that the corporate tax does not shift forward—increases the overall adverse effect of the tax upon the willingness to undertake risk.

The picture is complicated by the possibility that forward shifting of the tax from the firm to consumers of the products may restore profits. If real investors believe this to be possible, they will not regard the tax as a source of reduced returns and it will have effects on risk-taking comparable to those of a sales tax.

2. Tax Treatment of Capital Gains. Most countries provide favorable tax treatment for capital gains—realized increases in the value of assets. Many do not tax them at all, while the United States provides a maximum rate of 25 percent (on assets held more than six months). The net effect is to favor this type of income over regular income. The type of property that offers greatest potentiality for capital gains is stock in enterprises undertaking risky types of investments. Accordingly, given the progressive nature of the tax structure, strong encouragement is given to shift in the direction of this type of investment and away from lower yield, lower risk investments.

3. Other Differential Treatment of Certain Types of Income. The very favorable treatment given to investments in oil and mineral production—among the most risky types of investments—in the United States and many countries favors risk-taking. The exemption from tax of interest on state and local bonds has the opposite effect, by channeling the investments of the very wealthy, those most inclined to take risk, into minimum risk forms. Present taxes give added incentive to invest in one's home, and to set up trusts for minor children, a practice that lessens risk-taking.

Consumption-Based Taxes

When a tax is related to consumption, the direct connection between the yield and risk of an investment and the tax is broken. No longer, in the eyes of the investors, is the tax directly linked to the investment. This difference in itself is likely to affect behavior and lessen the overall influence of the tax. While the income effect of the tax is still present because real income from given dollar consumption is reduced, the substitution effect is relevant only to the extent that the person seeks to spend the earnings upon taxable consumption. Thus its significance is dependent upon relative preferences for consumption and savings and elasticity of substitution between them, or, in other words, upon the goals for the earning of income. This form of tax favors the investor who wishes to build up his total wealth quickly from high-yield investments, since he can do so without loss of the gains in current taxation. At the other extreme, the investor who wishes income solely to consume it is subject to the same substitution effect as he is with an income tax having the same distributional pattern, although he may not recognize the relationship so clearly.

For corporate financial investors, the consumption-based tax is likely to have no effect whatever; the income effect in its usual form is not operative, and the substitution effect is not relevant directly. Consumption-based taxes also are likely to have less direct impact on real investment than income taxes. No tax is paid directly by the business firm, which is not a "consumer," and management decisions are less likely to be influenced by a tax on expenditures of the owners of the business than by one on the profits of the enterprise. The major influence upon risk-taking is through the possible adverse effect of consumption-based taxes on sales and thus on yield. Also, the sales tax form of consumption-based tax frequently applies to some capital investment items, increasing the amount of capital being risked by the amount of the sales tax less the immediate write-off permitted of the tax paid.[13] If the yield is not increased accordingly, some disincentive to investment results.

On the whole, the consumption-related taxes would appear to have less effect upon the willingness to undertake risk than the income tax. Much of the difference, however, is a product of the absence of progressivity; as noted, a proportional income tax with loss offset

---

[13]Many firms in fact do not write off the tax element currently, but include it in the capital sum that they depreciate over the life of the equipment.

is not likely to have significant effects upon risk-taking. Furthermore, as explained in Chapter 9, the consumption-related taxes may lessen the assurance of attainment of full employment compared to income taxes of equal yield, and thus in fact investment may be less with the consumption-based tax despite its weaker influence on risk-taking incentives.

Wealth-Based Taxes

If a tax is imposed upon all wealth, including cash, incentive is given to cease holding cash and shift toward higher yield, more risky investments. There is no substitution effect (except indirectly through the subsequent tax upon investments made from the earnings), and the income effect leads the investor to seek to restore the yield. This influence is presumably greatest with cash and investments with negative after-tax yield; the tax will ultimately absorb the entire capital sum. The tax rate on income-yielding investments will be less relative to income than that of the income tax, since the base of the tax is broader.

As wealth taxes operate, however, there are several complications. In the first place, cash may not be taxed, either by law or practice; if so, the effect of the tax in encouraging shift from cash to income-yielding investments is lost and the tax more closely resembles an income tax in its effects. A second complication relates to the approach to valuation for tax purposes of high-yield, high-risk property. If property which does in fact provide a high yield is valued on yield alone for tax purposes without regard to the high element of risk, the tax resembles even more closely a tax on income.

Many property taxes apply only to real property, not directly to either money or securities. From the standpoint of the individual planning his financial investment program, the tax has no direct significance at all, except to render less attractive investments in taxable real property, especially ones that have little or no current yield, such as vacant land purchased for possible increases in value. Only if the person anticipates that the tax on corporate real property will reduce the earnings and sale price of securities of the company will the tax reduce his willingness to buy the securities. Since additional investment in real property will increase tax liability, less real investment will be undertaken. Since the base of the wealth tax is greater than that of an income tax, however, the rate is lower and the marginal impact is less. Precise comparison of the relative effects of the two taxes is impossible.

Estate Taxes. On the whole, taxes payable by heirs at death are less likely to affect willingness to take risk than ones affecting income currently earned. Incidental effects, however, tend to reduce risk-taking. An estate tax of any magnitude causes persons to increase liquidity of their estates so that heirs can meet death tax obligations. Even more significant, death taxes, by encouraging the use of trusts (also encouraged by income tax legislation) and of life estate systems and skipping of generations make investment policies more conservative, lessening both total risk-taking and the fluidity of investment from one type to another.[14] During settlement of estates, the investment policies are still more conservative.

Money Creation, Borrowing, and Governmental Debt

Financing of governmental expenditures by money creation or borrowing and the existence of governmental debt may lessen risk-taking in the economy below the level with tax financing by increasing uncertainty. If investors fear that deficits financed by borrowing or money creation will give rise to "governmental bankruptcy" in the future, higher taxes in the future concentrating on return from investment, or a depression consequent to an initial period of inflation, their uncertainty about the future will be increased and they will be less inclined to take risks. Some of these fears may be completely groundless, such as those of "national bankruptcy" or depression; others may have some basis, such as a higher level of taxes over a long-range period. The former fears, however groundless, may be significant for decision making, as they were in the thirties. On the other hand, if persons primarily fear that the use of money creation or loans will increase the danger of inflation, the attractiveness of holding cash or fixed-dollar-value investments will be reduced, and the willingness to take the type of risk involved in equity investment will be increased, as well as that in purely speculative holdings of commodities expected to increase in value.

Question may also be raised about the significance for risk-taking of an increase in the quantity of relatively riskless government bonds available to investors. Tobin and others[15] have argued that the governmental debt increases the amount of risk capital available by causing

[14]See C. S. Shoup, *Federal Estate and Gift Taxes* (Washington, D.C.: Brookings Institution, 1966), chap. iii, iv.

[15]See J. Tobin, "An Essay on the Principles of Debt Management," in Commission on Money and Credit, *Fiscal and Debt Management Policies* (Englewood Cliffs, N.J.: Prentice-Hall, 1963).

persons to seek more of the latter investment, given their relative preferences for risk and return. They will seek more risky investments to balance their larger holdings of high-security, low-return government bonds. In reverse, it is argued that the availability of a greater quantity of low-risk investment outlets pulls funds away from outlets that involve more risk. This question cannot be resolved on an analytical basis.

Governmental Activities, Expenditures, and Risk-Taking

Governmental activities in many ways reduce risk and uncertainty, and in doing so lessen the attractiveness of holding wealth in the form of money and increase total investment. This activity does not actually increase the amount of risk which persons undertake but lessens the total amount of risk and uncertainty that must be undertaken to obtain a given level of investment.

The basic protective functions of government are obvious examples. The protection of life and property and the enforcement of contracts are essential for the conduct of business activity; without them investment virtually ceases, as it has in some countries in recent years—the Congo, for example. Insurance of freedom to undertake economic activity is also important if investment is to be maintained in a market economy. Protection against foreign invasion is likewise important. Provision of what is today commonly called infrastructure—building of roads and other transport facilities, provision of mail service and other communications facilities—increases the profitability of private investment.

One of the most significant effects in reducing uncertainty is the lessening of fluctuations in business activity. A major hazard to any firm is the danger of a severe depression; to the extent that governments can prevent them from occurring, the dangers of loss of investments are reduced. In industries in which the government continues to make purchases on a regular basis the uncertainty of the firms is lessened somewhat because of the certainty of continued purchases, although the hazard that the cessation of the governmental purchases or contract may destroy the market completely is always present. Government mail contracts, for example, made or broke individual stagecoach companies; without the mail contract a company could not continue to operate, just as in later years loss of railway mail contracts has made it impossible for the railways to continue certain passenger trains. Governmental lending activities and operation of insurance systems such as FHA reduce risk by pooling in a fashion not feasible for private enterprise and increase the attractiveness of investments financed by the programs.

Governments at times increase uncertainty—partly on the part of their suppliers, as noted above, partly by undertaking activities competing with private enterprise, such as electric power plants, or by providing services that benefit competitors of existing firms. Land grants to the railroads helped put wagon freighters out of business in the last century, and highway construction increased uncertainty for the railroads.

Empirical Studies

Two major empirical studies have been made of investment effects, both based on the interview approach, persons in higher income levels being asked about the effects of present United States federal income taxation upon their investment policies. The first, undertaken under the auspices of the Harvard Business School in 1949,[16] consisted of interviews of 746 "active investors" to ascertain the effects of taxes upon their investment policies. The second was the Brookings study referred to earlier in the chapter, in which 957 individuals with incomes in excess of $10,000 were interviewed about the effects of taxation on their work and investment behavior.[17] While there are some differences in conclusions of the two studies the basic ones are similar:

1. Present U.S. taxes have limited overall significance for financial investment policies and risk-taking. In the Brookings interview a majority of the respondents never mentioned taxes at all in discussing influences on their investment policies. The Harvard study showed that a majority of the overall group was not influenced, but a majority of those in the over-$25,000 income bracket were, one group in the direction of more conservative investments, the other toward more risky outlets. Several explanations of the limited influence of taxation were suggested in the interviews:

a) The basis of decisions about use of savings was not primarily the rate of return. Savings were made primarily by younger persons for education of children, by middle-aged groups for retirement, by older persons for bequests, with great emphasis at all levels on the desire for security and for safety and liquidity of investments. These goals of savings and investment policies were not directly affected by the tax.

---

[16]J. K. Butters, L. E. Thompson, and L. L. Bollinger, *Effects of Taxation: Investments by Individuals* (Boston: Harvard University Graduate School of Business Administration, 1953).

[17]Barlow *et al., op. cit.*

b) At least a third of the respondents were not aware of the marginal tax rates to which they were subject.

c) Most respondents did not seek to make use of tax savings devices that are available.

2. The most significant positive influence of the tax structure, revealed in both studies but particularly in the Brookings inquiry, was the encouragement given by the favorable tax treatment of capital gains for purchase of growth stocks instead of other forms of investments. The combination of relatively high income tax rates and low taxes on capital gains without doubt increases the overall willingness on the part of the investors to take risks. Common stock constitutes a major and growing element in investment portfolios.

3. Other tax influences were noted:

a) The extremely wealthy indicate greater preference for state and local bonds because of their tax-exempt status.

b) Gifts to children and relatives are increased for both income and estate tax reasons. The Harvard study also showed an increase in the use of trusts, as have other studies of estate taxation.

c) The capital gains provisions to some extent lock investors in existing securities on which a gain has been made and encourage the sales of assets that have declined in value.

d) Many investors ignore loss offset provisions in their investment decisions.

Studies of the effects of accelerated depreciation rules and the tax credit for new investment showed significant influence. Norman Ture concluded that in 1959 business investment was increased by the accelerated depreciation rules by at least $1.3 billion, and perhaps as much as $5.7 billion.[18] The study by R. E. Hall and D. W. Jorgensen concluded that accelerated depreciation increased investment substantially, that more liberal depreciation guidelines authorized in 1962 had considerable effect on investment in equipment, and that the investment tax credit of 1962 had a very great influence on investment, being responsible for 41 percent of all investment in manufacturing equipment in 1963 and 10 percent of all investment.[19]

LAND

By definition land consists of resources provided directly by nature; any improvements, such as clearing, drainage, or irrigation, constitute

[18]Norman Ture, *Accelerated Depreciation in the United States* (New York: National Bureau of Economic Research, 1967), pp. 95–96.

[19]R. E. Hall and D. W. Jorgensen, "Tax Policy and Investment Behavior," *American Economic Review,* Vol. LVII (June, 1967), pp. 391–414.

capital goods. Therefore governments cannot affect the potential supply of land—the total quantity in existence—except by conquest of territory from other countries, although they can make existing land more usable by the development of transport, drainage, irrigation, and other facilities.

Governments, by their tax systems or by direct measures, can affect the willingness, in an imperfect world, of landowners to make their land available for optimal economic use. Owners of large estates may prefer to use the land in a very nonintensive fashion, as for example, for cattle grazing, simply because such use is traditional and requires less effort on their part. Taxes based on actual income allow them to continue this practice, whereas a tax on potential income or land value based upon use for the most profitable purpose may compel them to cultivate the land more intensively or rent or sell it to persons who will. Similarly, within urban areas persons may hold land idle in anticipation of price increases, rather than building on it currently, in the belief that gain can be maximized in this fashion. Or landowners may prefer to keep the land in a large personal estate. The consequence may be serious interference with the development of effective land utilization in the city. Tax measures, placing a heavy burden on such vacant land, can make continued holding of it disadvantageous if not impossible.

MAJOR CONCLUSIONS

While neither analysis nor empirical work give conclusive answers about the effects of taxes upon supplies of labor and risk taking, the following conclusions appear to be warranted:

1. The present tax structure in the United States, despite heavy reliance on progressive income taxes, does not appear to be having serious effects on supplies of either labor or risk taking. Empirical evidence shows relatively little impact on either.

2. Most taxes have both income and substitution effects, the former leading to increased factor supply, the latter to reduced supply. The net effect is usually difficult to predict.

3. Progressive rates increase the significance of the substitution effect relative to the income effect and therefore are likely to have somewhat greater influence in reducing factor supplies than proportional rates. The actual difference may not be great.

4. Consumption-based taxes are likely to have less effect on factor supplies than income taxes, since the direct relation between earn-

ing of income and payment of tax is broken, and in practice the taxes are less likely to be progressive. The extent of the difference depends upon motives for savings and other considerations.

5. The potential adverse effects of taxes on risk taking are greatly reduced or eliminated by loss offsets, which result in the government's sharing losses as well as incomes; by liberal depreciation rules; and by the typically favorable tax treatment given to capital gains.

6. Taxes related to wealth are less likely to reduce factor supplies than income taxes, because the importance of the income effect is increased relative to the substitution effect.

7. Estate taxes have less potential effects on risk taking incentives than most other taxes, but do increase liquidity and conservativeness of wealthy investors.

8. Governmental expenditures may have significant influence on supply of various types of labor, and both adverse and favorable effects on risk taking.

REFERENCES

BARLOW, R., BRAZER, H. E., AND MORGAN, J. N. *Economic Behavior of the Affluent.* Washington, D.C.: Brookings Institution, 1966.

BUTTERS, J. K., THOMPSON, L. E., AND BOLLINGER, L. L. *Effects of Taxation: Investments by Individuals.* Boston: Harvard University Graduate School of Business Administration, 1953.

CANADA, ROYAL COMMISSION ON TAXATION. *Studies:* No. 3: *Taxation and Investments,* by JOHN F. HELLIWELL; No. 4: *The Effects of Income Taxation on Work Choices,* by ROBIN BARLOW.

HALL, R. E., AND JORGENSEN, D. W. "Tax Policy and Investment Behavior," *American Economic Review,* Vol. LVII, June, 1967, pp. 391–414.

HARBERGER, A. "Taxation, Resource Allocation and Welfare," in *The Role of Direct and Indirect Taxes in the Federal Revenue System.* Princeton, N.J.: Princeton University Press, 1964.

KALDOR, N. *An Expenditure Tax.* London: George Allen and Unwin, 1955.

MUSGRAVE, R. A. *The Theory of Public Finance,* chaps. xi, xiv. New York: McGraw-Hill, 1959.

SHOUP, C. S. *Federal Estate and Gift Taxes,* chaps. iii, iv. Washington, D.C.: Brookings Institution, 1966.

Chapter 8

DISTRIBUTIONAL EFFECTS OF GOVERNMENTAL EXPENDITURES AND REVENUES

Governmental activities and revenue programs inevitably alter the overall pattern of distribution of real income in the economy. Some of the effects are intentional; welfare programs seek to increase the real incomes of the recipients, and progressive taxes are designed to lessen the relative real income of the highest income groups. Many of the effects, however, are neither deliberately sought, nor, in fact, commonly recognized.

BENEFITS AND BURDENS

Direct distributional effects result from receipt of benefits of governmental services and transfer payments and from reduction in disposable income available for purchase of private-sector output due to the financing of the activities. Indirect effects on income distribution are created by the influence of governmental expenditure and revenue programs upon relative factor prices and upon the level of employment in the economy.

Direct Increases in Real Income

Governmental expenditures of a welfare nature directly increase incomes. Governments provide a variety of forms of assistance, primarily to persons in the lower income groups, that increase the real incomes of the beneficiaries. Welfare programs include direct relief, old-age assistance, aid for dependent children, other antipoverty programs, and, in many countries, family allowances. Farm price supports have welfare characteristics.

Governmental services with partial direct benefits, such as education, likewise directly increase the real incomes of the beneficiaries. When governments provide these services to the users free of charge or at charges less than cost, persons acquire larger quantities than they would (or perhaps could) purchase at prices covering all costs, and their real incomes are increased. Lower income, large-family groups

194

receive very significant increases in real income from education, and they gain from public health and recreational measures. Real incomes of persons of the community as a whole are also increased by provision of public goods and by community benefit elements of goods also providing direct benefits. Since these benefits do not accrue separately to individuals, total increases in real income experienced by individuals cannot be measured, and any allocation of benefits, as for example under the assumption that all persons benefit equally, is arbitrary. As a consequence, any attempt to measure overall changes in real income resulting from governmental expenditures requires arbitrary decisions that greatly lessen the significance of the results.

The lack of direct individual benefits from public goods, which comprise a large portion of governmental activities, also has significant implications for the overall effects of governmental activities. Individuals experience a reduction in real income from the financing of the programs without receiving individual benefits, even though they, as a group, seek the provision of the public goods. Accordingly, the burden aspects of the financing are not offset by benefits from the expenditures as seen from the individual point of view, which determines behavior.

Direct Reductions in Real Income

The transfer of resources from private-sector to governmental-sector use or to certain groups of individuals through welfare programs reduces the real private-sector incomes of various individuals in society, at a given level of national income. This reduction, which may be called the direct burden of the governmental activities, results from governmental use of the resources and thus from governmental expenditures, rather than from the revenue measures. The latter, however, control the patterns of distribution of burden—that is, of reduction in real incomes—among the various persons in society, and thus we often speak of the burden or incidence of a tax, even though the tax does not produce the primary burden.

The burden or reduction in real income may take several forms. First, factor incomes may fall, with commodity prices unchanged (consumption goods and capital goods); or disposable income may decline, with factor incomes and commodity prices unchanged, the decline being related to income received. The reduction in both these instances is related to factor income received; a person may alter his tax burden only by altering his income. The reduction may be uniform with all incomes, limited to a few types, or all-inclusive but not uniform; it may be proportional, progressive, or regressive relative to income. Second, disposable income may fall in a pattern related to some other measure than income, such as wealth owned, expenditures, or inheritances received. The individual cannot alter his tax liability by changing his income; he can do so only by altering behavior related to the measure of the tax.

Third, real income may decline through an increase in consumption goods prices relative to factor incomes, whether the former rise in price, factor incomes remaining the same, or factor prices fall while the prices of consumption goods remain unchanged.

Temporal factors in distribution are also significant. Reductions in real incomes may occur at the time the expenditures are made, as they will if the latter are financed by current taxes or charges. If voluntary borrowing is used to finance the activity, however, individuals do not experience reductions in real income currently but will do so in the future as interest and principal obligations are met. Currently, some savers acquire government bonds instead of other assets; while private-sector output is reduced, those who would otherwise obtain ownership of the amount no longer produced receive government bonds instead, and do not experience a lower real income.

Prices of assets with unlimited life and a sale value dependent upon expected yield will fall in value as a result of a continuing tax on the value of the yield. For example, suppose that a 10-acre parcel of land yields, and is expected to yield, net, $4,000 a year. With a 5 percent interest rate, the land will sell for $80,000. If a tax reduces the net yield to $3,000 per year, the sale price will fall to $60,000. Thus the owner at the time of the imposition (or increase) in the tax will suffer a reduction in real income by the capitalized sum of the current tax, whereas subsequent purchasers of the property will be freed of any reduction in their real incomes, since the purchase price has been reduced by the tax. This analysis assumes that the overall rate of return on capital, and thus the capitalizing factor, is not altered by the tax.

Indirect Distributional Effects

In addition to these direct increases and decreases in real income, governmental activities may redistribute real income in several other ways.

In the first place, a decline in real factor incomes due to tax measures will not be uniform unless the elasticities of factor supplies (the response of quantities of the factors available to changes in their prices) are uniform for all types of factors. Otherwise, the more elastic the factor supply the greater the rise in factor incomes net of tax, and thus the less the decline in the real incomes of the owners.

Secondly, relative factor prices may be affected in several other ways. Shift from private to governmental production will alter the relative demands for various types of factors and alter their prices, unless they are perfect substitutes. Prices of factors specialized in the production of certain commodities (for example, copper ore resources) are most significantly affected, but the relative incomes of large factor groups, such as labor and capital, may be affected as well. If, for example, governmental production is more labor-intensive than private production, the share of labor in real income will be increased and that of capital owners decreased. Governmental civilian activities are on the whole more labor-intensive than private production, and thus a shift from private to governmental production is likely to increase labor's share of total income.

Thirdly, relative factor prices and thus incomes will be altered if governmental activities alter the quantities of the factors available, as analyzed in Chapter 7.

Finally, governmental expenditure and revenue programs may affect the level of unemployment and thus significantly influence real income distribution. A program that reduces unemployment will increase the real incomes of those formerly unemployed without necessarily reducing the absolute real income of anyone else.

The Basis for Measurement and Comparison of Distributional Effect Patterns

The most inclusive approach to analysis of distributional effects considers the influence of both governmental expenditures and revenues on income distribution patterns. Several empirical studies of this type, noted in later sections of this chapter, have been made.[1] The significance of such studies, however, is impaired by the arbitrary assumptions required about distribution of benefits of public goods. Their usefulness for policy decisions is also limited by the marginal nature of most decisions as contrasted to the complete overhaul of expenditure and revenue programs. While marginal studies that analyze the distributional effects of a particular change in governmental activities and the financing measures can be made, they do not escape the problem of arbitrary allocation of benefits of public goods. Furthermore, expenditure programs are rarely related to certain revenue measures.

[1]See pp. 233–35.

The approach that is most precise analytically because it avoids the allocation of benefits problem and is most useful for framing revenue policy compares the relative distributional effects of alternative revenue sources, given the program of governmental expenditures. This is the *differential* approach to the question. In turn, the simplest norm for comparison is a proportional income tax applying uniformly to all income without exception. Such a tax may itself have some effects on factor prices that will produce deviation from complete proportionality relative to income, but presumably it approaches proportionality more closely than any other levy.

Analysis requires the exclusion of distributional considerations arising out of fiscal (level of employment) effects, which cannot appropriately be assigned to the particular revenue measure but relate to the overall expenditure-revenue program. The assumption is therefore made that the taxes being compared leave aggregate real factor demand and thus the level of factor employment unchanged; the government would obtain the same command over factors from the various alternative revenue sources, but not necessarily the same monetary yield.[2]

Comparison can be made on the basis of three classifications. The first, as traditionally emphasized, concerns sources of income, the relative reductions in real income experienced by various classes of factor owners—workers, landowners, suppliers of money capital; or particular subdivisions of these, as for example owners of businesses as contrasted to those supplying money capital on a contractual basis, or certain types of labor. Secondly, comparison can be made in terms of use of income received: consumers versus savers, or consumers of certain goods versus those of others. Thirdly, burdens can be compared on persons classified by income group. The usual technique for this approach is measurement of the deviation, under various alternative taxes, from a uniform distribution.

These approaches are, of course, related. A sales tax related to consumption will place a relatively greater burden on the lower in-

---

[2]An opposite point of view, developed by Earl Rolph and his disciples, maintains that analysis of distributional effects of a tax can appropriately be based only on the assumption that the use of the tax revenue is ignored. Accordingly aggregate demand falls as a result of a tax, and factor prices decline; the tax is distributed in proportion to factor incomes and is not "borne by consumers." This position is developed in the article by E. R. Rolph, "A Proposed Revision of Excise Tax Theory," *Journal of Political Economy*, Vol. LX (April, 1957), pp. 102–17. A similar point of view was expressed in earlier work by H. G. Brown.

The difficulty with the Rolph analysis is that it mixes fiscal (employment) effects with distributional effects and considers only a portion of the reactions to the tax. The differential approach to incidence is more useful for analytical and policy purposes.

come groups than on the higher, and thus produce a regressive pattern of burden distribution; the percentage of reduction in real income is greater at the lower income levels than at the higher. A progressive income tax will produce a progressive pattern: the percentage reduction in real income will rise as income rises.

Similar studies can be made of distributional effects of various expenditure programs, given the revenue sources.

THE PERFECTLY COMPETITIVE MARKET STRUCTURE MODEL

Analysis of the patterns of income redistribution resulting from the various taxes requires the use of models of market behavior. Initially we will employ the perfectly competitive (PC) model, a very simple and precise analytical tool with which to express certain basic relationships. The similarity of the assumptions upon which the model is based to contemporary market conditions is not sufficiently close, however, for the results to have a high degree of significance. In subsequent sections, a more realistic but more complex nonperfectly competitive model will be introduced.

The PC model, characterized by inability of either individual buyers or individual sellers to influence price, is based upon the assumptions of (1) standardized product, with no preferences for the products of particular sellers, (2) sufficiently large numbers of buyers and sellers that changes in the action of any one will not perceptibly influence market price, and (3) free entry and exit of firms. The following relationships are developed in this model:

1. For each household: marginal rate of substitution between each pair of commodities equals the ratio of the commodity prices. This equality is necessary to maximize satisfaction.
2. For each commodity:
   a) Price equals marginal cost, for profit maximization.
   b) Price equals average cost, for equilibrium of the industry.
3. For each factor:
   a) Quantity utilized by each firm such that value of marginal product (VMP) equals factor price.
   b) Factor price equates total quantity used and total quantity available at the equilibrium price.

With the entire economy in equilibrium each commodity price will equate quantity demanded with the rate of output and will equal both average cost and marginal cost (the sums of the various factor costs).

For each factor the factor price will equate the quantity of the factor available at the equilibrium price with the quantity required by all producing units, each following the rule of equating VMP of each factor with the factor price.

Proportional Income Tax

Let us now introduce a proportional income tax into the system, full employment being maintained by governmental absorption of the factor units freed. If factor supply schedules are perfectly inelastic—that is, if the number of factor units available to the economy is independent of the factor prices within the relevant ranges—there are no further readjustments. As shown in Figure 8–1A real incomes fall in proportion to factor incomes. A progressive income tax will likewise, under the assumptions, be distributed in relation to the actual tax payments at each income level. The direct burden is distributed according to income received, with no additional burden arising out of reduced quantity of factor units available.

Given the level of employment and perfectly inelastic factor supplies, shifts in relative demands for various types of specialized factors due to the replacement of private-sector output by governmental production are the only potential source of indirect real income redistribution. If the commodities purchased in smaller quantities as disposable incomes fall require different factor combinations than the goods produced by government, relative factor prices will change.

When factor supply schedules are not perfectly inelastic, the relative prices of various factors will shift since at the original factor price minus tax (p_f^{-t} on Figure 8–1B), quantity demanded exceeds quantity available. Equilibrium is restored only when price (including tax) rises to $p_f t,$ and the price received by the factor owner is p_f^{t-t}. Relative factor price increases are determined by the elasticity of factor supplies, the greatest increases occurring with the most elastic supplies. With a perfectly elastic supply (Figure 8–1C) factor price will rise by the amount of the tax. Suppose that profit receivers would not continue to supply money capital unless they receive a given real income per unit of capital, perhaps 10 percent on investment. As a consequence, the given level of employment could be maintained only if adjustments restored the original rate of profit, and thus other groups of factor owners experienced a relatively greater reduction in real income. If the quantity of certain types of labor available falls sharply as the net return is reduced by the tax, the equilibrium factor price will rise very sharply.

With differing elasticities of factor supply, therefore, a proportional-rate income tax will not, in fact, reduce all incomes proportionately.

FIGURE 8-1

RESPONSE OF FACTOR PRICE TO INCOME TAX

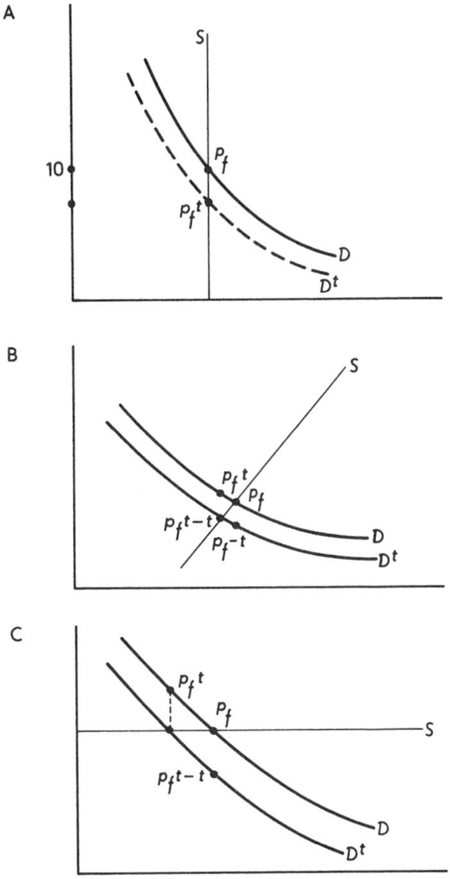

p_f: Equilibrium factor price, pretax.
$p_f t$: Equilibrium factor price, after tax.
D: Demand curve before tax.
D^t: After-tax payment to factor.

Excise Taxes

Suppose that an excise tax is employed as a substitute for a portion of the income tax revenue. The relative magnitudes of the two taxes being compared must be such as to insure the same level of employment in order to exclude fiscal effects of the substitution, that is, changes in the level of national income arising from changes in aggregate demand. The excise tax places a wedge between the selling price of the product and its factor cost. Accordingly the output and supply will fall and the price of the product will rise. The extent of the rise will be determined by the elasticity of demand and supply schedules, and the reaction of demand to elimination of the income tax, an influence not likely to be significant for an individual excise-taxed product.

FIGURE 8–2

RESPONSE OF COMMODITY PRICE TO EXCISE TAX

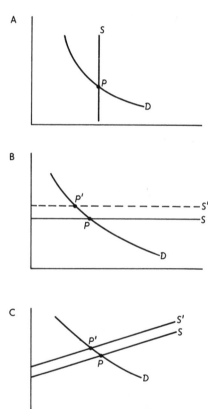

If the supply is perfectly inelastic and demand does not increase as a result of the income tax elimination, price will not rise and the owners of the firms will experience the entire reduction in real income (Figure 8–2A). The best example is a perishable commodity in a short period of time. If the supply is perfectly elastic, as it would be over a period of time in a constant cost industry, price will rise by the amount of the tax (Figure 8–2B) regardless of the nature or behavior of demand. If certain factors are specialized to the industry, their prices will fall as output falls, and the owners will share a portion of the decline in real income. This is the traditional increasing cost situation (Figure 8–2C). Any shift in demand to the product from the income tax reduction (not shown on Figure 8–2C) would lessen the fall in the factor prices.

To the extent that the price of the product rises, the reduction in real income is distributed in relation to consumption of the taxed article; in this sense the tax "rests on consumers" of the product. The pattern of reduction relative to total income is determined by consumption expenditure patterns on the taxed article by income groups, and an individual can reduce his tax only by curtailing consumption of the taxed good. Reduction in real income is not related to the type of factor income received.

When prices of specialized factors fall, a portion of the real income reduction is shared by the owners of these factors. The extent of the reduction in output due to the tax and the extent of decline in the prices of specialized factors are therefore a function of the elasticity of demand for the product (which has no relevance if elasticity of supply is either zero or infinite). To take an extreme example: if a product were produced solely with a specialized factor having no productivity in other uses (mineral springs from which consumers, for a fee, fill their containers), if the demand is highly elastic, and if consumers do not buy more of the product because of the income tax reduction, the real income of the owners of the specialized factor (the springs) will be almost entirely eliminated by the tax.

In the rare instances in which a reduction in output causes the loss of some type of economy of scale related to the output of the whole industry and not to that of individual firms, prices to consumers will rise by an amount in excess of the tax. Such instances are theoretically possible but appear to be very rare in practice.

As compared to a proportional income tax, those persons who spend more than average amounts on the taxed commodity will lose income as a result of the change; those who spend nothing on the commodity or less than the average will gain. To the extent that persons reduce purchases as a result of the tax, they suffer an *excess burden* arising from the shift in consumption, in addition to the reduction in real income due to the higher prices on the units that they continue to buy.

Presumably an excise tax will affect total quantities of factors available in the same fashion as the income tax, with one qualification: persons may react less to a decline in real income due to higher commodity prices than they do to a reduction in disposable income because of the money illusion. In an analogous situation, workers typically resist a cut in money wages more than they resist a reduction in real wages due to a rise in prices. Furthermore the persons involved are not the same unless the taxed item is universally consumed by persons subject to the income tax. The consumers of fur coats may be less inclined to reduce work hours because of a tax on fur coats than are income receivers as a whole because of a reduction in disposable income, partly because of the potential escape hatch; they can cease buying fur coats and avoid the tax.

An increase in the price of one commodity due to a replacement of a proportional income tax by an excise tax, with other prices remaining unchanged, can occur only if appropriate monetary adjustments, in the quantity or velocity of money, are made. Otherwise, the general level of commodity and factor prices must fall slightly to offset the increase in the price of the taxed good, which would remain relatively higher than other prices. In a perfectly competitive world, the distributional effects will be the same whether the general price level is permitted to rise or not, since the relationship between commodity and factor prices will be the same.[3] In the real world, long-term contracts and money illusions would produce a difference in the two situations. The most reasonable assumption to make is that monetary policy will permit a rise in the price level, in light of the usual intent that excises be shifted forward.

A General Sales Tax

A completely general sales tax, imposed upon all consumption goods at the retail level without exception at a uniform rate, but to no intermediate or capital goods, drives a wedge between the prices to the consumer and the factor costs of all consumption goods. Consumption goods prices must therefore rise relative to factor prices to restore equilibrium; the direction of absolute change depends upon monetary considerations noted subsequently. We will assume for the moment that commodity prices rise.

Price increases will uniformly equal the amount of the tax if all industries are of constant cost nature and thus the long-run supply schedules of all commodities are perfectly elastic, while the supply schedules of all factors are perfectly inelastic. The increases will also

---

[3]The importance of relative, rather than absolute, price changes for distributional effects was first stressed by R. A. Musgrave; see *The Theory of Public Finance* (New York: McGraw-Hill, 1959), chap. xv.

be uniform if the reduction in sales of each commodity due to the higher price is exactly offset by the increase in sales that results from the elimination of the income tax. This is unlikely, although the general influence of the income tax reduction in increasing purchases reduces significantly the output reductions that result from the sales tax.

Deviations from perfect elasticity of supply and thus from constant cost conditions will destroy the uniformity of burden distribution. When factors are specialized to particular industries, the prices of those specialized for the products whose sales fall are reduced, while the prices specialized for those with increasing sales rise. Thus prices of commodities produced in the former industries will rise by amounts less than the tax and those in others will rise by more. How significant these shifts are in practice is an empirical matter and no generalizations are possible. We commonly assume, however, that they are not highly significant for the overall pattern of income redistribution.

When factor supplies are not perfectly inelastic and have differing degrees of elasticity the reductions in real income experienced by various factor owners will not be the same as they would be with a proportional income tax, if the relative direct burden on various kinds of factor units differ, or persons react differently to equal real burdens of the two forms of tax. If a sales tax has relatively greater direct impact on the lower income workers compared to the income tax and these persons have more inelastic factor supply schedules than other factor groups, they will gain less from increases in factor prices and will experience a disproportionately greater decline in real incomes. In addition, because of the money illusion, persons may react very differently to a reduction in real income that occurs because of commodity price increases than to a reduction involving lower disposable income; on the whole they are less likely to react at all with the former as contrasted to the latter, and the effect on quantities of factors available will be less. If this difference is more significant with some factor-owning groups than others, alteration in the relative declines in real income will occur.

Thus, under the assumptions, the primary difference between a proportional income tax and a general sales tax is that the primary pattern of real income reduction with the former is directly related to income received, while that with the sales tax is related to consumption expenditures. In both instances there are deviations from this general pattern as a result of factor price changes, which are not likely to be identical with the two taxes. The magnitudes of these deviations are unknown. If the ratio of consumption expenditures to income declines as income rise, the sales tax will, apart from the factor price changes, be distributed in a fashion regressive by income group.

We have assumed that monetary policy will permit an increase in the general price level so that consumption goods prices rise relative to factor prices and relative to capital goods prices. In a perfectly competitive, frictionless world the direction of change would not be significant; if monetary policy held the price level constant, prices of factors, capital goods, and assets would fall relative to consumption goods prices, and the real income reduction would be related to consumption. In the real world, however, long-term contractual commitments and money illusions, in addition to frictions and imperfections, make the direction of change significant. Given these restrictions and the typical governmental intent that sales taxes rest on consumers, the assumption of a monetary policy that allows a price level increase is the only reasonable one.[4]

Two variations from the assumed coverage of the tax warrant attention:

1. *Exemptions.* Sales taxes are virtually never completely uniform, various types of consumption expenditures usually being exempted from tax. The effect is the introduction of an element of excise tax characteristics. The pattern of real income reduction will be related to consumer expenditure patterns on taxed and nontaxed items, which are now relatively cheaper. Factors specialized to the production of nontaxed items will experience a gain in real income and those specialized to the production of taxed items will experience a net loss.

Similar effects are introduced by rate differentiation and by levying the tax prior to the retail level, since the ratio of tax to final retail price will vary with differences in distribution margins on various products, and, with the turnover tax, the number of sales through which the commodity passes on its path to the final consumer. Otherwise, under the assumption of perfect competition, levying the tax prior to the retail sale would not affect the pattern of distribution.

[4]One school of thought has long maintained that general increases in the price level can appropriately be attributed only to monetary policies, not to taxes. See, for example, J. M. Buchanan, *Fiscal Theory and Political Economy* (Chapel Hill, N.C.: University of North Carolina Press, 1960). If, as many persons further assumed, sales taxes can be borne by consumers only with forward shifting, the possibility of any tax burdening consumers was effectively barred. Following Musgrave, it is now generally recognized that the direction of change is not of paramount importance, and thus even if the price level does not rise, consumers bear the burden of a sales tax in large measure. The argument that only monetary changes can cause general price level increases is purely a terminological one that is not helpful for purposes of analysis. Monetary adjustments must, of course, occur if the general price level is to increase.

2. *Taxation of Capital Goods.* Greater complexity is introduced into the analysis by the assumption that capital goods are subjected to the sales tax, as in practice they often are to some extent. Taxation of these goods increases the amount of money capital required for a given real investment. Accordingly, under the assumption of a perfectly inelastic supply of money capital, the return to owners of capital would be reduced by the amount of tax. If the supplies of labor and savings are both perfectly inelastic, the combination of a tax on all capital goods and all consumption goods at a uniform rate will have the same distributional effects as a proportional income tax. Departure from perfect inelasticity of factor supply should produce equivalent reaction in factor prices with a proportional income tax and a sales tax covering capital and consumption goods, apart from effects of the money illusion.

Taxation of some capital goods and not others—the usual practice—will reduce the rate of return from capital and will also affect the relative prices of commodities produced with taxed-capital-goods-intensive methods of production and those produced with nontaxed-capital-goods-intensive methods, and thus introduce excise tax effects as well. In addition the relative incomes of factors specialized to the production of the taxed capital goods will be altered.

Differential Tax on Business Profits

Taxes on earnings from operation of businesses as a part of a general uniform rate income tax were noted early in the chapter. Suppose, however, that a tax is imposed on the profits from business or from corporate businesses over and above the basic personal income tax. Under the assumption of perfect competition, firms cannot directly shift the tax forward in the form of higher prices since they have no direct control over market prices. So long as a tax of this type is uniform, there is no possibility of escaping it by shifting production to other activities, as there would be if the tax were levied only upon certain industries. If real investment is independent of the return received, the tax will be distributed in relation to income from profits from business. If, however, a decline in return reduces investment, the return must rise to maintain employment, and the real income of the profit receivers is at least partially restored.

With the PC model, the reasoning applied to a differential tax on business income applies to a differential tax on any type of income. If the supply of the factor is perfectly inelastic, the income of the taxed factor will be reduced by the amount of the tax. If it is not, a portion of the income reduction will be borne by other factor owners.

Taxes on Wealth

The pattern of reduction in real income of a tax on wealth is not easily defined. Wealth consists of a great many diverse items and the reactions of the holders to a tax may vary greatly. Since the tax has the effect of reducing the return from savings its influence is equivalent to that of any tax having a differentially higher impact on savings; if the supply is perfectly inelastic, incomes of capital owners will be reduced but in relation to the amount of accumulated savings, not current savings. If not, a portion of the burden will be shared. Much of the tax rests upon owner-occupied housing, and thus is not easily transferred to anyone; the reduction in real income is directly related to ownership of this type of property.

The substantial portion of property taxation that has direct impact on business property has much the same redistributive effects as a nonuniform sales tax, subject to the qualification that the overall return to capital may fall, and that a portion of the tax on improvements may fall on the owners of the land.[5] The portion of the tax on land and other nonreproducible assets will reduce the net return from land and directly reduce the real income of the landowners. Since the total supply of land is perfectly inelastic the owners cannot escape from the tax. Furthermore, such a tax will capitalize, that is, reduce the selling price of the land by the capitalized sum of the tax. Taxes on existing buildings on sites having no attractive alternative uses may also be shifted to the landowners through reduced rent that the landlords can collect.

PURE MONOPOLY MODEL

Brief attention will be given to the model of complete monopoly: one seller of a product with no close substitutes.

Tax on Net Income

If tax is imposed upon the net income of a monopolist who is maximizing profits, he will not raise price. The price that previously maximized profit will continue to do so; if a series of numbers is reduced by a given percentage, the figure that was previously the highest will continue to be the highest, as can be demonstrated by the simplest

---

[5]See R. L. Richmond, "The Incidence of Urban Real Estate Taxes," *Land Economics*, Vol. XLIII (May, 1967), pp. 172–80. Richmond argues that virtually all the tax on improvements will fall on the owners of the land.

arithmetic. In other words, neither marginal cost nor marginal revenue are affected by the tax. If the seller was seeking a satisfactory rate of profit only, and his actual price was below the optimum profit level, he will increase price by an amount necessary to restore profits to the level regarded as satisfactory and thus by the full amount of the tax.

Taxes on Sales

If an excise tax is imposed upon the sales of the firm, the price will be raised by only a portion of the amount of the tax: half of the amount if the demand curve for the product of the firm is linear and marginal cost constant, as shown in Figure 8–3. The firm seeks to

FIGURE 8–3

RESPONSE OF PRICE TO EXCISE TAX
MONOPOLY

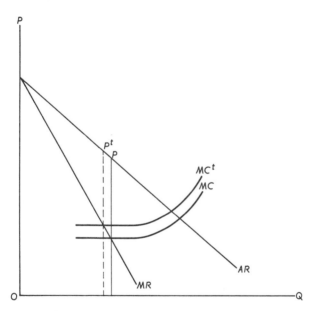

re-equate marginal cost and marginal revenue by reducing output so that MR rises by the amount of the increase in MC. But a given increase in MR involves a substantially smaller increase in price. With a satisfactory-profit goal, price will be raised by the entire amount of the tax, under the assumptions that the price after the increase does not exceed the maximum-profit price and the average cost of the firm remains unchanged.

These conclusions ignore the influence upon prices and income distribution of changes in specialized factor prices as output changes or of losses of economies of scale, which will cause departure from constant average and marginal costs, and any generalized response of factor prices to the tax. These influences can easily be added.

NONPERFECTLY COMPETITIVE MODEL

Neither the perfectly competitive nor monopoly models are sufficiently representative of the functioning of the modern economy to be adequate for explaining distributional effects of taxation. Such an explanation requires a nonperfectly competitive (NPC) general equilibrium model. Unfortunately, and for good reason, no such model with general acceptability is available. Imperfectly competitive markets are characterized by a wide range of variation in precise behavior; no single model of firm behavior yet devised appears to be reasonably typical. In other words, no single set of assumptions about behavior in NPC conditions will provide a model that is both usable and adequately representative of the contemporary economy. A set of models would be required, with a large number of alternative assumptions applicable to particular segments; not only do we lack empirical information for establishment of these assumptions, but the system would be extremely complex, perhaps to the extent of being unusable, with present techniques, for analyzing reactions to a tax. The explanation of determination of factor shares is particularly unsatisfactory with nonperfectly competitive conditions in factor and commodity markets.

Accordingly, the analysis is limited to one simplified model that on the basis of available empirical data appears to provide a more realistic tool of analysis than the models of perfect competition or complete monopoly. No claim is made for universal applicability of this model. The NPC model has the following features:[6]

1. Dominance of "satisfactory profit" or "target return" as the immediate objective, with maximization of joint profits for the group of firms as the ultimate long-range goal, but one that may have little effect on policy. Other goals clearly are significant in nonperfectly competitive situations: maximization of sales (gross revenue), higher share of the market, combined maximum profit and amenities for officials, and the like. But the satisfactory profit goal appears to be the most significant single assumption for the model. The level that con-

---

[6]For somewhat similar models presented in mathematical form, see R. J. Gordon, "Incidence of the Corporation Income Tax," *American Economic Review*, Vol. LVII (September, 1967), pp. 731–58.

stitutes satisfactory profits depends on attitudes of management and may be far higher than the average rate of return on capital.

2. Markets characterized by differentiation of product and by significant mutual interdependence among the firms; each is aware that its policies may affect those of its competitors. Seldom is interdependence strong enough to allow attainment of maximum joint profits for the group.

3. Setting of prices by individual sellers with emphasis on average cost, including a satisfactory rate of profit, with some recognition of demand elements. Output is adjusted to the rate of sales at the prices set; average cost is assumed to be more or less constant within the usual ranges of output. Average cost pricing often takes the markup form, a percentage being added to direct costs to distribute "overhead" and establish the price.

4. Wide variation in actual relationship of price to average cost among products, in light of the precise nature of market relationships and concept of satisfactory profit and ease of entry into the industry, and therefore wide and varying divergences between profits earned and the interest rate.

5. Wages, the major factor-cost element, determined by bargaining between employer and union. Given the wage rate, firms acquire workers to the level at which the additional gain (marginal revenue product) equals cost of the worker.

6. Interest rates on borrowed money determined by supply and demand of loanable funds, greatly influenced by governmental monetary policy except at full employment.

Proportional Income Tax

The reactions to a proportional income tax will differ from those with the PC model. Fiscal effects are ignored, since these are not appropriately attributable to the tax as such.

With imperfections in commodity and factor markets, persons will seek to shift their tax burdens directly onto others in order to avoid reduction in real income. This is, however, easier said than done. The typical worker cannot directly obtain higher wages because of the tax, but his union may, and from many indications does, consider the income tax in bargaining demands. Whether the tax will result in a higher wage cannot be determined; all that can be said is that the tax does become an added element in the bargaining picture. Because of the typical union emphasis on take-home pay, the use of withholding probably increases the impact of the tax on wage levels. Individuals in strategic bargaining positions, particularly executives with direct influence on corporate policy, likewise may be able to use the tax as an instrument for obtaining higher pretax salaries. Interest and dividend receivers have much less direct influence, since the markets for money capital are more nearly perfectly competitive. Corporation policies will be analyzed in a subsequent section.

The net result is greater departure from the initial proportional-to-income distribution pattern than is found with the PC model. To the extent that some persons free themselves of loss in real income through superior bargaining power, others must suffer a greater loss. The magnitude of the departure from the initial pattern is indeterminable with present knowledge.

Excise Tax

An excise tax constitutes a direct and immediate addition to average cost, one that, in its usual form, strikes all competing firms in similar fashion. Accordingly, under the assumptions, price will be increased immediately by the amount of the tax. So long as the firms selling the product follow the same policy, all will gain by raising, provided the original price did not maximize the profits of the firms as a group. If it did, increase by the full amount of the tax will reduce profits, as under monopoly. Output will be adjusted accordingly. Changes in prices of specialized factors may modify the initial pattern. The primary difference between the NPC and PC models is the nature and speed of adjustment; firms will readjust immediately and thus the price increase will not be delayed by the need for prior reduction in market supply.

There undoubtedly are some exceptions to this reaction. With relatively weak degree of interdependency among the firms, some may seek to gain through greater sales volume and thus not increase price when the tax is imposed. All firms in an industry may believe the demand for the product to be so elastic that an increase is not desirable; in other words, because of demand elasticity the present price appears to maximize joint profits of the group. With one-product firms and a pretax average rate of return, shifting would eventually occur through departure of some firms; this would allow the remaining ones to raise prices or to benefit through the effect of greater volume on per unit cost. With the common multiple-product situation, however, or pretax profits above the necessary figure, the taxed product may continue to sell indefinitely at a price less than the pretax price plus tax. The importance of these exceptions can be determined only by empirical studies. On the other hand, if the firms are operating on the declining portions of their average cost curves, they may seek to raise prices in excess of the amount of the tax to compensate for higher per unit cost.

The markup approach to pricing, as assumed in the model, introduces a further modification. If an excise is imposed upon a manufacturer who raises his price by the amount of the tax, the distributors, applying percentage markups to purchase prices increased by the amounts of the tax, will raise their selling prices in excess of the tax. There is some empirical evidence of this phenomenon. Thus consumers of the taxed products will not only have their real incomes reduced by the amount of the tax but by an additional amount as well, which either raises the profits of the owners of the distributing firms or allows factor units to continue to be employed in the industry when they would otherwise shift to other fields. Were competition sufficiently strong this tendency toward markup of tax would be eliminated, but in the non-perfectly competitive model this may not occur, or occur only very slowly.

Sales Tax

The initial reactions to a sales tax will be the same as with excises, with less concern about demand elasticity, since all prices are rising. Firms therefore shift the tax forward directly and immediately by simultaneous adjustment of price and output without the need for prior reduction in market supply. Over time, however, the pattern of redistribution of burden is more comparable to that with the PC model. Secondary readjustments in the prices of specialized factors would also be comparable. As with the perfectly competitive model, some industries will have greater output with the sales tax than with the alternative personal income tax, while others will have less. Higher demand is less likely to bring price increases with imperfect competition than with perfect competition. But this is primarily a short-run difference. Over a longer period, with either PC or NPC models, increased output in an increasing cost situation will lead to higher prices for the specialized factors and thus additional price increases. The reverse is true for firms with lower sales under the sales tax than under the income tax. Unlike the PC market, however, there may be long-continuing resistance to declines in prices of specialized factors when demand for them has fallen. If their owners have strong bargaining power, they can prevent owners of unemployed factors from bidding the factor price down. Furthermore, workers are likely to seek wage increases to offset the higher cost of living due to the tax. The significance of varying elasticities of factor supply is the same as with PC, except to the extent that bargaining considerations affect the determination of factor price levels.

Other elements influencing pricing may alter the overall distributional effects:

a) *Influence of Separate Quotation.* With the typical retail sales tax in the United States and Canada and some other countries, the prices of individual commodities are not readjusted to reflect the tax, which is applied at the cash register to the customer's entire bill. There are two major consequences. One is an increase in the likelihood of uniformity of price adjustments by all firms; for this reason vendor groups have often favored legislation requiring quotation of tax separate from the price. Secondly, demand considerations affecting particular commodities are less likely to influence the shifting pattern, partly because consumer reactions may be substantially different when the tax is applied in this fashion than when it is reflected in price adjustments for each commodity separately. Separate quotation may also lessen the likelihood that prices of some products will be raised in excess of the tax. Obviously the mere fact of separate collection does not "prove" that the tax has been shifted; prices net of tax might be changed. But this response is not to be expected in terms of our model, and there is no empirical evidence that it occurs.

b) *Tax-Free Competition in Geographically Limited Jurisdictions.* Exceptions to the shifting rule are likely when firms are subject to competition of firms in nearby tax-free jurisdictions. Shifting may prove to be unprofitable.

c) *Nonretail Taxes.* The level of imposition of the tax will have more significance than in perfect competition. If the tax is levied at preretail levels, the use of different pricing techniques may alter the burden pattern. Use of percentage markups is likely to cause pyramiding of tax, that is, increases in prices by amounts in excess of the tax.

d) *Direction of Price Change.* The imperfectly competitive features of factor markets are highly significant for the *direction* of change in the price level in response to a sales tax. Under the assumptions, wages are inflexible downward, since reductions are strongly opposed by unions as well as individual workers. Thus downward adjustment in factor prices with commodity prices remaining unchanged is virtually impossible. The only reasonable assumption that can be made about monetary policy under the circumstances is that it will permit forward shifting of the tax. Any attempt to do otherwise would produce intractable unemployment.

e) *Taxation of Capital Goods.* The significance for distributional effects of inclusion within the tax of capital goods is altered significantly by the use of the NPC model. The difference results partly from the divergence between the basic return to capital and the typical profit rates of business firms, and partly from the costing and pricing policies of businesses. A tax that increases the prices of capital goods does not automatically reduce the return to savers. Under the assumptions of the model, equipment-using firms will either depreciate the larger capital sum or treat the tax as a current expense; in either event the cost of the product is raised. Interest on additional working capital necessary to pay the tax on capital equipment will also be included in cost. Accordingly, consumption goods prices can be expected to rise, although uniformity among firms will be less than with a tax levied directly upon their sales. Thus much of the tax will pass on, directly or indirectly, into the prices of consumption goods, and this portion of the tax as well as that on consumption goods will be borne in relation to consumption. The capital goods portion will be distributed in an uneven fashion because of the nonuniform ratio of tax on capital goods to sales of consumption goods. The return on capital is not directly affected, nor will profits necessarily fall. A proportional income tax and a sales tax applying to both consumption goods and capital goods are not identical in a nonperfectly competitive world.

The Corporation Income Tax

The most striking difference between the distributional pattern with NPC and PC models is found with the corporation income tax. More specific definition of the nonperfectly competitive model is required, by adding the following assumptions:

1. Treatment by the firms of a tax on corporate net income as an expense for purposes of price determination.

2. Relatively uniform ratio of tax to sales among the firms in the industry; or acceptance by all firms of the prices set by those paying relatively high ratios of tax to sales (the umbrella doctrine). In other words, the high-tax firms are the price leaders in the industry.

3. Nonmaximization of joint profits of the firms as a group prior to the tax.

With these assumptions the tax, or at least a large part of it, will be reflected in the prices of the products, and the consequences for real income distribution will be similar to those for a sales tax, with differences among products due to the varying ratios of taxable profits to sales. The assumptions are not necessarily universally relevant, and many exceptions are likely. Firms having disproportionately high earnings are unlikely to be able to shift all of the tax. Competition of the less heavily taxed noncorporate businesses may impair shifting. Some fields of economic activity, such as agriculture, operate under conditions far removed from the assumptions of the model. The significance of the model can be determined only through further empirical work. But the model suggests that some shifting is inevitable.

Over a longer period, the differences between the patterns with PC and NPC models will be less if the reduced rate of return with the PC model slows the rate of capital formation and reduces the ratio of savings to labor in the economy, permitting shifting from capital owners to workers.

Wealth Taxation

The primary significance of the NPC model for distributional effects of a tax on wealth is the greater ease with which business firms can treat the tax as an expense and include it in selling prices, thus producing a sales tax effect. The ratio of tax to selling prices will vary among sellers of particular products, and widely among products. The former difference will check complete forward shifting while the latter will produce an uneven burden on various products. Both consumption and capital goods are affected, in contrast to those sales taxes that are limited to consumption goods.

Dynamic Approach to Income Redistribution

Our analysis to this point has been of a comparative statics nature, concerning income distribution in a given situation with alternative taxes. The world is, of course, dynamic; the real incomes of various groups follow different paths as the economy expands. Various taxes will affect these growth paths differently and thus produce various patterns of change in per capita real income. A proportional income tax that reduces the rate of savings materially but not the rate of increase in labor supply may reduce the rate of growth of labor income compared to that of property income and alter the pattern of income distribution in a progressive fashion over a period of years.[7] At present, however, neither analysis nor empirical work permit scientific determination of what the actual dynamic effects of alternate levies will be, and policy must be based on more static comparisons without direct regard to effects on growth patterns.

---

[7] See D. Dosser, Tax Incidence and Growth," *Economic Journal*, Vol. LXI (September, 1961), pp. 572–91.

Conclusions

Complete analysis of distributional consequences requires consideration of direct and indirect effects of governmental expenditure and revenue programs on real income. Such an approach, unfortunately, is of limited usefulness because of the inability to allocate benefits of public goods on any basis except purely arbitrary ones. Accordingly, more useful analyses are confined to the pattern of real income redistribution resulting from particular revenue systems, or from one type of revenue compared to another, with given patterns of governmental expenditures and given levels of employment. Redistributional patterns can be analyzed in terms of factor or income level groups, or factor owners versus consumers.

A proportional income tax is the most useful norm for comparing distributional effects of other taxes, although such a tax itself does not produce a completely proportional pattern of real income reduction because of varying elasticities of factor supplies, and, in NPC markets, varying ability of persons and groups to recoup their real income losses at the expense of other persons with weaker bargaining positions.

A sales tax on consumption goods at the retail level reduces real incomes in proportion to consumption expenditures, with some variation arising from changes in prices of specialized factors and factor groups that differ—partly because of the money illusion—from the pattern with a proportional income tax. Price adjustments are likely to occur much more quickly with the NPC model than with one of perfect competition. If capital goods are also subject to the tax, the distributional pattern is, with the PC model, similar to that of proportional income tax since the real return from savings is reduced as well as that from consumption. With NPC markets, however, a substantial portion of the tax on capital goods purchases will be reflected in the prices of consumption goods produced with them, and the tax more closely resembles a consumption goods sales tax in its distributional effects.

The direction of change in absolute prices is not significant for distributional effects of a sales tax in a perfectly competitive world. In an NPC world with long-term contracts, money illusions, and inflexible factor prices the direction of change is highly significant. The only reasonable monetary policy assumption is one that allows an upward adjustment in the price level.

An excise tax will reduce real income in proportion to expenditures on the taxed commodity, except for the effect of factor price adjustments; prices of those specialized to the taxed industry will fall. Excise tax shifting is likely to be much more rapid in NPC industries. A profit-maximizing monopolist will not find complete shifting of an excise advantageous.

The corporate income tax would reduce the rate of return on capital, the overall redistributional effects being determined by the elasticity of supply of capital in a PC model. If this supply were perfectly elastic, over a long-run period the real income of capital suppliers would be restored. In NPC models, direct and immediate forward shifting of the tax is possible if firms follow uniform policies of treating the tax as an expense, and either the ratio of tax to sales is relatively uniform among competitors or all follow the pricing policies of high-profit firms. The importance of the satisfactory profit goal increases the likelihood of shifting. Forward shifting produces a burden comparable to that of a nonuniform-rate sales tax.

Generalizations about distributional effects of taxes on wealth and property are difficult because of the diversity of types of wealth subject to tax. Such taxes primarily reduce disposable income in relation to personal wealth owned. The portion of tax on many types of business property will reduce real income relative to the consumption of the products, in fashion similar to that of a nonuniform sales tax.

APPENDIX—EMPIRICAL STUDIES OF DISTRIBUTIONAL EFFECTS

Empirical studies of distributional effects may be grouped into two classes: those that ascertain reactions of commodity and factor prices to particular taxes, and those that measure overall changes in patterns of income distribution resulting from revenue and expenditure measures, given various assumptions about initial price effects. Despite the limitations of the studies, use of this approach, facilitated by continuing refinements in econometric techniques, is imperative if further information is to be gained about the actual distributional effects of present and proposed revenue and expenditure programs.

Price Responses to Sales and Excise Taxation

Empirical studies of price reactions to commodity taxes have been relatively rare, even though initial attempts were made as early as the 1880's. The technique is simple: prices of taxed commodities are compared before and after a tax change. This technique measures only immediate commodity price adjustments and not factor price or longer period adjustments. The major limitation is the inability to isolate the tax influence from other sources of price change. Statements made by business firms at the time of excise tax changes often suggest that the tax has served as a stimulus to make changes that had previously been under consideration; thus the actual change reflects not only the tax influence but that of other accumulated forces as well.

Several studies relate to excise tax changes. Analyses were made of responses of prices of electrical appliances to 1954 legislation that reduced the tax rate from 10 to 5 percent. The studies utilized list prices of manufacturers; while by no means all sales were made at list, the behavior of these prices was a reasonably good measure of overall behavior. A study made at the time with information supplied by manufacturers and mail-order houses indicated that of 274 models, prices were immediately reduced on 94 percent. In addition the data showed strong evidence of pyramiding, especially on larger appliances; the median reduction was 4.8 percent of the retail price, although the tax alone constituted only about 2.5 percent of the price.[8] A study made a decade later by H. L. Johnson[9] with more complete data and a larger number of models (676) showed generally similar results, although with a somewhat smaller percentage of price changes: (91 percent of small appliances, 76 percent of larger) and somewhat less tendency toward pyramiding. The extent of pyramiding was shown to be related to the degree of concentration in the production of the particular model.

Further evidence of the reaction is provided by a study of Bureau of Labor Statistics data of changes in prices of various items affected by the 1954 reductions, as shown in Table 8A–1. These are data of actual, not list, prices. Although the overall price index rose slightly between March and June, 1954, during the period in which the reduction became effective, the indices of the taxed items fell in all instances, and with several types of appliances by percentages in excess of the price reduction.

Following the reduction in excise taxes in 1965, the Council of Economic Advisers requested the Bureau of Labor Statistics to collect detailed information on price responses to tax reductions. A series of reports were issued; one of September 22, 1965, showed that 90 percent of the tax reduction had been reflected in lower prices. On a num-

[8] John F. Due, "The Effect of the 1954 Reduction in Federal Excise Taxes upon the List Prices of Electrical Appliances," *National Tax Journal,* Vol. VII (September, 1954), pp. 222–26.

[9] Harry L. Johnson, "Tax Pyramiding and the Manufacturer's Excise Tax Reduction of 1954," *National Tax Journal,* Vol. XVII (September, 1964), pp. 297–302.

ber of items, such as women's handbags, reductions by the amount of tax were universal. Manufacturers of a few items raised their prices to offset the tax reduction (pens, pencils, matches), but these were of minor consequence in the overall picture. While most retailers passed the tax reduction forward, from 30 to 50 percent of those of electric ranges, movie cameras, and TV tube replacements did not do so. Table 8A–2 summarizes the changes.

TABLE 8A-1

BEHAVIOR OF PRICE INDICES OF ITEMS ON WHICH EXCISE TAXES WERE REDUCED
ON APRIL 1, 1954

	1953				1954			
Commodity	March	June	Sept.	Dec.	March	June	Sept.	Dec.
All items in index.	92.6	93.3	93.9	93.6	93.6	93.8	93.5	93.2
Water heaters	96.6	97.2	97.7	97.7	98.1	96.3	96.3	96.3
Telephone service.	95.0	96.9	98.6	98.6	98.6	93.9	93.9	94.0
Refrigerators.....	149.6	146.6	146.7	144.4	142.1	135.6	135.3	132.4
Ranges..........	101.8	103.7	103.6	104.6	104.8	101.2	100.2	98.2
Toasters.........	134.7	135.1	136.3	136.1	134.6	129.1	129.1	128.3
Fur coats........			123.9	118.6			101.0	98.9
Face cream......	86.6	86.7	86.9	86.9	87.5	80.1	80.2	79.7
Sporting goods...	103.3	103.3	102.3	101.2	101.7	97.5	97.8	97.8

SOURCE: U.S. Department of Labor, Bureau of Labor Statistics, *Consumer Price Index* (1957–59 = 100), *Price Indexes for Selected Items and Groups,* 1947–61.
Compiled by Mrs. Paulette Graziano.

Subsequently two detailed studies were made of the immediate reactions of prices of commodities on which excises had been reduced in 1965. The more extensive study, by O. Brownlee and G. L. Perry, examined Bureau of Labor Statistics price data by commodity class over the period in which the excise reduction became effective.[10] The study concluded that prices of commodities subject to retail excises fell immediately by the amount of the tax, except for admissions and club dues. Prices of goods subject to manufacturers' excises also fell immediately, with a few exceptions, typically by the amount of the tax, with little evidence of pyramiding. The failure to find extensive evidence of pyramiding may be attributed in part to greater encouragement for price increases that other determinants of pricing were giving in 1965 than in 1954. An alternative explanation is that the additional 11 years of operation of the tax may have resulted in squeezing out of more pyra-

[10]Oswald Brownlee and George L. Perry, "The Effects of the 1965 Federal Excise Tax Reduction on Price," *National Tax Journal,* Vol. XX (September, 1967), pp. 235–49.

miding. Finally, the earlier studies were based on list prices, the 1965 study on actual prices, in which less pyramiding would be expected.

TABLE 8A-2

APPROXIMATE PERCENTAGE OF SELLERS WHO PASSED ON FEDERAL EXCISE TAX CUT
BY AUGUST, 1965

| | Retailers* | | | Percentage of |
	Completely Passed on Tax Cut	Partially Passed on Tax Cut	Did not Pass on Tax Cut	Manufacturers Who Passed on Tax Cut
Retailers' excise tax				
Women's handbags.........	100	†	—	—
Men's wristwatches........	100	†	—	—
Home permanent kit.......	95	—	5	—
Manufacturers' excise tax				
New automobiles..........	100	—	—	100
Optional auto equipment				
(factory-installed)........	100	—	†	100
Air conditioners...........	80	†	20	100
Television sets.............	80	†	20	100
Refrigerator-freezers........	75	†	25	100
Ranges...................	60	5	35	100
Movie cameras............	60	5	35	95
Typewriters...............	95	5	†	100
Adding machines...........	95	5	†	100
Small TV replacement tubes.	40	5	55	100
Phonograph records........	n.a.	n.a.	n.a.	‡
Gold equipment...........	n.a.	n.a.	n.a.	30
Pens and mechanical pencils.	n.a.	n.a.	n.a.	0
Matches..................	n.a.	n.a.	n.a.	0
Stamp tax				
Playing cards.............	30	15	55	100

*Based on a nationwide sample of retailers.
†Less than 5 percent.
‡Excise tax was partially passed on by all major manufacturers.
n.a.—Not available.
SOURCE: *Report to the President on Excise Tax Reduction from the Council of Economic Advisers,* September 23, 1965.

The second study was confined to automotive accessories and replacement parts, utilizing price schedules developed and used in the industry.[11] The analysis showed a peculiar result. Prices of about half the items, primarily accessories, were reduced by the pyramided amount of the tax reduction—the same result found in the 1954 study. A group of items periodically replaced, such as spark plugs, showed some down-

[11]F. O. Woodard and Harvey Siegelman, "Effects of the 1965 Excise Tax Reduction Upon the Prices of Automotive Replacement Parts," *National Tax Journal,* Vol. XX (September, 1967), pp. 250–58.

ward adjustment. The prices of irregularly replaced parts remained unchanged. Demand for these items is inelastic without question, and the sellers saw no reason, therefore, to reduce prices at all. This reaction illustrates one of the exceptions noted in preceding sections to the basic NPC shifting model: demand elasticity may affect shifting in some instances. The firms may have been charging the maximum joint profit price before the tax was imposed; they made no increases in prices when the tax went on and did not reduce prices when it was repealed. Or, alternatively, they saw in the tax reduction the possibility of moving closer to the maximum joint profit level.

No study of the reactions of prices to retail sales taxes has been published since the work of Haig and Shoup in the early thirties. The authors of that study obtained information from a number of retailers in New York, Illinois, and Michigan about their responses to the tax. They found that a majority of the retailers were shifting (92 percent) in Detroit and nearly half (47 percent) in Chicago.[12] The New York study showed a lesser tendency to shift, but the rate was lower and the tax thought to be temporary. Separate quotation was much less common in this early period. In more recent years with universal separate quotation casual evidence suggests clearly that (1) retailers do add the full tax to the sale price as a separate item, and (2) they apparently do not make substantial changes in their pretax figures following the introduction of the tax or an increase in the rate.

The Corporation Income Tax—Rate-of-Return Studies

There have been two major approaches to the analysis of reactions to a corporation income tax to determine whether the tax reduces corporate profits or is reflected in the prices of the products with distributional consequences similar to those of a sales tax. The first stresses the behavior of the rate of return to investment capital in the corporate sector, the second, changes in the relative shares of income going to capital and labor.

1. *Earlier Rate-of-Return Studies.* Several studies were made prior to 1960 of the behavior of the rate of return on capital in the corporate sector. For example, the analysis by E. M. Lerner and E. S. Hendriksen showed a relatively constant rate of after-tax return in the period 1927–52, despite a sharp increase in the corporate income tax.[13]

---

[12]R. M. Haig and C. S. Shoup, *The Sales Tax in the American States* (New York: Columbia University Press, 1934).

[13]"Federal Taxes on Corporate Income and the Rate of Return in Manufacturing, 1927 to 1952," *National Tax Journal*, Vol. IX (September, 1956), pp. 193–202.

The before-tax return roughly doubled over the period. The study also showed that the gross rate of return did not adjust immediately to tax changes in either direction.

The Lerner-Hendriksen and similar studies suffer from a basic limitation well recognized by their authors: they do not exclude non-tax influences upon the rate of return on capital. The period following the tax increases of the early forties was one of higher level economic activity than in the previous years. Thus the higher rate of return cannot be attributed to the tax alone. The key question is: how does the rate of return in recent years compare with the figure which would have been attained without the higher taxes?

2. *Krzyzaniak-Musgrave.* In an effort to avoid this limitation, Marion Krzyzaniak and Richard Musgrave sought, in the early sixties, to analyze the problem by an extensive econometric study designed to ascertain the influence of the corporation tax variable on the rate of return. By the use of a profit behavior model and multiple regression techniques they sought to isolate the effects of the corporate tax rate from other exogenous variables influencing the rate of return, comparing the actual return in the 1935–59 period with the figure that would have prevailed without it, other variables being unchanged. This was strictly a short-run analysis, seeking to determine the effects of the tax year by year, by comparing actual behavior with the behavior that the model suggests without the tax element.[14]

The primary conclusion was that the entire corporate tax (not merely the differential over the personal income tax) was fully reflected in prices and thus did not reduce after-tax income of the corporations; in other words the rate of return on capital was maintained at the level that would have prevailed without the tax. The study also reveals a "ratchet" effect; when the tax is reduced the rate of return rises rather than remaining constant. The basic study shows not only full shifting but overshifting to the extent of 34 percent. However, the authors grant that these results overstate actual shifting, partly because of the lag of capital value figures in the face of inflation, and partly because of the correlation between the tax rate and government expenditures produced by the stimulative effect of the latter upon profits. Even with adjustments made for these two considerations, the authors find

---

[14]The other elements in the model are (1) increase in consumption, expressed as a percentage of GNP, for the previous year, (2) ratio of inventory to sales in manufacturing for the previous year, (3) current-year ratio to GNP of all federal, state, and local taxes (excluding the corporation income tax and deducting transfer payments and grants-in-aid to the states).

that the tax is at least fully shifted.[15] A study by Robert W. Kilpatrick of the relationship between increases in rates of return and the concentration ratios in a number of industries during the Korean War period, when the corporate income tax rate rose from 38 to 52 percent, showed a very high correlation, thus substantiating the shifting thesis.[16]

The Krzyzaniak-Musgrave (KM) work has been subjected to substantial criticism. One question centers around the adequacy of the model as a means of isolating the tax influences from those of other variables. In the period under study, there were a number of forces that tended to produce a correlation between tax rates and profit levels; tax rates tend to be high in periods in which forces in the economy make profits high. Operation at a high level of capacity and strong "economic pressure," that is, a high level of aggregate expenditures at full employment, were two such forces. The KM model sought to exclude these other forces, but many critics believe that it did not do so adequately. Working within the KM framework but introducing a cyclical variable (the employment rate) and a dummy variable to represent wartime mobilization, John C. Cragg, Arnold C. Harberger, and Peter Mieszkowski reach the conclusion that the tax is not shifted at all but rests entirely upon capital owners.[17]

Another question is the lack of any similarity between the KM profit behavior model and those developed for other purposes in recent years; several of these appear to explain profit behavior adequately in the period without reference to the corporate tax rate at all.[18]

The Factor Shares Approach

One basic question raised about the KM analysis is that of the appropriateness of behavior of rates of return as a measure of redistributional effects of the tax. A constant after-tax rate of return does not

[15]A study by Karl W. Roskamp of the reactions to the West German corporate income tax, 1949–62, using the KM model, produced similar results. See "The Shifting of Taxes on Business Income: The Case of the West German Corporation," *National Tax Journal*, Vol. XVIII (September, 1965), pp. 247–57.

However, a simpler economic model developed by Gerald Brannon in 1960 showed that the corporate tax had very little influence on before-tax profit behavior. This study was presented to the Econometric Society in 1960, as "Some Investigations on the Incidence of the Corporate Income Tax" (unpublished).

[16]Robert W. Kilpatrick, "The Forward Shifting of the Corporate Income Tax," *Yale Economic Essays*, Vol. V (Fall, 1965), pp. 355–422.

[17]John G. Cragg, Arnold C. Harberger and Peter Mieszkowski, "Empirical Evidence on the Incidence of the Corporation Income Tax," *Journal of Political Economy*, vol. 75 (December, 1967), pp. 811–21.

[18]For a summary, see R. Goode, "Rate of Return, Income Share, and Corporate Tax Incidence," in M. Krzyzaniak (ed.), *Effects of Corporation Income Tax* (Detroit: Wayne State University Press, 1966), pp. 220–21.

demonstrate shifting of the tax if changes in capital-output relationships were tending to raise this ratio during the period. This problem had led to use of the alternative factor shares approach. This approach is based on the assumption that shifting of the tax from corporate owners occurs only if the pretax share of profits in income originating in the corporate sector increases. If it does not, the tax is not shifted, regardless of the behavior of the rate of return.

The first of these factor-share studies, made by M. A. Adelman and published in 1957,[19] concluded that in the period between the twenties and 1946–55, the ratio of total corporate profits (before payment of tax) to GNP originating in the corporate sector remained constant. As a consequence, he concluded that the tax was not shifted.

In the sixties, Challis Hall, Jr.[20] under National Bureau of Economic Research auspices, undertook an econometric study of the behavior in the 1919–59 period of relative factor inputs, factor outputs, and income shares, seeking to determine whether the corporate tax altered these relationships. He employed two highly simplifying assumptions: a Cobb-Douglas production function, involving constant cost, and technological neutrality, that is, that technological change had not altered the relative marginal productivity of capital and labor. He concluded that the actual data agree more closely with those of a non-shifting model than with those of a shifting model. In other words, Hall concluded that the tax does not alter input-output relationships among the various factors and profit receivers do not escape from the tax.

In a more recent study, R. J. Gordon sought to reconcile the two approaches.[21] He used a different model based on markup pricing techniques and included changes in productivity of capital as an input in the analysis. With this model, his analysis shows that the tax was not shifted, on the whole, as determined by either the rate-of-return or share-of-income approaches, although some shifting occurred in particular industries. The rate of return remained relatively constant, but for reasons other than tax shifting; without the tax the rate would have risen. The productivity of capital rose rapidly during the period and the capital-output ratio fell, less capital being needed per unit of out-

[19]M. A. Adelman, "The Corporate Income Tax in the Long Run," *Journal of Political Economy*, Vol. LXV (April, 1957), pp. 151–57.

[20] Challis Hall, Jr., "Direct Shifting and the Taxation of Corporate Profits in Manufacturing, 1919–59," *Proceedings of American Economic Association for 1963*, pp. 258–71.

[21]R. J. Gordon, "The Incidence of the Corporation Income Tax in U.S. Manufacturing, 1925–1962," *American Economic Review*, Vol. LVII (September, 1967), pp. 731–58.

put. Accordingly, the ratio of after-tax profit to income originating in the corporate sector fell even though the rate of return remained constant. Firms were able, through the markup technique, to raise the ratio of profits to sales so as to retain the same ratio of profits to assets. But they were not able to go farther and shift the tax as well, and the share of corporate income minus tax fell. Gordon argues that the KM conclusions are wrong because of the use of a defective model, which resulted in the conclusion that maintenance of the old rate of return on capital was attributable to tax shifting whereas actually it was attributable to other sources.

A Canadian study, using both approaches, concluded that there is substantial evidence of shifting, estimated to be about 70 percent of the tax.[22]

STUDIES OF CHANGES IN INCOME BY INCOME LEVEL

The other type of analysis of distributional effects is concerned with the reduction in income by income class which results from various governmental expenditure and revenue programs. These studies are of necessity based on certain assumptions about the price reactions to the tax: is the income reduction related to all or certain consumption expenditures, to factor incomes, or to profits alone?

The Individual Tax Studies

Several studies have been made of the distribution by income class for individual taxes, and particularly the sales tax, since the distributional pattern is less obvious than with income taxes and the claimed regressivity is the basis of opposition to the tax. The studies assume price increases by the amount of the tax but unchanged factor prices. With this assumption the typical tax burden at each income level is determined from data of consumer expenditures by income level, and these burdens are expressed as ratios of the average incomes of the income groups. Studies of this type have been made for the sales taxes of the United States, Canada, and other countries, and broader studies have included analyses of sales taxes. Typically, the results indicate a regressive relationship of tax to current income if food is taxable; the relationship is more nearly proportional if food is exempt except at the lowest and highest income levels, where some regressivity

---

[22]R. J. Levésque, *The Shifting of the Corporate Income Tax in the Short Run, Studies of the Royal Commission on Taxation*, No. 18 (Ottawa: Queen's Printer, 1965).

is encountered. The explanation is obvious: higher income families save and spend on nontaxable items higher percentages of their incomes than do those in the lower income levels. Figures 8A–1 and 8A–2 give typical examples of these results.[23]

FIGURE 8A–1

PERCENTAGE OF INCOME SPENT ON TAXABLE GOODS
Illinois Sales Tax, 1950 Data

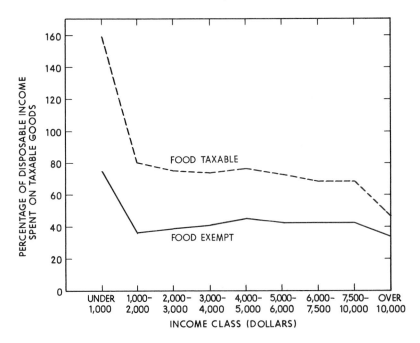

SOURCE: *Study of Consumer Expenditures, Income and Savings*, (Philadelphia: University of Pennsylvania Press, 1955).

The development of the Friedman permanent component doctrine raised doubts about the usefulness of the technique of comparing tax to income at various income levels. Many families in the lower income levels are in these brackets either temporarily or as a result of retirement, and determine their expenditure levels on the basis of income

[23]For examples of other studies, see the article by G. N. Rostvold, "Distribution of Property, Retail Sales, and Personal Income Tax Burdens in California," *National Tax Journal*, Vol. XIX (March, 1966), pp. 38–47, which summarizes the work on the question in California by W. H. Hickman; D. G. Davies, "An Empirical Test of Sales Tax Regressivity," *Journal of Political Economy*, Vol. LXVII (February, 1959), pp. 72–78; J. F. Due, *Provincial Sales Taxes* (rev. ed.; Toronto: Canadian Tax Foundation, 1964), pp. 105–8.

viewed from a longer time point of view—the permanent component. Those with temporarily high incomes behave in similar fashion. If the tax-income ratio is established in terms of permanent income, the sales tax is progressive whether food is exempt or not.[24] While the permanent component doctrine helps to emphasize a relevant issue, there are serious doubts about its overall significance for distributional questions. There are many persons who are permanently poor and many who have high incomes throughout their lives. Furthermore, taxes must be paid out of current income.

FIGURE 8A–2

STATE OF MARYLAND
SALES TAX PAYMENTS AS PERCENT OF MONEY INCOME
By Income Classes, 1961
(Food Exempt)

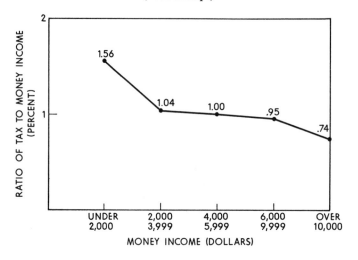

SOURCE: Bureau of Business and Economic Research, University of Maryland, *Maryland Tax Study* (College Park, Md.: 1965), p. 81.

Excises

Few independent studies have been made of distributional effects of excises, outside of the U.S. Treasury, whose conclusions have never been published. Excises have been included, however, in overall studies such as those of Musgrave and Rostvold. The various studies suggest the following conclusions for major excises:

[24]See D. G. Davies, "Commodity Taxation and Equity," *Journal of Finance*, Vol. XVI (December, 1961), pp. 581–90; D. C. Morgan, Jr., *Retail Sales Tax* (Madison, Wis.: University of Wisconsin Press, 1963), chaps. iii, iv.

1. Cigarettes: highly regressive, the most regressive of all major taxes. In the Musgrave study, expenditures on cigarettes as a percentage of income were only one-fifth as great in the highest income bracket as in the lowest.
2. Liquor: progressive relative to income.
3. Beer: slightly progressive in the lower income brackets; regressive in the higher.
4. Motor vehicles: roughly proportional in most brackets; regressive at high levels.

Property Taxation

Many studies have been made of the relationship between property tax payments and income, particularly for residential housing, based upon consumer expenditure surveys. These studies, which are summarized in the recent Brookings Institution volume on property taxation,[25] show the tax to be highly regressive in the lowest income brackets, and with slight regression or near proportionality for the middle- and upper-income segments. Fig. 8A–3 shows the results of a typical study. Similar results, although with continuous regression, are provided by an analysis of property tax deductions shown on federal income tax returns at various income levels. The ratio of property tax to income declines steadily as income rises, from a 4.46 percent figure for the $3,000–$4,000 income class (adjusted gross income) to 1.48 percent for the over-$50,000 income group. Studies that include both tenants and homeowners show progression in the middle-income brackets, a product of the fact that most persons in these brackets are homeowners while those in the lowest brackets are predominantly tenants; the absolute property tax burden of homeowners at a given level is substantially greater than that of tenants. The reason for the regressivity is obvious: housing expenditures do not rise in proportion to current annual incomes as incomes rise, partly because there is little correlation of the need for space with the income level, partly because housing decisions are made at very infrequent intervals.

Devotees of the permanent component doctrine question the significance of the analysis that relates property tax payments to current income on the grounds that housing decisions are made on the basis of long-term income considerations that vary less than year-to-year incomes. Studies by Margaret Reid suggest that the elasticity of housing expenditures relative to "normal" or long-term income is high

---

[25] D. Netzer, *Economics of the Property Tax* (Washington, D.C.: Brookings Institution, 1966), chap. iii.

(around 2.0).[26] Accordingly, property taxes on residential property are distributed in a progressive fashion relative to "permanent income." While the permanent component doctrine is, as noted, open to serious question, it does suggest that the regressivity of the property tax may be regarded as less than the data relative to current income suggest. Many of the low-income, high property tax families consist of older persons living on retirement pensions and accumulated capital, their housing facilities having been acquired in earlier high-income years. Nevertheless current taxes must be paid out of current incomes, and the traditional measures of regressivity are not without significance.

FIGURE 8A–3

RELATIONSHIP OF PROPERTY TAX ON RESIDENTIAL PROPERTY
TO MONEY INCOME

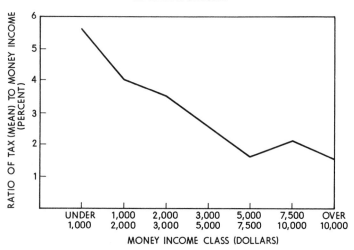

SOURCE: Based upon work of Survey Research Center, presented in D. Netzer, *Economics of the Property Tax* (Washington, D.C.: Brookings Institution, 1966), p. 47.

The portion of the property tax that rests upon business property is likely distributed in a quite different fashion. Various empirical studies have been made, but their results are conditioned to so great an extent by the assumptions made about direct shifting that they lack general acceptability.

Overall Tax Studies

A number of studies have been made of the overall effects of tax structures upon the distribution of income. The significance of the re-

[26]M. G. Reid, *Housing and Income* (Chicago: University of Chicago Press, 1962).

sults is dependent upon the assumptions made about the distributional effects of particular taxes, the corporate income tax and the portion of the property tax on business property being the sources of greatest question. A few major studies will be noted.

1. The most significant pre–World War II studies were those of G. Colm and Helen Tarasov[27] in the United States and Tibor Barna in Great Britain.[28]

FIGURE 8A-4

DISTRIBUTION OF OVERALL TAX BURDEN BY INCOME CLASS,
ALL LEVELS OF GOVERNMENT, UNITED STATES, 1954

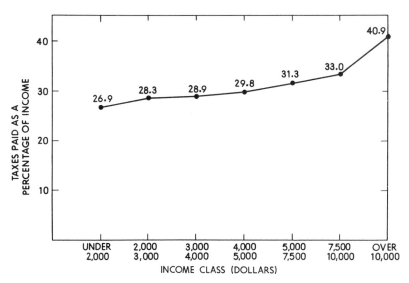

SOURCE: R. A. Musgrave, "The Incidence of the Tax Structure and Its Effects on Consumption," in Joint Committee on the Economic Report, *Federal Tax Policy for Economic Growth and Stability* (Washington, D.C.: U.S. Government Printing Office, 1955), p. 98.

2. In the early fifties, Richard Musgrave and a group of associates at the University of Michigan undertook a detailed study of the question. The first results were published in 1951,[29] with a revised version in 1955.[30] Breakdowns were shown for each major type of tax; the

[27]G. Colm and Helen Tarasov, "Who Pays the Taxes?" *TNEC Monograph No. 3* (Washington, D.C.: U.S. Government Printing Office, 1941).

[28]Tibor Barna, *Redistribution of Incomes Through Public Finance in 1937* (Oxford: Oxford University Press, 1945).

[29]R. A. Musgrave, *et al.*, "Distribution of Tax Payments by Income Groups: A Case Study for 1948," *National Tax Journal*, Vol. IV (March, 1951), pp. 1–53.

[30]R. A. Musgrave, *et al.*, "The *Incidence* of the Tax Structure and its Effects on Consumption," Joint Committee on the Economic Report, *Federal Tax Policy for Economic Growth and Stability* (Washington, D.C.: U.S. Government Printing Office, 1955), p. 98.

FIGURE 8A-5

EFFECTIVE RATES OF CANADIAN TAXES BY INCOME CLASS BY
LEVEL OF GOVERNMENT, 1957

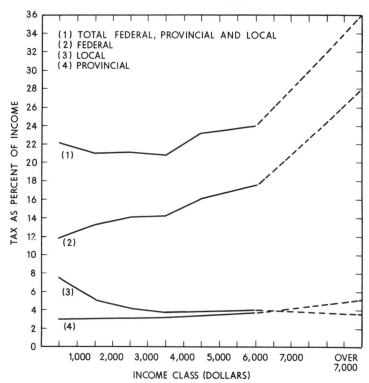

SOURCE: I. J. Goffman, *The Burden of Canadian Taxation* (Toronto: Canadian
Tax Foundation, 1962).

overall pattern, dominated by the federal income tax, is shown on Figure 8A–4. The overall pattern is progressive, with only a slight degree in the lower income levels.

3. A study of the distribution of Canadian taxation by income class by I. J. Goffman, using 1957 data, showed an overall picture comparable to that in the United States, the progressivity of the federal structure overcoming the regressivity and proportionality at the provincial-local level, as shown in Figure 8A–5.[31]

4. A Norwegian study of 1960 data, which compared the actual tax burden at various income levels with a proportional income tax.[32] The tax system was substantially progressive, particularly for married

[31]I. J. Goffman, *The Burden of Canadian Taxation* (Toronto: Canadian Tax Foundation, 1962).

[32]Norway, Statistisk Sentralbyra, *Progressiviteten I Skattesystemet,* (Oslo: 1965).

couples with children, although with a substantial range of proportionality for families without children.

Relatively few expenditure-distribution studies have been made, primarily because of the difficulties of measuring benefits by income class. Apart from those included in the overall studies noted below, the following are typical examples:

1. A study of distribution of benefits from the property-tax-financed activities, made by Netzer,[33] in which he concludes that the distribution of benefits is highly "regressive". By the nature of local government property-tax-financed activities, the lower income groups presumably benefit much more than the higher, relative to income.

2. A study of redistribution of income from public housing expenditures, by Hugh Nourse.[34]

3. Analysis of redistribution of income under the social security system, by Elizabeth Deran.[35]

Overall Tax and Expenditure Studies

Several major attempts have been made to ascertain the overall impact of both expenditure and revenue programs upon the distribution of income.

1. The first was the pioneering study by John Adler, the results of which are shown in Figure 8A–6. The 45° line represents a perfectly equal distribution; the degree of curvature of the line showing the actual pattern of distribution demonstrates the degree of inequality. The line showing the distribution after taxes and benefits from governmental activities are taken into consideration is much closer to the 45° line than the curve of distribution before these items are included. Accordingly, inequality is reduced by the tax and expenditure system. The lowest income groups gained very substantially; the under-$1,000 income class experienced an estimated 73 percent increase in real income as a result of the expenditure-tax program, whereas the over-$7,500 income class experienced a 22 percent decline. In other words, for this group the money values of the benefits received were much less than the taxes paid. The higher income groups experienced a still greater decline. The positions of the income groups between $2,000 and $7,500 were almost unchanged, since the gains from the governmental activities offset the burdens of the taxes.

2. A study by A. M. Cartter, published in 1955, of the effects

[33]Netzer, *op. cit.,* pp. 59–62.

[34]Hugh Nourse, "Redistribution of Income from Public Housing," *National Tax Journal,* Vol. XIX (March, 1966), pp. 27–37.

[35]Elizabeth Deran, "Income Redistribution under the Social Security System," *National Tax Journal,* Vol. XIX (September, 1966), pp. 276–85.

in postwar Britain.[36] Both the tax structure and the pattern of expenditure benefits were found to be highly progressive relative to income, producing a much greater overall redistributive effect than in the United States.

FIGURE 8A–6

REDISTRIBUTION OF INCOME THROUGH THE FISCAL SYSTEM, 1946–47

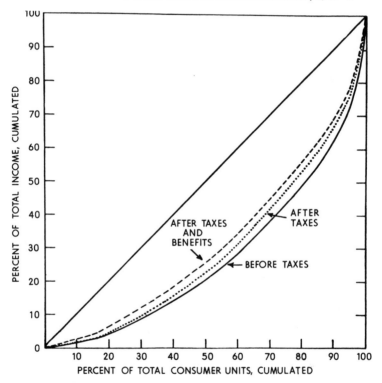

PERCENT OF TOTAL INCOME, CUMULATED

AFTER TAXES AND BENEFITS

AFTER TAXES

BEFORE TAXES

PERCENT OF TOTAL CONSUMER UNITS, CUMULATED

SOURCE: Kenyon E. Poole (ed.), *Fiscal Policies and the American Economy* (copyright, 1951, by Prentice-Hall, Inc., New York), from chap. viii, by John H. Adler, p. 399. Reproduced by permission of the publisher.

3. A 1966 study by W. Irwin Gillespie of the United States,[37] together with one of Canada.[38] As shown in Figure 8A–7, the results

[36]A. M. Cartter, *The Redistribution of Income in Postwar Britain* (New Haven, Conn.: Yale University Press, 1955).

[37]W. Irwin Gillespie, "Effects of Public Expenditures on the Distribution of Income," in R. A. Musgrave (ed.), *Essays in Fiscal Federalism* (Washington, D.C.: Brookings Institution, 1966), pp. 122–86.

[38]W. Irwin Gillespie, *The Incidence of Taxes and Public Expenditures in the Canadian Economy, Studies of the Royal Commission on Taxation,* No. 2. (Ottawa: Queens Printer, 1964).

are different from those of other studies, showing limited redistribution in the lower and the highest income levels. Those in middle-income levels experienced no net gain or loss. In Canada, the poor gain substantially; the rich experiences some net loss.

FIGURE 8A–7

NET REDISTRIBUTIONAL EFFECTS BY INCOME GROUP, 1960

United States

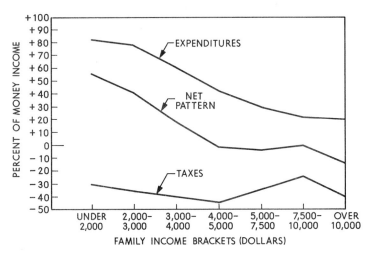

SOURCE: W. Irwin Gillespie, "Effect of Public Expenditure on the Distribution of Income," in R. A. Musgrave (ed.), *Essays in Fiscal Federalism* (Washington, D.C.: Brookings Institution, 1966), p. 165.

The conclusions of these various studies warrant little confidence, since the limitations are so serious:

1. No consideration is given to possible changes in factor prices net of tax.

2. The benefits of many governmental expenditures can be allocated only on an arbitrary basis. Even those such as education conveying significant direct benefits have community benefits as well.

3. The distributional effects of several major taxes, especially the corporate income tax, are not known.

4. The allocation of several major taxes is based primarily upon consumer expenditure surveys, which are by no means entirely reliable. There is a common tendency to understate income and certain types of expenditures, such as those on liquor. Even where there is no deliberate bias, information is often not complete.

REFERENCES

DUE, J. F. "Sales Taxation and the Consumer," *American Economic Review,* Vol. LIII (December, 1963), pp. 1078–84.

HARBERGER, A. C. "The Incidence of the Corporation Income Tax," *Journal of Political Economy,* Vol. LXX (June, 1962), pp. 215–40.

MIESZKOWSKI, P. M. "On the Theory of Tax Incidence," *Journal of Political Economy,* Vol. LXXV (June, 1967), pp. 250–63.

MUSGRAVE, R. A. *The Theory of Public Finance,* chaps. x, xiii, xv, xvi. New York: McGraw-Hill, 1959.

ROLPH, E. R. *The Theory of Fiscal Economics,* chaps. vi, vii. Berkeley: University of California Press, 1959.

Note also the footnote references to the empirical studies.

Chapter 9
STABILIZATION AND GROWTH EFFECTS

The effects of governmental expenditures and revenues upon the level of national income and the rate of growth of the economy are distinct from the allocational and distributional effects although affected by them. These effects are called stabilization and growth effects, or, more simply, *fiscal effects.*

THE MODEL OF NATIONAL INCOME DETERMINATION

Explanation of the effects of government upon national income requires the use of a model of national income determination. The usu-

FIGURE 9-1

EQUILIBRIUM LEVEL OF NATIONAL INCOME

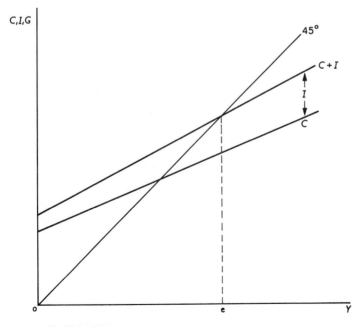

Y: National income.
C: Consumption.
I: Investment.
oe: Equilibrium level of national income.

ally accepted model today is that based upon the work of J. M. Keynes, often referred to as the Keynesian model. In this system, given the rate of money wages and the supply of money, national income attains equilibrium at the level equal to total spending in the economy (consumption *(C)* plus investment *(I)*, ignoring government for the moment). Only at this level will total purchases of final products (consumption and real investment spending) equal the rate of output of final products (consumption goods and capital goods). Equilibrium is thus defined by the equation: $Y = C + I$. The equilibrium is illustrated by the simple diagram on Figure 9–1; $C + I = Y$ at the level of national income at which the $C + I$ line crosses the $45°$ line. At equilibrium, planned savings *(S)* and planned investment *(I)* are of necessity equal; otherwise total spending $(C + I)$ could not equal Y, which equals $C + S$.

Equilibrium and Full Employment

The equilibrium thus determined may be one that allows full employment of all resources whose owners wish to have them employed at current factor prices; in other words there is no continuing unemployment, although on any one day there will be transitional unemployment of persons shifting jobs, laid off because of seasonal fluctuations, and so on, and there may be pockets of unemployment of unskilled or technologically displaced workers. On the other hand, the equilibrium level of income thus defined may be too low to allow employment of all resources (Figure 9–2A). The unemployment would be eliminated if money wage rates and interest rates were flexible downward and investment responsive to interest rate changes. The unemployed would offer to work for lower wages; prices would fall and reduce the transactions demand for money and the interest rate, and stimulate investment. The adjustment would be facilitated by the wealth or "Pigou" effect: as the price level and interest rates fell the value of most forms of accumulated wealth would rise relative to income and persons would be encouraged to save less and consume more.

Unfortunately, the assumptions of flexible money wage and interest rates are not realistic. Money wages are resistant to downward adjustments, particularly with unions but even without, as are many commodity prices. From all indications interest rates cannot fall indefinitely because of the "liquidity trap"; below a certain figure persons seek to hold their wealth in money form rather than making it available for investment because the compensation for parting with it is too low. Investment appears to be relatively unresponsive to declines in the in-

terest rate, especially in a period of unemployment in which many firms
have excess plant capacity. The decline in the price level in itself tends
to discourage investment as long as the decline is expected to continue; firms delay investment in the expectation that prices will fall
still more.

FIGURE 9–2A

EQUILIBRIUM WITH UNEMPLOYMENT

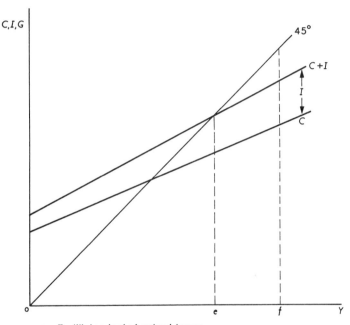

oe: Equilibrium level of national income.
of: Full-employment level of national income.

Accordingly, the economy may stabilize below full-employment
levels, as it did in the thirties and to a lesser extent in the early sixties.
Unemployment equilibrium can be attributed basically to inadequate
investment opportunities relative to the amounts that persons wish to
save at full employment. Or, alternatively, the difficulty may be stated
in terms of inadequate consumption and therefore excessive savings
relative to investment opportunities. At full employment, total spending—$C + I$—is inadequate to buy all goods that the economy is capable of producing at this level of national income, and output must
fall to restore equilibrium.

On the other hand, at full employment $C + I$ may exceed total
output (Y) which, by definition of full employment, cannot increase

except over time as resources increase and technology improves. Accordingly, prices are raised by excessive demand arising out of the inflationary gap; persons are seeking to buy more goods than are or can be produced, and prices are bid up (otherwise, shortages would appear). Ultimately, however, as prices rise, equilibrium is restored by the rise in interest rates caused by the increase in total dollar value of transactions and, perhaps, by the influence of higher prices in discouraging purchasing. Figure 9–2B shows the new equilibrium position.

FIGURE 9–2B

INFLATION

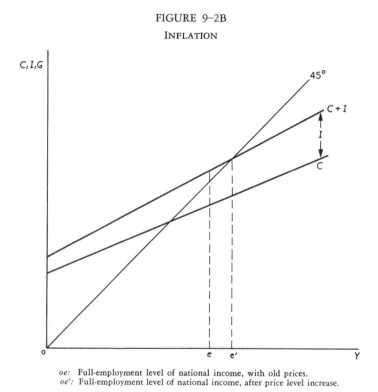

oe: Full-employment level of national income, with old prices.
oe': Full-employment level of national income, after price level increase.

In the earliest simplified models of national income determination, the assumption was typically made that an increase in $C + I$ would affect only output so long as full employment had not been reached; once this point was attained, excess of $C + I$ over Y would have full impact on prices, since output could no longer rise. This conclusion was based upon the assumption that output of goods was perfectly elastic throughout the economy until full employment was reached; at this point it became perfectly inelastic. This was an oversimplification. As outputs of various industries continue to increase, increasing costs will be encountered; firms will operate beyond the point of lowest average cost and will lack sufficient time to increase plant capacity. Time is inadequate for new firms to enter the industry. Some industries will reach full capacity before others. Accordingly, some prices rise and the general price level will commence to increase before full employment is attained.

A significant modification in the analysis reveals another source of inflation. We have assumed thus far that money wage rates are given, except as they may be forced up by demand-supply relationships at full employment. Labor markets, however, are not perfectly competitive. Strong labor unions may succeed in pushing money wage rates upward by amounts in excess of increases in productivity per worker even if full employment is not attained, but particularly as full employment is approached. With typical present-day markup methods of pricing, wage increases are reflected directly and immediately in price increases, and in some instances in amounts in excess of the wage increases because of application of percentage markups to higher purchase prices (in the same fashion that manufacturers sales taxes are pyramided). This source of inflation is often called "cost-push." Because of wage reactions attainment of both full employment and price stability may be impossible, and society must accept some unemployment to keep inflation to a tolerable rate.

Determinants of the Allocation of Income between Savings and Consumption

Analysis of the determinants of the two elements in total spending, C and I, is necessary to complete the explanation of the national income model, as a basis for explaining the reaction to governmental expenditure and revenue.

The overall allocation of income between consumption and savings is dependent upon the relative preferences that persons have for present consumption and future availability of funds. While motives for present consumption are relatively simple and obvious, those for future availability are complex.

First, the goal of accumulation may be a specific objective. Future availability is frequently desired as a reserve for use in emergency, arising either from unexpected decline in income or unexpected increase in expenditure needs, due, for example, to illness or accident. The person does not necessarily expect to consume the amounts; he merely wishes to have them available in the event of need. Alternatively, saving may be motivated by desire for specific future consumption. Education of children is a purpose of major importance for the overall volume of saving, as is the financing of consumption during retirement years when income is low. In some instances a person accumulates to make an expensive purchase: a new car, a trip around the world, in some societies a wife. Closely related is the goal of accumulation of funds to bequeath to heirs.

Some persons save for the purpose of increasing future income, through financial or real investments. While all savings, regardless of motive, will increase income if placed in investments other than cash, only a small portion of savings is apparently motivated directly by this goal. The motive is particularly important for operators of small businesses, including farmers; evidence shows these persons to have relatively high S/Y ratios compared to others with comparable incomes, as they save to provide funds for real investment in their businesses.[1]

Savers influenced by specific motives for accumulation may be *calculating* savers who carefully balance relative advantages of present consumption and future accumulation of funds, or they may be *target* savers, seeking to save a specific sum for future use or to attain a specific income in the future; a special case is the family that saves only enough to meet specific savings commitments such as life insurance premium payments. The final group consists of *residual* savers. Some—descendants of Silas Marner—prefer accumulation to present consumption simply because they enjoy accumulating money per se, in place of collecting stamps, old paintings, or rare books; they consume a bare minimum and save the rest. Other persons spend as much as they wish on consumption and save the residual with no particular purpose in mind.

Circumstances Affecting Savings Patterns. A number of circumstances affect a person's allocation of income between consumption and savings. The level of current income relative to expenditure needs is significant. In general, the higher the income, the greater is the margin over and above the expenditure level regarded as essential, although there are many individual exceptions. Families in the lowest income groups typically dissave, spending more than their incomes. These persons do not have sufficient income to maintain minimum living standards or ones they regard as imperative. No family can continue to spend more than its income indefinitely, but many families in the lower levels are so located only temporarily and thus can spend in excess of

---

[1]See R. Ferber, "Research on Household Behavior," *American Economic Review,* Vol. LII (March, 1962), pp. 33–34.

income for a considerable period of time. Many elderly families deliberately use up their wealth.

Evidence indicates that both average and marginal propensities to consume fall as incomes rise, although to a lesser extent than was long believed.[2] The available data are by no means entirely satisfactory. Table 9–1 reproduces data presented by Goode, based on an article by Lansing and Lydall. Studies by Musgrave[3] and U.S. Bureau of Labor Statistics data show comparable results.[4]

TABLE 9–1

DISPOSABLE INCOME AND SAVING, BY MONEY INCOME
DECILES, 1950

Money Income Decile	Mean Disposable Income (1)	Average Saving Ratio (3)
Lowest.....................	$ 479	−88.9%
2nd......................	1,112	− 4.0
3rd......................	1,653	0.2
4th......................	2,121	1.0
5th......................	2,635	[− 0.8]
6th......................	3,089	3.6
7th......................	3,568	[7.2]
8th......................	4,122	7.5
9th......................	4,957	11.1
Highest....................	$8,606	23.5

SOURCE: R. Goode, *The Individual Income Tax* (Washington, D.C.: Brookings Institution, 1964), p. 335, based on data in the article by John B. Lansing and Harold Lydall, "An Anglo American Comparison of Personal Saving," *Bulletin, Oxford University Institute of Statistics,* Vol. XXII (August, 1960), p. 242.

A person's estimate of a "necessary" level of consumption is influenced by many elements, material and psychological. The extent to which the family has already accumulated consumer durables is a major element, as well as the number and ages of the children and

[2]As real income has risen over the years, the overall S/Y ratio has not risen, remaining remarkably stable, between 18 and 20 percent. In other words, as general income levels rise, expenditures keep pace with them. The statement in the text above refers to a cross-section analysis at a particular time.

See S. Kuznets, *Modern Economic Growth* (New Haven, Conn.: Yale University Press, 1966), p. 237.

[3]R. A. Musgrave, "Effects of Tax Policy on Private Capital Formation," *Fiscal and Debt Management Policies, Research Studies for Commission on Money and Credit* (Englewood Cliffs, N.J.: Prentice-Hall, Inc., 1963), pp. 145–47.

[4]U.S. Bureau of Labor Statistics, *Consumer Expenditures and Income, Urban United States, 1960–61* (April, 1964).

other dependents and the standard to which the person has become accustomed. Families strongly resist reductions in their living standards. Age plays a part; older persons are less concerned about increases in standards than are younger families.

Savings-consumption behavior is also influenced by the attitudes of persons toward the future, their estimates of future needs and incomes, and the extent to which they have already accumulated for the future, that is, their present assets. Some attach great importance to security, to responsibility for dependents, to education of their children and bequests to them, and to the ability to support themselves in old age. Other persons are content to live from day to day. Estimates of future needs, for example, the costs of educating children and living during retirement, and of retirement income from other sources influence their desire to save, as does the present value of their assets relative to their incomes and estimates of future needs.[5] The relationship between present and estimated future cost of a given real income is also relevant; an expected rise in prices gives incentive to consume now; an expected fall in prices tends to increase current saving.

Finally, persons may be influenced by the return on money capital; the higher the return, the greater the gain from saving, in terms of future real income or accumulated sum, relative to sacrifice of present consumption. On the other hand, the sum required to attain a given retirement income or other specific objective in the future is reduced.

Calculating savers will increase savings in response to a higher rate of return, since the compensation for forgoing present consumption is greater, unless the income effect of the higher return outweighs the substitution effect.[6] Target savers reduce savings if the return is higher, since less is needed to accomplish their objective. Residual savers are not affected at all by the rate of return.

A portion of total savings is made directly by corporations rather than individuals; in a sense corporate savings represent collective savings on the part of stockholders, but the decisions are made by corporate management. The choice between paying out earnings as dividends and holding them is based upon the desirability of keeping additional earnings for reserve and real investment, on the one hand, and the desire to keep the stockholders satisfied, on the other. The more attractive the real investments, the greater will be the incentive

---

[5] See Ferber, *op. cit.*

[6] J. R. Hicks and others argue that income effects of prospective lenders and borrowers tend to cancel out, leaving only the substitution effect. See R. Goode, *The Individual Income Tax* (Washington, D.C.: Brookings Institution, 1964), p. 330.

to hold additional amounts and the higher the overall S/Y ratio of the economy.

In summary: the S/Y ratio is not significantly affected by the level of the rate of return. Some persons will save less if the rate falls; some will save more; many are not affected.

The Volume of Investment

The volume of real investment—the purchase of new capital goods—is controlled by several major determinants:

1. Marginal productivity, or earnings from acquisition of additional capital goods. This, in turn, is dependent upon present and expected changes in the stock of capital goods compared to other resources, the rate of technological change, and changes in the level of national income.

If the stock of capital goods is rising relative to other resources, other determinants given, the marginal earnings from additional capital will fall because of the Law of Diminishing Returns. Rapid increase in availability of natural resources or in the supply of skilled manpower will raise the marginal earnings from capital and increase investment. The more rapid the rate of technological change, the greater the profitability of investment opportunities, since a substantial portion of all investment is undertaken to embody technological change. The nature of the change is also significant; some technological developments are capital-saving, others labor-saving. The latter result in a relatively greater volume of investment. Changes in the level of national income affect the profitability of investment through the accelerator effect; increased output of consumption goods increases the profitability of investment in capital equipment to produce them.

The profitability of additional capital goods is also affected by the cost of the capital goods; the lower the cost the greater the earnings per dollar of investment, given the level of other variables.

2. The degree of certainty of expectations about future earnings. The greater the doubt, the less willing firms are to invest.

3. The availability and cost of money capital. Capital owned by a firm, arising, for example, out of retained earnings, is particularly significant because of the reluctance of many firms to borrow or sell additional stock, or the impossibility of their doing so. The significance of interest cost for investment is not clear, although many studies, analytical and empirical, suggest that it is not highly important. Marginal investment appears to be a relatively small portion of the total. Much investment is undertaken with internal capital not di-

rectly subject to an interest rate. Other investment is so highly profitable that usual changes in the rate have little effect. Sharp increases in interest rates and lessened availability of money capital in 1966–67 had primary impact upon building construction financed largely by borrowing, and limited effect upon industrial investment.

Finally, gross investment is dependent upon the size of the existing stock of capital equipment and the average life of the equipment, which determine the rate of replacement of old capital equipment by new.

THE INFLUENCE OF GOVERNMENTAL EXPENDITURES AND REVENUES

Given the level of national income (Y) and the basic wage rate and price level, the introduction of government into the analysis may alter the level of national income in real terms and the general price level in several potential ways:

1. By directly altering aggregate spending ($C + I + G$) through its own spending (G).

2. By affecting private consumption (C), by altering:
   a) Funds available for C.
   b) Relative preferences for savings (S) and consumption (C).
   c) Expectations of future prices.

3. By affecting private investment (I), by altering:
   a) Supply of money capital available.
   b) Willingness of persons to take the risk of supplying money capital for I.
   c) C, since volume of sales is a major determinant of I.
   d) The direct net return from I, given the level of C.
   e) Expectations about future returns from I.
   f) Rate of technological change.
   g) Supplies of other factors.

4. By altering the basic wage rate, a determinant of the price level.

A given net initial change in total spending will alter national income by the magnitude of the *multiplier,* equal to the reciprocal of MPS (marginal propensity to save). The multiplier is defined as the numerical relation between an increase in spending and the consequent increase in national income. For equilibrium, planned S and planned I must be equal. Any change in total spending will destroy this relationship; an initial rise in aggregate spending will cause an equivalent excess of I over S, and S must rise until it again equals I. If persons on the whole are saving one fourth of additional income (MPS $= \frac{1}{4}$), Y must rise by four times for S to rise by the amount of the increase in I.

This framework provides the basis for examining effects of government expenditures and revenues on national income.

Governmental Spending and the Equilibrium Level of National Income

Purchase of goods and services by governments constitutes a form of spending on final products (G), and therefore is added to total private spending in the national income determination model; the basic equation becomes: $C + I + G = Y$. Transfer payments by govern-

FIGURE 9–3

EQUILIBRIUM, WITH GOVERNMENT SPENDING

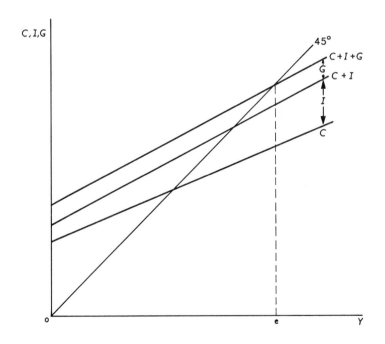

ments merely shift money from some persons to others and do not directly enter into spending in the national income equation. Thus on the national income diagram (Figure 9–3), the significant line for determination of equilibrium is $C + I + G$; the intersection of this line with the 45° line indicates the equilibrium position.

An increase in G, so long as it does not lower C and I, will raise Y by the amount determined by the multiplier. Increased governmental spending directly increases incomes; in turn, individuals spend more and output of consumption goods rises. Equality of S and I, necessary for equilibrium, is destroyed, and Y must rise sufficiently to restore equality.

The rise in Y is likely to stimulate some increase in I—the accelerator effect—and the multiplier effect will operate on this increase as well. Thus the final increase in Y will be greater than that indicated by the application of the multiplier to the increase in G. This analysis ignores effects of income taxation in absorbing a portion of the increased income, which will restrict the rise in Y.

The increase in governmental spending may give rise to changes in C and I other than those arising through the multiplier and accelerator effects. First the ratios of C and S to Y may be altered. If the additional government spending results in increased production of goods yielding direct benefits to individuals, such as education, which are substituted for private-sector output, persons will lessen consumption and increase savings, thus reducing the net increase in national income —2a.[7] If the governmental goods are ones that would otherwise be acquired from the private sector in the future (education for one's children) the effect will be the reverse; persons will feel less obligation to save and will increase consumption.

Governmental spending may affect I by altering expectations about the future (apart from the effects of the financing noted below) —3e. If the expenditures are undertaken for activities competitive with the private sector (power plants, river improvements) uncertainty will be increased and profit expectations reduced and I will fall. If the activities are regulatory in nature the effect may be even greater.

Transfer spending by governments, such as welfare payments, does not in itself constitute an element in G or $C + I + G$. The recipients, however, may increase their own spending, and thus increase C and I. If the payments are of welfare nature the primary impact is on C, because MPC of welfare recipients is likely to be high. The higher the average income of the recipients, the smaller the impact on C and the larger the possible impact on I. Thus retirement of bonds held by high-income groups will have little or no effect on C at all but may facilitate I by increasing equity investments. The establishment of wel-

[7]Numbers refer to number in list of determinants of Y, p. 246.

fare programs may alter preferences between savings and consumption, reducing S/Y as persons have less need to accumulate for the future.

Taxation, Savings, and Consumption

When a government increases its total spending, the funds must be obtained from some source; the revenue, in turn, may affect C and/or I. We will first consider the effects of taxation, and subsequently of borrowing and money creation. Taxation may affect the S/Y and C/Y ratios and the volume of investment.

Absorption Effect—2a. The first and most obvious influence of taxation is the "absorption" effect: taxes lessen the amounts persons have available for savings and consumption and force a reduction in either or both, the relative reductions depending on relative MPS and MPC figures. Let us ignore for a moment the effects of the tax upon the relative advantages of saving and consuming. If the person is not saving or is saving less than his tax, he has no alternative but to reduce consumption, unless he is willing temporarily to go into debt or to use reserves. Target-return savers will act in the same fashion, if they hold strictly to their savings goals; the entire reduction will occur in consumption. On the other hand, if savings are sufficiently great the person may absorb the entire amount of the tax from them. This last approach will be followed by the residual savers, whose relative preferences are not affected by the tax.

As a consequence, taxes that concentrate primarily upon the lower income groups and persons in groups spending high percentages of their income will primarily reduce consumption. Sales taxes and payroll taxes with low cutoff points are major examples. By comparison, progressive income taxes will be borne out of savings to a greater extent, since a larger portion of tax will be borne in income levels in which the propensity to save is high. The difference, however, is not as great as might be anticipated because the propensity to save apparently does not rise rapidly with increases in income. Goode concludes that, with 1950 data, 33 percent of the federal income tax was absorbed out of savings, as contrasted to 28 percent of a proportional rate income tax and 27 percent of a flat rate consumption tax.[8]

A tax on corporations, if not shifted forward to consumers of products and not reflected in lower dividends, must be borne entirely out of savings, since a corporation does not consume. In practice, divi-

---

[8] Goode, *op. cit.,* p. 67.

dends and thus the incomes of the stockholders may be affected to some extent. High-income stockholders may encourage the corporation to hold earnings instead of distributing them so as to benefit through the favorable treatment of capital gains.[9]

Relative Preferences for Consumption and Saving. Taxes may also affect the relative real gains from consumption and saving—2b. A tax on all income reduces the return on savings and thus the net gain from giving up present consumption for accumulation. The *calculating* saver is subject to the usual two influences: the income effect, which leads him to save more to restore his income, and the substitution effect, which encourages him to consume more and save less, since the reward for saving is less. Both income and substitution effects are relevant in evaluating the effects of the overall expenditure and revenue program; generalization about the relative significance of each is not possible. When comparison is being made among the effects of alternative forms of taxation, the income effect ceases to be relevant, since all taxes, by reducing income, will have this effect. For this comparison, the substitution effect is dominant and an income tax, which directly reduces the return from additional saving, is likely to lessen savings more than a sales tax, which has a less direct impact on the return and can be avoided so long as the person continues to accumulate. The more progressive the income tax, the greater is the difference in effect, as the greater is the reduction in the gain from additional saving. If a person saves solely with the intent of purchasing consumption goods in the future and the sales tax is expected to be permanent, the effect will be similar to that of a proportional income tax, except for the delay in payment that the sales tax permits. A wealth tax may have even greater effect in reducing preference for savings, since its impact is entirely upon sums saved. Since the base is very broad, including all wealth accumulated in the past as well as newly made savings, however, the tax rate necessary to raise a given sum is lower than that of an income tax.

Target savers seeking to accumulate a sum sufficient to attain a specific level of real income or to finance specific real purchases or bequests in the future will tend to save more as a consequence of any change that reduces their ability, at present savings rates, to attain their goals. Income taxes, which reduce the return on their savings, and sales taxes, which make the attainment of the future objectives more

[9]See John A. Brittain, *Corporate Dividend Policy* (Washington, D.C.: Brookings Institution, 1966).

expensive in real terms, will both raise S/Y. If the future objective is viewed in terms of a given sum of money, the income tax will lead the savers to raise S/Y, the sales tax will not. Preferences of residual savers are not affected by taxes; taxes will be absorbed entirely from savings so long as they do not exceed savings in amount.

Taxes will alter the relative advantages of present and future consumption if the tax rates are expected to be different in the future—2c. If a consumption-related tax is believed to be temporary, incentive is given to defer purchases until sometime in the future when the tax is no longer in operation. A progressive-rate spendings tax would have strong effects of this type. If the tax is believed to be temporary and is steeply progressive according to the amount spent, it can discourage inflation-stimulating consumption drastically. This tax, unlike most, is not limited to a rate under 100 percent; the rate could go to 1,000 percent or any desired figure on consumption spending in larger amounts.

Taxes related to specific uses of savings will alter the relative advantages of savings for these purposes. The best example is a tax on bequests (inheritance or estate tax); if a person knows that the bequest will be taxed heavily he may be less interested in saving to be able to make the bequest (as would obviously be true if the death tax rate were 100 percent). On the other hand, if he follows a target approach, seeking to bequeath, net of tax, a certain sum, the tax will lead him to save more rather than less.

Money Illusion.   The relative effects of different taxes may be affected by the *money illusion.* A person may become accustomed to spending a certain amount of money on consumption regardless of the price level and may continue to do so after a sales or excise tax is imposed. Accordingly, he absorbs all of the tax out of consumption, his savings remaining unchanged. If this reaction is significant, consumption-related taxes will have even more effect in reducing consumption than otherwise.

Summary of Tax Effects.   1.   All taxes reduce capacity to save and consume; given consumption and savings preferences, a substantial portion must be absorbed from consumption spending, perhaps 70 percent. However, the overall S/Y ratio will be reduced, since the percentage of tax absorbed from savings is presumably greater than the percentage of income saved, because MPS and tax liability rise as income rises.

2.   The relative effects of different taxes depend primarily upon the distributional effect by income group, since the propensity to save

rises with the income level. Thus a progressive tax will be absorbed from savings to a greater extent than a proportional or regressive tax.

3. A corporation income tax will reduce savings more than most taxes, so long as it is not shifted forward, because most of the tax is likely to be absorbed from retained earnings, which of necessity are saved.

4. With most taxes, the effects on relative *incentives* to consume and save are probably not great. A proportional income tax gives a slight incentive to calculating savers to save less because the gain is reduced, while target savers will save more to attain given objectives. Residual savers will not be affected. A consumption tax will have the opposite effect, favoring accumulation and providing a slight gain from postponement of consumption. A consumption tax, particularly a high-rate excise on consumer durables or a progressive spendings tax believed to be temporary, may have significant positive influence on savings. The money illusion may also increase the effect of an excise or sales tax in restricting consumption.

5. A tax on wealth, although penalizing the saver, may give less encouragement to curtail saving than an income tax since the rate affecting marginal savings is less.

6. A once-and-for-all capital levy would increase the incentive to save as persons sought to restore their accustomed ratios of assets to income. Belief that the levy will be repeated will have the opposite effect.

7. Death taxes probably reduce savings more than any other tax, per dollar of revenue, since they concentrate on the higher income groups and are most likely to be paid by the heirs out of the sum received. Heirs are unlikely to reduce their consumption to pay the tax. The existence of a death tax will lead some persons to seek to save more to bequeath, others to save less.

Taxation and Real Investment

Taxation affects real investment in several ways:

1. Availability and costs of money capital—3a, b. All taxes take funds from business firms and individuals that would otherwise be available for investment and reduce the actual amount of real investment, if it is closely restricted by funds available. Thus taxes, in reducing savings, may also reduce investment, although this result will not follow if the persons who would otherwise save these amounts did not make them available for real investment. Of the major levies, the corporate income tax and the portion of the personal income tax applying to the owners of noncorporate businesses would appear to have

the greatest impact on investment, because the availability of these funds determines the ability of businesses to expand without resorting to outside capital. The personal income tax with progressive rates is also likely to have greater impact than consumption-based taxes, by reducing the amounts of money capital wealthy families have available to place in equity investments and by facilitating real investment. Estate taxes have the same effect, taking substantial sums from wealthy groups more prone to risky investments.

Taxes also may have some effect in lessening the willingness of persons with liquid wealth to make it available for real investment, as explained in Chapter 7. With loss offset, however, this influence is not likely to be great.

2. Earnings from additional investment—3c, d. Taxes may affect the marginal earnings from additional investment in two ways: through the accelerator effect by reducing consumption, and by absorbing a portion of additional earnings made. Taxes on sales or lower bracket incomes have the greatest effect, per dollar of revenue, on consumption and thus on I via the accelerator reaction; personal and corporate income taxes have the greatest effect in absorbing a portion of profits. An investment expected to yield 10 percent before tax will yield only about 5 percent after corporation income tax, if the tax is not shifted. The responsiveness of I to changes in the prospective rate of return is not known; loss offset reduces the impact.

As noted in Chapter 7, the significance of income taxes for the net gain from investment is dependent upon the depreciation treatment allowed for tax purposes. An investment tax credit reduces the cost of new capital goods and increases the yield accordingly; accelerated depreciation reduces the overall capital costs as the investment can be recovered tax-free at an earlier date. The Hall-Jorgensen study indicates that changes in depreciation provisions have substantial impact upon investment decisions.[10]

3. Certainty—3e. Taxes may affect the certainty of expected returns. Rigid restrictions on depreciation deductions, for example, lessen the certainty of recovering capital tax-free.

The Overall Fiscal Effects of Governmental Expenditures and Taxes

The net fiscal effect of the overall program of governmental expenditures and taxes is the composite of the effects of the various indi-

---

[10]R. E. Hall and D. W. Jorgensen, "Tax Policy and Investment Behavior," *American Economic Review*, Vol. LVII (June, 1967), pp. 391-414.

vidual expenditures and taxes in the structure. In general, expenditures are expansionary, adding to total spending; taxes are contractionary, reducing C and I. Equality of revenues and expenditures, or equal increases in expenditures and tax revenues from an equilibrium situation, is not necessarily neutral in its effect on the level of national income. The effects of the expenditures and revenues do not necessarily balance merely because the totals are equal in magnitude. The exact effect depends upon the nature of the taxes and the effects they have upon C and I. At the one extreme, a progressive spendings tax might curtail spending by an amount substantially in excess of the tax revenue collected; a progressive income tax with impact confined to the higher income groups and paid primarily out of accumulated savings without restrictive effect on investment would have little contractionary effect and the overall program would increase C + I + G by virtually the full magnitude of G. Broad-based income taxes probably have greater impact on investment and less on consumption than general sales taxes, but the latter, while placing no direct burden on the returns from investment, may, by restricting consumption, reduce investment as much or more. There is no obvious advantage of one over the other.

It is often argued that a balanced budget or an equal increase in expenditures and revenues is certain to have a net expansionary effect because the entire sum of the government spending constitutes an element in total spending, whereas some of the tax revenue, coming from savings otherwise idle, will not directly reduce consumption or investment. This rule is not necessarily valid. Taxes that sharply reduce present and future earnings from investment or give persons strong incentive to curtail C may reduce C + I more than the amount of G. This is unlikely, however, with usual taxes.

Budget Deficits and Borrowing

If tax revenues fall behind expenditures, the difference must be made up by borrowing or money creation. Borrowing is almost certain to reduce savings more and consumption less than taxation. Families spending high percentages of their income—those in the lower income groups particularly—must reduce their consumption when the tax method is used (or go into debt, which they will be unlikely or unable to do for any lengthy period), but are unaffected by governmental borrowing. Target savers will reduce consumption to meet tax obligations, and other savers are likely to reduce consumption to some extent. By contrast, since persons buy bonds voluntarily, the availability of additional government bonds is unlikely to cause them to alter consumption. Only if the government bonds have some unique feature that makes them more attractive than existing forms of financial investments could their issuance increase the S/Y ratio.

The relative effects of borrowing and taxation on I are less clear. Taxes may reduce I by altering the net return and the availability of money capital; borrowing does so only by absorbing funds and by reducing confidence of businessmen in the future. If the deficit and resort to borrowing create serious fear about higher taxes in the future or "government bankruptcy," I may be reduced drastically, even more so than by taxes. The net effect depends primarily on popular reactions to deficit financing.

On the whole, a program of government spending financed by borrowing is almost certain to be more expansionary than one (with the same G) financed by taxation, except in the event of drastic adverse effect of the borrowing upon business confidence.

Economic Significance of the Debt

Distinct from the effects of borrowing are those of existence of the debt once it is created.

The fiscal effects of governmental debt are influenced by the possibility of a fiscal illusion relating to the debt. Persons who own government bonds regard them as personal wealth, which most certainly they are. If persons as taxpayers regard the debt as a source of future obligations and discount these back to the present, the sum would equal the current value of the debt[11] and the total net personal wealth of the country would appear neither greater nor less than it would be without the debt. Do people do so? Apparently most do not, and thus the personal net wealth of the country appears to society to be greater by the amount of the debt. Apart from the purely illusory aspects, persons are inclined to minimize the significance of future tax liability, partly because they do not know precisely what their own liability will be, partly because they, as a group, hope that other persons may share a portion of the burden. This fiscal illusion and deemphasis of future burdens will, under the assumption that current rates of savings are influenced by the total value of existing assets, reduce the volume of saving and facilitate attainment of full employment, but it will encourage inflation once full employment is attained. The high liquidity of governmental debt facilitates a sharp rise in consumption as occurred at the outbreak of the Korean War in 1950.

---

[11]With the assumption of a discount rate equal to the interest rate on the bonds.

The debt not only increases the propensity to consume but also may encourage investment by reducing the cost of money capital on an equity basis. The existence of a large quantity of government debt will lead to a reduction in the required yield on equity investments as persons seek more of the latter—given their relative overall preferences for government debt and equities. The lower required return on equities makes investment more advantageous.

The overall effect of the debt upon I also depends upon the attitudes of the business community toward the significance of the debt in the future. If there is great fear about the consequences, uncertainty will be increased and I reduced, just as it will be by borrowing itself. Today the fear of the debt appears to be negligible; in the thirties the fear was much greater, although the debt was only a small fraction of the present figure.

A final consequence of the governmental debt is the possible effect of interest and/or principal payments upon $C + I$. Taxes are normally used to meet the interest obligations and to provide funds for retirement of the debt, if retirement is undertaken. The effects of taxes upon C and I incentives are not offset by the receipt of the interest and principal payments by the bondholders, and thus any depressing effects of the taxes upon $C + I$ will reduce the level of national income. Only if the interest and retirement program transfers money to persons with higher propensities to consume and to invest than the taxpayers will it have a net expansionary effect.

Local debt may have somewhat similar, and less groundless, effects on expectations and thus upon investment in the area. Large debt relative to that of other local units may discourage industrial, commercial, and residential investment. The net effect is influenced by the purposes for which the money was borrowed.

Money Creation

If the government simply produces the money with which to increase its spending, there is no curtailment of private funds available for consumption and investment. Therefore $C + I$ can remain the same as G increases. Money creation, however, may alter $C + I$ by changing expectations about the future. If the business community greatly fears the ultimate consequences of money creation and thus uncertainty increases, investment may be reduced. The fear may be irrational, but nevertheless it may be very real and influence behavior. If consumers and businessmen believe that money creation will generate inflation, the effects will be the reverse; consumption and investment spending will increase immediately in anticipation of the price increases. In a full-employment situation this reaction could lead to open-end—run-away—inflation. Spending can increase so rapidly that it feeds on itself since no one wishes to hold money or fixed-money-value investments, and prices rise progressively faster.

Financing by money creation has one further expansionary effect; by increasing commercial bank reserves it increases the ability of the banks to expand loans and encourages private investment. This effect can be offset by appropriate monetary policy to prevent net increases in reserves.

The Consequences for National Income

In a period of unemployment, with national income below the full-employment level, a governmental budget with a net expansionary

FIGURE 9–4

EQUILIBRIUM, WITH GOVERNMENT SPENDING AND TAXES

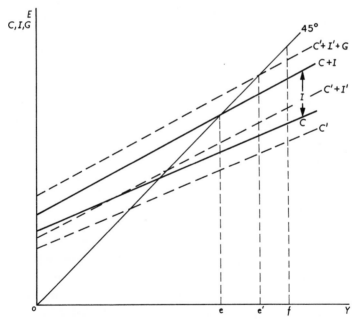

oe: Equilibrium level of national income, before governmental program.
oe′: Equilibrium level of national income, after governmental program.
of: Full-employment level of national income.
′:   Indicates level after taxes.

effect will raise the level of national income toward the full-employ-ment level, as shown on Figure 9–4. Increase in G raises $C + I + G$

if C and I remain unchanged or fall by a lesser magnitude. If G remains unchanged and taxes are replaced by borrowing or money creation, $C+I$ will rise, and therefore $C+I+G$, given the magnitude of G. The less deflationary the revenue sources used and the less adverse effect the expenditures have on expectations, the more easily the program will bring the economy to full employment. Thus a program of expenditures financed by money creation will have the greatest expansionary effect, unless fears generated by the deficit and the printing of money reduce confidence so that investment is curtailed. Financing by borrowing will result in greater expansionary effect than financing by taxation; the type of tax used will affect the net influence. If a government adheres strictly to a balanced budget, the total expenditures must be larger to eliminate a given deflationary gap than with a budget involving financing by money creation or borrowing.

With an inflationary gap situation the reverse is true; the more contractionary the revenue, the greater the effect in restraining inflationary pressures. In this instance also, equivalent results may be obtained by a sharp reduction in total governmental spending with financing by relatively noncontractionary taxes or a smaller reduction with tax changes that drastically reduce spending: elimination of depreciation allowances, for example, or a progressive spendings tax. The effectiveness of the program will also depend on the effects of the taxes upon wage rates and other costs. If the taxes lead to greater wage increases, the lessening of the inflationary gap will not bring inflation to an end. Those taxes that may be most effective in lessening spending may be the ones that have greatest impact on wages, as for example a general sales tax with broad coverage. This form of tax, by raising the cost of living, will increase union demands for higher wages.

When inflation is caused by wage increases, governmental budget adjustments cannot eliminate it without creating substantial unemployment. Fiscal measures are effective only against demand-pull forces creating an inflationary gap; they have no influence in restricting union wage demands unless they drastically reduce the level of employment.

Thus the net expansionary or contractionary effect of a program of governmental expenditures and revenues, given the size of the multiplier and the determinants of C and I, as noted earlier in the chapter, will depend upon:

1. The magnitude of G.
2. The effect upon C, through:
    a) Absorption of funds otherwise used for C.

     b) Changes in relative preferences for *C* and *S*.

     c) Changes in expectations about future prices.

3. The effect upon *I*, through:

     a) Changes in the supply of money capital.

     b) Changes in the willingness of persons to take the risk of supplying money capital for *I*.

     c) The effects upon *C*, a major determinant of the profitability of *I*.

     d) Change in direct net return from *I*, given the level of *C*.

     e) Changes in expectations about future returns from *I*, through the effects of governmental expenditures or revenues.

4. Effect upon wage rates, which affect the general price level.

Accordingly, a program designed to be expansionary will be more effective, other things given:

1. The greater the increase in *G*.

2. The less the absorption of funds otherwise used for *C*, and the less the extent to which the revenue and expenditure programs increase the relative preference for *S* relative to *C*. The less the reduction in *C*, the less the decline in profitability of *I*.

3. The greater the increase created in expectations of future price increases.

4. The less the restrictive effect upon the supply of money capital and the willingness of persons to make it available for *I*.

5. The less the reduction in the direct return from *I*, and in certainty of expectations about future returns.

The net restrictive effect of a governmental program designed to check inflation will be more effective,

1. The greater the reduction in *G*.

2. The greater the curtailment of *C*, which not only reduces the *C* element in *C* + *I* + *G* but also reduces the profitability of *I*.

     Curtailment of *C* will be greater, the larger the relative tax burden on those spending most of their incomes; the greater the incentive given to consume less and save more; the greater the increase in belief that prices will be lower in the future; and the more important the money illusion.

3. The greater the curtailment of *I*, through the effects of the curtailment of *C*, the absorption of a portion of the earnings from *I*, the absorption of money capital otherwise available for *I*, the greater incentive given to hold money instead of

making it available for real investment, and the greater uncertainty created for investors about the future.

4. The less the effect of the programs in raising money wage rates.

Thus, for example, a steeply progressive spendings tax not affecting wage rates would have the greatest restrictive effect; a sales tax would have greater restrictive effect than an income tax so long as it does not affect wage rates, and particularly if the money illusion is strong. Higher revenues from sources such that neither C nor I are affected have no restrictive effect. Reduction in G will have more restrictive effect than equivalent tax increases unless the latter give great incentive to reduce. $C + I$.

ECONOMIC GROWTH

In all countries today, the objective of a high rate of economic growth is regarded as of fundamental importance. Government expenditure and revenue programs may facilitate attainment of a higher growth rate or they may lower the rate. Analysis requires a sharp distinction between the potential path of economic growth—the annual increase in Y permitted by the determinants of real national income—and the actual rate of growth. The latter lags behind the former if full employment is not attained and output is therefore less than the potential.

The Potential Growth Path

The annual potential increase in Y (or GNP) is a function of:

1. The rate of capital formation: the annual increase in the total stock of capital goods. The potential rate is limited to the amount of savings made at full employment; real investment cannot outrun full employment savings, since this magnitude measures the amount of goods available for capital formation at full employment.
2. The capital-output ratio: the relationship between an increase in real investment and the consequent increase in output.
3. The rate of technological change, which allows greater output with given resources.
4. Increase in total resources available (natural resources and manpower).

The *actual* path of growth depends upon the ability of the economy to expand at a full-employment rate and thus upon maintenance of adequate total demand $(C + I + G)$ to insure that total expenditures rise at the same rate as potential output.

The analysis of the preceding pages suggests possible influences of governmental expenditures and revenues upon both potential and actual economic growth.

Governmental activity almost certainly alters the private-sector S/Y ratio in a downward direction, since a substantial part of the tax revenue will be absorbed from savings and some incentives may be given to consume more and save less. The extent of the influence depends primarily upon the types of taxes; progressive income, corporate income, and estate taxes will have greater depressing effect on S/Y than expenditure-related taxes with greater impact on consumption and less likely to increase preference for consumption. A progressive spendings tax has the greatest potential effect in increasing S/Y.

While the governmental program reduces private-sector saving, some governmental expenditures constitute capital formation. Thus the reduction in private saving may be offset by an increase in governmental saving. Governmental investment in power plants and highways, for example, constitutes capital formation and will contribute as much to economic growth as private investment provided the marginal returns are as great. Governments in developing economies may significantly supplement private savings in this fashion, raising taxes above current expenditures and investing in capital formation.

To the extent that governmental activities do reduce total net savings, private and governmental, the rate of capital formation possible at full employment is reduced. The significance for economic growth depends upon the capital output ratio, or, in other words, the effect of additional I for increases in Y. The Dennison estimate for the United States indicates that an increase in the growth rate by one tenth of one percentage point (for example, from 3.3 to 3.4 percent) requires an increase in the percentage of national income saved of 1.4 percentage points.[12] In other words, a very substantial change in the savings ratio is required for any significant change in the growth rate and any reduction due to governmental activities is not serious. This figure, however, does not take into consideration the supplementary effect that investment may have on growth through the embodiment of technological change. If the conclusion is reached, as by Harberger,

---

[12]E. F. Dennison, *The Sources of Economic Growth in the United States* (New York: Committee for Economic Development, 1962), p. 277.

that primary embodiment of technical change occurs in the intramarginal investment, the type so profitable that it is not affected by usual changes in the savings rate, and is negligible in marginal investment, the supplementary effects are not significant, and the net influence is limited to that based upon the contribution to output of additional stock of capital goods.[13] Accordingly, tax influences are not likely to be substantial, and the differences among various taxes even less so, most being attributable to variations in distributional patterns, rather than to the nature of the levies.

Governments may be able to facilitate increase in technological change through tax policies that encourage research and development, such as supplemental tax deductions for expenditures for these purposes, or by financing research directly. In the United States federally financed research primarily designed to aid national defense has made important contributions to nondefense technology. For a century, a large portion of agricultural research has been financed by government.

As noted in Chapter 7, governments make significant contributions to economic development through expenditures for education. Investment in human resources may appropriately be regarded as a portion of total investment, which, up to a certain level, may make a greater contribution per dollar than other forms of investment. Improvements in management skills are also highly significant. Finally, governments through their own investment and other expenditure programs may increase the availability of other resources, including farmland through irrigation facilities, and may have some influence via tax policy, such as, for example, by encouraging exploration for new mineral deposits.

The Actual Growth Path

Governments influence the extent to which the potential growth path is attained and the trend in the general price level by their effect upon $C + I + G$, and thus upon the level of output and employment. Present-day expenditure and revenue programs provide a substantial element of built-in stabilization in the economy, through automatic responses to declines or increases in private-sector spending $(C + I)$. As $C + I$ and therefore Y commence to fall below full-employment levels, income tax revenue falls much more rapidly than Y because of exemptions and progressive rates. Welfare programs automatically

---

[13]A. C. Harberger, "Taxation, Resource Allocation, and Welfare," in *The Role of Direct and Indirect Taxes in the Federal Revenue System* (Princeton, N.J.: Princeton University Press, 1964), pp. 62–70.

pay out more money under established rules as more persons become eligible for benefits and seek them. Both of these reactions check the decline in total spending and thus the decline in Y. When total spending rises above Y at full employment, fixed income tax exemptions and rate brackets cause tax revenue to rise more rapidly than Y and check the inflationary pressures. These automatic stabilizers, however, can merely check a downward or upward trend; set into action by autonomous forces, they cannot, with existing programs, completely counteract the initiating force. Accordingly, to attain full-employment growth, more deliberate changes in revenues and expenditures may be required.

If an economy is suffering from a tendency toward inadequate total demand, any change in G or in the revenue structure that reduces S/Y will facilitate attainment of full employment but at the same time lessen the full-employment rate of capital formation and the potential rate of economic growth. Changes that increase I without affecting S/Y, on the other hand, will increase the actual rate of growth without reducing the potential rate. This result may be difficult to attain, however.

Some Obstacles to Attainment of the Potential Growth Path. Continued attainment of the potential growth path may prove to be difficult. One source of trouble is a possible chronic tendency for investment to lag behind the rate of savings that persons wish to make as national income continues to rise, because the increasing stock of capital goods relative to other resources reduces the marginal productivity of capital and the rate of profit. In other words, the larger the stock of capital goods, the more difficult it is to maintain a high rate of earnings from additional investment, because of the increasing ratio of capital goods to other factors. Only continued technological change can prevent this phenomenon from lowering investment below full-employment levels; otherwise, governments must either continue to curtail savings and increase consumption (thus reducing the potential growth path), or undertake more and more investment themselves, with declining contribution to society. This thesis suggested in various writings for centuries was most fully developed by Challis Hall.[14] Its relevance remains to be tested.

Governments may design tax and expenditure programs in such a fashion that they automatically check the rise in the actual level of Y before it attains the potential full-employment level; the automatic

---

[14]Challis Hall, *Fiscal Policy for Stable Growth* (New York: Holt-Rinehart, 1960).

stabilizers that check inflation may operate too soon, stopping expansion. This will occur if, given the expenditure programs, tax rates and exemptions are set at such levels that the net restrictive effect on $C + I + G$ more than offsets the expansionary effect of rising $C + I$ before full employment is reached. This reaction, known as *"fiscal drag,"* apparently occurred in 1962–64. A reduction in tax rates is necessary to allow attainment of full employment before expansion is choked off.

REFERENCES

BARLOW, R., BRAZER, H. E., AND MORGAN, J. N. *Economic Behavior of the Affluent*, chap. iv. Washington, D.C.: Brookings Institution, 1966.

FERBER, ROBERT. "Research on Household Behavior," *American Economic Review*, Vol. LII (March, 1962), pp. 33–34.

GOODE, R. A. *The Individual Income Tax*, chaps. iii, iv, and Appendix C. Washington, D.C.: Brookings Institution, 1964.

HARBERGER, A. C. "Taxation, Resource Allocation, and Welfare," in *The Role of Direct and Indirect Taxes in the Federal Revenue System*. Princeton, N.J.: Princeton University Press, 1964.

MUSGRAVE, R. A. *The Theory of Public Finance*, chaps. xii, xiv, xvii, xviii, xix, xx. New York: McGraw-Hill, 1959.

PEACOCK, A. T., AND WILLIAMSON, J. "Consumption Taxes and Compensatory Finance," *Economic Journal*, Vol. LXXVII (March, 1967), pp. 27–47.

PART III

Overall Expenditure and Revenue Policy

Chapter	FISCAL POLICY
10	

Fiscal policy considerations play a major role today in the shaping of governmental expenditure and revenue policy at the national level. Acceptance of fiscal policy adds another dimension to the determination of optimal governmental expenditures: the effects of the expenditures upon the equilibrium level of national income and employment. Revenue structures and levels are determined not solely on the basis of financing of governmental expenditures but also with regard to their impact upon total spending and national income. By the term *fiscal policy* (or stabilization and growth policy) is meant, therefore, adjustment in governmental expenditures and revenues to attain greater economic stability and the desired rate of economic growth. Fiscal policy has the same objectives as monetary or credit policy, which seeks to attain the goals by changing the availability and cost of money capital, primarily by altering commercial bank reserve positions. Fiscal and monetary policies are not mutually exclusive; presumably both will be used in coordinated fashion to attain the desired goals.

THE GOALS OF FISCAL POLICY

As usually conceived, fiscal policy has three major objectives: to insure that the actual rate of growth of the economy coincides with the potential rate of growth through maintenance of full employment; to attain a reasonably stable general price level; and to increase the potential rate of growth if possible without interfering with attainment of other objectives of society.

Full-Employment Growth. An economy can attain the potential rate of growth permitted by the full-employment rate of capital formation, the rate of technological change, the improvement in levels of skill and education, and increased availability of other factor units only if full employment is maintained. Total spending $(C + I + G)$ must at all times keep pace with rising national income (Y), or unemployment will develop. Figure 10–1 shows the estimated gap between

267

the actual path of economic growth and the potential path in recent years. The evils of unemployment are so obvious that no elaboration is needed. From the standpoint of the economy, real per capita income is less than it could otherwise be, and the individuals involved experience drastic reduction in real income.

Price Level Stability. The maintenance of a reasonably stable general price level is also regarded as a major objective. A decline in the general price level is incompatible with the maintenance of full employment and would generate bitter labor strife, as well as injuring debtors. Inflation—a rising price level—does offer the limited advantage of aiding investment because some costs lag and therefore profits are increased, so long as firms do not commence to delay capital equipment purchases in anticipation of declines in equipment prices. Continued inflation of any magnitude, however, produces several re-

FIGURE 10-1

RELATIONSHIP OF THE ACTUAL AND POTENTIAL GROWTH RATES, 1955-66

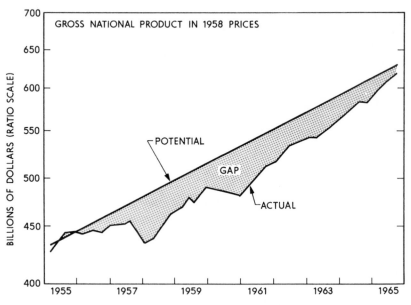

SOURCE: *Economic Report of the President,* 1966.

sults that society regards as undesirable. Fixed-income groups, particularly older, retired persons, suffer reductions in real income, while persons speculating in commodities and land experience gains. Investment is distorted toward speculative forms instead of those providing long-term aid to economic development. Saving is discouraged; persons seek to buy now before prices go still higher. Acquisition of money capital through any fixed-monetary-value security becomes impossible. Costs lose their effectiveness as measures of performance and many nuisance problems are created (for example, operating of vending machines).

Labor strife is likely to increase; each group is constantly striving to raise its wages faster than the price level rises. Once a country becomes accustomed to sharply rising prices and escalation is built into many facets of the economy, the task of bringing inflation to an end becomes an almost impossible one, certainly for a democratic government. When unions become accustomed to large money wage increases each year, they strongly resist restraints. The experience of such countries as Chile in seeking to bring long-continuing inflation to an end illustrates the problem.

Stability in the price level does not require stability of all individual prices. Commodities experiencing more than average increases in productivity will decline in price; those with little change in productivity will rise as money wages rise to reflect the higher productivity in the other fields. Thus in the United States in recent decades the prices of many manufactured goods have remained more or less stable or have even declined while the prices of services, with little change in productivity, have risen. If money wages keep pace with productivity in manufacturing, the general price level will rise slowly.

Compatibility of Full Employment and a Stable Price Level. A major question is the compatibility of the goals of full employment and a stable price level; as full employment is approached unions may tend to push money wages up faster than productivity and prices will rise. Some tradeoff between the two objectives may be necessary, that is, society may have to accept some unemployment in order to avoid inflation. The Phillips Curve is now used to show this tradeoff: the amount of inflation occurring with various levels of unemployment. One study concludes that 4 percent unemployment is required if the increase in the general price level (consumer price index) is to be held to 1½ percent; with 3 percent unemployment the price level increase will be 2.5 percent or more.[1] A major difficulty in ascertaining a Phillips Curve with predictive value is the continuing change in the size of structural unemployment that cannot be eliminated by fiscal policy:

[1] Note the paper by M. E. Levy, *Full Employment without Inflation* (New York: National Industrial Conference Board, 1967).

the unemployment of persons lacking education and skills necessary for them to find jobs even in a period in which many job opportunities are available. Increases in aggregate demand will not increase employment for these groups; structural unemployment can only be eliminated by provisions for training and in some cases relocation of the persons. Increased percentages of teen-agers in the population and increased automation tend to increase the figure of structural unemployment and thus the percentage of unemployment consistent with a stable price level.

Potential Growth Rate. The third goal, increasing the potential rate of economic growth, is much less clearly definable. Given factor supplies and the rate of technological change, a higher rate of growth requires a higher rate of capital formation and a higher S/Y ratio at full employment. But additional saving requires reduction in consumption; accordingly the definition of the optimum rate is essentially dependent upon choices between present and future consumption. Thus to define the optimum on any basis other than that reflecting society's preferences between present and future consumption can be justified only on grounds that warrant overruling popular preferences. One is the argument that individuals in society may prefer a higher rate of overall growth, but each knows that change in his own S/Y will not have a measurable effect; he would be willing to save a higher percentage if he knew that other persons would do so as well.

The other argument, of primary importance in a developing economy, is the recognition by the government that an increase in S/Y will allow more rapid attainment of a prime goal of society, namely, higher per capita real income, whereas the people of the society lack sufficient information to recognize this relationship. In the United States the second justification is not relevant; only on the basis of the first can a case be made for increasing the sacrifice of present consumption for future consumption, and the case does not appear too strong.

The Techniques of Fiscal Policy

The actual path of national income is controlled by the relationship between total spending $(C + I + G)$ and the level of Y. Accordingly, the primary avenue of influence of the government upon the level of national income and the actual path of growth is through policies that affect the level of $C + I + G$. The government may alter its own spending (G) and affect the total, provided perverse changes in $C + I$ do not offset the changes in G; or it may seek to influence the level of C and/or I. Government may influence C either by altering the funds persons have available for consumption spending or by altering preferences between consumption and savings. Governmental policies may affect I by altering the supply of money capital and the willingness of its owners to make it available for real investment, or by altering the return from investment, present and future, and the certainty with which the return is expected.

The effectiveness of a given program, therefore, will depend upon the net change in $C + I + G$, given the multiplier and the accelerator effects. The former, equal to $\frac{1}{MPS}$, determines the magnitude of the increase in Y consequent to an initial increase in $C + I + G$; the accelerator determines the extent of response of I to a change in Y. Accordingly, the program will be more effective, the lower the marginal propensity to save (and the higher the multiplier) and the greater the accelerator reaction.

Secondly, the effectiveness of the program will be affected by the extent to which it affects the basic money wage rate. This is not a relevant aspect in antidepression fiscal policy, but it is significant for control of inflation.

FISCAL POLICY TO ALLOW ATTAINMENT OF POTENTIAL GROWTH

In a period in which unemployment is preventing the economy from reaching the potential level of Y and thus the potential growth path, the immediate aim of fiscal policy is to raise the total level of spending in the economy. This may be approached via changes in G or changes in policy designed to alter C and/or I.

Increases in Governmental Spending

An increase in G in excess of any induced decline in $C + I$ will increase total spending and thus the level of Y, the magnitude of the increase in Y being controlled by the size of multiplier and by the accelerating influence of the rise in Y upon I. This latter will be of limited significance when unemployment is severe because of excess plant capacity; it will rise in importance as full employment is approached.

The fiscal impact of an increase in G is largely independent of the purposes for which the money is spent, since G constitutes purchase of final products. The purpose, however, has importance in three respects. First, the size of the multiplier is dependent upon the MPS of the initial recipients of the governmental payments. If the payments go primarily to persons in the lower income groups in the form of wages for work on governmental projects, the MPS will be lower and the multiplier higher than if the payments go in large sums to a few wealthy persons whose MPS is high.

Second, the nature of the expenditures may affect expectations about returns from private investment. If the money is spent for governmental investment in projects competitive with private enterprise, I may fall sharply, particularly if business firms regard the governmental activity as a forerunner of greatly increased governmental participation in traditionally private-sector spheres. Alternatively, governmental expenditures on activities that appear to be completely wasteful—some of the WPA projects of the thirties—tend to lessen community confidence in the governmental programs generally; persons do not realize that the wastefulness is not significant in terms of the ultimate objective of full employment, even though production of something useful would be preferable.

Finally, the expenditures may adversely affect consumption, if the governmental activities provide services that substitute for private consumption expenditures.

Financing. The primary potential source of offsetting influence upon $C + I$ is the raising of the revenues to finance the increase in G. Creation of money in itself has no direct restrictive effect upon private spending and has the secondary effect of increasing commercial bank reserves and facilitating an increase in bank lending. The only potential adverse effect is indirect: lessened certainty of investors about the future because of belief that money creation is a dangerous practice. This reaction can largely be avoided if the government nominally borrows the money while the Federal Reserve simultaneously buys an equivalent value of government bonds in the open market. The net effect is exactly the same as if the Federal Reserve bought the bonds in the first place. A major criticism of fiscal policy in past depressions has been the failure to rely on money creation for financing.

Governmental borrowing has a somewhat more restrictive effect than money creation, since the supply of money capital available for private investment is reduced. The extent of the restrictive effect depends upon the reserve position of the commercial banks, the extent to which interest rates rise as money capital becomes less plentiful, and the signifiance of the reduced supply of loanable funds for business investment. If most investment is undertaken with internal funds or if investment is unresponsive to changes in the interest rate, the restrictive effect will be small.

Borrowing, while regarded by many persons as less dangerous than money creation, may also reduce expected earnings from investment. It does this by creating fears of higher taxes in the future to service the debt—there is no similar fear with money creation—and by creating fears about the future stability of the economy, a fear that has little foundation but may nevertheless have significant influence.

Tax financing probably has the greatest restrictive effect, since taxes not only take funds otherwise available for C and I but may also reduce the return from I and thus lessen the amount still more, and may even provide incentive to consume less and save more. The aim, if taxes are used, is to employ the forms that have minimum restrictive effect upon C and I: taxes on the higher income groups so devised that they are absorbed primarily from accumulated savings without restricting either the funds available for investment or the willingness to undertake investment. Such taxes are difficult to devise; some form of levy on idle balances of individuals and financial institutions, or a progressive tax on sums saved but not used directly for real investment could best accomplish the desired results but would be difficult to implement. In practice a government is forced to chose between a tax with primary impact on C (personal income tax on the lower income levels) with little direct adverse impact on I, or taxes on the higher income groups with greater restraining impact on I. Taxes on consumption are particularly objectionable because of their heavy impact on those consuming all their income and the possible incentive they give to consume less. In a severe depression in which I is almost nil, taxes on the higher income groups are clearly preferable since I cannot be reduced any further, but income levels may be so low that the potential base is limited.

The logical conclusion is that the increase in G should be financed by money creation, rather than borrowing or taxation. Borrowing gives rise to unnecessary interest charges that may produce undesirable consequences for development in the future and has some restrictive effect on the availability of funds. Taxes, while avoiding the adverse effect of other methods upon business expectations, have maximum restrictive effect on $C + I$ and impair the effectiveness of the overall program. To accomplish a particular expansionary impact, total spending must be much higher if financed by taxation, with consequent adverse effect on business confidence. The economic function of taxation and borrowing is to restrict private spending in order to prevent governmental expenditures from causing inflation. In a period when the primary goal is to increase total spending, this function is no longer relevant; any restrictive effect arising out of the financing reduces the effectiveness of the program in attaining the desired goals.

Selection of Outlets for the Expenditures. As noted, the expansionary effect of the program depends to some extent upon the purposes for which the additional spending is undertaken. On the one hand the government must seek to minimize activities that increase fear of competition of government with private enterprise; on the other hand clearly the greater the contribution that the activities make to society, the more fully the overall objectives of society are attained. But the number of potential objects of spending in this intermediate zone may be limited, particularly in a severe depression. The regular routine activities of government, such as education, are as a rule not suitable for temporary expansion; the levels should be determined on the basis of longer period estimates of costs and benefits in terms of the preferences of society. The most suitable activities are ones of a capital nature that can be undertaken at an earlier date than would otherwise be warranted, such as school buildings, post offices, highways, rapid transit lines, and recreational facilities. In addition some capital projects that might never be regarded as warranted in periods of full employment, such as certain marginal roads, transit lines, or monuments, can justifiably be built if resources would otherwise be idle. Improved housing facilities offer great possibilities but create greater fear of governmental competition with private enterprise. One advantage of a system in which governmental conduct of a relatively wide range of activities is generally accepted is the greater base of potential projects with which to work in a period of unemployment.

Apart from the limited number of potential projects is the problem of timing. Capital improvement projects of any magnitude require substantial time to initiate and complete. Meanwhile the decline in business activity may reach such levels that general pessimism and high uncertainty makes revival difficult to attain. Geographical limitations may be serious; the locations of the most feasible projects may not be those of greatest concentration of unemployment. Once the projects are under way, they may require considerable time to complete; meanwhile full employment may already be reattained. Careful advance planning of prospective projects so that time necessary to initiate them will be reduced and use of a number of smaller projects rather than a few large ones will facilitate their effectiveness. But the limitations suggest that other measures must be utilized as well, especially in the early period of the decline in Y.

Increased Transfer Payments by Government

An alternate to increases in G is a program of increased governmental transfer payments. While these constitute increases in governmental spending, they do not constitute a portion of G in the total expenditure picture $(C + I + G)$ because they are not purchases of final products. Their stimulative effect upon the economy arises through their influence in increasing $C + I$ by increasing disposable income. The increases may take various forms: additional unemployment compensation payments over and above usual amounts, higher old-age pensions, increased direct relief payments, establishment or increase of negative income tax payments, or some form of general family allowance under which all families would be paid specified amounts each month. For that matter, paper money coud be dropped from planes flying across the country. Presumably, however, most effective results are obtained from concentrating the payments in the lowest income groups.

This program involves less direct increase in $C + I + G$ than do increases in G since, regardless of distribution some of the funds would not be spent. But with optimal distribution the difference might not be great. The program has two major advantages over increases in G. Maximum assistance is given to those in the lowest income groups, thus according most closely with usually accepted standards of equity, and the problems of selection of appropriate projects and possible competition with private enterprise are avoided. Furthermore, resources would be used to produce goods that persons sought to buy, rather than governmental projects with lower preferences on the part of society. Delay would be minimized; payments could begin immediately following authorization of the program, especially if they involved extension of payments of existing programs such as unemployment compensation.

On the other hand, these programs, directly and immediately, involve payments to persons with nothing given in return. While governmental projects may be of limited usefulness to society, they presumably convey some benefits, whereas transfer payments provide nothing directly. Closely related is the morale impact; providing persons compensation on a liberal basis without requiring anything in exchange can impair morale and incentives. To some persons, failure to be able to work, to utilize one's skills, is demeaning and leads to deterioration of morale. To others, living off the government is a pleasant existence which they are only too willing to continue. The former reaction is likely to be much more widespread than the latter, but neither is regarded by society as desirable. For these reasons, governments, while regarding direct relief and other transfer payment programs as necessary to provide immediate assistance to those most urgently in need and as justifiable permanent programs to aid unemployables, prefer to minimize their use as means to stimulate attainment of full employment.

Tax Reduction

Reduction in taxes, with given or increased levels of G and governmental transfer payments, is the major alternative approach, one ignored until after 1950. Tax reductions increase funds available for both C and I in the hands of the taxpayers; they may remove deterrents to both C and I, and they may provide incentive for immediate C and I expenditures to escape higher taxes in the future.

Availability of Funds. Availability of funds for consumption is increased by tax reductions affecting individuals directly; the greatest increase in C arising out of greater availability of funds will be provided by tax reductions primarily benefiting those persons spending high percentages of their incomes. Thus reduction in consumption taxes and in income taxes affecting the lowest income brackets have the greatest impact on C, per dollar of tax reduction. Greatest impact on availability of funds for investment is provided by reduction in corporate income taxes and in personal income taxes affecting the profits from business firms and the higher income groups generally.

Incentives to Spend. Repeal of high-rate excise taxes on commodities with elastic demand will have the greatest influence in removing deterrents to consumption spending; reduction or removal of sales taxes would have some influence in lessening deterrents, as would elimination of a progressive spendings tax were one employed. Reduction in taxes affecting C will in turn also stimulate I via the accelerator effect. Reduction in corporate income tax rates will have some effect in reducing deterrents to invest, as will accelerated depreciation and investment tax credits. Allowance of more rapid depreciation lessens uncertainty about the ability to recover capital tax-free and restores money capital to the firm more quickly, thereby not only increasing its availability but also lessening total interest cost. Any form of accelerated depreciation reduces the total tax burden of a firm continuing to expand; while the firm "catches up" on particular pieces of equipment since it reaches the fully depreciated figure sooner (and thenceforth has no further deductions on the particular equipment), it never "catches up" on its total tax liability as long as it continues to expand. Investment tax credits, which provide a credit against tax of a portion of the cost of new equipment in the year in which the equipment is acquired and do not diminish the base for subsequent depreciation, reduce the cost of new equipment by the percentage of credit (7 percent in the United States). They may have considerable impact on investment, as shown by the Hall-Jorgensen study.[2]

Effectiveness of Stimuli. The effectiveness of the various stimuli to *I* is dependent upon the severity of the decline in national income below full employment and the consequent attitudes of persons toward the future. If a decline is severe, firms typically have excess plant capacity, and the accelerator effect of an increase in *C* is negligible. Tax reductions affecting the return from *I,* including tax credits, will have little effect. When prospects for increasing sales are negligible, no amount of adjustment of tax on the earnings from *I* will be significant, since no earnings are foreseen. Accordingly, in a period of severe decline, the government must rely on measures that have primary effect on *C.* When *Y* is lagging only slightly below the full-employment level, however, adjustments in taxes on return from *I* may significantly affect total spending.

The effectiveness of the incentive influence of tax changes is also dependent upon attitudes about the permanence of the changes. If an investment credit or a reduction in high-rate excises is expected to be temporary, strong incentive is given to purchase capital equipment or consumer durables immediately while the reduction is in effect. If the changes are expected to be more permanent, the reaction to them may be less. When the changes affecting *I* are introduced there may also be considerable temporary impact, especially if the changes have been anticipated, as investment that has been postponed in anticipation of the changes is undertaken. The longer period impact will be weaker. The restoration of the investment tax credit in 1967 caused a sudden jump in investment that had been delayed in anticipation of the restoration; the longer range impact was apparently considerably less.[3] These considerations suggest that changes in taxes affecting *I* are much more helpful in restoring full employment following a temporary decline than they are in holding *I* to a higher level when there is continuing deflationary influence.

In developing an optimal tax reduction program, therefore, a government must seek to assess the relative impact of various forms of tax reduction; the program optimal in one period is not likely to

---

[2]R. E. Hall and D. W. Jorgensen, "Tax Policy and Investment Behavior," *American Economic Review,* Vol. LVII (June, 1967), pp. 391–414.

[3]The effects of the 1967 change were summarized in the *Wall Street Journal,* December 26, 1967, in cursory fashion.

be optimal in another. Information is required on several questions:

1. The extent to which C will rise in response to reduction in various taxes.

2. The accelerator relationship; how much will I react to given increase in Y? The answer depends in part upon the size of the gap below full employment and thus the amount of idle capacity, and in part on the attitudes toward the future.

3. The responsiveness of I to changes in the rate of return on investment.

4. The relative effectiveness of changes in income tax rates, increased acceleration of depreciation allowances, and investment tax credits in stimulating I.

5. The nature of the lag in Y below full-employment levels, particularly whether it is of temporary or continuing nature.

Financing the Deficit. Reduction in taxes, given the level of G, will produce a deficit, just as will an increase in G, given the level of taxes. Financing of the deficit by money creation will allow maximum stimulating effect of the program unless strong fears generated about the future reduce the expected returns from I, or increase uncertainty and lessen the willingness of businessmen to undertake investment. Use of borrowing lessens the stimulating effect somewhat and creates an interest obligation; its use can be justified only on the basis that adverse effects on confidence are less. This is by no means necessary; the business community may fear the deficits per se much more than the particular source of money employed to finance them. Borrowing, in addition, creates fear of higher taxes in the future and reduces the expected long-range returns from investment. On the whole, the main offsetting influence that restricts the effectiveness of the tax reduction program, just as one of increasing G, is the possible adverse influence of the deficits on confidence of the community. Future effectiveness of such programs depends in large measure on their acceptability by the business community—acceptability that is much greater today than it was in the thirties.

The argument, widely advanced in political circles in the early sixties, that effectiveness of a tax reduction will be increased if it is accompanied by an equivalent reduction in government spending has no validity, except in the very rare eventuality that the effect of reduction in G would have such a strong favorable effect on business confidence that it would stimulate I more than the decline in sales due to reduced G would reduce it. Otherwise, such a program would have a dampening effect on the economy. Total spending would fall by the full amount of the decline in G whereas a portion of the tax reduction would be absorbed in savings without an equivalent increase in real investment. There is strong reason to believe that I is influenced much more by current trends in sales of products than it is by confidence-altering effects of reduction in government spending.

The Merits of a Tax Reduction Program Compared to One of Increased Governmental Spending

Emphasis on tax reduction rather than upon increases in G or transfer payments probably minimizes adverse reactions to the overall program that deter I. An increase in G increases the scope of the governmental sector of the economy relative to the private sector, an increase that may become permanent. Higher levels of welfare payments may also become permanent and bring higher tax levels in the future. On the other hand, tax reduction does not enlarge the governmental sphere or create long-term commitments, and dangers of governmental spending for purposes competitive with the private sector are avoided.

Implementation of tax reductions is much simpler. They can be made effective within a month via the withholding system, without the establishment of new administrative staffs or the long advance planning necessary to start governmental projects. So long as Congress can be persuaded of the necessity for the tax reduction, very prompt action is possible; Congress can enact a tax measure within a few weeks if it wishes to do so. Similarly, the tax increase can be ended quickly, assuming Congressional cooperation, without problems relating to partly finished projects. All in all, tax reduction is a much simpler device. It has less disturbing effects upon confidence, and avoids commitments to long-range projects that might not be regarded as justifiable if evaluated in full-employment periods, but once introduced cannot easily be eliminated.

One limitation to the tax reduction approach is the smaller direct expansionary effect per dollar involved. Regardless of the care in the designing of the tax reduction program, the expansionary impact is likely to be somewhat less per dollar because some of the tax saving will not be reflected in either consumption spending or additional investment, whereas an increase in G involves an equivalent increase in total spending and a high percentage of additional transfer payments will be spent. The overall effects per dollar of deficit created, however, may bring a greater increase in Y because of the weaker disturbing effects upon business confidence. A second limitation is the failure of the program to give financial assistance to those most needing it:

the persons losing their jobs or incomes as a result of the decline in Y. Accordingly, some supplementing of tax reduction by increases in G or in transfer spending by government would appear to be imperative.

One final problem that may arise is purely political; Congress may be less willing to increase taxes once full employment has been restored than it was to reduce them. This problem, which is less serious in countries with the parliamentary form of government, may or may not prove to be significant.

ANTI-INFLATIONARY FISCAL POLICY

In a period of inflationary pressure, fiscal policy seeks to lessen total spending, but its task is complicated by the wage-rate problem; the reduction in total spending must be accomplished in such a way as to minimize the additional pressure placed upon wages and thus upon prices from the cost side. There is no equivalent complication confronting fiscal policy designed to lessen unemployment.

Reduction in Governmental Spending

A reduction in G, given the tax level, will reduce total spending and cut anti-inflationary pressures by an equivalent amount, whereas tax increases are unlikely to have dollar-for-dollar effect in reducing spending. Reduction in G likewise offers the great advantage that it places no added pressure upon wage rates or other costs. Inevitably, reduction in G is favored by the elements in society that constantly fear the expanding role of government.

The difficulty with this approach is to find suitable objects for reduction. If the basic governmental services have been extended to levels that reflect community preferences for them compared to private-sector output in optimal fashion, reduction is undesirable. Reduction in defense, protection, education, and similar activities is usually unwarranted in terms of the preferences of society. The primary scope for reduction is to be found in the postponement of various capital improvements such as new post offices, replacement of old school buildings, and marginal highway construction which can be delayed until inflationary pressures have died down. Mild inflationary pressures may be eliminated by such postponement alone. Careful examination of longer range programs of questionable merit is also important in periods of inflation. If the inflation is strong and long continuing, however, these actions will be inadequate and other techniques must be used.

Welfare payments tend to fall automatically in periods of inflationary pressure, and reexamination of the programs to find abuses or elements of doubtful merit is warranted. Again, however, to the extent that programs reflect community preferences for income redistribution and elimination of poverty, little change in the programs is likely to be warranted.

Tax Increases

Strong inflationary pressures can be restrained, if at all, only by tax increases, given the limitations to reduction in G and in transfer payments. The aim of the program is to maximize anti-inflationary pressure per dollar of revenue so that adverse incentive effects of the tax structure are minimized, in such a fashion as to place the least possible upward pressure on wages. This is, unfortunately, a difficult task, because the taxes that have maximum effect on spending are likely to be the same as those that place maximum pressure on wages. Increases in income taxes on the lower income levels would be the simplest to implement and would maximize the reduction in consumption spending, since persons in these levels spend high percentages of their income, but the reduction in take-home pay would increase pressure for wage increases. Objection can also be raised against this policy, if used alone, on equity grounds as well, and political considerations may make enactment of the policy difficult.

Introduction of a sales tax might be even more effective in reducing consumer spending because of its greater concentration on families spending high percentages of their incomes and the limited incentive given to spend less and save more, particularly if the tax is regarded as temporary. The tax would, however, increase the cost of living and produce even stronger demands for wage increases. In addition a new administrative structure to operate the tax would be required, and there would be danger that the tax would not be eliminated once inflationary pressures had declined. Much the same can be said about an extensive system of excises. In addition, these taxes discriminate on the basis of consumer preferences for various goods. They may be useful, however, in periods of severe inflation to avoid rationing of goods in very scarce supply, provided that they are not placed on necessities widely used in the lower income groups. If they are, "rationing" through taxes would be regarded as highly inequitable.

Tax Increases to Check Investment. Alternatively, increases in higher bracket income taxes and the corporate income tax could be used to check investment spending; elimination of investment tax credits and denial of the privilege of making any depreciation deductions at all on new equipment could drastically reduce I. The depreciation techniques are likely to be the most effective, since a firm is not necessarily deterred from continuing to invest by high taxes on its earnings if it has ample funds and future prospects are regarded as excellent. A tax on profits that might seriously affect investment incentives under more normal conditions may go unnoticed in a boom period characterized by extreme optimism.

Unfortunately even if I can be curtailed by various tax policies, the inflation may not be controlled. $C + G$ alone may be so high that even if all I were eliminated, total spending would exceed full-employment Y. Furthermore, curtailment of I may perpetuate bottlenecks that add to inflationary pressures, as, for example, shortages of steel and other basic materials due to inadequate capacity. Additional I in these fields, while temporarily adding to inflationary pressures, may very quickly bring forth additional output in critical sectors and reduce pressure on prices. This possibility suggests the need for selective restrictions on investment that can be provided through curtailment of depreciation deductions. Such deductions can be permitted for those industries in which additional capacity is urgently needed and denied in fields where it is not. Such a policy places a premium on administrative integrity and good judgment, but it may be the most effective approach to the problem.

A Spendings Tax. An essentially untried alternative that offers great possibilities for inflation control is a progressive-rate spendings tax. A basic minimum level of consumption expenditures, reflecting typical family expenditures and adjusted according to family size, would be exempted, as well as certain types of spending—for example, for education. A steeply progressive rate would be applied to spending over and above the exemption figure, commencing with perhaps a moderate rate such as 5 or 10 percent, but increasing to figures well over 100 percent on larger sums in periods of severe inflation. Particularly if the tax were regarded as temporary, it would give strong incentive to reduce spending. This type of levy would minimize pressure on wages because of the exemption figure and the ability to escape the tax by curtailing spending. Without question some enforcement problems would be encountered, especially at very high rates, and families long accustomed to high levels of spending would regard the burden as inequitable. But the approach nevertheless deserves more attention in periods of strong inflation than it has received in the past.

Weaknesses of Anti-Inflationary Fiscal Policy

Fiscal policy, like monetary policy, can play a part in restricting inflation, but is subject to serious weaknesses that limit its effectiveness. First, most tax increases that are effective in curtailing consumption also place pressure on wages, and, unless drastic controls are placed on wage levels, may provide no net restrictive effect at all. Tax increases that do not place pressure on wages (such as higher corporate income taxes that are not shifted) are effective only against investment and may be inadequate in overall impact to restrict inflation. Even these levies may place some upward pressure on prices. The potentially most effective tax device, a progressive spendings tax, is untried and would be subject to adminstrative problems.

The second problem is related: anti-inflationary fiscal policy, whether involving tax increases or reduction in governmental spending, is not effective against cost-push inflation caused by union activity and markup pricing, unless it is extended so far as to create substantial unemployment, a consequence society may regard as intolerable. Otherwise, lessening demand will not be effective in checking upward pressures on prices.

Tax increases may also reduce incentives, as discussed in Chapter 7. The effects are difficult to predict, but sharp increases that raise tax rates well above usual levels may have serious effects. The curtailment of output is contrary to the goals of society and is regarded as particularly objectionable in a wartime inflationary period.

SUMMARY EVALUATION

The determinants of national income are significantly influenced by governmental expenditures and revenues. Accordingly deliberate adjustment of these expenditures and revenues can aid in the attainment of full-employment growth patterns and general price level stability. There are, however, significant limitations to complete effectiveness to fiscal policy measures, at least with the present state of knowledge, and proposals relating to "fine tuning" of the economy by governmental action—a popular phrase of recent years—must be viewed with great skepticism.

Limitations

Several of the major limitations have been noted in preceding sections. In periods of unemployment, the greatest problem relates to uncertainty and to general psychological attitudes, particularly on the part of the business community. Policies that are most expansionary, in terms of direct effects, such as increased governmental spending financed by money creation, may produce the most serious adverse reactions on the part of investors, and thus there may be no net gain at all. The government may be forced to use measures with less direct expansionary impact to avoid this consequence.

In periods of inflationary pressures the primary limitation relates to money wage rates. Tax measures that are most effective in reducing total spending are those that are likely to have the greatest impact upon money wage rates. Even more seriously, to the extent that inflation is primarily a product of the development of a cycle of substantial periodic money wage rate increases followed by price increases, no fiscal policy or monetary policy may be effective in checking the increases without a level of unemployment regarded as intolerable. A related danger of use by fiscal policy is an attempt to eliminate structural unemployment by fiscal means; this inevitably generates inflation.

An overall difficulty not thus far mentioned is that of adequate forecasting and timing of fiscal policy measures. The art of forecasting is still in its infancy, and the government can never be certain at any time about the direction in which the economy is headed or the strength of the trend. Thus it faces a dilemma. If the trend is allowed to go far enough to eliminate doubt about its direction, reversal may be much more difficult than it would have been earlier. The alternative of acting quickly will have undesired results if the forecast was wrong. Interpretation of a minor downward adjustment as the beginning of a major decline and introduction of major anti-depression policies may quickly lead to strong inflation.

A closely related problem is that of obtaining congressional approval. This may not be required for minor adjustments in expenditures, but it is for major ones and for tax changes of any sort. Given the usual forecasting difficulties, the tendency to inertia on the part of Congress—particularly if the changes proposed may be politically unpopular—and the inevitable clash that arises if the President lacks majority support in both houses of Congress, the delay in obtaining action may be very substantial. Meanwhile the trend may have become much more severe and difficult to eliminate. Congress can act very quickly on fiscal matters if it wishes; the problem is that it often is not convinced of the need for speed. This problem is avoided with the parliamentary form of government and a strong majority.

A distinct problem of major concern in the United States with its federal system of government is the danger that the states and local governments will sabotage the fiscal policy action of the federal government. Since subordinate governments lack the power of money creation and are severely restricted in their borrowing powers, they tend to raise taxes and reduce expenditures as unemployment develops and their revenues fall. As prosperity continues they raise expenditures and gain popular support for bond issues for capital improvement and consequently contribute to inflation. The depression of the 1930's provides an excellent illustration of the danger. Expenditures for new state and local capital construction fell from $2.5 billion in 1930 to $0.6 billion in 1935, and virtually all states raised taxes during the mid-thirties. A detailed analysis of the experience during the thirties by E. Cary Brown shows that the actions of the state and local governments combined during the thirties very largely offset the positive fiscal policy of the federal government; thus there was virtually no net stimulating effect.[4] Possible solutions to the problem are noted in Chapter 12.

Fear of Discretionary Action

Much of the opposition that remains in the United States today against the use of fiscal policy is based on the substantial element of discretion involved in its use. Persons responsible for policy formation introduce programs with potentially great effects upon the economy; in so doing they increase uncertainty, which may sabotage the effectiveness of the programs. The policies may even aggravate the trends; if the government suddenly undertakes anti-inflationary policy, this may be a signal for persons to start buying in anticipation of inflation. The introduction of antidepression policy may be a signal for loss of confidence. There is the further danger that drastic action, especially if based on wrong forecasts, may do serious harm and may result in permanent increases in the size of the governmental sector that would otherwise never have occurred.

Monetary Policy. Accordingly, persons with this general point of view stress the use of monetary policy, which is much less disturbing to business confidence and does not involve increased size of the governmental sector. Unfortunately, however, while monetary policy can increase the effectiveness of fiscal policy and may be able to smooth

---

[4]E. Cary Brown, "Fiscal Policy in the Thirties: A Reappraisal," *American Economic Review,* Vol. XLVI (December, 1956), pp. 857–79. An article by A. M. Sharp, "The Counter-Cyclical Fiscal Role of State Governments during the Thirties," *National Tax Journal,* Vol. XI (June, 1958), pp. 138–45, shows that the states themselves did not actually pursue a perverse policy; the local governments were the source of the perversity.

out minor deviations in total spending, it has not proven to be effective against strong downward or upward trends. The impact is limited to I; once unemployment has become serious, earnings prospects from additional I are so limited that firms will not borrow regardless of the interest rate or availability of money capital. Great difficulty is encountered in driving the interest rate below certain levels because of the liquidity trap, and low rates may lead to increased drain of gold from the country.

In periods of strong inflationary pressures monetary policy is likewise of limited effectiveness. In usual form it has no impact upon C and little direct impact on I financed by retained earnings, by far the largest portion of the total. As a consequence, as clearly revealed in 1966–67, most of the impact rests upon the few types of investment largely financed by borrowing, particularly building construction. The net result is limited impact on inflationary pressures and the creation of unemployment in the industries affected. Restrictive monetary policy also raises the interest cost of governmental debt and can interfere seriously with state-local borrowing for urgently needed improvement.

Strengthening of Built-in Stabilizers. Groups fearful of discretionary fiscal policy also favor increased use of built-in-stabilizers to provide automatic deterring effects against upward and downward pressures. Present income taxes exert substantial automatic effect because of fixed dollar exemptions and rate brackets. The effectiveness could be increased by providing automatic changes in tax rates if unemployment exceeded a certain percentage, on the one hand, or the price level rose more than a certain percentage, on the other. Such a system would eliminate delays and discretionary action and presumably have less disturbing effect on the economy, especially that arising during a long period of discussion of proposed changes. Additional automatic stabilization could also be built into expenditure programs as, for example, by providing for automatic increases in various welfare payments as unemployment rose. Or, automatic adjustments could be made in some form of broad negative income tax or family allowance system.

These proposals are not without some merit, but they are based upon mechanistic concepts of national income determination: if unemployment exceeds a certain percentage, automatic turning of an expenditure valve by a certain amount will restore full employment. National income determination, with important psychological determinants and shifting importance of structural unemployment, cannot be reduced to purely mechanical relationships and quantitative adjustments. Furthermore, in the United States, Congress is hostile to any such delegation of its powers, especially over taxes. The most that Congress could possibly sanction would be greater discretion over timing of capital improvement expenditures.

GOVERNMENTAL POLICY AND ECONOMIC GROWTH

Fiscal policy that succeeds in maintaining full employment will automatically keep the actual rate of economic growth to the level of potential growth. Growth, however, may produce a constant tendency for total spending to lag behind Y; if it does, fiscal policy must be planned in terms of this situation, rather than being utilized as necessary on occasions when $C + I + G$ falls below or rises above full employment Y.

Lag in Investment

The chief potential difficulty is a possible tendency for I to lag as growth continues because of the growing stock of capital goods relative to other factors. Two primary alternative policies may be considered. The first is provision of gradually increasing stimulus to investment by fiscal and monetary policy measures: gradually increasing tax credits and acceleration of depreciation and gradually declining interest rates. High tax credits, accelerated depreciation, and low interest rates help to sustain a somewhat higher level of I than otherwise, but most of their impact arises out of their introduction. Tax credits make some investment advantageous when it would not otherwise be, but the main influence arises when the change is made, making profitable an additional segment of previously submarginal I. Under this approach, occasional inflationary pressures would be dampened by tax measures to cut C rather than I. The primary question is whether or not such a program can continue to be effective. If the marginal return from additional I does continue to fall, policies designed to keep the volume at a high level will eventually reach a point beyond which they cannot go. There are limits to reduction of the interest rate, and continuous increases in tax credits may result in completely worthless investment. Alternatively, the government may continue to increase its own investment (or other spending) to absorb the savings that cannot find outlet in additional private investment. This approach avoids the problem encountered with continued efforts to increase private investment, but it does not overcome the difficulty that the additional investment may contribute little to society.

The other alternative is a reduction in the S/Y ratio by tax measures that impinge on funds saved. This must, of course, be accomplished in such a way that adverse impact on investment is kept to the minimum—a result not easily attained. The reduction of S/Y makes the attainment of the potential growth rate easier, but the consequent reduction in the potential growth rate is contrary to the goal of maintaining a high rate of economic growth. Nevertheless this may be the only alternative to a continuing tendency toward unemployment on the one hand or useless governmental investment on the other.

This problem may never be encountered; continued technological progress may allow investment to remain at sufficiently high levels to avoid the need for governmental intervention. The problem is presented as a possible one, not as an inevitable one.

Potential Growth Rate

The other question relating to growth is possible governmental action to increase the potential rate of growth if society seeks this objective. One approach is through increases in governmental activities that have direct impact upon growth: higher levels of education; elimination of poverty pockets of unskilled persons who contribute nothing to the economy; provision of funds for research, including ones for public health; attempts to improve relations with other countries to lessen defense expenditures; and action to prevent unions from barring introduction of new techniques or requiring employers to use unnecessary personnel. Provision of facilities for retraining of persons displaced by automation not only facilitates growth directly but also lessens the resistance of workers to introduction of new techniques. Tax adjustments can likewise encourage research activities.

The other approach would increase the S/Y ratio, thus permitting a higher rate of capital formation at full employment. The potential success of such a policy depends on the capital-output ratio; evidence cited in the previous chapter suggests that in the United States any attempt to increase growth by raising S/Y does not appear to be fruitful, whereas it would be in many developing economies urgently requiring additional capital goods. If such a policy is attempted in a developed country, the simplest approach is to shift the relative impact of the tax structure from S to C. Unfortunately such a policy is likely to run counter to widely accepted standards of equity since more of the burden would be transferred to the lower income groups.

The basic problem is that increasing S/Y would aggravate the problem of attaining the potential growth path. Reduction in consumption, for example, makes the attainment of a continuing high level of investment more difficult. Most developed economies will probably do well if they succeed in attaining the potential growth path based on the present S/Y ratio rather than seeking to increase the potential rate.

EMPIRICAL STUDIES

Several studies have sought to ascertain the actual effects of fiscal policy measures.

1. The study of experience during the depression of the thirties by E. Cary Brown, referred to above, indicated that the failure of the government to bring recovery was due to the failure to use fiscal policy effectively, not to inability of such policy to succeed.[5] The combined federal-state-local spending during the depression years was actually greater than the 1929 figure only in two years, 1931 and 1936. The general trend of governmental spending was downward throughout the thirties; thus the government was aggravating the depression rather than facilitating recovery. The federal government did increase its expenditures, but this increase was roughly offset by the tax increases in 1932 that doubled the potential full-employment revenue yield, and the small net expansionary effect was more than offset by decline in state-local spending.

2. A long-range study by J. M. Firestone, covering the period 1879–1958, showed that in peacetime cycles in business activity, other than those immediately after wars, changes in government receipts produced deficits in depressions, thus providing some automatic stabilization.[6] Introduction of the income tax greatly increased the magnitude of the countercyclical influence of the budgetary position. In contrast to other cycles, in those immediately following wars changes in governmental expenditures rather than in revenues provided a stabilizing influence.

3. A study by Wilfred Lewis examined fiscal policy in the post–World War II period in detail, with the following conclusions:[7]

a) Built-in stabilizers, particularly the personal income tax, unemployment compensation, and payroll taxes, made a significant contribution to economic stability with relatively good timing, producing

[5] Brown, *op cit.*

[6] J. M. Firestone, *Federal Receipts and Expenditures during Business Cycles* (Princeton, N.J.: Princeton University Press for National Bureau of Economic Research, 1960).

[7] Wilfred Lewis, *Federal Fiscal Policy in the Postwar Recessions* (Washington, D.C.: Brookings Institution, 1962).

deficits when business activity declined, surpluses during prosperity. Reversal of the stabilizing influence tended to check recovery, however, once it began.

b) Deliberate fiscal policy during the period contributed much less toward stability. During the period covered (prior to the tax cuts of 1963) expenditure measures, rather than tax changes, were used, partly because they could be justified more easily politically and did not require the administrations to admit publicly the need for corrective action. Typically the changes were so delayed that recovery had started before they were under way.

c) Major constraints to effective use of fiscal policy included campaign pledges requiring contrary action, uncertainty of forecasting, fear of losing business confidence by admitting that a decline had commenced, concern over balancing the budget, and failure to consider the effects of trust fund financing. Over the years, however, the need for use of fiscal policy became more widely accepted.

4. A study by Robert Rafuse of state-local revenue and expenditure policy in the postwar period showed that state-local tax receipts provided a stabilizing influence during inflationary periods by rising rapidly, but had a perverse effect during declines in business activity by continuing to rise.[8] State-local expenditures provided the opposite effect, aiding recovery in declines but contributing to inflationary pressures. State, but not local, revenue receipts increased in stabilizing effect over the last two decades, primarily because of growing importance of income and sales taxes, and expenditures declined in perverse effect during inflationary periods. Considering revenues and expenditures together, the overall effect has been stabilizing in periods of decline and has promoted recovery once under way, the expansionary effect tapering off toward the end of the inflationary period. These results are very different from those of the thirties.

5. A study by P. Eilbrott of the significance of automatic stabilizers in the United States in the period 1948–60 concludes that they prevented from 36 to 52 percent of the decline in income in recessions that would otherwise have occurred, and from 25 to 42 percent of the increases in expansions. Thus they provided a significant countercyclical tool, but tended to place excessive restraint on expansion.[9]

[8]R. W. Rafuse, Jr., "Cyclical Behavior of State-Local Finances," in R. A. Musgrave (ed.), *Essays in Fiscal Federalism* (Washington, D.C.: Brookings Institution, 1965), pp. 63–121.

[9]P. Eilbrott, "The Effectiveness of Automatic Stabilizers," *American Economic Review*, Vol. LVI (June, 1966), pp. 450–65.

As yet no scientific study of the effects of the 1963–64 income tax reductions and the 1965 excise tax reductions have been made, but limited evidence suggests that they were effective in accomplishing the objectives. These were the first deliberate uses in the United States of a policy of tax reduction to stimulate economic activity.

APPENDIX—MORE EXTREME PROPOSALS TO AID ECONOMIC GROWTH

Much more drastic proposals to aid economic growth have been advanced from time to time. One was developed by K. Knorr and W. J. Baumol[10] and used in Canada in modified form for a short time. The original proposal called for replacement of the U.S. corporate income tax by a value added tax, with tax concessions made for firms increasing output and tax penalties placed on firms failing to increase output. As a result, firms would be given stronger incentive to expand and transfer of resources to growing firms would be facilitated. The authors argued that mere insurance of adequate total spending in the economy was inadequate for growth—that more drastic measures were required. The major question that can be raised about the proposal of course is whether the placing of this form of pressure on firms can actually bring about expansion, or whether growth depends primarily on sales trends that are beyond control of the firms.

In 1963 Canada introduced a modified version of his proposal, providing corporate income tax concessions to firms that increased sales over the previous year. Apparently the plan was designed to increase current employment and use of existing capacity as well as to aid long-range growth. Many objections were raised against it, partly because of complexities, and it was repealed a year later without any careful examination of its effects, which appear to have been small.[11]

Another proposal, that of the Social Credit movement, was based upon the argument that total purchasing power is inevitably inadequate to buy all goods produced. This thesis was popularized in the writing of Major C. H. Douglas, a retired British electrical engineer, who argued that purchasing power is inadequate because depreciation charges and payments for materials are elements in prices but do not become incomes. He proposed "social credit"—a program of regular payments

---

[10]See K. Knorr and W. J. Baumol, *What Price Economic Growth?* (Englewood Cliffs, N.J.: Prentice-Hall, Inc., 1961).

[11]See R. Bird, "A Tax Incentive for Sales: The Canadian Experience," *National Tax Journal,* Vol. XVIII (September, 1965), pp. 277–85.

by government to all persons, to be financed from printing paper money to offset the continuing deficiency in purchasing power.

The Douglas movement gained no significant following in the United States, but in Canada it became a force of some moment. The center of the Canadian movement was Alberta. William Aberhart, a Calgary high-school principal and director of the Prophetic Bible Institute, became a convert to the Douglas ideas and formed the Social Credit Party, which gained power in Alberta in 1935 on a platform of paying $25 a month to all adults. The problem of how to make these payments, in the light of the bankrupt condition of the province and the lack of power of the provinces to issue money, was an immediate dilemma and nothing was accomplished. The coming of the war and prosperity diverted attention from the "social dividends."[12]

The fallacy in the Douglas reasoning is obvious; to the extent that amounts equal to depreciation charges are reinvested in new capital equipment, there is no shortage of purchasing power. Failure to reinvest such amounts, if not offset by equivalent new investment, will, of course, reduce aggregate demand and lead to a decline in output. The difficulty is one not of a basic inadequacy of purchasing power but of insufficient profitability of investment. Any program of continuous payments of substantial sums of printed money could easily produce serious inflation.

REFERENCES

JOHANSEN, L. Public Economics. Chicago: Rand McNally, 1965, chap. iii.

LEWIS, WILFRED, JR. Federal Fiscal Policy in Postwar Depressions. Washington, D.C.: Brookings Institution, 1962.

MUSGRAVE, R. A. The Theory of Public Finance, chaps. xvii–xxii. New York: McGraw-Hill Book Co., Inc., 1959.

PERRY, GEORGE L. Unemployment, Money Wage Rates, and Inflation. Cambridge: MIT Press, 1966.

[12]The Social Credit Party remains in power in Alberta and has gained control of the government in British Columbia, but relatively little is said today about the social credit doctrines, except in occasional reference to the basic defects in the monetary system and the fact that the federal government has prevented the provinces from carrying out the proposals.

Chapter 11 DEBT POLICY

Since borrowing is a significant source of governmental revenue, debt policies—selection of the forms of borrowing, credit instruments and refunding and retirement policies and determination of other aspects of the structure of the governmental debt—are significant for the economy and for the attainment of the objectives of the borrowing program and of governmental activities generally. Before debt policies are considered, however, a brief review of the objections to borrowing and the justifications for it is necessary.

Primary Objections to Borrowing

The objectionable features will be summarized first, since governments typically follow the rule that expenditures should not be financed by borrowing except in those specific circumstances in which its use is warranted in preference to other means. The first and most obvious disadvantage is the interest cost that is created; the interest increases the total cost to the taxpayers of the expenditure programs financed by debt. The taxes employed to meet the interest costs are almost certain to have some adverse effects on the economy and retard economic development; the receipt of the interest by the bondholders does not offset the adverse incentive and allocational effects of the taxes. The tax and interest payment program may produce undesired redistributional effects (transferring wealth to higher income groups) and may make the attainment of the potential growth path more difficult. The higher taxes will interfere with attainment of optimal levels of governmental activities in future years.

Secondly, financing by borrowing is less anti-inflationary than financing by taxation; thus large-scale borrowing in periods of full employment is likely to permit inflationary pressures to continue. Borrowing is less objectionable from the standpoint of inflation than money creation.

Thirdly, to the extent that persons suffer from debt illusion, viewing the bonds as personal wealth but ignoring the tax liability to which they give rise, their decision making on allocation of income between consumption and savings will be distorted. They will spend relatively too much on consumption, compared to their long-range preferences, as they ignore the future reduction in their personal wealth from higher taxes and the future tax liabilities of their heirs. Likewise, taxation forces many persons to reduce consumption, whereas borrowing does not. This relatively greater reduction in the S/Y ratio in turn lowers the full-employment rate of private-sector capital formation and thus the potential rate of economic growth compared to those with tax financing.

Fourthly, if governments borrow freely without regard to the future consequences and voters are relatively shortsighted, large obligations will be built up for future taxpayers from the financing of activities that do not benefit them and the major restraining force will be taken off increases in government spending. The real burden in the sense of reduced private-sector output resulting from governmental use of resources will not appear as a current burden to the taxpayer-voters and they may be unaware of the burden that they will bear through inflation. Accordingly the preferences of the community will not determine resource allocation and governmental activities will be carried too far relative to private-sector activities. Presumably this will not continue indefinitely; voters will not remain myopic as the debt catches up with them. But this may take time.

Justifications for Borrowing

Despite these objectionable features, governmental borrowing is regarded by voters and by governments as justifiable in several circumstances.

First, the postponement permitted by borrowing of the need for taxes to finance specific governmental activities may be advantageous in two major situations. When governmental activities rise very sharply, particularly to conduct a major war, borrowing permits the cushioning of the reduction in consumption, allowing some persons who prefer not to reduce consumption immediately to continue consuming at the old levels. A larger portion of the impact of increased G rests on I, and the impact on C is spread out over a longer period. Accordingly, society will tolerate a higher level of governmental spending, partly because individuals know that they can escape a portion of the burden temporarily, and partly because they may hope that they can escape it permanently by shifting it to others. At the same time GNP can be held to a higher level if increases in taxes would reduce incentives to work.

Sharp increases in taxes over accustomed levels may have drastic effects on work incentives that can be avoided if the tax increases are more gradual. Furthermore, when expenditures increase sharply equity considerations become more serious. At usual levels of taxation some inequity is tolerable. But if a country is seeking to reduce private-sector output to the lowest possible level in order to maximize defense activities, complete financing by taxation would place intolerable burden on those persons discriminated against by the tax structure, since persons benefiting from the structure would be forced to curtail consumption less than is feasible. Financing of a major war entirely out of taxation could lead to a breakdown of the war effort; more realistically, no government could undertake such a program and survive politically.

The second situation justifying postponement of tax financing is the nonrecurrent expenditure of large sums on capital projects that will yield their benefits over a period of years, sums of such magnitude that they raise total expenditures well above prevailing levels. This is of primary importance at the state and local level, since national government capital expenditures typically do not cause sharp variations in total expenditures. A small school district, however, may build a new high school once in 50 years, at a cost several times as great as regular annual expenditures. Were borrowing not possible for such purposes, voters would be biased against long-range improvements conveying benefits to persons in the future, compared to those yielding all benefits currently.

The justification for borrowing is particularly strong if the investment will be financed out of charges on the users rather than out of taxes; obviously charges cannot be raised sufficiently in one year to cover all capital costs or persons would not use the services.

Thirdly, borrowing constitutes a second-best alternative to money creation to finance governmental activities in periods of unemployment, if money creation is barred by institutional restriction (for example, borrowing by subordinate units of government) or by widespread fear by society of its use, with potential adverse consequences for business confidence and the volume of investment.

Borrowing and the Shifting of Burden to Future Generations

Justification for borrowing to postpone payment of taxes is based on the assumption that borrowing actually allows present taxpayers to spread the costs of current expenditures over a period of years, instead of meeting them all in the current year, and to transfer costs to future generations of taxpayers. These may be persons moving into the taxing area, or persons not yet born or liable for tax.

This assumption requires reconsideration, in light of the now widely accepted argument that real costs of governmental activities cannot be shifted from one period to another. Distinction is necessary between "external" and "internal" borrowing. External borrowing, that is, foreign borrowing on the part of a national government, clearly does shift real burden forward in time, regardless of the definition of burden employed. This type of borrowing enables the economy to obtain additional resources from outside during the period of borrowing. Subsequently the economy suffers a loss of resources, because an export surplus is necessary for payment of interest and principal. Borrowing by subordinate units of government is very similar in nature to foreign borrowing, since funds and resources are primarily obtained from outside the area and the funds are repaid to the outside.

Burden as Transfer of Resources. The major question relates to national government internal borrowing; the answer depends upon the concept of burden employed. If burden is defined as the transfer of resources out of private-sector production to governmental-sector use, and thus as the reduction in private-sector output, the burden (assuming full employment) of the governmental activities is borne at the time the expenditures are made, whether the expenditures are financed by taxation or borrowing. Thus in this sense the cost of World War II was borne during the war through reduced output of goods for civilian use,[1] as resources were diverted from the manufacture of automobiles and other civilian goods to national defense items. The burden was borne at the time regardless of use of taxation or borrowing; borrowing did not permit a shift of resources from future periods to the war period.[2] In turn, persons in subsequent generations have no fewer resources available because of the borrowing and real private-sector GNP is not reduced. The future generations inherit both the bonds and the obligations that they represent. When interest and principal payments are made, funds are merely transferred from some persons to others in the same generation. Given these definitions and assumptions, there is no forward shifting of real costs and future generations are not bur-

[1] That is, output of goods was reduced below potential levels. Since there was substantial unemployment when the war began, little overall cutback in civilian production was required. Much of the burden was borne from use of idle resources and, indirectly, by persons serving in the armed forces instead of in preferred occupations.

[2] Burden suffered by future generations from more rapid depletion of natural resources is not related to the use of the borrowing method of financing.

dened with the expenditures of the present.[3] Admittedly certain problems are created for the future that may reduce real income. The taxes necessary to pay interest and principal may deter economic development and the debt illusion may reduce the rate of capital formation, as previously explained.[4] But these problems do not constitute forward transfer of the burdens of the activities.

Effect on the Rate of Capital Formation. This argument ignores the relative effects of borrowing and taxation upon consumption and savings and thus on the potential rate of capital formation. Borrowing will typically reduce savings more and consumption less than taxation, for reasons outlined in earlier chapters. Accordingly, with borrowing, future generations inherit a smaller stock of capital goods, and output and consumption are lower than they would be if the taxation method had been employed. The only exception is a situation in which persons save solely for the purpose of bequeathing to heirs a sum sufficient to insure a given real income. If borrowing were used for financing, persons would supply the entire sum out of consumption in order to be able to bequeath the same sum. However, this is a most unlikely objective for all saving; accumulation per se, without regard to heirs, is a significant motive and many persons are subject to the debt illusion: they regard government bonds as wealth but do not consider the additional future tax liabilities (on themselves or their heirs).[5]

Accordingly, through the effect on capital formation, the burden of governmental activities financed by borrowing is in part shifted to the future (including persons in future generations) as a result of the relatively greater curtailment of savings and real investment compared to that with the taxing method. Persons can thus succeed in postponing real burden, as they seek to do. This analysis is based upon the assumption of full employment. If this is not attained, the use of borrowing instead of taxation, by increasing aggregate demand, may result in a higher actual rate of capital formation despite the lower potential rate; if so, burden is not actually transferred forward, but both present and future generations are benefited, or at least are subject to no burden.

---

[3]This is the traditional argument of economists relating to shifting of burden to future generations, as expressed first by H. G. Brown and Pigou. See J. M. Buchanan, *Public Principles of Public Debt* (Homewood, Ill.: Richard D. Irwin, Inc., 1958), chap. ii.

[4]This consideration is developed by J. E. Meade, "Is National Debt a Burden?," *Oxford Economic Papers,* Vol. X (June, 1958), pp. 163–83.

[5]This argument is developed by J. G. Head, in "The Theory of Debt Incidence," *Rivista di diritto finanziero e scienza finanze,* Vol. XXVI (June, 1967), pp. 175–213.

Individual Reactions to Debt. Alternatively, burden may be defined as reduction in personal satisfaction resulting from the financing of governmental activities. With this definition, no burden is incurred at the time the money is borrowed.[6] The bondholders purchase bonds voluntarily, exchanging liquid wealth for them and presumably increasing, not decreasing, their satisfaction. The taxpayers pay no tax currently for the activity and suffer no burden. Bondholders have either given up consumption voluntarily to buy the bonds, or, more likely, have purchased the bonds in lieu of other assets. At the time the debt is retired, a burden is placed on the taxpayers. Tax is collected from them and their consumption or saving is reduced. The bondholders, on the other hand, experience no gain; they merely exchange their bonds for money, which in turn they may place in other assets. A net burden has been placed upon the future generations, shifted forward from the borrowing generation. If the debt is not repaid, no burden is created except from the payment of interest; if governments borrow in perpetuity, no one bears burden other than interest charges.

The significant issue on the question of shifting of burden is the relative usefulness of the alternative definitions. The first two definitions (the second being essentially a refinement of the first) stress that borrowing does not enable one generation to pull resources from another to use in conduct of its activities, although methods of financing that reduce the rate of capital formation will reduce the potential real income and consumption of future generations. The difference between the effects of taxation and borrowing on capital formation is one of degree, but the difference may be substantial. The definition related to individual satisfaction, on the other hand, is useful in analyzing individual decision making relating to borrowing and debt retirement. Thus borrowing does shift burden to future generations as individuals view the burden, but it does not shift resources to the present and it does not reduce future real income and consumption except insofar as it affects the rate of capital formation.[7]

[6]J. M. Buchanan is the leading exponent of this approach. See his *Public Principles of Public Dept, op. cit.,* and the collection of articles in J. M. Ferguson, *Public Debt and Future Generations* (Chapel Hill, N.C.: University of North Carolina Press, 1964).

[7]Another approach to the question is presented by W. G. Bowen, R. G. Davis, and D. H. Kopf, "The Public Debt: A Burden on Future Generations," *American Economic Review,* Vol L. (September, 1960), pp. 701–6. Their analysis assumes an overlap of generations. Generation A, alive at the time of the government spending, reduces consumption in order to buy the bonds, and thus temporarily bears the burden. However, ultimately persons in Generation A sell the bonds to persons in Generation B, spend the amount on consumption, and maintain their lifetime consumption levels. If Generation B retires the debt, it will bear the burden in the form of reduced consumption; however,

BORROWING POLICY

Governments—especially national governments—have extensive choice of borrowing methods, relating to maturity, to marketability and redemption, and to retirement. Once a debt is incurred, changes in its form may be possible, at least as existing securities mature. An optimal program can be defined only in terms of the situation in which borrowing is undertaken and thus in terms of the goals of the particular program. Several general issues warrant initial attention.

Internal versus External Borrowing

External borrowing allows a country to increase the quantity of resources available for use at the particular time, but creates a liability requiring greater exports in future years. This type of borrowing is particularly advantageous to a newly developing economy in need of additional imports of capital goods for economic development and having very limited foreign exchange. If the capital goods acquired speed economic development, the rise in output will facilitate payment of interest and principal. The limitations to external borrowing are two: the ability to obtain foreign loans, and the danger of building up so much liability that interest and principal payments become impossible, with consequent international difficulties. Foreign domination of the economy and of governmental policy may also be feared. A more developed economy, except in periods of catastrophe, does not require foreign borrowing to obtain resources and would merely create unnecessary external obligations.

Interest Cost and Liquidity

In full-employment periods, the primary goal of national debt policy is to lessen liquidity, that is, to encourage holders of personal wealth to avoid consumption or real investment spending. Taxation would eliminate the possibility of spending the given sums by taking them; debt policy seeks to discourage spending by inducing persons to acquire government securities and hold them. At the same time the government seeks to minimize its overall interest cost, because of the adverse effects of interest payments upon the attainment of optimal levels of governmental spending and upon economic development.

---

it may sell the debt to Generation C, and so on. This result is not obtained if Generation A gives the bonds to B instead of selling them. The approach may be regarded as a version of the reduced-capital-formation method of forward transference of burden.

Thus the borrowing program, or program of refunding existing debt, seeks to find a satisfactory balance in the attainment of these two objectives. Policies that would maximize illiquidity could result in an intolerable total interest cost; deliberate minimization of interest cost per dollar borrowed could easily result in greater total interest burden since issuance of more securities (in place of money creation) would be required to attain the desired restriction of liquidity. Complete disregard for liquidity would be contrary to stabilization goals.

Ascertainment of the best combination of forms of borrowing to attain these goals is unfortunately a difficult task, primarily because the antiliquidity effects of various borrowing techniques are unknown. Since attitudes of investors differ, it is reasonable to assume that various forms of securities (that is, combination of interest rates, periods of maturity, and other features) will have varying appeal to different persons. Thus a variety of security offerings is likely to produce better results than use of a single form.

In a period of unemployment, the objectives of debt policy are altered drastically. The aim is to maximize liquidity, to encourage persons to spend as much from accumulated sums as possible, the debt being replaced by money creation. The goal of interest minimization remains the same.

Short-Term versus Long-Term Borrowing. The length of time for which securities are issued is of major significance for liquidity and interest cost. Short-term borrowing offers several advantages. The interest rate on long-term loans is typically higher than that on short-term loans, primarily because of the greater uncertainty involved in long-period loans and the greater hazard that the lender may suddenly require liquid funds and be unable to get them without suffering a capital loss. The differential widens greatly in periods when GNP drops well below full-employment levels. In such a period there is substantial idle money capital that persons are unwilling to commit to long-term investments at low interest rates. Many of these funds belong to business firms that want them readily available for real investment once recovery commences. Short-term loans have an additional advantage of giving the government frequent opportunity to readjust the debt structure.

On the other hand, long-term loans typically reduce liquidity more effectively. Since they are not automatically maturing at short intervals, greater inertia must be overcome by the owners to use the funds, and sale involves some cost. More significantly, bonds can be reduced in price by Federal Reserve action at any time; many bondholders, especially financial institutions, are reluctant to sell bonds that have dropped below par, even though continuing to hold them may not be entirely logical. Furthermore, long-term borrowing minimizes the nuisance and cost of refunding as well as governmental vulnerability to increases in interest rates due to monetary policy or other causes. The government also avoids the danger of possible borrowing crises if refunding becomes necessary in a period of financial stringency when for other reasons the Federal Reserve system does not wish to liberalize credit. Possible opposition of the Treasury to Federal Reserve anti-inflationary monetary policy is lessened.

While interest rates on long-term loans are usually higher, overall interest cost may not be greater because the total amount of long-term securities necessary to accomplish a given restriction of liquidity will be less. The rate will be higher, but the total base will be lower. The exact optimal pattern, in terms of the two objectives, therefore, will depend on the schedule of the relationship between increases in interest and reductions in liquidity, a schedule difficult to ascertain.

Changes in Rates. So far the discussion has considered the situation at a particular time, without regard to expectations of interest rate changes. Experience suggests that the interest rate level will not remain stable, particularly since variations in rate appear to be imperative for economic stabilization. Accordingly, in a period in which rates are relatively high, any new borrowing or refunding in long-term securities at current rates will saddle the government with high rates for a long period to come. Accordingly, short-term borrowing, even though less effective in reducing liquidity, has the important advantage of allowing the government to shift to long-term securities when the rate falls. Or, in other words, the government, in determining policy, must consider not only the present rate differentials but the possible differentials over the life of the securities as well.

In periods of less than full employment, on the other hand, when interest rates are low, borrowing or refunding on a long-term basis will give the government the advantage of the low rates over a long period. The extremely low rates on short-term loans in such periods are unfortunately tempting to governments, since their use would allow very low current interest cost. But such use would sacrifice the opportunity to make long-term loans at low cost.

In summary: a government inevitably faces a dilemma on the question of term of borrowing. In inflationary periods, long-term borrowing will be most effective in dampening inflationary spending by providing greater illiquidity, but such borrowing will commit the government for a long period to high rates. In depression, while short-term borrowing will maximize liquidity, the government has the opportunity of making long-term loans at very low rates. The most logical conclusion is that long-term debt should be incurred in depression periods, while short-term borrowing should be utilized in periods of high interest rates in anticipation of lower rates in the future. The long-term borrowing in depressions will insure that the central banking system has a good supply of long-term bonds to depress in price in inflation, thus decreasing liquidity. The most significant element in debt policy in inflation is not the nature of the new borrowing as much as it is the ability to make existing bond holdings nonliquid. This is much more significant than an overall lengthening of the term of debt in inflationary periods, as was once widely advocated.[8]

Restrictions on Marketability

The most nonliquid form of bond is the type that is not negotiable and therefore nonsalable. Nonsalability, as such, makes the bonds unattractive to most bondholders, since the bonds cannot be converted to money until maturity. In order to sell them, therefore, a much higher interest rate must be paid; at progressively higher rates, progressively more investors can be induced to buy them.

Nonsalability does have one advantage to investors: since sale value cannot decline there is no danger of capital loss. This feature is of little advantage if the bonds cannot be redeemed prior to maturity. But the combination of redeemability and nonsalability is attractive to many investors. These dual features, characteristic of U.S. savings bonds, may allow sale of the bonds at relatively low interest rates to investors who fear a general decline in security values. The redemption privilege, unfortunately, destroys the liquidity reducing effect, unless steps are taken to preserve it by discouraging redemption. A simple method, as used in the United States with savings bonds, is to make the interest payable in a lump sum at redemption, with the rate progressive according to the period the bond is held. Thus redemption prior to maturity is discouraged. In severe inflationary periods, other methods could be used, such as popular appeals to hold the bonds, or publication of lists of redeemers.

Fixed Purchasing Power Bonds

Guarantee against decline in bond prices does not protect the purchaser of bonds against decline in their real value as a result of infla-

---

[8]The desirability of long-term borrowing in depressions in preference to shift to long-term debt in periods of inflation was developed effectively by Warren Smith in *Debt Management in the United States* (Study Paper No. 19, Joint Economic Committee, U.S. Congress, 1960).

tion. Once an economy has experienced considerable inflation, persons may become reluctant to buy fixed-income securities.[9] Therefore bonds issued with fixed purchasing power, that is, with adjustment of interest payments and maturity value by the index of the general price level, appear more attractive to many bond buyers and can be sold at lower interest rates.

Provision of such bonds, however, would in effect be a tacit admission on the part of the government that more inflation was likely and could lead to additional anticipatory buying and aggravate inflation. All such "escalator" provisions tend to strengthen inflation, in part by raising the monetary value of the wealth of the bondholders as prices rise and lessening savings (to the extent that the rate of savings is a function of the total value of wealth) and in part by raising government interest payments. Shift to the system in a period in which inflation was anticipated would cause substantial transfer of investments from other government bonds to the new ones and would disorganize the bond market.

Pressures to Buy and Mandatory Lending

Particularly during war, direct pressures can be employed to persuade persons to buy bonds: advertising, bond drives, payroll deduction plans, and the like. The deduction system is particularly effective, as the forces of inertia favor continued purchasing of bonds rather than the reverse. Too much pressure will lead persons to redeem bonds at the same rate at which they purchase them, with no net gain.

Mandatory Lending. Mandatory lending or refundable taxation is a hybrid of taxation and borrowing. The system has often been called compulsory savings, a complete misnomer.[10] Mandatory lending requires persons to lend a certain amount to the government, the sum based upon income or other criteria. Or, in the other words, the government would promise to refund in the future a portion of the tax paid during the period.

The potential advantage of mandatory lending over tax increases

---

[9]One of the principal early advocates of fixed purchasing power bonds was Sumner Slichter. See R. Goode, "A Constant Purchasing Power Bond," *National Tax Journal*, Vol. IV (December, 1951), pp. 332–40.

A more recent plea for fixed purchasing power bonds is made by James Tobin; see his "Principles of Debt Management," in Commission on Money and Credit, *Fiscal and Debt Management Policies* (Englewood Cliffs, N.J.: Prentice-Hall, Inc., 1963).

[10]A system appropriately called compulsory savings, whereby persons would be required to add, net, a certain amount to their savings in each time period, related presumably to income, could be devised, but it would be extremely difficult to administer because of the necessity for ascertaining net wealth of the taxpayers each year.

is the lessened incentive effect; if persons know that the amounts will ultimately be refunded to them after the inflationary period is over, their work incentives are less likely to be impaired. Unfortunately, however, persons may not clearly distinguish between refundable and nonrefundable taxes. Experience suggests that they are more likely to do so if they are issued securities to represent their future claims against the government, rather than merely being given tax receipts and a promise of refund. Other advantages are based on equity grounds. The burden on the lower income groups, almost imperative if inflation is to be checked, could be lessened over a period of time by refunds. The squeeze that sharp tax increases places on persons with heavy savings commitments could be mitigated by allowing credits against refundable taxes for certain forms of savings. The program offers the fiscal policy advantage of giving persons a backlog of purchasing power to use in a subsequent period of unemployment. On the other hand, the program would be somewhat less effective from the standpoint of inflation control than tax increases to the extent that persons regard the refundable taxes as a portion of their accumulated savings, and therefore reduce voluntary savings.[11]

Interest Rates, Consumption, and Investment

In periods of severe inflation, when the curtailment of C and I are of great importance, interest and debt policy may affect total spending by influencing incentives to save and to buy government securities. If the total volume of savings is positively related to the rate of interest, deliberate interest increases, although raising the government's interest cost, could reduce consumption. The motives for savings are such, however, that the relationship is probably negligible; very great increases would be necessary to induce a small additional amount of saving.

[11]World War II experience with refundable taxes was somewhat limited. There were minor features of this nature in the United States with the so-called victory tax (a supplement to the income tax) and the excess profits tax, but general use of the proposal received little serious attention. Great Britain employed compulsory savings after 1941, largely confined to the lower income groups because of a maximum on the amount refundable. Evidence suggests that the workers did not distinguish sharply between refundable and regular taxes. Canada provided for refund of a portion of the income tax. As in Great Britain, taxpayers did not appear, on the whole to recognize the refundable feature, and because of continued adverse incentive effects, particularly on willingness to work overtime and on absenteeism, tax rates were cut back in 1944 and the refund system eliminated.

One of the few nonwar uses of the system has been in Ghana, where the program was introduced as a supplement to the income tax in 1961, to increase the availability of funds for economic development.

For review of experience, see W. W. Heller, "Compulsory Lending: The World War II Experience," *National Tax Journal*, Vol. IV (June, 1951), pp. 116–28.

Increasing the rate paid on government securities might also lure some funds away from private investment. Again, however, in periods of good business prospects, probably little investment is sufficiently close to the margin to be affected significantly by rate differentials. Nevertheless, increased availability of certain forms of governmental securities may alter funds available for private investment of particular types. Increased availability of long-term government bonds may reduce the funds available for long-term private investment; increased short-term obligations would reduce the funds available for short-term business use.

Depression Borrowing Policy

The aim in depressions is to keep the government securities as liquid as possible and to minimize any restraining influence that borrowing may have on C or I. The danger of restraint is not great since few persons will cut C merely because more government bonds are available, and any tendency for interest rates to rise can be offset by Federal Reserve action. Depressions offer the opportunity to refund short-term obligations by longer term bonds, even though temporarily interest costs may be higher as a result.

State-Local Borrowing

State and local government borrowing is primarily employed to finance nonrecurrent capital improvements lasting over a period of years. Of necessity long-term bonds are issued to avoid the problems of constant refunding, which could prove disastrous because these governments have no power to create money or control over monetary policy. The typical policy is to issue bonds for roughly the period of expected life of the investment or a somewhat shorter period, depending in part upon expected ability to repay principal. Likewise, systematic provision is almost always made for retirement of the debt. For many years a sinking fund system was employed, a certain sum being set aside from charges or taxes each year and invested to provide the means to pay off the debt at maturity. Because sinking fund reserves sometimes were diverted to other purposes, serial bonds have become standard; a certain portion of the original issue is paid off each year from tax revenues or charges. Since states and local governments have no control over interest rates, they must pay the current rate for securities of the particular type if they are to obtain the money and the actual rate particular governments must pay depends in part on their own credit standing.

Revenue Bonds. A major issue that subordinate governments face is the choice between revenue bonds, which are not obligations of the taxpayers and are met from revenues from the investment, and general obligation bonds, which are liabilities of the taxpayers. Traditionally revenue bonds have been used to finance commercial enterprises, with interest and principal paid from commercial charges. They are used for two primary reasons. First, they are not usually subject to the requirement of a popular vote or other debt restriction. Second, opposition to their issuance is less since they create no future tax liability, and taxpayers are not forced to carry the risk of failure of the project. On the other hand, revenue bonds require payment of a higher rate of interest, often about one percentage point. The choice between the two forms must therefore be made on the basis of these conflicting considerations.

In more recent years, revenue bonds have been employed in some states to finance noncommercial activities, particularly school construction. The bonds are issued by a building authority that constructs the buildings and rents them to school districts and other local governmental units, which in turn meet the obligations out of taxation. This use is purely and simply a device to bypass constitutional limitations on borrowing. Taxpayers appear to be willing to pay a higher tax rate in order to avoid modifying the constitutional rules. Or, a majority may favor borrowing but is not strong enough to insure approval of constitutional change.

RETIREMENT OF DEBT

Governments, like corporations, do not necessarily retire debt. They may continue to refund particular issues as they mature and maintain the debt at a given level, and national governments, at least, may cancel outstanding debt if they wish. Rarely will a government do so, however, partly because of equity, partly because of the fear of the consequences for any subsequent attempts to borrow.[12]

A primary purpose of debt retirement is the desire for elimination of the interest cost and undesirable consequences of the debt for the economy, particularly reduction in the potential growth rate. At the state-local level retirement is imperative to permit borrowing for new capital projects and to attain intergeneration equity. Failure to retire

---

[12]In the United States, states but not local governments can also repudiate debt. Holders of local government bonds can take legal action against the governments, although they cannot foreclose on local government property.

debt by the time that the investment is liquidated shifts burden forward to persons who do not benefit from the original expenditure.

Retirement of debt, per se, without regard to the sources of revenue, is expansionary to a limited extent. The effect on C is limited but not necessarily negligible. If bondholders had strongly desired to consume the sums invested in bonds, they would have done so prior to redemption by selling the bonds. Inertia, however, is a significant influence on human behavior; some persons are likely to spend the amounts received if the bonds they hold are paid off, whereas they would not have taken the trouble to sell the bonds to increase consumption spending. More significantly, the retirement of bonds will tend to increase C by raising the price of the remaining issues (if they are salable) since consumption is in part dependent upon the current value of a person's wealth (the wealth or Pigou effect). The retirement of debt will have some stimulating effect upon investment by making money capital more plentiful and thus cheaper—unless the effect of the retirement is offset by Federal Reserve action.

The entire picture of the effects of debt retirement must consider the source of funds as well. If the debt is retired by money creation, there is no offsetting effect whatever (except possibly indirectly through adverse reactions of the business community to the money creation). If the debt is retired from taxation, the taxes will restrict $C + I$, almost certainly by an amount in excess of the expansionary effect of the payment of the bonds. The exact net effect will depend upon the form of taxes employed. Any continuing program of bond retirement from a surplus is almost certain to make more difficult the maintenance of full-employment growth—unless the economy is constantly subject to net inflationary pressures in the absence of the debt retirement program.

What, therefore, is the best policy relating to retirement? A budgetary surplus to permit retirement is desirable in periods of inflationary pressure, but the actual retirement would counteract to some extent the restrictive effects of the taxes. Accordingly, the surplus should not be used to retire the debt, but be "held" (in effect the purchasing power cancelled) and then "used" (the purchasing power created) to retire the debt when GNP falls below the full-employment level. Such a program, however, amounts to nothing more than one of a budget surplus in inflationary periods and retiring debt from money creation in periods of unemployment. On the other hand, political considerations may dictate the retirement of the debt at the time of the budget surpluses; legislative bodies are much more likely to hold taxes to levels above current spending to retire debt than to produce budget surpluses. The damage is not great, however, as most of the expansionary effect of bond repayment can be offset by monetary policy.

The extent to which systematic debt retirement through money creation (that is, Federal Reserve purchase and retention of government bonds) is desirable in periods of depression is a question for which answers are not easily forthcoming. Such bond purchases facilitate investment directly and also increase commercial bank reserves. If bond purchases are very extensive, the commercial banks may accumulate such great excess reserves that sudden attainment of full employment would lead to bank credit expansion difficult to control without restoration of government debt—that is, Federal Reserve sale of bonds—thus cancelling the debt retirement. Lessened reliance on open-market operations and more reliance on changing bank reserve requirements may allow this problem to be avoided; if so, the case for debt retirement in depression through Federal Reserve purchase of bonds has great merit. While other programs of government expenditures financed by money creation are even more expansionary, retirement of debt does not necessarily reduce the amounts that may be spent for other purposes.

APPENDIX I—PUBLIC DEBT IN THE UNITED STATES

Total Public Debt. Figure 11A–1 shows the absolute amounts of federal, state, and local debt outstanding in the United States in 1966. Of the total of private and public debt, federal debt accounts for 18 percent of the total, state-local for 7 percent, and private debt for 75 percent. Figure 11A–2 shows the trend in governmental and private debt since 1942; private debt has increased much more rapidly.

Figure 11A–3 shows the behavior of the ratio of total federal debt to GNP in the United States since 1942; the ratio has declined greatly, from 134 percent to 41 percent. While the debt itself has grown slowly, real GNP has increased rapidly and the general price level has risen. Accordingly, the real significance of the debt for the economy has fallen drastically.

Figure 11A–4 shows the ownership of federal debt in 1967. About 15 percent of the total is held by the Federal Reserve and therefore is not actually a portion of the debt in any meaningful sense since it involves no obligations for the government. Twenty-three percent is

owned by government trust funds and therefore is not in the hands of
the public.

Figure 11A–5 shows the federal debt by type of security.

Figure 11A–6 shows the composition of state-local debt by general
obligation and revenue bonds.

FIGURE 11A–1

FEDERAL, STATE, AND LOCAL DEBT OUTSTANDING
UNITED STATES, 1966

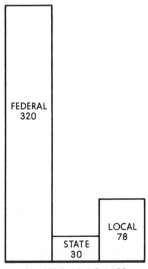

BILLIONS OF DOLLARS

SOURCE: U.S. Department
of Commerce, Bureau of the Census, *Governmental Finances in the
United States in 1965–66.*

FIGURE 11A-2

NET PUBLIC AND PRIVATE DEBT IN THE UNITED STATES, 1942–68

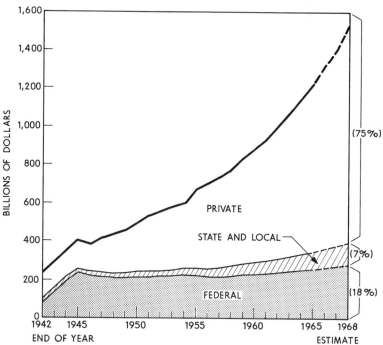

SOURCE: U.S. Bureau of the Budget, *The Budget in Brief, 1968,* p. 16.

FIGURE 11A-3

RATIO OF FEDERAL DEBT TO GNP
UNITED STATES, 1942-68

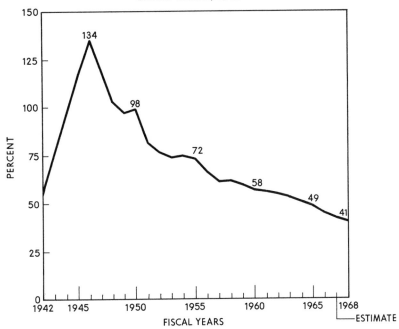

SOURCE: U.S. Bureau of the Budget, *The Budget in Brief, 1968.*

FIGURE 11A-4

OWNERSHIP OF UNITED STATES
FEDERAL DEBT, 1967

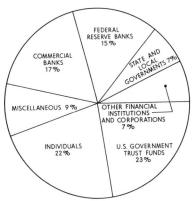

SOURCE: *U.S. Treasury Bulletin,* September, 1967.

FIGURE 11A-5

FEDERAL DEBT BY TYPE OF SECURITY,
UNITED STATES, 1967

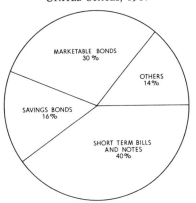

SOURCE: *U.S. Treasury Bulletin,* November, 1967.

FIGURE 11A–6

STATE AND LOCAL DEBT BY TYPE, UNITED STATES, 1965

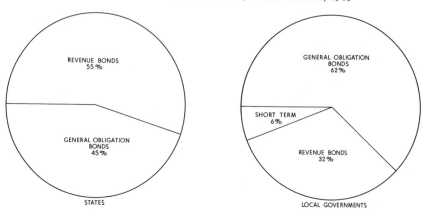

SOURCE: Tax Foundation, *Facts and Figures on Government Finance,* 1967.

APPENDIX II—PUBLIC DEBT IN CANADA

Figure 11A–7 shows the trend of national debt in Canada as a percentage of GNP for selected years since 1940; the debt is somewhat smaller relative to GNP than the United States federal debt, but the difference is not great.

Figure 11A–8 shows the total composition of governmental debt in Canada, and Figure 11A–9 shows the ownership of Canadian federal debt.

FIGURE 11A–7

CANADIAN PUBLIC DEBT EXPRESSED AS PERCENTAGE OF GNP,
SELECTED YEARS 1940–67

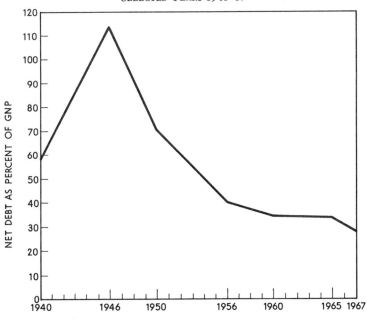

SOURCE: Canadian Tax Foundation, *The National Finances*, 1967–68 (Toronto, 1967).

FIGURE 11A-8

GOVERNMENTAL DEBT IN CANADA

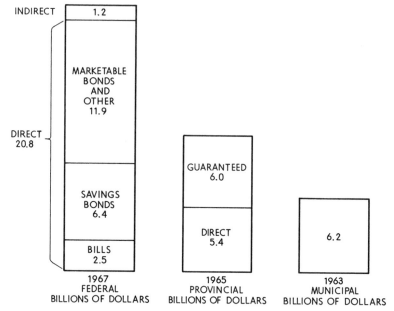

SOURCE: Bank of Canada, *Statistical Summary,* December, 1967; Canadian Tax Foundation, *Provincial Finance,* 1967; *Canada Yearbook.*

FIGURE 11A-9

HOLDINGS OF CANADIAN GOVERNMENT DEBT,
JUNE, 1967

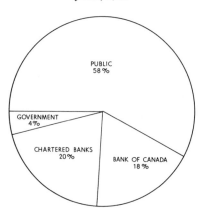

SOURCE: Bank of Canada, *Statistical
Summary,* September, 1967.

REFERENCES

MURPHY, H. C. *National Debt in War and Transition.* New York: McGraw-Hill Book Co., Inc., 1950.
A summary of World War II debt policy.

MUSGRAVE, R. A. *The Theory of Public Finance,* chaps. xxiii, xxiv. New York: McGraw-Hill Book Co., Inc. 1959.

ROLPH, E. R. "Principles of Debt Management," *American Economic Review,* Vol. XLVII (June, 1957), pp. 302–20.

SMITH, W. L. *Debt Management in the United States.* Study Paper No. 19. Joint Economic Committee, U.S. Congress. Washington, D.C., 1960.

TOBIN, J. M. "Principles of Debt Management," in COMMISSION ON MONEY AND CREDIT, *Fiscal and Debt Management Policies.* Englewood Cliffs, N.J.: Prentice-Hall, Inc., 1963.

Chapter

12

INTERGOVERNMENTAL
FISCAL RELATIONSHIPS

All governmental functions may be concentrated in a single unit of government, as they occasionally are in a very small country,[1] but more commonly they are divided between two levels of government, or, in a federal or semifederal country,[2] among three levels. Such division has significant advantages, but it gives rise to a number of problems relating to levels of functions and to their financing.

Advantages of Multiplicity of Governmental Units

A significant advantage of division of functions is the better adaptation of the conduct of activities to the preferences of the people. Those activities of strictly national concern must be kept exclusively in the hands of the national government. But the area of benefits of many activities is much smaller—regional or local. Many public goods directly affect only the persons in particular communities. When preferences differ among various communities for the activities, the amounts can be adjusted in light of local preferences, if the functions are locally conducted. In fact, persons may tend to congregate in those local units that provide the mixture of activities and taxes they prefer—the Tiebout effect, named for the economist who first popularized it.[3] Local conduct of activities also involves much greater popular control over the precise manner in which the service is provided.

A second element relates to economies of scale of production. Some activities cannot be carried on efficiently at the local level, particularly outside of metropolitan areas, and thus state (or national) provision is necessary. Intercity highway systems, universities, and various regulatory activities are examples. But evidence suggests that most gov-

[1]Newfoundland prior to its inclusion in Canada in 1948 approximated this situation.
[2]A truly federal structure involves constitutional allocation of activities and taxing power between federal and state governments; one of semifederal nature involves some separation of activities but without constitutional allocation of powers.
[3]Charles M. Tiebout, "A Pure Theory of Public Expenditures," *Journal of Political Economy,* Vol. LXIV (October, 1956), pp. 416–24.

ernmental activities attain full economies of scale in local units (unless the units are excessively small) or at state level. Conduct of these activities at higher levels would encounter greater danger of diseconomies of large-scale operation than possibilities of greater efficiency and would lessen flexibility in operation and adaptation to changing conditions. The labor-intensive nature of most nondefense governmental activities lessens the significance of large-scale production.

Finally, division of functions among various levels of government provides greater chance for popular participation in government and governmental policy formation and for small-scale experimentation; if policies are successful they can be adopted by other governments.

This discussion suggests the basic rule of allocation of functions by level of government: allocation should coincide with the area of the scope of the primary benefits, subject to the constraints of (1) attainment of economies of large-scale production and (2) performance of the activities at as low a level of government as possible consistent with the other requirements. Activities of such nature that they can be conducted effectively only at the national level because the benefits are nationwide in character, such as national defense, must be assigned to the federal government. Activities whose benefits are primarily local in character, such as sanitation and street lighting, are appropriately assigned to local units. In some instances, economies of large-scale operation dictate allocation to a unit higher than that indicated by area of benefit, and compromise between conflicting requirements is necessary.

Despite the advantages of division of governmental activities among several levels of government, this division, particularly in a federal country, interferes with the attainment of optimal government expenditure and revenue programs. These difficulties in turn have led to a variety of solutions, some of which have produced new problems.

EXTERNAL BENEFITS AND COSTS

Many governmental services that can be performed most efficiently at lower levels of government and primarily benefit persons in the particular jurisdictions nevertheless result in *spillovers*—external benefits—to persons in other areas. Education is the classic example. Higher levels of education promote more stable and effective political processes and effective functioning of democracy; they bring more rapid technological change and economic growth, and higher levels of per capita real income. These benefits extend to the country as a whole, not merely to the particular school district or area. Secondly, persons are highly mobile, especially in countries such as the United States; persons educated in one area migrate to other areas, which benefit from the education. This effect is illustrated by the migration of large numbers of poorly educated persons from southern states to northern cities in recent years, bringing to the cities many problems that would have been avoided if the migrants had been better educated. There are numerous other examples; visitors to a city or state benefit from roads and police protection; treatment of sewerage by one city avoids pollution of the water supply of another; preservation of forests in one state lessens floods in its neighbors.

When some benefits are external, the level of the activity is likely to be too small relative to the interests of the country as a whole, if the activity is financed locally and decisions about quantity to produce are left in local hands. In making decisions about the activity, persons will, we assume, consider only those benefits they themselves receive and ignore those spilling over into other communities.[4]

There is an exception to the rule that activities with spillovers will be underproduced. If a community has very strong preference for a particular level of a certain activity and some of the benefits are lost to other areas, the community will spend more, rather than less, than it would if there were no spillovers, in order to attain the desired levels.[5] This reaction is comparable to the income effect reaction of an individual to a change in a factor price.

Equivalent spillins from governmental activities of other jurisdictions will not bring adjustment of expenditures to the optimum, unless the spillins are induced by the spillouts. Otherwise, persons will enjoy benefits of the spillins without considering the spillouts in determining expenditure levels; in fact, awareness of spillins may reduce still more the amount of the activity provided by the unit. Why produce as much as otherwise if the area benefits from services produced by other areas? Likewise, ability to shift cost of governmental activities to out-

---

[4]Several empirical studies provide evidence. See, for example, the article by R. F. Adams; "On the Variation in the Consumption of Public Services," *Review of Economics and Statistics,* Vol. XLVII (November, 1965), pp. 400–405; and B. A. Weisbrod, *External Benefits of Public Education* (Princeton, N.J.: Princeton University, 1964), pp. 107–15. These studies show significant correlation between expenditure levels and the extent of subdivision of local governments into small units.

[5]Alan Williams in "The Optimal Provision of Public Goods in a System of Local Government," *Journal of Political Economy,* Vol. LXXIV (February, 1966), pp. 18–33, demonstrates this possibility.

siders will not necessarily be regarded as an offset against external benefits, but rather as a means of attaining a net increase in benefits for the community. In fact, if substantial revenue can be obtained from outsiders,[6] the overall level of activity may become excessive relative to the optimum but without increase in activities that yield external benefits.

Functional Grants[7]

If the residents of each jurisdiction were to base expenditure decisions upon benefits to the entire country rather than to their own areas alone, the problem would be avoided. This is not a realistic assumption. The only feasible solution, short of transferring the activity to higher levels of government, is the *conditional* or, more appropriately, *functional,* grant. The higher level of government grants funds to the subordinate unit for a particular function to induce it to raise the level of the service. For the attainment of the desired goal, the amount of the grant must be adjusted on the basis of the magnitude of external benefits, and the grant must be established in such a way as to insure an increase in the local activity rather than a reduction in local support for the activity. The value of the spillover benefits cannot be measured exactly but can be estimated. Functional grants may serve one other purpose: to encourage subordinate units to overcome inertia on activities that directly benefit them provided they develop cooperation with adjacent units. This is an aspect of the metropolitan area question discussed in a later section.

To insure that the recipient units do not lower their own support of the activity, the matching rule is necessary, the percentage of matching support being adjusted on the basis of the relative external and internal benefits. That is, a grant is made only if the subordinate unit provides a specified percentage of the total expenditure on the activity. The open-end type of grant, whereby the expenditures of the recipient unit will be matched without limit as to amount, has justification since the external benefits may be expected to rise in total as the internal benefits rise. Grantor governments are often reluctant to provide this form of blank check because of their own budgeting problems.

---

[6]Examples include localities with extensive outside-owned industrial property and few residents; the residents can easily increase the services that benefit themselves at the expense of the outsiders. Or, if a local government operates a commercial facility such as a toll bridge used largely by outsiders, expenditures may be increased beyond the optimal level.

[7]See George F. Break, *Intergovernmental Fiscal Relationships in the United States* (Washington, D.C.: Brookings Institution, 1966).

With the grants inevitably go some measure of control of use of the funds, to make certain that the recipient unit employs them effectively. Extensive debate has occurred over the extent to which controls interfere with the autonomy of the recipient unit. The rule that controls should go no farther than is essential for accomplishment of the purposes is not easy to interpret, and reasonableness of the controls in the grants program in the United States has been debated extensively.[8]

The related complaint, that grant programs distort state-local expenditure patterns from the optimum, is not valid if the grants are properly designed; on the contrary by financing the costs of the external benefits, they enable the recipient units to approach the optimum more precisely. Improperly designed grants may well lead states and local governments to spend more than the preferred optimum simply to obtain the grant money and to spend less than optimal amounts on other activities.

Over the years the United States federal government has developed an extensive grant program (summarized in Appendix I). Many questions have been raised about the programs. Some reflect lack of understanding of the basic role of the grants, such as the charge that nothing is gained and much is lost by having funds channeled from local areas to Washington and back again. Other more legitimate complaints have centered around the questions of whether grants are limited to situations of significant external benefits, whether magnitudes are properly adjusted in terms of the external benefits, and whether the nature and extent of controls are acceptable. The large number of separate programs has been criticized. Consolidation of grants, which would simplify operation, would be warranted for activities with similar ratios of internal and external benefits.

FRAGMENTATION OF TAXATION

Division of governmental activities among several levels of government requires fragmentation of the overall tax structure in the sense that portions of the overall structure are levied and administered by several units of government. Fragmentation is necessary if each level is to have autonomous financial resources, rather than merely serving as an agency to spend money collected by the national government. Division of taxation between the central government and the sub-

---

[8] *Ibid.* pp. 79–83.

ordinate units results in collection at both levels (vertical fragmentation) and by a number of separate subordinate units (horizontal fragmentation). In addition to allowing fiscal autonomy, tax fragmentation does offer certain advantages. It allows adaptation of tax structures to voter preferences and facilitates experimentation. In the United States, for example, several states pioneered in the use of EDP equipment long before the Internal Revenue Service. Some taxes may be administered more effectively by a small unit than by a larger one, and possible diseconomies of scale are avoided. These diseconomies are apparently less serious than those of expenditure activities.

Consequences of Fragmentation

On the other hand, fragmentation gives rise to a number of major difficulties:

Attainment of Optimal Tax Structures. When tax policy is determined independently by various levels of government, attainment of an optimal *overall* structure is obviously complex. The optimal tax structure for each unit depends upon the policies of the others, and a simultaneous adjustment is required. In practice, this is virtually impossible to attain. Some units must act first; others consider this action in making their decision, and then the first may readjust, requiring further adjustments in the others. The largest jurisdictions may preempt certain fields, making use of these taxes by other units politically difficult and economically dangerous. Yet these forms may be well suited to the subordinate units, whereas other types are not. The subordinate units will be forced to use unsatisfactory taxes, or the combined burden on some levies may be so great as to produce adverse consequences, and, at the minimum, duplication of collection facilities. At state or local levels, the failure of some units to use a particular tax may make it difficult for others to do so and agreement on uniform action may be impossible.

Reduction in Tax Capacity. Fragmentation of the tax structure reduces the total tax capacity of the subordinate units compared to the ability of a unified government to finance the same level of activity. This reduction is a reflection of the basic rule that the larger the taxing jurisdiction relative to the country as a whole, the more effectively it can operate a tax, for both economic and administrative reasons. First, some types of taxes cannot be administered by relatively small jurisdictions because these governments do not have access to the information necessary to assess the taxpayer or the ability to reach the taxpayer by legal means to enforce payment. A local government cannot discover property owned by residents but located in other areas and cannot require a vendor located outside of the unit and having no property or activity in the unit to collect and remit sales tax on a sale to a resident of the area. While payment could legally be enforced against the purchaser, this procedure is usually too costly to be worthwhile.

Second, various subordinate units are fearful of tax competition of other areas. Given the levels of taxation of other states, a particular state will be reluctant to raise its tax rates above these levels for fear of loss of business and population. The real danger may be small but the governments are greatly influenced by the possibility. State legislatures are more fearful of locational effects of income taxes than of sales, excise, and other taxes. Or a state may deliberately hold tax levels below those of other states to attract industry to the state, or may seek to do so by special tax concessions, such as exemption of new firms from property tax for a period of years. These policies aggravate the problems of the other states. While legislators exaggerate the dangers of locational effects, substantial differentials may have some influence.

This reduction in fiscal capacity has several consequences. The most serious is the restriction in the level of services of the states and local governments below desired levels. Another is the disproportionate reliance placed upon forms of taxes least effected by interstate competition. Many states undoubtedly rely more heavily on sales taxes and less heavily on income taxes than they would prefer were it not for fear that income taxes will impair economic development of the state.

Unequal Fiscal Capacity. Given the division of functions among various levels of government, the fragmentation of the tax structure results in varying tax capacity of local units relative to their expenditure needs. Potential tax base and expenditure needs are unevenly distributed by local unit. One local unit may contain only low-income families, with large numbers of children and heavy demands for funds for welfare, education, and housing, but very little tax capacity. A neighboring community may contain only wealthy persons with high incomes and little need for welfare services, while another may have very few inhabitants but extensive business property and thus substantial per capita wealth. Even among the states, the per capita income of the highest income state (Nevada) is two and one-half times that of the lowest (Mississippi); within states the difference of per capita income, sales, or property among local units is very much greater. This difference in tax capacity has several consequences. The overall pattern of adjustments of activities will be very different from that arising if the central government conducted all activities and raised all revenue. Activities will be carried farther in wealthy areas than in poor. Taxes must be higher in poor areas even to maintain levels of activity that are far lower than those in the wealthy areas. Not only may these differences be regarded as inequitable but by retarding development in the poor areas they perpetuate and aggravate the differences. If school districts were required to finance all of their own activities except for the assistance of functional grants reflecting external benefits, taxes would be higher and quality of education lower in poor districts than in wealthy areas, thereby interfering with economic development and making the poor areas still poorer.

Administrative and Compliance Problems. Fragmentation of the tax structure between higher and subordinate units of government results in duplicating tax administration and compliance activities. Two sets of administrative staff are required and two sets of returns must be filed by taxpayers. Overall costs of administration and compliance are increased. The tasks of taxpayers are aggravated if the bases of the two taxes are not identical.

Operational problems arising at subordinate levels from the interjurisdictional nature of economic activity will be discussed in a subsequent section, since the solutions are different from those of vertical fragmentation.

Fiscal Capacity and Unconditional Grants.[9] The reduction in overall fiscal capacity and the unequal fiscal capacity of various subordinate units are so closely related that solutions must be considered in terms of both problems. Functional grants determined solely on the basis of external benefits make only limited contribution to the solution of these problems, which are related to the financing of the services that benefit the residents of the local area. Functional grants could be extended to meet the problem by increasing the payments beyond the amounts related to external benefits. To lessen inequality of fiscal capacity the functional grant programs would require equalizing features; the amount of the grant would be adjusted on the basis of a measure of the local unit's capacity to finance the activity itself, relative to need. For example, state grants to school districts often are established on the basis of the figure of assessed value of property per child in school in each district. Use of functional grants to meet the tax capacity problem is open to the basic criticism against any func-

[9]See Break, *op. cit.,* chap. iv.

tional grant program not directly related to external benefits; the grants are accompanied by controls that are unjustifiable in terms of relative responsibilities of the donor and recipient governments, and they distort expenditure patterns of the recipients away from those regarded as optimal in the local area.

The logical solution of the fiscal capacity problem is the unconditional or block grant, adjusted in terms of fiscal capacity and provided without specifications as to use or control. The allocation formula can be based upon population weighted by the reciprocal of per capita income, and perhaps also by an index of the tax effort of the recipient unit, to lessen the danger that the recipients simply reduce their own tax levies and to give a bonus to units that prefer a higher level of activity. Tax effort can be ascertained by a comparison between actual tax collection and the potential yield of a "standard" tax program in the area.[10]

While all units would receive some money, the payments to the poorer units would be relatively greater. Accordingly, not only would the overall fiscal capacity of the subordinate units be increased, but the inequality in fiscal capacity would be lessened or eliminated. The absence of specification of use and of controls would protect the financial autonomy of the recipient governments and avoid distorting their budget patterns. Substantial use of the unconditional grant system has been made for many years in Canada, at both dominion and provincial levels. Little use has been made of it in the United States although considerable attention has been given in recent years to the Heller-Pechman proposal[11] whereby the federal government would make unconditional grants to the states from income tax revenues.

One objection raised against unconditional grants, which also applies to a lesser extent to functional grants, is the danger that governments are less careful to attain efficiency in the spending of money given to them than they are in spending their own money, especially if they are not subject to supervision. This argument is difficult to evaluate but is probably of limited merit. Waste in the use of granted funds means higher taxes if given functions are to be performed, since taxes imposed by the jurisdiction must provide the marginal revenue. Standards of efficiency developed for use of the government's own funds are likely to be applied to granted funds as well. Furthermore, pro-

---

[10]See Advisory Commission on Intergovernmental Relations, *Measures of State and Local Fiscal Capacity* (Washington, D.C.: U.S. Government Printing Office, 1962).

[11]See Walter W. Heller, *New Dimensions of Political Economy* (Cambridge, Mass.: Harvard University Press, 1966), chap. iii.

vision of granted funds may make effective planning feasible since without them the government may be forced into a hand-to-mouth existence that produces inefficiency and use of inexpensive, incompetent personnel.

Another question relates to the general utilization of the funds; will they be allocated to attain overall optimization of use of governmental resources? If subordinate governments are to continue to play a role in the overall structure, they must be allowed some freedom in the choice of expenditures, except for those supported by functional grants because of external benefits. If the states are not to be allowed discretion, the federal structure might as well be eliminated.

The final question is the danger that unconditional grants (as well as functional grants) will perpetuate poor areas that have lost their economic base, such as mining or timber resources. The best use of national resources may require that people move out of these areas, whereas grants may enable them to stay, supported by the government. Minimum welfare grants may produce this result. But grants for such purposes as education will facilitate movement out of the area since educated persons are much more mobile than the uneducated. Furthermore, elimination of poverty areas does not necessarily require outward movement of population because of inadequate resources; some need additional skilled workers to bring about development of resources that are available, and the grants may facilitate inflow of such persons. Poverty tends to be self-perpetuating; some stimulus to better utilization of resources, rather than outmigration, may be the best answer.

Alternative Solutions

These questions, and particularly the argument of financial responsibility, have led to search for alternative solutions to the problems that would provide greater financial resources for the subordinate governments and reduce duplicating of administration yet preserve financial autonomy. Some use is made of these alternatives, in part because of the unwillingness to make adequate unconditional grants.

Tax Sharing on Origin Basis. The higher unit of government may share a portion of a tax that it imposes and administers on the basis of the origin of the revenue. This procedure increases the fiscal capacity of the subordinate units by giving them access to revenue from taxes barred from their direct use at equivalent rates by competitive and administrative considerations and avoids the distorting effects on location that might arise from differential use of the levies. But the technique does not meet the problems of unequal fiscal capacity and varying preferences among communities for use of the particular revenue source. Nor does it meet the argument that governments are less careful about the use of taxes they do not themselves impose. While this technique lessens duplication of tax administration and compliance, taxpayers must still segregate tax liability by local units, with inevitable allocation problems. The origin basis of allocation, while satisfactory for the personal income tax once relative claims of the jurisdictions of residence and source of income are established, is unworkable with some forms of tax. For example, a motor fuel tax may be collected from refineries located in one county, whereas the motor fuel is used over a wider area.

Tax Supplement. To meet the problem of variation in need for revenue and the objection that governments are less careful in the use of revenue from taxes that they do not impose, a tax supplement system may be used in lieu of tax sharing. The larger unit collects, along with its own levy, a supplement imposed by the local unit. Several states employ this technique with sales taxes. Tax supplements allow for diversity in rates among local units; like tax sharing, the system avoids duplication of administration and compliance activities and insures uniformity of base of the tax. But it does not avoid the tax competition problem; some local units may be unwilling to impose the tax for fear of loss of economic activity to other jurisdictions. The system works best when rates of the supplement are so low that there is little fear of this result, or when use of the tax is universal.[12] Except where there is variation in need, the preference for the supplement system over shared revenue rests entirely on the rather questionable argument that units must impose the taxes that provide them revenue if the funds are to be used most efficiently.

Tax Credit[13]

Full credit of tax paid to the subordinate unit against tax due to the larger unit eliminates tax competition problems and thus increases tax capacity of the subordinate units, but does not, per se, eliminate duplication of administration.[14] This system has been used for many

---

[12]In California, local sales tax supplements to the state sales tax are universal and in Illinois most local units employ the supplement. Once a levy of this type becomes universal, the uniformity advantage of the shared revenue approach is attained.

[13]See J. A. Maxwell, *Tax Credits and Intergovernmental Fiscal Relations* (Washington, D.C.: Brookings Institution, 1962).

[14]The Canadian federal government has used this system for a number of years for income taxation; see *The Financing of Canadian Federation* (Toronto: Canadian Tax Foundation, 1966). The provinces are given the option of federal collection.

years for state inheritance and estate taxes in the United States (with a maximum deductible figure established in terms of a percentage of federal tax due) and is employed in Canada for both personal and corporate income taxes, with a maximum set in terms of percentage points of the federal rate. The fear of the smaller units to impose the tax because of loss of economic activity is eliminated; if a particular unit does not impose the tax, its residents will pay no less tax, but the central government will receive all the revenue. Introduction of the system without an increase in the central government tax rates increases the tax capacity of the subordinate units relative to that of the central government.

With credit of only a portion of the tax instead of the full amount, the tax competition influence is only partially removed. If the tax is merely deductible from income instead of from tax, for example, the larger unit government bears only a portion of the cost of subordinate unit tax increases.

Other Measures.[15]   Some of the compliance and administrative inefficiencies arising out of overlapping of taxes can be lessened by rather simple devices that do not reduce the fiscal autonomy of the smaller units. For example, a state may adjust the base of its income tax to correspond with that of the federal tax, or, as a few states have done, define the liability for state income tax as a percentage of federal tax. Joint operation of portions of tax administration or exchange of audit information lessen administrative duplication. The larger unit of government can also avoid using taxes that are suitable for the subordinate units yet unnecessary for its own use and avoid unnecessary departure from separation of tax sources and duplication of administrative effort. This consideration is a major argument against the use of a federal sales tax in the United States.

On the other hand, a proposal for complete separation of all revenue sources, whereby no tax would be used by more than one level of government, is unrealistic, unless supplemented by extensive grant programs, since there are not enough "acceptable" taxes available for the subordinate units. The result of attempted separation would be use by the subordinate units of less satisfactory levies.

Interjurisdictional Problems from Horizontal Fragmentation

Horizontal fragmentation of the tax structure creates major jurisdictional questions for the subordinate units, because much economic activity extends beyond the boundaries of a particular taxing jurisdic-

---

[15]See Break, *op. cit.*, chap. ii.

tion. When the base of the tax is in any way interjurisdictional in nature, not only do questions of principle arise about the allocation of the base among the various units but the task of compliance and enforcement may be more difficult and costly. Some retail sales are interstate in nature, made by a vendor in one state to a purchaser in another. Decision must be reached about the claim to the tax: does the state of the vendor or the state of the purchaser have jurisdiction? In terms of the principle of the tax as a levy on consumption the state of the purchaser is entitled to the tax, but effective enforcement by this state is possible only if the vendors can be made to collect and remit tax. Even when states have legal power to force payment by vendors, they find collection difficult from out-of-state vendors who make only a few sales in the state, and the firms selling into a number of states experience substantial cost in collecting and remitting tax. In practice the states are limited in their power to firms doing business in the state or selling through agents in the state.[16] Even when they have legal power, they usually do not enforce this power effectively; revenue is lost, inequity created, and interstate selling encouraged. Some double taxation arises when an article is purchased in one state subject to tax and then taxed again when transferred to another state. Most states now provide credit for sales tax paid another state.

With state personal and corporate income taxes, allocation and enforcement problems arise when a person lives in one state and earns income from work or investment in another, and when business firms operate in more than one state. With individuals, most states tax on the basis of both residence and source of income and double taxation would be widespread were it not for reciprocal provisions whereby credit is allowed for tax paid to another state. With corporations, there are two major questions of principle: determination of the nature of activity in a state necessary to give it jurisdiction over the corporation, and the allocation of the income among the various states. Most states use a three-element formula (property owned, payrolls, sales), but some do not, and the definition of sales varies; accordingly some companies may pay tax on more than their entire income and others on less.[17] Enforcement is a less serious problem than it is with sales taxa-

---

[16] Attempts of the states to require collection by firms selling only through mail-order catalogs and other advertising sent into the state were blocked by the U.S. Supreme Court action in 1967 in the National Bellas Hess case (*National Bellas Hess, Inc.* v. *Dept. of Revenue of the State of Illinois*, 386 US 753, 18th ed. 2d 505). The large mail-order houses collect tax because they also have places of business in the state. Previous court decisions barred the states from requiring firms merely delivering in the state to collect tax.

[17] See *State Taxation of Interstate Commerce*, Report of Special Subcommittee on State Taxation of Interstate Commerce of the Committee on the Judiciary, U.S. House of Representatives (Washington, D.C., 1965).

tion; the main source of additional cost is that of compliance with a number of state laws.

With estate and inheritance taxes, problems similar to those with personal income taxes are encountered, although the rule is usually accepted that the state of residence of the decedent, not that of the heir, has jurisdiction. On corporate securities, however, the state of incorporation has been held to have claim as well, although frequently this right is not exercised.

The consequences of these interstate collection problems include higher cost of tax administration and higher compliance costs for business firms, especially those operating in a number of states with diverse laws and subject to both income and sales tax requirements, and for individuals complying with the tax laws of several states. At the same time, effectiveness of collection is reduced and evasion is increased. Compliance problems may affect business decisions; a firm may decide not to place an office or distribution warehouse in a particular state because to do so would make the firm liable to collection of sales tax on sales made into the state. On the other hand, the inability of the states to enforce payment on certain types of interstate sales, such as those by mail-order catalog, encourages this form of business activity.

Excessive fragmentation reduces efficiency in tax operation by placing administration in the hands of governmental units too small to attain economies of scale. The most extreme example is assessment of property by jurisdictions too small to hire full-time trained personnel.

Reduction of Administrative and Compliance Problems of Subordinate Units. Some of the major difficulties encountered by both taxpayers and state and local governments can be lessened by cooperation of the units or by action of the higher level of government.

First, use of standard rules of allocation of tax lessen multiple taxation and escape from tax. With income taxation, a rule such as that providing for allocation of income in pending federal legislation in the United States is required. With sales and excise taxation, rules relating to taxation on the basis of origin or destination are necessary; the latter is more logical, given the consumption intent of the taxes, while the former is easier to administer.[18]

Second, cooperative administrative action can benefit all concerned except the tax evaders. Sales taxation offers many possibilities for joint effort; states may agree on cooperative audit, whereby each state, in its own audit work, insures that tax due another state has been paid. Or agreements can be devised whereby one state collects and remits to

---

[18]The destination-of-delivery rule is provided in proposed federal legislation.

other states the sales tax due them by vendors located in the state. Legislation providing that sales tax on mail-order sales is due the originating rather than the destination state would not only reduce tax evasion but also simplify the tasks of the vendor.[19]

Multiple taxation can be prevented by federal rules requiring the granting of credit for sales tax paid another state.

THE SPECIAL CASE OF METROPOLITAN AREAS[20]

Several of the basic problems arising out of fragmentation of governmental activities and taxation are most apparent in metropolitan areas, which typically include large numbers of local governments, often spreading across state lines. These areas witness the most spectacular failure of governments to solve the problems of the contemporary world: slums with substandard housing and juvenile delinquency and crime; poor quality of education in the core cities; traffic congestion and air pollution, largely a product of the motor vehicle; urban sprawl with its unsightliness and poor land utilization.

Inability to solve metropolitan area problems is in part a result of faulty governmental organization—the large number of autonomous local governments—in a metropolitan area. Many of the functions are areawide in nature. Some cannot be undertaken at all by small units, others only very inefficiently, without adequate regard to the interests of the area as a whole. Spillover benefits are widespread within a metropolitan area, yet no one local unit can take them into consideration in its own decision making. There is no means of balancing the overall governmental needs of the area. The tax base may be very unevenly divided, industrial suburbs having high-tax capacity relative to those of low-income residential character. Because of the limited size of the taxing jurisdictions and the relative equality of other forces affecting location within metropolitan areas, tax competition may have severe effects upon the tax capacity of each unit. The governmental structures are carry-overs from earlier years when they were more suitably adapted to the circumstances. Change is often difficult because of sheer inertia, vested interests of existing local units, and domination of state legislatures by rural representatives.

[19]Unfortunately, proposed federal legislation in the United States would restrict the power of the states to require out-of-state vendors to collect and remit taxes but not provide any satisfactory substitutes and therefore would give federal sanction to evasion of state taxes. The legislation was instigated by vendors selling in a number of states; they sought to lessen compliance problems.

[20]See Break, *op. cit.,* chap. v.

Several general solutions to the problem are available; all have been utilized in limited degree, with slow but definite trend in the direction of positive action.

Consolidation

An obvious solution is the merger of the various small units into a single metropolitan government. Consolidation, however, is difficult politically, and loses the advantages of smaller units: greater popular participation in government, and adjustment of revenues to the wishes of the people of the areas. Much of the political objection to consolidation centers around the fear of domination by the core city political machine, and in some instances the desire—much more questionable from the standpoint of welfare of society—to maintain nonintegrated schools.[21] As with any merger of governmental units, residents and officials of each city inevitably resist loss of their political identities, and merchants fear the loss of business. Despite these obstacles, some movement toward merger of contiguous small units could help to lessen the problems of metropolitan areas, increasing efficiency and the ability to meet some of the major problems.[22]

The Metropolitan Federation

A compromise, which retains the smaller units for purely local activity but establishes a metropolitan government to undertake functions requiring conduct and financing on an areawide basis, has more political appeal and offers some advantages of each system. The metropolitan government can undertake activities requiring areawide operation for efficiency and those with significant spillover benefits. The metropolitan government can also levy its own uniform tax throughout the area, thereby lessening tax competition. The local units retain the purely local activities, with continued popular participation and the important political advantage of retention of identity. Even if exact optimal allocation of functions cannot be attained, the system is an improvement over the present disorganization. The main difficulty is the political objection to transference of functions; there is also danger that the metropolitan government will be merely a confederation, with paralyzing veto powers retained by the various local units. When the

---

[21]Consolidation in rural areas would often increase governmental efficiency. Townships are too small for efficient operation, and in many states even counties are excessively small. The same identity and prestige concepts impede merger; lobbies of township officials are often very influential in state legislatures.

[22]One of the few examples of this type of merger was the formation of the city of Fremont, California, bringing together a number of towns and unincorporated urban areas.

metropolitan area covers more than one state, political obstacles to the formation of an overall metropolitan government are serious.

When one county covers all or a large portion of a metropolitan areas (as for example Los Angeles), the county may serve as the metropolitan government, with perhaps less political difficulty.

More common in practice than metropolitan governments or federations are metropolitan councils, representing the various local jurisdictions, seeking better coordination of policy. These organizations accomplish little because of lack of power.

Special-Purpose Districts

An alternative approach is the formation of special-purpose districts. Historically these first developed in the field of education, where they were often contiguous with the basic local governmental unit, because of the desire to free education from the control of local political machines. Other districts have frequently been formed to escape bond and tax rate limitations or restrictions on existing local governments and have contributed little except additional fragmentation, interfering with coordination of policies and optimal adjustment of activities.

Special districts covering an entire metropolitan area, however, can make significant contributions to the improvement of the conduct of governmental functions and financing. Such units can undertake areawide functions and provide a uniform basis of financing. They may even include parts of more than one state, as does the New York Port Authority. The districts are usually relatively easy to form, especially if no major functions are transferred away from existing governmental units. As a practical matter they constitute an effective device for improving governmental organization, but they are not without defects. Their formation to meet the most pressing problems may retard more basic reforms. Special districts interfere with evaluation of the benefits and costs of overall governmental activities. The officials of an aggressive special district, armed with substantial taxing powers, may push their activity far beyond the level reflecting comparative consideration of benefits from other activities as well. Other districts may lie moribund, accomplishing nothing. Voters may take little interest. An infinite number of elections for officials of special districts (on different days) is sufficient to discourage the most responsible citizen from voting. On the whole, special-purpose districts represent a feasible, simple method of accomplishing in part what broader approaches could do much better; they may gradually become metropolitan governments if diverse functions are given to them, or in time they may be replaced by broader units.

Other Devices.   Other techniques are used on a limited scale. One government may contract to supply certain functions for another government, as various communities of the Los Angeles area have done for one another (the so-called Lakewood plan). Several counties may set up joint multicounty health units, or other joint projects. These arrangements allow greater efficiency in specific instances but do little to meet the overall problems.

Stabilization and Intergovernmental Relations

A final problem arising out of the division of functions and revenue sources is the potentially perverse stabilization behavior of state and local finance, as explained in Chapter 10. To prevent this reaction from offsetting federal fiscal policy, adjustments are required in federal grant programs.

Unconditional grants to support basic state-local expenditures in depression would avoid cutbacks in these functions, even though in full-employment periods there was no justification for federal aid for these activities. Secondly, grants for public works expenditures, as a partial substitute for direct conduct of the public works by the federal government, would facilitate better project selection since many state-local functions offer good opportunities for capital investment.

Such an approach could be systematized by a formal program whereby the federal government would grant to the states and localities the difference between predepression revenues and expenditures, provided that the recipients did not raise taxes or cut expenditures. If the states would liberalize their debt limits they could themselves lessen their fiscally perverse behavior.

Restriction of increases in state-local expenditures in inflationary periods is more difficult. Monetary policy has some restrictive effect by increasing the total cost of state-local borrowing. Reduction in grants can also curtail spending, but must be employed in such a way as to avoid curtailing basic activity.

A DYNAMIC APPROACH TO INTERGOVERNMENTAL FISCAL RELATIONS[23]

The usual approach to the question of assignment of activities and revenues is based upon traditional specific allocation of major functions to each level of government. This approach stresses the problems

[23]A summary is found in the article by Selma Mushkin and R. F. Adams, "Emerging Patterns of Federalism," *National Tax Journal,* Vol. XIX (September, 1966), pp. 225–47.

arising from spillovers and inadequate and unequal tax capacity at the subordinate levels, and seeks to find solutions to them within the framework of given basic allocations of functions. More recently attention has focused on a more dynamic concept of federalism, in which society seeks continuing change in "government mix"—in allocation of functions—as well as in "product mix." Changes in functions and in voter attitudes dictate changing patterns, the allocation coming less and less to resemble a "layer cake" and more and more a "marble cake," with greater cooperation in performance of functions rather than sharp, rigid allocations.

Changing patterns in allocation reflect in part change in activities requiring governmental action, and in large measure the extent of responsiveness of governments to changing consumer preferences. Failure of local governments to meet strong demands leads to popular pressures to shift financing to states or federal levels, or vice versa. Urban areas complain that rural-dominated state legislatures will not listen to their demands and thus urge the federal government to take over the activities.

Thus federal participation in conduct or financing activities is by no means based entirely on spillover or inadequate tax capacity considerations but also upon voters' preferences for federal activity, in part because of failure of lower units of government to respond. Unfortunately, voter preference for federal financing is strengthened by the Santa Claus phenomenon—the belief that services provided by the national government cost the community nothing. In a sense this is of course true from the standpoint of any one community, but it cannot be from the standpoint of the country as a whole. The pressure to get the national government to undertake an activity instead of financing it locally, with clearly defined additional costs, is very strong.

INTERNATIONAL TAX RELATIONSHIPS

The fragmentation of tax structures within a country is paralleled in a sense by the use of separate tax structures by various countries, but the consequences are less serious. Economic activity of an international character is much less significant, relative to total economic activity, than that of an interstate or interlocal nature. While some persons gain incomes from outside the country, the percentage of total income so derived is less than the percentage gained outside state or local units. Furthermore, because of control over the borders of the country, the operation of fiscal frontiers, and the unrestricted taxing power of a country over its nationals and over all activity within or crossing its borders, the enforcement of tax on international activity is much easier than enforcement against interstate or interlocal activity. Nevertheless, several problems arise.

Income Tax Complications

Income earned in one country by residents of another is difficult for the country of residence to discover, although it has legitimate claim to tax the earnings. Frequently the country of origin will subject the income to at least partial tax, so the person will not escape completely. The opposite result is also possible: the person may be fully taxed by both countries. This result is usually avoided by tax treaties, under the terms of which each country frees from tax the income earned in the country by residents of the other. The United States allows a credit for tax paid other countries even without a tax treaty, but many countries are not so liberal. Corporate taxes give rise to less difficulty, since usually a separate subsidiary corporation must be formed for operation in each country, subject to the tax laws of that country. Questions do arise about such items as payments by the subsidiary to the parent company in excess of the commercial value of the service rendered.

Commodity Taxes

International transactions have for centuries been the object of discriminatory commodity taxation in the form of customs duties, partly because customs are relatively easy to enforce so long as smuggling can be prevented, partly because of protective aspects. National sales taxes can be applied to imported goods without great difficulty, either in conjunction with customs or at a later transaction, with problems less serious than those posed by interstate sales.

Countries usually free exports from sales or excise taxes in order to protect the international competitive position of their producers. On the other hand, developing countries frequently levy special export taxes on basic primary products designed to reduce the income of the producers of the products rather than to hamper the exports of the country.

Tax Harmonization[24]

Since 1960 increased efforts have been made to develop common market areas in Europe, in Latin America, and in Africa. With this development has arisen concern about harmonization of tax relation-

---

[24]This question is discussed at length in C. S. Shoup (ed.), *Fiscal Harmonization in Common Markets* (2 vols.; New York: Columbia University Press, 1967).

ships among countries forming the common market, that is, adjustments in the tax structures of the countries to insure that taxes do not interfere with attainment of the objectives of the common market. A common market requires, by its nature, the removal of internal tariffs among the countries so that trade can move freely and industry can develop on the basis of comparative advantage, as it does within a country. But removal of tariffs alone may not be adequate. Internal tax structures, particularly commodity taxes, can interfere with the free functioning of the common market and prevent full attainment of its advantages. Differences in rates of manufacturers sales taxes or value added taxes will affect location decisions. Turnover taxes are virtually impossible to make uniform in practice, because of differences in structures of industry and distribution. If a country seeks to eliminate turnover tax on sales into the other common market countries, it finds the cumulative amount of tax affecting export prices hard to determine. Inadequate refund of tax on exports will harm production in the country, while refunds in excess of the actual tax on export sales will give artificial advantage and invite retaliation. While these differences can be offset by tariffs in the absence of a common market, they cannot be within such a market.

Accordingly some uniformity of policy is imperative for sales taxes. The European Common Market countries have agreed upon the use of the value added form, which will allocate revenue among the countries automatically in terms of the value added within the country. Since a value added tax must be more or less uniform in all of the countries to avoid affecting location, the countries plan to use supplementary retail sales taxes to adjust for differences in revenue needs. Variations in retail taxes do not cause serious distortions. Retail activity is market oriented and cannot shift to any extent to escape taxes. The Central American common market countries are introducing retail sales taxes in preference to the other forms for the same reason.

With both the value added tax and the retail tax, decision must be made about the jurisdiction for taxation on intercountry sales; should the tax of the originating country or the destination country apply? The latter rule, as used within the United States, is most logical since the tax is intended to be a levy on consumption spending. But this rule requires the maintenance of fiscal frontiers, that is, control over goods coming into the country from other common market countries, or some alternative technique. The origin rule is much simpler to operate and with equivalent tax rates and comparable flows of goods in both directions will produce much the same overall distribution of revenues, even if the "wrong" country gets the tax on particular transactions. If the tax rates are not uniform, the tax revenue distribution will be different and producers in high-tax countries are placed at a competitive disadvantage. The European Common Market countries plan ultimate use of the origin base for the value added tax but do not expect to attain it until the rates are more nearly uniform.

Corporate Income versus Value Added Taxes

Interest in the value added form of sales tax for harmonization of the sales tax systems of the common market countries has led to consideration in other countries, including Great Britain, the United States, and Canada, of the replacement of the corporate income tax by the value added tax in order to stimulate exports. Proponents of the plan in the United States argue that the country has worsened the world position of its exporters by heavy reliance on the corporate income tax, which is not refundable on exports, instead of using the value added tax, which could be refundable. Accordingly, the exporters of other countries are able to undersell American firms (given the exchange rates). This argument has merit only to the extent that the corporation income tax results in higher prices of products; otherwise the U.S. producer is not placed at a disadvantage. Furthermore, the international comparisons are misleading; most of the industrialized countries use corporation income taxes of magnitude comparable to the U.S. tax in addition to the value added or sales tax. Were the United States to shift away from the corporate income tax, other countries would likely take retaliatory measures to prevent what they would regard as an unfair advantage.

APPENDIX I—GRANT PROGRAMS IN THE UNITED STATES

Federal Grant Programs

The United States federal government uses only the functional (conditional) grant system, the grants primarily designed to stimulate state activity in fields in which externalities are important. The programs have expanded over the years, the payments constituting in 1967 about 10 percent of total federal spending. Most of the programs are matching, but the traditional 50 percent is giving way to a greater variety of figures. All programs are accompanied by some control and supervision of the use of the funds.

As shown in Table 12A–1 most of the money is granted for a

relatively few programs, particularly highways (the largest single item), public assistance, and, to a growing extent, education. Some of the welfare grants have equalizing features, the amounts given being determined in part by the tax capacity of the recipient states. Most grants go to the states, but a few are made directly to the local units.

State Grant Programs

Three functions account for most of the state grants to the local governments: education, roads, and welfare; the first comprises 70 percent of the total. Grants to the school districts for education were established primarily because of their limited tax resources, the wide variation in tax capacity among districts, and the desire to stimulate

TABLE 12A–1

MAJOR FEDERAL GRANTS-IN-AID TO STATE AND LOCAL GOVERNMENTS,
1967 FISCAL YEAR

(In Billions of Dollars)

Education and Research	
Elementary and secondary schools.	$ 1.7
Other.	1.0
Welfare	
Public assistance (mainly old-age assistance and aid to dependent children).	3.9
Employment security administration.	0.5
Antipoverty and other programs.	2.9
Transportation	
Highways.	4.0
Other (airports, urban transport, etc.).	0.9
Other.	0.2
Total.	$15.1

SOURCE: *Budget of the United States, Fiscal Year 1968.*

them to provide better quality education. In many states part of the grant is on a uniform ADA (average daily attendance) basis, part on an equalizing basis. The districts with low figures of total assessed valuation of property per child in school receive larger sums, in order to obtain better equalization of fiscal capacity of the various districts.

Total state grants to local governments in 1966 totaled $16.8 billion, or 33 percent of total state spending. Grants by function are shown in Table 12A–2. Some states share revenues from particular taxes with the local governments, thus providing a payment very similar to an unconditional grant.

TABLE 12A–2

STATE GRANTS TO LOCAL GOVERNMENTS, BY FUNCTION, 1966

(In Billions of Dollars)

Function	*Amount*
Education	$10.2
Highways	1.7
Welfare	2.9
General support	1.6
Other	0.4
Total	$16.8

SOURCE: U.S. Department of Commerce, Bureau of the Census, *State Government Finances in 1966.*

APPENDIX II—CANADIAN INTERGOVERNMENTAL FISCAL DEVICES

Federal Conditional Grants

Canada was much slower to develop conditional grant programs than the United States, primarily because of greater fear of the effects of such grants on provincial autonomy. Quebec, until 1960, flatly refused to accept the grants for this reason. There is as yet, for example, no general highway grant program, and the number of grant systems is much smaller than in the United States. However, the programs have expanded rapidly in the last five years, and the total sum given in the 1968 fiscal year, $1,683 million, is three times as great as the unconditional grants. The major grants are those for hospital insurance, welfare, and higher education.

Federal Unconditional Grants

The story of the Canadian block grants and other intergovernmental techniques is an extremely complicated one and can only be summarized here. There are several distinct elements:

1. *The Statutory or Constitutional Subsidies.* When the Dominion was formed in 1867, the powers of the provinces to levy indirect taxes were taken from them. Since they had relied heavily on these taxes, the Dominion gave them annual subsidies to replace the lost revenue. The amounts were intended to remain fixed, but were increased somewhat and have continued down to the present time. The total in 1968 was only $32 million.

2. *Equalization Grants, Designed to Equalize the Relative Fiscal Position of the Various Provinces.* Under legislation effective in the period 1968–72, provinces receive equalization grants if the per capita

revenues they can derive from standard tax rates for some 16 taxes are less than the national average. In 1968 all provinces received equalization grants except Ontario, Alberta, and British Columbia.

3. *Stabilization Grants, Designed to Protect Provincial Revenues in Depression.* These are made when necessary to bring the current year's revenue at previous-year tax rates up to 95 percent of the previous year's revenues.

Payments under equalization and stabilization grants totaled $533 million in the 1968 fiscal year.

Federal Tax Collection and Tax Credits

In addition the federal government collects personal and corporate income taxes for all provinces that wish it to do so (all except Quebec, and, for Ontario, except corporate income tax). An abatement or tax credit is allowed for provincial income taxes against federal tax liability (personal income tax, 28 percent of tax, corporate income tax, 10 percent of taxable income). Similar provisions are made for estate taxes.[25]

Provincial Grants to Municipalities

Conditional grants to municipal governments totaled $1.6 billion in 1967, of which $1.2 billion was given for education. Unconditional grants totaled $218 million; over half of this was in Quebec.[26] The total figure was 29 percent of total provincial expenditures.

REFERENCES

BREAK, GEORGE F. *Intergovernmental Fiscal Relationships in the United States.* Washington, D.C.: Brookings Institution, 1966.
A good general survey.

MOORE, A. MILTON, PERRY, J. HARVEY, AND BEACH, DONALD I. *The Financing of Canadian Federation.* Toronto: Canadian Tax Foundation, 1966.
The developments in Canada.

NATIONAL BUREAU OF ECONOMIC RESEARCH. *Public Finances—Needs, Sources and Utilization,* pp. 79–274. Princeton, N.J.: Princeton University Press, 1961.

Revenue Sharing and Its Alternatives. Subcommittee on Fiscal Policy, Joint Economic Committee, U.S. Congress, 90th Cong. 1st Sess. Washington, D.C.: U.S. Government Printing Office, 1967.

[25]Canadian Tax Foundation, *The National Finances, 1967–68* (Toronto: 1967).
[26]Canadian Tax Foundation, *Provincial Finances, 1967* (Toronto: 1967).

PART IV

Revenue Policies

Chapter 13

CHARGES FOR
GOVERNMENTAL SERVICES
AND TAXES IN LIEU
OF CHARGES

Truly collective goods cannot be sold to the users, for reasons explained in detail in Chapter 1. They cannot be packaged and distributed directly to individuals, and no one can feasibly be excluded from the benefits of the services. But many governmental services are not purely collective in nature. Those undertaken by governments because of partial externalities convey some direct benefits to individuals as well, in the sense that the services are received separately by the individuals, and persons can be excluded from the benefits. Services provided by governments to avoid the undesirable consequences of monopoly, to insure desired standards of quality, or to avoid collection costs necessary with private enterprise may yield no externalities at all, all benefits accruing to the persons who acquire units of the services. Or governments may in practice conduct certain activities for reasons of tradition or the pressure of interested groups even though all benefits are direct and there are no economic advantages to governmental participation.

Any governmental service yielding at least partial direct benefits can be financed by charges instead of taxes, or if the use of charges per se is difficult, by a tax directly related to use. The key criterion for the possibility of use of a charge is excludability: the possibility that a person can be excluded, in a fashion tolerable to society, from benefits of the service if he does not wish to pay for it. Or, from the opposite point of view, excludability necessitates direct provision of the service to individuals, rather than in joint fashion to the community. Education, highways, parks, sewerage, among others, are activities for which charges can be made.

The Merits of Use of the Price System

The use of the price system offers significant advantages, in terms of both resource allocation and equity.

Resource Allocation. Financing by a charge instead of a tax allows the price system rather than the political process to determine the amount to produce. Accordingly, the complexities of political process decision making are avoided, with greater assurance of determination of output and resource use in conformity with the preferences of the community. The danger of producing goods for which there is little desire is avoided; goods will not be produced unless preferences are strong enough that persons are willing to pay for them. Output can be adjusted automatically to the amounts purchased at prices established; given appropriate pricing policies, discussed below, optimal resource adjustment can be attained. The political process may result in serious resource misallocation because of failure to interpret preferences correctly. When the demand for the service has any significant elasticity, the pricing mechanism is particularly useful to prevent "waste," that is, production and use of additional units that the person would not buy if he had to pay for them. Thus pricing of electric power and water service will reduce carelessness and use for purposes very low on preference scales. Other services (issuance of marriage licenses, recording of deeds) are not so easily subject to waste.

Use of the price mechanism facilitates optimal resource use in other ways as well. In a short period of time, with demand in excess of a fixed quantity of a service available at a zero price (given number of seats in a municipal auditorium for a concert), or over a longer period with unique resources (Yellowstone Park), the charging of a positive price rations available facilities among the users. Over a long-run period with adjustable facilities, charging of prices provides a key to decisions for expansion of investment.

Many governmental services are used for production purposes. Charging a price for these services, when the benefits are direct and exclusion is possible, facilitates the attainment of optimal factor combinations and optimal outputs of the commodities produced by firms using the services. If, for example, governments were to provide electric power free of charge to all users, production processes would use excessive amounts of electric power relative to other fuels, and output of commodities that are highly electricity-intensive in their production would be excessive. Failure to charge would result in prices that did not reflect all real costs for which production is responsible, and thus consumers would acquire relatively too much.

Finally, the use of charges avoids the almost inevitable distorting effects of taxation upon resource allocation, efficiency, and factor supplies. Taxes are mandatory, charges are not; presumably, therefore, the former have more adverse effect upon behavior.

Constraints. There are, however, restraints on the rule of charging for the services. The first is the cost of collection. With any service—just as with any sale by private-sector firms—some collection costs are incurred. Charges for electric service require meters, meter readers, billing, and action against persons who do not pay. Charges for rides on rapid transit lines require ticket sellers, turnstiles, and physical means to prevent access to trains without paying, while users are subject to the inconvenience of having to wait to make payment. Nevertheless, in both these examples, costs as a percentage of revenue are not high. But collection of tolls for use of city streets and rural roads, other than a few superhighways, would be extremely costly and a source of substantial nuisance to the users. If admission was charged to remote Forest Service camps and many state parks in off-season periods, the costs of collection could easily exceed the revenues.

With some services, high collection costs can be avoided by devising a tax that will operate as a charge; the user, instead of paying directly for the service, is taxed upon some action that is directly correlated with the gaining of benefits from the service. The gasoline tax, discussed later in the chapter, is the primary example. If collection costs are high and tax substitutes are not possible, the costs must be balanced against the gains from the use of charges to determine the desirability of imposing them. There is no particular rule of thumb to determine excessiveness of costs, except 100 percent of the revenues.

The other restraint is the need to insure that the charges do not cause loss of external benefits. If a charge is made on the basis of the ratio of direct benefits to externalities and the demand for the service is highly elastic, use will fall sharply, and most benefits from the externalities will be lost.

Equity. Use of charges also has merit on equity grounds. Except where special circumstances dictate otherwise, usual standards of equity dictate that persons pay for what they get. This is the rule of the private sector of the economy; with governmental services conveying direct benefits to individuals, the same principle can be applied. The question of the desirability of use of the rule involves a value judgment—but one that is widely accepted in a market economy and, in practice, in other economies as well.

Some services, however, are not regarded as suitable for sale on a pay-for-what-you-get basis because of distributional considerations and the desire of society that all persons receive the services as a matter of principle, even if not warranted by externalities. This may be true, for example, of city parks, or the direct-benefit portion of elementary education, as distinct from the externalities portion to be financed by taxation under all approaches. This equity question is the basic issue in the debate over tuition fees to state universities. Opponents of tuition argue that all qualified students are entitled to an education whether they can pay or not. The defenders of the use of tuition counterargue that abandonment of the price system is not necessary to meet distributional requirements. By establishing grants to cover tuition for those students meeting the necessary standards but lacking the funds to finance their education, the needs of persons in the lower income groups can be met without loss of the advantages of the price system. This approach, however, requires means tests to determine eligibility for scholarships. The need to apply for assistance may be sufficient to discourage many qualified persons from seeking aid— whereas society wishes to encourage qualified persons to obtain the services.

In summary:

Use of the pricing mechanism where possible instead of free distribution with financing by taxation is regarded as most justifiable when:

1. Benefits are primarily direct, so that charges will not cause significant loss of externalities.

2. Demand has some elasticity, so that the use of prices aids resource allocation and lessens waste.

3. Charges do not result in inequities to lower income groups, on the basis of accepted standards.

4. Costs of collection of charges are relatively low or alternate taxes measured by use can be employed.

Use of charges is more questionable when:

1. Externalities are significant and will be lost in part if charges are made.

2. Demand is perfectly inelastic, so that no waste is possible. Even so, charges may be regarded as warranted on equity grounds.

3. Equity standards require that the lower income groups be assured of obtaining the services.

4. Collection costs are relatively high and alternative tax measures related to usage cannot be devised.

Terminology of Charges

The terms applied to charges for governmental services vary with the type of service provided. The term *fee* is applied to charges for traditionally governmental services, that is, services which if to be available at all must be provided by government. Typically the user does not receive a good that he himself uses to satisfy wants. He may receive a privilege or authorization—to carry on a certain type of occupation, to incorporate a business, to marry, to hunt, to keep a dog, to drive a car. Those fees that authorize a continuing activity are often called license fees. Other fees are charged for recording titles and documents and for similar basically governmental services directly supplied to an individual. Charges for attending public educational institutions are universally known as *tuition* or tuition fees. Admission charges to use public property are also sometimes called fees. Charges for services that persons themselves use to satify wants, of a type that could be rendered by private firms, are designated as *prices, rates,* or *charges* (for water, electric power, transit service, postal service, and so forth). Charges for road use are universally designated as *tolls.* Those for use of government lands are often called fees; those for exploitation of natural resources are royalties.

Regardless of the terminology, however, all of these items have one characteristic in common: they place part or all of the cost of the service directly upon the user of the service. If the charge significantly exceeds the cost of providing the service, the excess may be regarded as a form of tax, although legally it does not take on this status.

Closely related to charges are taxes directly adjusted in terms of individual use of governmentally provided facilities. While legally taxes, they are closely related to charges in terms of economic effects and equity considerations. Motor fuel taxes and motor vehicle taxes (often called fees) are the primary examples.

PRICING POLICY

If governments are to attain their objectives from the use of charges, several rules must be followed in setting them.

Charges to Cover Direct Benefits Only

Charges must cover only the direct benefits as distinguished from the externalities; otherwise total output of the service will be too low in terms of optimal allocation of resources. If, for example, charges for education were set at levels to cover all costs, total output would be substantially less, and society would lose the advantages of the externalities from the larger output. If rapid transit facilities provide significant externalities in the form of reduced congestion and cost of urban expressways, rates set to cover all costs would sacrifice advantages of externalities. If no externalities are present, obviously all costs should be covered (as for example, the operation of a lunchroom in a public park).

Implementation of this rule involves several problems. First is the determination of the externalities; how significant are these to the community? Some externalities can be calculated rather accurately, as for example the effect of rapid transit on reduction in cost of expressway construction and in congestion and accident rates on existing expressways. With other services, such as education, determination of externalities requires use of the political decision-making process, to determine society's preferences for the externality benefits: more rapid economic development, greater political stability, and broader cultural advantages of higher levels of education. Delineation of direct benefits to road users and benefits to property owners and others from roads has always been troublesome.

The other major question is the relationship between usage of the service and externalities. At the one extreme the externalities are produced by making the service available to the public, and the total externalities benefit does not vary with the amount of the service utilized. Society, for example, may regard the availability of a road to Alaska as of vital importance; the externalities relate only to the availability, not to the actual use. Accordingly, the users could, in terms of resource allocation, be charged tolls high enough to cover all costs (assuming that some toll level would do so), since reduction in usage would not lessen the total gain to society from externalities. At the other extreme, the externalities may be proportional to usage: the externality directly depends upon use of the service, with no decline in the marginal gains to society as more is used. Gains from education may be considered to be of this nature. Or externalities may be considered to decline, per unit of use, beyond a certain level of service. Once highway use is reduced to the point that congestion and pressure for new expressways have been eliminated, there may be no gain from diversion of additional traffic to public transport.

Whenever externalities are related to usage of the service, to the extent that charges are imposed, some of the externality gains are lost. The problem, therefore, is to define the optimal level: the charge that, considering usage, behavior of externalities per unit of use, and economic effects of the taxes to finance the externality portion, is regarded by society as the optimum. While this decision can be made only on the basis of the political process, two economic relationships are significant for the decision: the behavior of the externalities as usage changes and elasticity of demand for the service. If the demand is highly inelastic, increases in charges will have little effect in reducing externalities, while reduction in charges will accomplish little in increasing consumption and the magnitude of externality benefits.

Inclusion of All Costs

In determining the sum of costs as a basis for determining charges, obviously all costs to society should be included, not merely those directly incurred by government in the production of the service. Thus state liquor stores can appropriately include not only the wholesale cost of the liquor and the costs of store operation but also an estimated figure for indirect costs to society arising out of excessive use of liquor. In establishing charges for highways (whether tolls or use-related taxes), indirect costs to society arising out of additional highway use (called spillover costs) must be included as well as costs of highway construction and maintenance. Spillover costs include those caused other users by contributions of additional cars to congestion, those of additional air pollution, and the aesthetic effects of the noise and unsightliness of many urban expressways.

The Marginal Cost Pricing Rule

For attainment of optimal economic welfare, prices must equal both marginal cost and average cost—if this is possible. Marginal cost reflects the real cost to society (in the sense of sacrifice of production of other goods) of additional output of the governmental services (provided the private sector is operating at the optimum). If price fails to cover marginal cost after adjustment for externalities, as indicated, consumers are paying too little for the good compared to others and thus too much will be produced. If price exceeds marginal cost, price exceeds relative real factor cost and too little will be produced. In both cases it is assumed that demand is not perfectly inelastic.

Prices must also equal lowest possible average cost, with maximum efficiency in provision of the services; $MC = AC$ only at the level of lowest AC. If price does not cover average cost, the deficit must be made up from taxes, with distorting effects upon the economy. If price exceeds short-run average cost, plant capacity is too small and output is too low in terms of long-run adjustments. If price exceeds long-run average cost, production is encountering diseconomies of scale.

The optimal adjustment is shown in Figure 13–1, with the assumption that there are no external benefits, the entire cost being placed on the users. In the example there is a substantial range of constant average cost (as is probably typical); $MC = AC$ in this range, and price (P) equals both MC and AC. From a long-run standpoint this situation may be approximated in the operation of city water systems with water provided from local wells, and in the operation of public hospitals and of municipal power plants when optimal production methods involve local generation with diesel engines. As explained subsequently, with some governmental services price cannot equal both MC and AC and compromise is necessary.

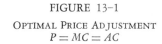

FIGURE 13-1

OPTIMAL PRICE ADJUSTMENT
$P = MC = AC$

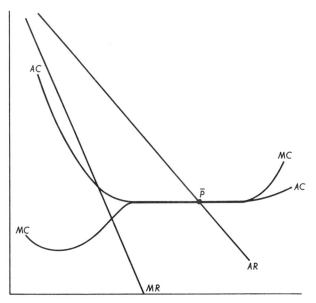

The Significance of Non-optimal Private-Sector Operation. Even if the optimum is attained, it is possible that the results are not best in terms of the preferences of society, since private-sector adjustments may not be optimal in terms of economic welfare. Factor prices may not reflect supply-demand conditions for the factors, and private firms may not be operating at $MC = P$ levels. Under such circumstances, in light of the Theory of the Second Best, government enterprise might provide greater economic welfare by operating at some point other than the optimum as defined. As a practical matter, however, the impossibility of determining the extent of private-sector departures from the $P = MC$ rule suggests that there is a prima facie case for seeking to adhere to the rule in the governmental sector.

Failure of MC *Price to Cover* AC.[1]   Some of the most important governmental activities for which charges are made are in fields in which economies of scale are highly significant. Governments have undertaken provision of the services to avoid the evils of private monopoly or to insure greater attainment of economies of scale. Under these conditions, given the demand for the product, there may be no level of operations at which $P = MC$ and covers AC. In other words, at the output range of lowest AC, demand is inadequate to allow the output to be sold at a price equal to MC or AC. If $P = MC$ ($\bar{p}''$), AC is not covered; if $P = AC$ ($\bar{p}'$), it exceeds MC, as illustrated on Figure

FIGURE 13–2

MARGINAL COST PRICING DILEMMA

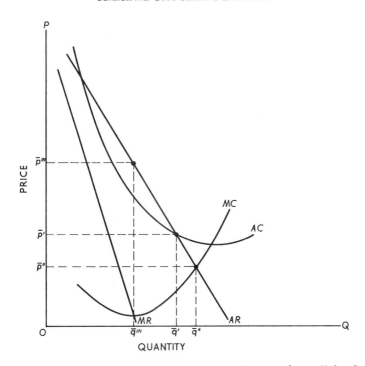

13–2. The extreme example is the traditional one of a toll bridge not used to capacity. The marginal cost for another person to cross is nil or virtually so; the average cost (total cost divided by the number of persons crossing it) is substantial. If the charge is set to equal AC,

[1]The literature on this issue is very extensive. See, for example, R. W. Harbeson, "A Critique of Marginal Cost Pricing," *Land Economics,* Vol. XXXI (February, 1955), pp. 54–74; I. M. D. Little, *A Critique of Welfare Economics* (2d. ed.; Oxford: Oxford University Press, 1967), chap. xi.

use will be greatly restricted; many persons will be barred from using the bridge when the marginal cost to society of their using it would be nil. Optimal welfare is obviously not being attained. The same situation in lesser degree is encountered with utility systems, especially in nonpeak periods. The marginal cost of additional kilowatts of electricity may be very much lower than the average cost of the entire output.

Distinction is necessary between short-run and long-run relationships. A marked difference between MC and AC is a short-run phenomenon; a bridge is built, and for its lifetime, which may be a century, short-run AC is greatly in excess of short-run MC. The long-run problem arises from economies of scale; since further increase in plant size would reduce average cost, long-run MC is less than long-run AC in the range of operations. But the difference is likely to be much smaller.

One solution to the dilemma is to establish price on a marginal cost basis and cover the difference between AC and MC out of general tax revenues. But taxes themselves have distorting effects on the economy that reduce economic welfare; any such effects must be weighed against the disadvantages of restricting use of the facility by charging prices in excess of marginal cost. From a longer range standpoint, failure to cover AC lessens the effectiveness of the pricing system as a guide to governmental investment policy. Covering deficits from tax revenue also reduces pressure on management to maximize efficiency and to resist efforts of unions to push money wages out of line with those in other fields.

Use of the marginal cost rule is also criticized on equity grounds. The particular project (for example, a toll bridge) is undertaken with the intent that the users—who directly benefit—should pay for it. But once it is built, the MC rule requires that most of the cost be covered by general taxation. Accordingly the users experience a net improvement in real income compared to taxpayers as a whole, a result not intended when the facilities were built.

Alternatives to MC *Pricing.* These objections to strict adherence to the MC rule suggest the need for an alternative approach to pricing that will make the users as a group pay all costs of the direct benefits, but with the charge for each use covering only marginal cost. The primary technique involves an annual standby payment unrelated to use. Thus persons who wish to use the toll bridge during the year pay an annual charge for a bridge pass; on each crossing they pay only a small amount equal to marginal cost. Similar methods could be used with electric power and other utility services. Casual users would be given the option of a relatively high charge for individual use of the facility. The system will accomplish the desired goals if the total demand for the service is such that an adequate number of users will pay the annual charge. If many of them will not, the average cost cannot be covered in this fashion. The approach, however, offers potentialities that have rarely been explored.

This approach constitutes a modified form of perfect discrimination in the setting of charges—a system whereby each purchaser is required to pay the maximum that he is willing to pay to obtain each unit of the service. Perfect discrimination is in practice impossible to implement since rates cannot be varied so precisely. But in addition to the standby charge approach, there are other systems of limited discrimination that facilitate the coverage of AC without setting prices above MC. Rates for electric power are often varied by type of use, with low rates on marginal uses for which higher figures will not be paid. Quality of service may be varied slightly with sharp differences in rates; the Paris subway system carried first-class cars for this purpose. Admission charges to events in municipal auditoriums and stadiums are varied with the location of the seats, even though costs are the same.

Price in Excess of Marginal Costs. There are three types of situations in which price equal to MC exceeds AC or may appear to exceed AC:

1. Inadequate plant capacity in the short run. If at the price equal to AC, the quantity demanded exceeds output, price must be raised to ration output, or, in other words, to equal the higher marginal cost of producing output in excess of the amount allowing lowest average cost. This situation requires longer period expansion of investment to provide greater capacity, so that demand can be met at the price equal to MC and AC.

2. Decreasing returns to scale over a long-run period. The governmental activity may reach a condition in which additional output causes a more than proportional increase in total costs because of decreasing returns to scale—primarily the diseconomies of large-scale management. Accordingly, price equal to MC is in excess of AC. If the government is to continue to provide the service there is no escape from this situation if all avenues of decentralization of operations have been explored. Such situations may not arise.

3. Increasing cost conditions due to scarcity of certain resources relative to use in producing the service. If certain resources used are

specialized to the particular product, increases in demand for them by government may raise their costs. This is a true increasing cost situation, such as that encountered in perfectly competitive extractive industries. The average cost schedule of the production of the service will rise because of the higher factor costs until $P = MC = AC$, so excess profits are not actually earned. If the government owns the scarce specialized factors, it gains additional income in its capacity of factor owner.

Varying Marginal Costs

Troublesome issues in pricing are encountered when marginal cost varies greatly by time period, a phenomenon known as the peak load problem. While the marginal cost of carrying an additional passenger on subway and commuter trains during off-peak hours is almost nil, it may be substantially in excess of average cost during peak periods. Directly and immediately an additional peak-load passenger causes inconvenience to other passengers by adding to overcrowding of cars and causing delays.[2] Additions to traffic also require additional cars and personnel, which cannot be used effectively at other times of the day. A rapid transit system requires several times as many cars at rush hours as at off-peak times. Airlines, intercity bus lines, and railroads face the same problem with seasonal peaks. The same phenomenon also arises with highways, particularly urban expressways. While an additional car driven on an expressway adds very little to costs in non-peak hours, it contributes substantially to total cost in rush hours; by adding to congestion, it causes time loss by other persons and increases accident hazards. From a longer run standpoint, additional peak-hour traffic leads to expensive expressway construction.

In theory, charges should be varied by time of day to reflect the varying marginal cost. Therefore transit fares should be high during rush hours and low in off-peak periods, and higher on lines used to capacity than on those not so used. Special charges should be imposed on persons driving on expressways during the peak periods. Such a program encounters problems of implementation, but it is not impossible.[3] Use of expressways during rush hours, for example, could require a special permit checked automatically at various points; casual

---

[2]In the opening days of Expo 67 in Montreal, overcrowding of subway lines became so great the trains could not operate; platforms were so jammed that train doors could not be closed.

[3]William Vickrey developed a plan for fare variation on the New York subway system; see *The Revision of the Rapid Transit Fare Structure of the City of New York*, Mayor's Committee on Management Survey of New York (New York: 1952).

users would either be barred and required to use other roads or subjected to a special toll. In the urban transport field use of the principle for one mode of transport must be accompanied by use with other forms or the problems of the latter will be compounded. To use the principle for commuter trains and not for expressways would merely shift traffic to the expressways and probably aggravate the overall problem.

The other obstacle to use of such systems is popular objection. Especially on rapid transit facilities, many rush hour users are lower income workers while nonrush hour users may be on the average persons of higher incomes. Accordingly, there is usually strong resistance to fare or toll differentiation; extensive education of the public to the need for differentiation is imperative before its use becomes politically possible.

Deliberate Profit Maximization

Maximization of profit requires the adjustment of output to the level at which marginal revenue is equal to marginal cost ($\overline{q}'''$ on Figure 13–2) and setting the price at which this output can be sold ($\overline{p}'''$). The price figure may be substantially higher than the figure set on an $MC = P$ or $AC = P$ basis. Some communities deliberately maximize profits from electric utilities as a means of lowering taxes. Such a policy involves distribution of the costs of general governmental activities on the basis of usage of the particular utility service. Thus evaluation of this technique must be based upon comparison of relative economic effects and equity of this method of taxing compared to others. Viewed in this light the policy may not appear to be acceptable; consumption of electricity or water may not be regarded as a suitable measure of ability to pay tax, and the heavier charges on these services may deter location of power- or water-intensive industries more than would taxes of other types. Overall resource allocation is distorted, in the same fashion as by private monopoly. Unfortunately not all governments following this policy evaluate it carefully.

The greatest temptation to maximize profit arises when outsiders are the primary users of the facility provided: a municipally owned toll bridge primarily used by nonresidents, for example. Profit maximization is advantageous from the standpoint of the particular community, but not for the entire economy.

Charges for Use of Resources

When charges are made for the use of governmentally owned resources rather than for governmentally produced goods, rules of pricing are different. In the United States the federal government owns extensive ore and timber resources, as well as land used for grazing and other purposes. Failure on the part of the government to price these at the level at which supply and demand are equal would result in either excessive production of the final products (since factor prices would not equate factor supply and demand) or excess profits for those firms fortunate enough to be able to obtain their resources from the government. Competitive bidding, as used for logs from national forests, may be the best procedure to insure this result, although when the number of buyers is small there is danger of collusion and under-payment.[4] To go beyond this level and seek to maximize profits would distort prices for the resource from the optimum.

Deficits

Governmental enterprises will show justifiable deficits in two situations: with MC pricing and MC less than AC, as explained, and when externalities warrant pricing below the figure that would cover all costs. In this situation, failure to show a deficit would indicate failure to attain optimal output, if demand has any elasticity. If deficits are incurred in other situations, one explanation is failure to attain maximum efficiency in operation. The solution is obvious.

Alternatively, the deficit may arise from inability to adapt rates to take differences in preferences into consideration. If an enterprise would cover all costs with perfect discrimination in rates (that is, every customer being required to pay the maximum that he would pay to obtain each unit of the good), it is economically justifiable, even though the rates cannot be adjusted in this fashion and costs actually covered. If, however, costs minus external benefits could not be covered even with perfect discrimination, the enterprise is not economically justifiable. Once the equipment wears out to the point that variable costs are no longer covered, the activity should be abandoned. Political considerations may make this action difficult, however.

Another Exception to the Marginal Rule: Distributional Considerations

Society may seek some deviation from optimal pricing rules in the interests of distributional objectives. One example was given above: the resistance to charging higher transit fares in rush hours because of

---

[4]Forest Service techniques are explained and evaluated in W. J. Mead's *Competition and Oligopsony in the Douglas Fir Lumber Industry* (Berkeley: University of California Press, 1966), Part III.

the large volume of lower income travelers in this period. Distributional and allocational elements must be weighed in reaching a decision. The issue also arises with services such that availability to all persons is regarded as essential, yet those who can afford to pay are expected to do so. Municipal hospitals are an example. The usual aim is to set the basic price at average cost (and in practice probably marginal cost also), but to reduce the charges for persons unable to pay. An alternative approach, much preferred by persons who stress the resource allocation role of charges, would apply uniform rates and finance hospital care of lower income groups by outright payments to them or payments of the hospital bills by relief or charitable agencies.

TAXES IN LIEU OF CHARGES: THE FINANCING OF HIGHWAYS

In one major field—the financing of highways—governments in the United States and a few other countries have followed the policy of charging for the use of roads through the application of taxes directly related to highway use instead of through tolls. Highway service is a type of governmental activity for which charges can justifiably be made. The service is rendered directly and separately to individuals, and those not wishing to use the roads can be excluded from them. While externalities are present, they are not of primary importance; most of the secondary gains from highways arise through their use rather than indirectly to the community and are not externalities. Highways are used extensively for production purposes in competition with railway and other transport systems. General tax financing would thus produce economic distortion. Charges are acceptable also on equity grounds, since payment by the users does not work a hardship on the lower income groups.

Direct collection of tolls, however, is expensive to the government and a nuisance to the user, particularly on less heavily traveled roads or city streets. Accordingly a substitute for tolls was developed: a tax on motor fuel used for highway operation, plus a license fee for the privilege of operating on the highways.[5] These taxes are inexpensive to collect, and, at least so far as automobiles are concerned, are as good or better measures of usage than tolls would be. They vary not only with mileage traveled but also, at least to a limited extent, with the weight of the car. Motor fuel taxes were made possible by

---

[5]Historically license fees came first, initially being regarded merely as charges to finance the issuance of licenses for regulatory purposes.

the fact that motor fuel consumption varies with road usage; should the electric car develop, the simple system would break down as there would be no equivalent base for taxation.

The height of the charge is determined through the political process, although in a rough way reflecting the preferences of road users for road construction and their willingness to pay for the roads. Actual expenditures on roads are dictated largely by the amount of tax revenue received at the rates set. The system worked very well in earlier years, in part because it was strongly favored by the road-using groups, who saw it as the only means of getting suitable highways built relatively quickly. This is one of the few taxes in history that was sought by the persons who were going to pay it.

Problems of Implementation

Several problems have arisen in the implementation of the principle of user charges. One is the exclusion from tax of motor fuel used for nonhighway purposes. Fortunately gasoline has few such uses, the principal one being for farm purposes. A refund system is typically used, although with some evasion by persons claiming refund on fuel used on highways. The development of the diesel truck complicated the problem because diesel fuel and its close relative, stove or fuel oil, are widely used for other purposes, and some evasion is almost inevitable. The diesel vehicle created another complication: mileage per ton is greater for diesel fuel than for gasoline, and thus a higher tax per gallon is necessary. The users of diesel fuel fight this differential, arguing for equality of rates, whereas equality does not mean equity.

The much more serious problem of implementation of the principle arises with larger vehicles generally. Regardless of the approach employed, presumably larger vehicles should pay higher per mile charges than passenger automobiles. They are responsible for substantially greater highway maintenance and construction costs than automobiles, for slowing traffic on many highways, and for increasing accident hazards. Appropriate charges are particularly important because the larger vehicles are directly competitive with other forms of transport. The most logical rule, in terms of optimal pricing methods, is adjustment of charges in conformity with the added highway costs for which the heavy vehicles are responsible. Unfortunately these are very difficult to calculate, although a number of studies have been made over the years, including an exhaustive federal study published in

1961.[6] More frequently relative burdens have been compared on a ton-mileage basis, under the assumption that, in the absence of better knowledge, a uniform charge per ton-mile is a reasonable rule. In practice the relative charges have been based upon guesswork and political considerations as much as on anything else.

The license fees are flat annual amounts and accordingly are unrelated to mileage, thereby favoring the commercial vehicles that travel extensively and discriminating against those used relatively little. Accordingly, some states have supplemented the other levies by a ton-mileage tax, based upon the number of miles traveled. This form of tax is much more satisfactory in terms of pricing principles but it is more difficult to enforce.

Allocation of Funds

Whereas tolls would be collected on each road and therefore would be directly related to costs of that road, highway user levies are allocated through the political process, and thus not necessarily in terms of origin of revenues by road or type of road[7] In practice, because of the traditional domination of state legislatures by rural areas, far too much has typically been allocated to secondary rural roads compared to the revenues they produce, thus leaving too little for roads in urban areas and major intercity routes. This, in turn, led, in the 1950's, to growing inadequacy of intercity roads and urban arterial routes. Reallocation of funds was difficult, given the makeup of the legislatures, and strong opposition developed on the part of user groups to further increases in tax rates without better allocation; they felt that they were paying too much for what they were getting. This source of lag in highway spending relative to preferences was accentuated by the specific rate nature of the motor fuel taxes, which prevented automatic increases in yields in response to rising price levels, and to the general bias against higher taxes of any type that developed in this period. The opposition to higher taxes became so emotionally

[6]U.S. Department of Commerce, Bureau of Public Roads, *Final Report of the Highway Cost Allocation Study* (House Doc. 54, 87th Cong., 1st sess.) (Washington, D.C.: U.S. Government Printing Office, 1961).

A good summary of the approaches and issues is found in the article by R. W. Harbeson, "Some Unsettled Issues in Highway-Cost Allocation," in *Public Finance and Welfare: Essays in Honor of C. Ward Macy* (Eugene, Ore.: University of Oregon Books, 1966).

[7]R. W. Harbeson, "Some Allocational Problems in Highway Finance," in *Transportation Economics* (New York: National Bureau of Economic Research, 1965), pp. 139–65.

blinded that it failed to distinguish between user charges and regular taxes.

This problem led to two consequences of importance in the 1950's. One was the revival of the use of toll roads, in order to permit immediate construction of major interstate routes for which existing roads were completely inadequate. Some states were also motivated by the desire to obtain payment from out-of-state motorists for the costs of through routes. About 3,000 miles of toll roads were built. The second development was the establishment in 1956 of the federal interstate highway system, whereby the federal government accepted for the first time the principle of user charges (in the form of motor fuel and other highway-related taxes) in the highway field and assumed financing of a much larger portion of the costs of the major highway routes (90 percent). One consequence was virtual cessation of toll road expansion.

The Relationship of Charges and Costs on Particular Roads

The various road user charges have always been set up in a uniform fashion within a state, and, with the federal taxes, the entire country. Actually, the costs for which additional vehicles are responsible are greater, per vehicle mile, on some roads than on others and differ according to the time of day. The highest marginal costs are created on urban expressways and arterial streets at rush hours. From a short-run standpoint each additional car adds to congestion and therefore slows down traffic and lessens the carrying capacity of the roads, as well as causing time loss for other drivers and increasing accident hazards. From a longer run standpoint, this congestion leads to the building of more expressways, which in turn soon become congested. The continuing difficulty arises in part because the highway charges are based upon the average cost of the road system, ignoring the spillover costs and the effects of additional traffic upon highly expensive expressway construction. The response of governments—now aided by federal funds—has been to try to meet the problem by building more expressways. But the traffic estimates are based upon the present congestion-burdened routes and inevitably prove to be loo low for the initially congestion-free new routes.[8]

One solution to this problem now recognized more widely than in the past is to adjust charges in terms of these factors: as noted above, to restrict the traffic on urban expressways during peak hours

---

[8]See C. O. Meiburg, "An Economic Analysis of Highway Services," *Quarterly Journal of Economics*, Vol. LXXVII (November, 1963), pp. 648–56.

by special charges. Governments, however, are very slow to do this, partly because of the long-accepted principle that anyone is free to drive at any time on any road free of charge (except routes built specifically as toll roads and not at the taxpayers' expense). But the principle must, sooner or later, give way under the urgency of the situation. In other words, the charges need to be related more specifically, so far as is administratively feasible, to the costs created by travel on particular types of roads at particular periods.

Another long-ignored cost created by rising metropolitan area motor vehicle use is air pollution; as this grows in seriousness, the case for restricting urban car use by higher charges is strengthened still more.

Highways versus Public Transport in Urban Areas

Urban area expressway and arterial congestion, plus increased concern over air pollution, has led to renewed attention to the possibility of increasing urban transit use. Over recent decades public transport facilities have declined rapidly in relative importance and in some areas in absolute availability and use. The decline can easily be explained. Private motor vehicle ownership has rapidly increased. Once a person has a car or two cars, he has a strong bias in the direction of using his own car.[9] One element is the declining per mile cost as use increases; once he has bought the car, the marginal cost of additional driving is much less than the average cost and thus average cost falls. The average cost to him of public transit is constant per ride (even though for the transit service, cost per passenger would fall with increased travel). Many persons find a car more convenient and faster; to others it is a source of prestige and pride; others dislike the crowding of public transit in rush hours. Frequently, the use of a car is timesaving. The tendency toward decentralization of shopping and industry in large cities has made the provision of rapid transit more difficult and expensive and less convenient so that many persons have no choice but to drive. To aggravate the problem, motor vehicle use is often underpriced, in the sense that user charges do not reflect all costs created by driving on city streets and expressways in rush hours.

On the other side of the picture, public transport has been allowed to deteriorate. Much commuter service was operated by the railways; they were unable to realize on the gains from externalities (less crowd-

---

[9]This argument is developed by R. Sherman in "A Private Ownership Bias in Transit Choice," *American Economic Review*, Vol. LVII (December, 1967), pp. 1211–17.

ing of streets) and have often been subject to heavy taxes on their facilities. As a consequence covering of costs has been difficult, and the service has declined and in some instances has been abandoned. Some of the commuter roads were in such financial difficulties that they had no choice, and others were unwilling to continue covering the losses from freight revenue. Private city transit systems were in much the same situation, and even municipally owned systems were frequently forced to operate on a cost-covering basis, so that fares were too high in light of externalities. Fares often substantially exceed marginal costs.

There is little wonder, therefore, that public transport has been underutilized and the streets overcrowded. Only in the last five years has any effort been given to restoring a balance. This is often difficult to do; the demand for transit service is not highly elastic, and various studies have shown that riders cannot easily be lured away from the motor vehicle by fare reductions.[10] But as the congestion problem becomes progressively worse, and as cities resist more and more the carving up of developed areas for more expressways, governments are gradually coming to recognize that expenditures to insure continuance of existing transit facilities and to provide additional ones are imperative. But the resistances are still strong: well-organized pressure groups, the motor vehicle manufacturers and automobile associations particularly, fight for continued expansion of expressways and oppose rapid transit.[11]

[10]L. M. Moses and H. F. Williamson, Jr., "Value of Time, Choice of Mode, and the Subsidy Issue in Urban Transportation," *Journal of Political Economy*, Vol. LXXI (June, 1963), pp. 247–64.

[11]One of the most successful experiments has been the Government of Ontario train service along the lakeshore into Toronto from east and west. This was introduced in 1967 for the expressed purpose of luring persons from the use of cars and was expected to operate at an annual deficit. Thus far traffic has been substantially greater than anticipated, and further expansions are planned. The deficits were regarded as entirely justified by the externalities of the service.

A number of studies of the urban transport problem have appeared in recent years; see, for example, W. Owen, *The Metropolitan Transportation Problem* (rev. ed.; Washington, D.C.: Brookings Institution, 1966); L. C. Fitch, *Urban Transportation and Public Policy* (San Francisco: Chandler, 1964); J. R. Meyer, J. F. Kain, and M. Wohl, *The Urban Transportation Problem* (Cambridge, Mass.: Harvard University Press, 1965).

APPENDIX 1—REVENUES FROM CHARGES AND TAXES IN LIEU OF CHARGES

TABLE 13A-1

REVENUES FROM CHARGES AND TAXES IN LIEU OF CHARGES,
UNITED STATES, 1966 FISCAL YEAR

Billions of Dollars

Charges		*Taxes in Lieu of Charges*	
Federal			
Natural resources	$3.1	Motor fuel	$3.0
Housing and urban re-		Other highway taxes	2.7
newal	0.5		
Postal services	4.6		
Water transportation	0.2		
Other	1.4		
Total	9.8	Total	5.7
State			
Tuition and other charges		Motor fuel	4.6
for education	2.0	Motor vehicle licenses	2.2
Hospitals	0.4		
Liquor stores	1.4		
Other	1.2		
Total	5.0	Total	6.8
Local			
School lunches	1.0	Motor vehicles	0.1
Other education	0.7		
Hospitals	1.1		
Sewerage and sanitation	0.8		
Parks	0.2		
Housing	0.4		
Air transportation	0.3		
Utilities	5.1		
Liquor stores	0.2		
Miscellaneous	1.3		
Total	11.1	Total	0.1
Total	$25.9	Total	$12.6

SOURCE: U.S. Bureau of the Census, *Governmental Finances in 1965–66*.

APPENDIX II—ACTUAL PRICING POLICIES

In the actual setting of prices, almost no direct attention has been given to marginal cost considerations. Typically, government-owned utilities have followed the same general patterns as the rate regulatory policies applied to private utilities: they have set rates sufficiently high to cover average cost, in many cases including an "average" rate of return. A few seek to maximize profits. Controlling legislation often requires the enterprises to cover costs, denying them resort to taxes to cover deficits. In setting rates on particular types of service, marginal considerations have played a part, as is manifest in the low rates charged industrial users by municipal power systems and the developmental rates of the TVA[12] But even in most of these cases the the overall goal has been the covering of average cost. In Canada the Canadian National Railways has essentially no independent rate policy of its own at all, merely following the rates of the Canadian Pacific, which serve as the yardstick.

The United States postal system has used a type of pricing discriminatory by class of mail, based on the implicit (and apparently largely incorrect) assumption that the marginal cost of handling additional second- and third-class mail is relatively low. As a matter of actual policy, the low rates on second-class mail (periodicals, etc.) have reflected congressional policy, which is to facilitate dissemination of information, and thus are based on externalities. The low rates on third-class mail (advertising circulars and the like) have rarely been explained and are attributable to the pressure brought upon Congress by the benefited groups. The net result of the low rates on these two classes of mail is a continuing overall postal deficit, which is due to the setting of rates well below marginal cost, not to a deviation between marginal cost and average cost. Justification for most of the deficit in terms of indirect benefits is difficult to find. As one student of the question concludes, "Postal pricing policy is chaotic, if not bizarre."[13] Much of the difficulty has arisen out of the unwillingness of Congress to permit the postal system greater freedom in rate setting, and from the influence of pressure groups on congressional action.

The operation of the federal reclamation projects presents an example of the problems of pricing with a decreasing cost operation. The general procedure has been to set the charges for water on an average cost basis after deducting cost elements attributed (in rather arbitrary fashion) to other functions, such as flood control. But none of the projects can cover their costs on a strictly uniform average cost price, given the capacity of the farmers to pay and continue farming. As a consequence, the Bureau of Reclamation has established a block pricing system, which constitutes a step in the direction of marginal cost

[12]A detailed account of the pricing policies of the French national electric power system is given in J. R. Nelson (ed.), *Marginal Cost Pricing in Practice* (Englewood Cliffs, N.J.: Prentice-Hall, 1964).
[13]See Jane Kennedy, "Structure and Policy in Postal Rates," *Journal of Political Economy*, Vol. LXV (June, 1957), p. 208.

pricing. The lands served by a project are grouped into blocks, and the rate for water for each block is adjusted in terms of the net increment in farm income resulting from the use of the water. Unfortunately, however, the diversity of land in the various blocks prevents any close adjustment of benefit and charge and interferes with efficient use of the water. But the resistance of the farmers to more complete classification prevents the use of more scientific pricing that would permit the projects to cover their costs. Congress has, in practice, not insisted that they do so and, as a consequence, has allowed perpetuation of unsatisfactory pricing methods.[14] Federal electric power projects typically price on an average cost basis.

Policies on indirect benefits have varied widely. Municipal utilities usually ignore them and attempt to make the users pay all of the costs.[15] As suggested in the examples above, the federal government has frequently established rates that do not cover costs, and thus has in a sense recognized indirect benefits, although the motive for setting the relatively low rates was often quite different.

In contrast to the utilities, the government liquor monopolies have aimed at the earning of a high rate of profit.

REFERENCES

THE USE OF PRICES AND PRICING POLICY

BROWNLEE, O. H. "User Prices vs. Taxes," in *Public Finance: Needs, Sources and Utilization*, pp. 421–38. New York: National Bureau of Economic Research, 1961.

HOTELLING, H. "The General Welfare in Relation to the Problems of Taxation and of Railway and Utility Rates," *Econometrica*, Vol. VI (July, 1938), pp. 242–69.

THOMSON, P. "Prices versus Taxes in the Allocation of Public Resources," *Proceedings of the National Tax Association for 1955*, pp. 140–56.

VANDERMEULEN, ALICE "Reform of a State Fee Structure," *National Tax Journal*, Vol. XVII (December, 1964), pp. 394–402, based on her study, *California's Fee and License Structure*. Sacramento, Calif.: Assembly Interim Committee on Revenue and Taxation, 1964.

[14]See J. Margolis, "Welfare Criteria, Pricing, and Decentralization of a Public Service," *Quarterly Journal of Economics*, Vol. LXXI (August, 1957), pp. 448–63.

[15]In some cases an attempt is made to require the users to pay for aspects of the service that are provided for purposes other than benefit to the users, as such. Thus, San Francisco retains its cable cars primarily for reasons of tradition and tourist attraction, but attempts to cover the somewhat higher costs of this form of transport from the users of the system, not from general tax revenues, as would be appropriate.

The Canadian government has sought in recent years to support deficits of those Canadian National Railways activities justified on the basis of externalities from tax revenues rather than from freight charges.

Highway Finance

Bulletin of the Oxford University Institute of Statistics. *Symposium on the Economics of Roads,* November 1960.

Burch, Philip H. *Highway Revenue and Expenditure Policy.* New Brunswick: Rutgers University Press, 1962.

Friedlaender, Ann F. *The Interstate Highway System.* Amsterdam: North Holland Publishing Co., 1965.

Mohring, H., and Harwitz, M. *Highway Benefits.* Evanston: Northwestern University Press, 1962.

Chapter
14

AN OPTIMAL
TAX STRUCTURE

Actual tax structures reflect the interplay of a number of forces. A primary influence is the evaluation by legislative bodies of various forms of taxation in light of the objectives of society as they interpret them. The executive and the administrative organization play a significant role, both by influencing community and legislative attitudes toward various forms of taxation and by their recommendations to the legislative body of specific tax measures. At the state level and in the Commonwealth countries, study commissions of outsiders play a role, as do experts in all countries. At all levels of government, interested pressure groups exert considerable influence. All groups, other than interested ones seeking to reduce their own tax burden, are presumably striving for a structure that is optimal in terms of the goals of society. Definition of such a structure, therefore, requires a restatement of the goals of society and consequent development of the requirements that the tax structure must meet if it is to facilitate to the maximum the attainment of these goals. These requirements are often called principles or standards of taxation.

PRIMARY GOALS OF SOCIETY

Contemporary society has many objectives, two of which are of primary relevance to tax policy. The first objective is attainment of the highest possible level of per capita real income and the highest feasible rate of economic growth consistent with the constraints (technology, resources, skills), with the product mix (resource allocation) adjusted to the optimum in terms of consumer preferences. As explained in deail in earlier chapters, attainment of this goal requires:

1. Allocation of resources so that the marginal rate of substitution (MRS) between each set of commodities is equal to the marginal rate of transformation (MRT) in their production; with this relationship, shifting of resources from one product to another will not increase the satisfaction of some persons without reducing that of others.

2. Maximum quantity of factor units available, given the preferences of factor-unit owners for their use in production; and maximum attainable quality of factor units.

3. Optimum efficiency in production, so that maximum output is obtained from given inputs; and maximum rate of technological development.

4. Full employment of available resources.

5. A full-employment rate of capital formation that reflects relative preferences of society for present consumption and economic growth.

The second objective is equity: a pattern of distribution of real income that contemporary society regards as most equitable. This pattern is impossible to define precisely, but broad guidelines of attitudes are discernable.

Tax Requirements for Optimal Per Capita Real Income

If the tax structure is to facilitate the attainment of the goal of maximizing per capita real income, it must be designed in such a way as to avoid excess burdens, on the one hand, and to give maximum incentive to changes in economic behavior that increase real income, on the other. By *excess burden* is meant reduction in private-sector real incomes (including in real income gains from leisure) caused by taxes over and above those required to make resources available for governmental-sector production. There are several areas of behavior in which beneficial effects and excess burdens may occur:

Consumption Patterns and Resource Allocation. Taxes will improve resource allocation if they lessen barriers to attainment of the optimal pattern in the private sector. If, for example, production and use of a commodity create external costs, consumption and output of the commodity will be excessive if the government does not interfere. Excessive consumption of liquor is the traditional example; such consumption creates costs to society that are not reflected in the prices of the products. Or, greater departures from perfect competition in some lines of production than in others will result in relatively greater excess of price over marginal cost in the former, with consumption and therefore production too small in terms of the optimum. If taxes can be devised to raise the relative prices of goods that are underpriced in terms of all costs and lower those that are excessive, resource allocation can be improved.

On the other hand, taxes can easily create *consumer excess burden,* by causing a readjustment of consumption and resource allocation away from the optimum. In nontechnical terms, if a tax alters the relative prices of various goods, it will cause consumers to shift away from the taxed goods to untaxed ones; as they do so, they lose satisfaction, since they are buying less preferred goods, yet the government gains no revenue. For simplification, let us assume that all markets are perfectly competitive and all factor supplies perfectly inelastic. Under the former assumption, for each commodity, the marginal rate of substitution between each set of commodities will be equal to the marginal rate of transformation in the production of the two commodities, or, in other

FIGURE 14–1

EXCESS CONSUMER BURDEN OF AN EXCISE TAX

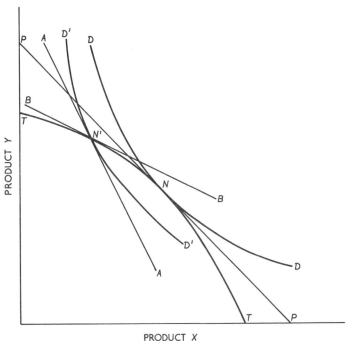

PRODUCT X

TT: Transformation curve.
DD: Equilibrium indifference curve, with income tax.
D'D':   Equilibrium indifference curve, with excise tax.
PP: Price ratio, before excise tax.
AA: Price ratio confronting consumer, after excise tax.
BB: Price ratio, net of tax, to producers after excise tax.

words, shifting of resources from one commodity to another will not increase want satisfaction. This relationship is illustrated by the tangency between the transformation curve *(TT)* and the indifference curve *(DD)*. On Figure 14–1, the curves are tangent at *N*, indicating that the individual is attaining the maximum satisfaction possible from given resources. PP indicates the ratio of prices of the two goods.

If a tax is levied uniformly on all commodities, on total income, or on a per capita (poll tax) basis, the equilibrium adjustment is not disturbed, although the level of consumption of each commodity will be reduced because of lower disposable income. If, however, one commodity is taxed and another is not, one commodity will now be more expensive than the other, relative to input costs, regardless of the absolute direction of change in prices. Thus equality of marginal rate of transformation and marginal rate of substitution is lost. In a sense a tax wedge has been inserted between the market price and the factor cost of one commodity but not of the other; the consumer bases his decisions on the market price, the producer on price net of tax. Thus relatively too little of the taxed commodity will be consumed and produced, and too much of the untaxed commodity. On Figure 14–1, when an income tax is replaced by an excise, the new equilibrium is at N', on a lower indifference curve, which is tangent to the price ratio curve after excise tax (AA) but not to the transformation curve, since producers' decisions are based on price relationships net of excises (BB). Thus consumer satisfaction is less.

Factor Supplies. As analyzed in detail in Chapter 7, taxes may alter the relative supplies of various factors. The changes in factor supplies may bring greater attainment of the objectives of society. If, for example, a society wishes to induce additional persons to enter the labor market, as many developing economies do, a substantial flat sum tax unrelated to actual income may force persons to seek jobs instead of living off subsistence production. If a society wishes, as a matter of policy, to encourage wives to stay out of the labor market, it can do so by adjustment in tax structures. If a country wishes to alter the birth rate it may, at least theoretically, do so by adjusting the system of allowances for dependents in income tax structures.

Tax structures may also create *factor excess burden*—changes in factor supplies that bring an undesired reduction in per capita real income. Any income tax, particularly of a progressive nature, may have this effect. If persons work less because of the tax, they lose income; total output and per capita real income fall, without gain to anyone. Evidence summarized in Chapter 7 indicates that the actual effects of the present tax structure are not nearly as great as is often argued.

Efficiency. Taxes may on some occasions stimulate businesses to greater efficiency in production, as noted in Chapter 6, especially when the satisfactory-profit motive is dominant and the tax reduces the actual profit below this figure. To the extent that the private sector attains maximum efficiency—and there are always strong pressures in this direction—taxes may lessen efficiency and thus produce an *efficiency excess burden* by altering choice of techniques or organization of production, as explained in Chapter 6, or by lessening incentives to seek attainment of low-cost factor combinations.

Collection. Resources used in the administration of taxes, in compliance with them, and in devising methods of escaping from them are not available for use in the production of goods and services. All taxes require some resources for these purposes; the lesser the extent to which resources are so used, the less is the administrative burden. Maximum convenience to taxpayers in calculating tax liability, in making payment, and in timing of payment aid in minimizing collection excess burden.

Stabilization and Growth. Taxes tend to reduce the S/Y ratio because taxes are absorbed in part out of savings. Therefore a deliberate policy of raising the potential growth rate by tax adjustments is difficult; the best that can be hoped for is that the structures will have minimum impact in reducing the potential growth rate. As previously explained, most developed countries find consistent attainment of the existing potential growth rate difficult; to the extent that taxes reduce the potential rate they make the attainment of it easier by increasing total spending relative to national income. Any tax, per se, tends to curtail spending $(C + I)$; the aim in establishment of the tax structure, therefore, in a period in which there is a tendency toward unemployment is to minimize the restrictive effect on C and I. Such restrictive effect of the structure can presumably be offset by overall fiscal and monetary policy (for example, by reducing the overall level of taxes), but these policies have some adverse effects of their own and are not necessarily fully effective.

Taxes, on the other hand, play a major role in restricting inflationary pressures. Some taxes are more effective than others, per dollar of revenue. Maximizing the anti-inflationary effect in a period of tendency toward inflation is an important goal in framing the tax structure. As with unemployment, inflation can presumably be controlled by overall fiscal and monetary policy, but these by no means work perfectly, and the greater the effect of the tax structure in restricting price increases per dollar of revenue, the less the required height of the tax structure (or extent of necessary expenditure reduction).

The extent to which a tax contributes to economic stability depends in part upon the revenue elasticity of the tax: the behavior of the yield of the tax in response to a change in national income. A tax whose yield rises and falls more rapidly than national income serves as an automatic stabilizing device, although too rapid increases can create fiscal drag. Secular behavior of yield is also significant, particularly in developing economies. If yield lags behind increases in real national income or the price level, frequent rate changes are required, with consequent time lags in growth of yield.

Equity

Questions of equity are of necessity ones involving value judgments and no scientific approach to the definition of equity is possible. Standards of equity for taxation are determined solely by consensus of thought in a particular society; the tendency to attach scientific validity to standards of equity is unfortunate.

For the financing of governmental activities that primarily convey direct benefits to persons who can afford to pay for them, equity is interpreted to require that persons pay on the basis of benefit received as they do when they buy privately produced goods. This is the basis for charging for such services and the basis for taxes employed in lieu of charges. More specifically, the benefit rule is regarded as equitable as the basis for taxation when (1) benefits from the services are primarily individual rather than collective in nature, (2) charges cannot effectively be used or would be more costly to collect than taxes, and (3) the benefit basis does not result in burdens on particular persons or groups that society regards as unreasonable. For most taxes, this basis does not conform with desired standards of equity, partly because the benefits received by individuals are not direct and any allocation would be entirely arbitrary, partly because this basis of financing would be contrary to the patterns of after-tax income distribution that society prefers. For redistributional activities the benefit approach is unworkable.

For most governmental activities, equity in distribution is interpreted by contemporary society to require that relative burdens be distributed according to *ability to pay,* that is, that the pattern of reduction in private-sector real incomes reflect the relative abilities of persons to pay taxes. Unfortunately the concept of ability has no clearly defined universally accepted meaning or measure. Basically the term refers to economic well-being—how well off the person is from an economic standpoint. Economic well-being is measured by income adjusted for various circumstances affecting tax capacity; by consumption expenditures, either in total or for certain purposes; and by wealth owned. Opinions differ widely, however, over how much relative reliance on each basis is desirable.

Equity is also commonly interpreted to require progression in the tax structure relative to income, because tax capacity is considered to rise more rapidly than income. Progression is also defended by many on the grounds of lessening inequality of income distribution. For many years progression was justified on the basis of the Law of Diminishing Marginal Utility applied to income; the more dollars gained, the less the utility from each successive dollar. This approach was subjected to severe criticism in terms of the "new" welfare economics, partly because of question about the applicability of the Law to income, but primarily because the reasoning was based upon the assumption of interpersonal utility comparison—the ability to compare satisfactions gained by various people. Such an assumption is meaningless; satisfaction gained by various persons cannot be compared.[1]

Political support for progression arises from at least two other sources in addition to equity. Some persons seek to shift their own tax burden from the present, when their incomes are low, to the future, when they will be higher. Others seek in progression a means of transferring burden permanently from themselves to others—specifically, to the wealthy. For this reason, conservatives tend to be hostile toward progression, which they see simply as a device whereby the poor exploit the rich, and condemn it for lack of any objective standard for determining the appropriate degree.

Regardless of the measure of ability employed, equity cannot be attained unless enforcement is effective. If some persons are able to evade taxes, the desired pattern of distribution is not in fact obtained.

Establishment of a tax structure on the basis of accepted standards of equity requires knowledge of the pattern of redistribution of income that results from various taxes. As noted in Chapter 8, unfortunately this knowledge is deficient, particularly for the corporate income tax. As a consequence, actual distributional effects may conform with desired standards of equity less than society believes.

Conflict of Standards

In practice, as a tax structure is framed or revised, conflict between various standards is almost inevitable. If society seeks a high degree of progression for reasons of equity, the consequence may be a significant

---

[1] H. Kalvin and W. J. Blum, *The Uneasy Case for Progressive Taxation* (Chicago: University of Chicago Press, 1953).

reduction in the rate of savings, investment, and economic growth. Provisions that increase equity may complicate administration and compliance to such an extent that evasion becomes substantial. To resolve such conflicts society must weigh the importance of the various conflicting considerations. These conflicts are apparent in any analysis of a tax structure as a basis for reform.

ELEMENTS IN THE OVERALL TAX STRUCTURE

The optimal tax structure of a country is dependent on the nature of the economic, political, and social structure of the country, and the attitudes of the people toward various objectives. Definition of the optimum is inherently difficult. Neither distributional patterns of particular taxes nor the economic effects of various measures are known. Society's equity objectives are not clearly revealed, nor is its ranking of various objectives. Actual tax structures therefore reflect a compromise among different attitudes of persons about effects and equity goals. Nevertheless there is a substantial consensus on the overall role of various major taxes; most of the dispute centers around marginal change in rates and structures.

Income Taxation

The important role played by the income tax in the tax structures of the United States and many developed countries is a reflection of its advantages compared to all other forms of taxation.

Equity. Acceptance is based primarily on equity considerations: the tax accords more closely than any other levy with usually (but not universally) accepted standards of equity. Income is regarded as the best single general measure of economic well-being and thus of tax capacity; furthermore, the relative tax liabilities of various persons can be adjusted according to other circumstances affecting taxpaying ability: number of dependents, medical expenses, casualty losses, and so on, and according to expenditures that a government may wish to encourage (for example, contributions to charity). Similar adjustments are not possible with other taxes. The income tax also permits the exclusion from tax of persons in the lowest income groups. The income tax is the only levy capable of introducing significant progression into the tax structure; much of the support for it reflects the attitude that progression is essential for overall equity in distribution of the tax burden. Other taxes are at best proportional and some are regressive.

To those who defend consumption rather than income as the best measure of ability, the income tax is inherently inequitable; these however appear to be a small minority. Those who regard progression as inequitable object to the usual income tax on this basis. Some of the equity of the income tax is admittedly lost by changes in relative factor prices resulting from the tax and by evasion. If some persons are able to restore pretax real income, others are burdened with the share of these persons as well as with their own. Some readjustments of this type are inevitable, but there is no evidence that they are serious. Despite these criticisms and limitations, the income tax is usually regarded as the most equitable tax.

Economic Effects. The income tax, properly designed, does not create excess consumer burden or reduce efficiency by altering the choice of production and organization techniques. On the other hand, the tax may lessen the incentive of business firms to maximize efficiency and may encourage firms to undertake some marginal activities of doubtful gain, such as additional advertising. The income tax gives rise to some excess factor burden unless factor schedules are perfectly inelastic, but the empirical evidence indicates that at present in the United States the effects upon supply of labor, executive talent, and risk taking are not significant. Virtually all taxes create some excess factor burden, but a progressive income tax may have more effect, per dollar of revenue, in altering factor supplies than consumption or wealth taxes.

An income tax, particularly with progressive rates, reduces the overall S/Y ratio more than other major taxes, because the burden concentrates more heavily upon the higher income groups and corporations and, unlike consumption taxes, gives no incentive to save more and consume less. Accordingly, the potential rate of economic growth is reduced somewhat, although evidence suggests that the difference is not a great as is often argued. The relative effects of income and other taxes upon full employment and thus the attainment of the potential growth rate are less clear. On the one hand, because of the lower impact on consumer spending per dollar of revenue, the income tax allows a higher level of national income, given overall tax levels. Because it restricts consumption less than other major taxes, it likewise has less repressive effect upon investment to the extent that investment is dependent on total spending in the economy. On the other hand, the income tax places a greater direct impact upon the returns from investment than do other taxes. On the whole, however, the income tax probably reduces $C + I$ less, per dollar of revenue, than other taxes, and thus allows a lower deficit to attain a given stimulus to total spending. By the same reasoning the income tax is a less effective anti-inflationary device than taxes that have more restrictive effect on C + I, but, as explained in Chapter 10, the income tax has less influence than sales taxes in inducing wage rate increases.

Revenue Elasticity. The revenue elasticity of the income tax, that is, the response of the tax yield to changes in national income, is relatively high compared to that of other taxes because of progressive rates and exemptions. Goode estimates the income elasticity in the United States to be 1.1 percent, that is, a 1 percent increase in national income produces a 1.1 percent increase in income tax payments.[2] J. O. Blackburn estimates a 1.4 to 1 relationship.[3] Other major taxes show somewhat lower figures, although the difference appears to be less, on the basis of empirical studies, than might be expected. Various figures for the property tax in recent years range from 0.8 to 1;[4] an earlier estimate was a very much lower figure, 0.22.[5] Studies of sales tax revenue elasticity indicate a figure of around 1 over a relatively long period, but well below 1 for shorter periods.[6]

Administration and Compliance. The income tax, with its large number of individual returns and payroll deductions by employers, requires substantial resources for effective operation, and causes much talent to be devoted to finding means of reducing tax liability. But other acceptable taxes that are major revenue sources have similar problems; in a developed economy, the income tax does not appear to be significantly worse. In a developing economy, however, with low levels of education and record keeping, administrative problems place a major obstacle in the way of use of a refined income tax applying to a large sector of the economy.

Actual versus Ideal Income Taxes. This analysis has related to an "ideal" tax applying uniformly to all forms of net income. As explained in Chapter 14, the framing of an income tax to accomplish this goal is difficult. Definitions of income, particularly with respect to increases in the value of assets and nonmarket gains, delineation of

[2] R. Goode, *The Individual Income Tax* (Washington, D.C.: Brookings Institution, 1964), chap. x.

[3] J. O. Blackburn, "Implicit Tax Rate Reduction," *American Economic Review,* Vol. LVII (March, 1967), pp. 162–69.

[4] D. Netzer, *Economics of the Property Tax* (Washington, D.C.: Brookings Institution, 1966), pp. 184–90.

[5] H. M. Groves and C. H. Kahn, "The Stability of State and Local Tax Yields," *American Economic Review,* Vol. XLII (March, 1952), pp. 87–102.

[6] D. G. Davies, "The Sensitivity of Consumption Taxes to Fluctuations in Income," *National Tax Journal,* Vol. XV (September, 1962), pp. 287–88.

consumption expenses from those of gaining income, treatment of the family unit, and adjustments in tax to attain greater conformity with accepted standards of equity give rise to questions that are not easily resolved. The existence of the corporate structure is a major source of complexity. As a consequence of these problems artificial lines that must be drawn cause departure from equity standards, distort behavior, and increase the amount of resources used for enforcement. Examples were given in earlier chapters. Any actual income tax, no matter how carefully designed, is likely to be far removed from the perfect tax. Many of these same problems arise with other taxes, but some are less serious; capital gains problems do not arise with consumption-related taxes, for example.

The Spendings Tax

The possible adverse effect of income taxes upon incentives to work, investment incentives, the S/Y ratio at full employment, and the potential rate of capital formation has led to consideration of consumption-based taxes, that is, taxes established in such a fashion that liability depends upon consumption rather than upon income. Support for this approach also comes from persons who regard progression in the income tax as inequitable.

One form of consumption-related tax is the spendings tax, long considered but not yet used to any extent.[7] The spendings tax has the merit of raising the potential rate of capital formation above that possible with the income tax by reducing the tax impact on savings and providing positive incentive to save, and of providing greater anti-inflationary influence per dollar of revenue, especially if it is believed to be temporary. At the same time use of the expenditure base may lessen the effects of the tax upon factor supplies. Unfortunately the qualities of a spendings tax that make it an excellent anti-inflationary tool give it a perverse effect in periods of inadequate demand; the incentive that the tax provides to save more is obviously contrary to the goal of increased spending and would make the attainment of the potential growth rate more difficult. This argument relates to automatic effects; deliberate reductions in the spendings tax in depression would provide effective stimulus to recovery.

From an equity standpoint, the spendings tax, unlike the sales tax, can be made progressive in rate and can provide an overall distribution

---

[7]The strongest case for the spendings tax has been made by the British economist Nicholas Kaldor; see *The Expenditure Tax* (London: George Allen and Unwin, 1956).

of burden more closely in line with accepted standards of equity than that of the sales tax. The defenders of the tax also argue that consumption expenditure is a more equitable measure of tax capacity than income, on the grounds that only consumption yields personal satisfaction. Therefore fairness requires taxation of persons according to the amount they drain out of the "common pool" of national product rather than according to the amount they put into it. From this point of view, taxation of all income constitutes double taxation of the portion saved because tax applies to the amount saved as well as to the return on it. This argument is rejected on usual grounds of equity; persons save because they prefer to do so and gain satisfaction from this use of income. Accordingly the spendings tax is criticized for favoring the miser—the person who saves unusually high percentages of his income. While an overall progressive distribution can be obtained as with the income tax, the burdens on individual families will vary unfairly with their consumption behavior relative to income.

Administratively the spendings tax suffers from even more complexities than the income tax, since not only must income be ascertained but the net increase in savings as well. Operation of the tax would require annual reporting of net wealth to ascertain net savings, which would be deductible from income to calculate consumption. Accordingly the tax, particularly with the high rates necessary to provide strong anti-inflationary effect, is not feasible for use in developing economies, which have greatest need for it. The only operational advantage, compared to the income tax, is the avoidance of certain problems relating to the concept of income, particularly capital gains.

Sales Taxation

The sales tax seeks to do in an indirect fashion what the spendings tax would do directly: tax persons in relation to their consumer spending rather than their entire income. Like the spendings tax, the sales tax should have less adverse effect on the full-employment rate of capital formation and upon factor supplies, although, as previously noted, most of the potential difference is a product of the lack of progression of the sales tax, rather than of the character of sales taxation per se. Like any consumption-based tax, a sales tax aggravates the task of attaining full employment because of its greater impact on consumption, unless the income tax has serious impact on investment decisions—which it does not appear to have. Like an income tax, a sales tax uniform relative to all consumption expenditures does not create excess consumer burden and if confined to consumer purchases does not reduce efficiency in production and distribution.

A second major advantage claimed for the tax is the easier and more effective administration, because of the small number of tax-paying firms, who are essentially tax collectors. This argument can be exaggerated. Sales taxes do not automatically collect themselves, but require extensive audit and delinquency control programs. They may have some net advantage over the income tax since the number of persons from whom the government collects tax is smaller, but the overall gain is not likely to be great. While sales taxes avoid some of the problems of implementation arising with income taxes (for example, capital gains), they give rise to many others. Experience has shown the difficulty of limiting the tax to consumer spending, since there is no sharp, administratively workable line between consumer and business spending (the same problem in slightly different form encountered with income taxes). Equality among various business techniques is difficult to attain, particularly with taxes that do not apply to all consumer spending. Exemptions, introduced for a variety of reasons, not only result in consumer excess burden but often complicate both administration and compliance.

The primary argument against sales taxation is the inequity—under usually accepted standards—created by regressivity; a sales tax covering all consumer purchases or all consumer commodity purchases tends to be regressive relative to income, as explained in Chapter 8, and places a relatively heavy absolute burden on the lowest income groups. Various kinds of exemptions lessen regressiveness, but with the consequence of administrative complications, other forms of inequity, and consumer excess burden. In addition to overall regressiveness, sales taxes are condemned on other equity grounds. The tax favors persons whose circumstances dictate their spending relatively small amounts of their income. The tax bears more heavily on large families than on small ones at given incomes, on younger couples acquiring consumer durables compared to older ones, on persons suffering misfortunes requiring unusually heavy spending.[8] The pattern of distributional effects is not as obvious as legislators believe; if the tax affects factor prices or residual incomes of business firms the pattern of distribution is haphazard.

By usual standards, accordingly, the sales tax is regarded as inferior to the income tax as the primary national government revenue source in a developed economy. The sales tax is a less effective means of reaching persons according to ability to pay under usual standards than the income tax. The advantages it offers relative to the rate of

___

[8]Reed R. Hansen, in "An Empirical Analysis of the Retail Sales Tax with Policy Recommendations," *National Tax Journal,* Vol. XV (March, 1962), pp. 1–13, demonstrates these inequities.

capital formation and factor supplies may not be significant in magnitude, and it makes more difficult the attainment of full employment. The greatest merit of the tax is its potential use to provide a significant revenue source for states in a federal system, when the national government relies primarily upon the income tax. The sales tax also offers the opportunity for additional revenue with little harm in a developing economy in which the yield of income tax is limited for administrative and incentive reasons, and in which increased savings are urgently needed. Use is possible only if wholesale and retail trading are sufficiently well organized to allow the collection of the tax.

Excise Taxes

Taxes imposed upon the sale of particular commodities allow the attainment of certain specific objectives not possible with sales or other taxes. First, such taxes provide substitutes for charges for governmental activities conveying direct benefits, when the consumption of particular commodities is significantly correlated to the benefit received from the activities.

Second, excises provide an instrument for reducing consumption of commodities that give rise to costs to society not reflected in the costs to the producers. Without the tax the price is too low, in terms of economic welfare, and excessive resources will be allocated to the commodity. The tax on liquor is the best example; use of liquor in excess gives rise to costs to society arising out of alcoholism that do not enter into the prices of the product. Similarly, excises provide a device whereby society may discourage the use of a product that is considered contrary to the best interests of the community as a whole, without outright prohibition of its use. A special case of this situation is one in which a government wishes to release specialized resources from the private sector for governmental use; an excise will be more effective than general revenue measures for this purpose.

Excises as General Revenue Measures. Excises have not only been used in these special situations but also as general revenue measures in lieu of sales taxes—as was true in the United States during and after World War II. A system of excises can provide an overall distribution of burden regarded as more equitable than a sales tax, since the excises can be confined to commodities regarded as unessential to a reasonable living standard. Excises permit individuals to adjust their tax burden, year by year, according to their own financial situation, altering the timing of purchase of goods subject to tax. This is not possible with income taxes, or, to any extent, with sales taxes.[9] If excises are confined to a few products produced or distributed by a small number of large firms, administration and compliance are less costly than they are with a sales tax.

There are, however, serious objections to the use of excises in lieu of sales taxes as general revenue measures, objections not relevant to the excises noted above designed to accomplish specific purposes in the economy. The basic objection is the consumer excess burden; the excise tax raises the prices of taxed commodities relative to those of untaxed ones and thus causes reallocation of consumer expenditures and excess consumer burden, whereas income, spendings, and broad-based sales taxes do not. This argument, however, is not a conclusive one against excise taxes. It is based upon the assumptions of substitutability of commodities, perfect competition in the private sector (so that marginal rates of transformation are equal to marginal rates of substitution), absence of other excises, and perfectly inelastic factor supplies. Each of these assumptions can be questioned:

1. Substitutability. If the taxed commodity is not substitutable for others and therefore has a perfectly inelastic demand relative to both price and income, the relative purchases and outputs of the two commodities will be unaltered. With given incomes, however, consumption of other goods is reduced and resource allocations distorted.

2. Imperfections in the Market. If the markets are not perfectly competitive, MRS and MRT are not necessarily equal prior to the introduction of the excise tax. Thus there is no a priori evidence that the levying of an excise will create excess burden.[10] Suppose that the tax is placed on a commodity sold in a perfectly competitive market, while other products are sold in markets characterized by oligopoly. The excise, by restricting the output of which there is relatively too much, pretax, will allow closer attainment of optimal economic welfare, with a net gain rather than an excess burden. If, however, the tax is placed on a product sold under conditions of monopoly or oligopoly while others are not taxed—as is often true—the misallocation of resources will be aggravated and an excess burden created.

3. Second-Best Solution. If the tax system includes one or more

---

[9] J. M. Buchanan and F. Forte, "Fiscal Choice Through Time: A Case for Indirect Taxation," *National Tax Journal,* Vol. XVII (June, 1964), pp. 144–57.

[10] This is the Rolph-Break argument. E. R. Rolph and George Break, "The Welfare Aspects of Excise Taxes," *Journal of Political Economy,* Vol. LVII (February, 1949), pp. 46–54.

excise taxes, levying of additional excises would move the system closer to a general tax, and possibly closer to equilibrium of MRT and MRS, whereas the use of an income tax would not, so long as the other excises were retained.

4. Elasticity of Factor Supplies. If factor supplies are not perfectly elastic, any form of tax may create excess factor burden by altering the quantities of various factors available for production. General income taxes may have greater effects than excises, per dollar of revenue. The fact that excises create both consumer and factor excess burdens does not prove that the combined excess burden is greater than that of a general tax raising the same revenue with only factor effects.

Accordingly, the excess burden argument is not a conclusive one against the use of excises in an imperfect economy, particularly if other excises are already imposed and factor supplies are not perfectly inelastic. Nevertheless, the excess burden argument remains a prima facie case against excises; the various types of excises employed, particularly in a system in which the total number is small, almost certainly cause some consumer reallocation of expenditures and there is no evidence that the changes increase economic welfare. Nor is there strong evidence that more general taxes do have more serious effects on factor supplies, per dollar of revenue. The decision on excess burden of particular excises must be made separately for each tax on the basis of analysis of demand elasticities, types of competition in the relevant market, and relative effects on factor supplies.

A second objection to general excises is based on equity. While excises may be more acceptable to society than sales taxes in terms of overall distribution of tax burden by income class, they discriminate among individuals on the basis of preferences, placing a relatively heavy tax burden on those persons with strong preferences (or need) for the taxed objects, compared to persons with higher preferences for nontaxed goods. The relatively heavy rates required by excises to raise significant revenue aggravate this effect. When forward shifting of the tax is incomplete, discriminatory burden remains upon the owners of the taxed businesses, and, over time, on owners of resources specialized to the industry.

A third objection to excises is the likely reduction in economic efficiency. Excises levied prior to the retail level may alter distribution channels, and taxation of producers' goods, which typically occurs to some degree, affects efficiency in the selection of production methods. Anticipation of rate changes affect consumption and production patterns over time. As an excise system is extended, the administrative and compliance advantage is lost, and a uniform rate sales tax becomes cheaper to operate, per dollar of revenue.

On the basis of experience there are serious practical difficulties in establishing a tolerable excise system. Excises, even those imposed for justifiable purposes, may become devices whereby a majority of the voters transfer tax burden from themselves onto a smaller group that makes extensive use of a certain commodity, justifying this behavior with a flimsy cloak of morality—"use of liquor is sinful." The distinction between legitimate use of an excise to accomplish a reasonable goal of society (for example, discouraging excessive use of liquor) and its use to transfer tax burden to other persons is a very fine one. Fortunately, commodities that yield significant revenue are ones very widely consumed; minority-use items that yield substantial revenue are rare. More seriously, excise systems have often been framed with little attention to objectives or burden distribution during "emergency" periods when the prime goal has been to raise as much revenue as possible and retained after the emergency was over. An extreme example was the United States excise system established early in World War II and retained with minor changes until 1965.

Customs Duties. Taxes on imports resemble excises in many respects and have in part the same advantages and disadvantages, so long as they are revenue producing rather than protective. They are of negligible importance revenuewise in the United States, but in many developing countries they provide an administratively simple means of taxing goods regarded as luxuries and aid in reducing imports of these goods. They are analyzed in Chapter 17.

Taxation on Wealth

While income is usually regarded as the best single measure of taxpaying capacity in the sense of economic well-being, it is not the sole determinant; accumulated personal wealth is also a significant factor. A person having a reserve is under less obligation to save than one who has not accumulated and thus has greater discretion over the use of his income. He has the means with which to make purchases in excess of his income, and the mere possession of wealth is a source of satisfaction. A tax on income does reach the earnings from income-yielding wealth, but the relative tax capacity may be considered to exceed the liability based on income. A tax on income does not reach nonincome-producing wealth at all and could not be made to do so without serious complications; it also favors the low-yield, low-risk type of investment. A tax on wealth can provide additional contributions from all persons who have accumulated wealth and a more reasonable relative burden on those with nonyield or low-yield investments.

From the standpoint of economic effects, taxation of wealth has the advantage that the base is very much larger than that of current income or current savings; accordingly the marginal rate is lower than that of an income tax necessary to raise the same revenue, and the danger of effects upon factor supplies is less. Labor supply, particularly, is not likely to be adversely affected; and because of the nature of the tax, pressures to work more and to increase efficiency of business operation are increased. From the standpoint of geographically small taxing jurisdictions, many types of property cannot move to escape tax, and migration effects are avoided. A tax on real property may also encourage more efficient use of the property, especially in developing economies, and can be used to lessen inequality.

While taxation of wealth can legitimately play a significant role in a tax structure, it suffers from several inherent limitations that restrict its appropriate role to one less than that of income and possibly consumption taxes. Considering society as a whole, income, much more than accumulated wealth, determines economic well-being. Primary reliance on property taxation would allow persons with large incomes and little accumulated wealth to escape taxation and would severely burden persons with some accumulated wealth, particularly if this wealth takes the form of homes, and little current income. The tax would bear with particular severity upon elderly retired persons, widows, and the unemployed who own their homes. Economic effects are not entirely beneficial; while real property cannot move, taxes can affect industrial location and use of property.

From an administration and compliance standpoint, a tax on wealth has several disadvantages. Certain types of property are highly volatile and difficult to find. Cash, bank deposits, and expensive jewelry are examples, especially if administration of the tax is in local government hands. Even with the tax at the national level, cash and jewelry are hard to locate and funds may flow abroad. As a consequence wealth taxes in practice concentrate on real property; as they do so, not only is equity lost but much of the rationale for the tax as well. Wealth taxes likewise suffer from their application to a stock rather than to a flow; since they do not apply to a market transaction, a constructive valuation is required: what would the property sell for if sold? For many types of property this is not a problem but for much real property it is a very serious one, resulting in considerable expense and inequity, since uniformity in assessment is difficult to attain. Related is the day-of-the-year problem; since continuous assessment is not possible, a date, usually once a year, must be selected for determination of tax liability. This rule is a source of both inequity and possible adverse economic effects.

Despite these limitations, there is an appropriate role for wealth taxation as a supplement to the income tax; the framing of a suitable wealth tax will be discussed in Chapter 16.

Death Taxes

Taxes on gifts and bequests can be regarded as supplements to the income tax, and could in fact be integrated into the income tax structure. Alternatively they can be viewed as taxes on accumulated wealth at time of transfer. The case for taxing gifts and bequests is strong; they add to the wealth of the recipients and thus reflect tax-paying ability, and they may be complete windfalls from the standpoint of the recipients. Death duties aid in attaining the common social objective of lessening excessive inequality of wealth. The taxes produce a minimum of excess factor burden, since a tax that applies after one's death is less likely to influence behavior than one that applies on a current basis. However, they probably reduce the S/Y ratio more than any other tax, per dollar of revenue, as explained in Chapter 8. Thus they reduce the potential rate of capital formation more than other taxes but they increase the likelihood of attaining it.

The major problems relate to the establishment of a suitable structure of tax to accomplish the desired goals, as explained in Chapter 16. In practice present death tax structures have substantial effects on resource use, affecting the manner in which property is transferred, increasing the liquidity of estates, and directing substantial effort to find means of escaping tax.

Payroll Taxes

Taxes levied on payrolls, either on the employee, employer, or both, are usually employed to finance social security programs, justified on the benefit principle: workers and their employers build up a fund during their working years to provide benefits at retirement or for support during unemployment. Since the benefit is related to the wage earned, the tax is based upon payrolls. Essentially these taxes are regarded as compulsory insurance premium payments; stress on the insurance feature was designed to lessen pressure by recipients for larger payments and to minimize the "charity" aspects.

The only possible justification for these levies, as taxes, is the benefit rule; they are objectionable in many respects, violating virtually all standards usually accepted for taxation. They are regressive relative to income, particularly when wages are subject only up to a specified figure (on the grounds that maxima are set for benefits relative to income). The employer may pass his portion of the tax on to employees since productivity of the workers is not increased by the tax; if he does not, the tax either rests as an uneven levy on profits or is reflected in uneven and haphazard fashion in the prices of the goods produced. With powerful unions, the portion of the tax on the employee may be reflected in higher wages and in higher prices of the products. The taxes increase the relative advantage of use of capital instead of labor and aggravate the task of maintaining full employment. Their use is on the whole justifiable only if they are regarded as insurance premiums, a very questionable point of view.

Business Taxes

The use of taxes on business, per se (more commonly, on corporate business), as distinguished from application of income taxes to businesses as well as individuals, is justified on the grounds that business firms have taxpaying capacity distinct from their owners. The argument is based upon the philosophy that modern businesses, especially large-scale ones, have command over extensive assets and are controlled by persons other than the owners (the professional managers). Accordingly they are considered to be taxable entities and can justifiably be regarded as taxbearers themselves, without respect to the individuals who own them or are otherwise involved with them. Beyond this basic argument, which is used in part to justify the federal corporate income tax, the states justify business taxation on the grounds that they supply extensive services to businesses and may receive little or no tax revenue under other levies if the owners live outside of the state and sales of products are interstate.

This latter argument, from the standpoint of the states, has obvious validity for moderate business levies. The former argument, however, is questionable. Any tax on a business firm must affect the real income of human beings—owners, managers, employees, stockholders, consumers. Equity considerations require that the distribution of burden be considered in terms of these persons, not the firms per se; from this point of view there is little or no justification for separate business taxation. As explained in Chapter 15, application of some form of income taxation to corporations is essential as a part of the overall income tax system. Differentially higher tax on corporations is a separate question.

Conclusion

The precisely optimal tax structure of a country depends upon a number of considerations: the primary objectives of society; the pattern of income and wealth distribution relative to the accepted standards of equity in distribution; the level of economic development; the administrative standards of the government; the path of economic growth relative to the one regarded as most desirable; the attitudes of persons toward various forms of taxation; the reactions of factor owners to changes in factor prices; and others. The issues of taxation in developing economies will be considered in Chapter 17. For the typical developed economy such as the United States several generalizations can be made on the basis of usually accepted standards:

1. The most significant element in the overall tax structure should be the income tax. The primary advantage is equity; income is a much better measure of tax capacity than other bases by usual standards, and the income tax alone can effectively introduce progression into the tax structure. The income tax avoids the distorting effects of many taxes on production efficiency and resource allocation. It may have somewhat greater effects upon factor supplies than other levies, but there is no evidence at present that these are serious. While the income tax may reduce the potential rate of economic growth somewhat more than other taxes, it facilitates the attainment of this growth path. Effective enforcement is possible in modern society. Adverse effects of the income tax, when they appear, are almost entirely attributable to the degree of progression, not to the income base per se.

2. A wealth tax has justification as a supplement to the income tax in order to place more adequate burden on those persons having substantial wealth but little current income. Per dollar of revenue, the potential effect upon factor supplies is probably less than that of the income tax. Use of the tax is restricted, however, by the dangers of placing intolerable burdens on persons with some wealth but little current income, and by the administrative problems relating to valuation.

3. Excise taxes are desirable in two situations: in lieu of charges to finance services primarily conveying direct benefits to individuals, and as a means to require consumers to cover indirect social costs arising from production and use of the commodities but not included in their prices. Use of other excises is objectionable on two primary grounds: the potential excess consumer burden and the discrimination according to consumer preferences.

4. Sales taxes provide an autonomous revenue source to the states

in a federal system. Excessive reliance on sales taxation is objectionable because of regressiveness and discrimination on the basis of consumer preferences. The case for a sales tax at the national level becomes strong only if income taxes reach a level at which they have serious adverse effects upon factor supplies and production efficiency.

5. Estate and inheritance taxes reach tax capacity reflected by gifts and bequests, with little effect on factor supplies or production efficiency. They are not likely to be highly productive of revenue.

6. A spendings tax, if it proves to be administratively feasible, would be justified in a period of strong inflationary pressure.

The next two chapters consider the optimal structures of the various major taxes in light of the objectives of society.

REFERENCES

KALDOR, N. *The Expenditure Tax.* London: George Allen & Unwin, 1955.

PECHMAN, J. A. *Federal Tax Policy.* Washington, D.C.: Brookings Institution, 1966.

Report of the Royal Commission on Taxation, Vol. 2. Ottawa: Queen's Printer, 1966.

The Role of Direct and Indirect Taxes in the Federal Revenue System. Princeton, N.J.: Princeton University Press for the National Bureau of Economic Research and Brookings Institution, 1964.

U.S. CONGRESS, HOUSE WAYS AND MEANS COMMITTEE. *Excise Tax Compendium,* Washington, D.C.: 1964.

AN OPTIMAL
INCOME TAX STRUCTURE

Framing an income tax structure that will maximize attainment of the goals of the tax system is a highly complex task, one that presents numerous problems for which there are no simple, obvious solutions consistent with all desired goals. Present income tax structures in the United States and most other countries reflect years of experience and modifications, some motivated by the desire to improve the structure in light of the goals, some resulting from the pressure of well-organized groups. The present structures suffer from many defects that, while recognized, continue, partly as a result of inertia and the pressure of groups they benefit, partly because better solutions are by no means obvious.

The Requirements

If income taxation is to play its role in the tax structure most effectively in conformity with the standards of economic effects and equity developed in the previous chapter, several requirements must be fulfilled.

First, the tax must apply uniformly to all income, after adjustments for various circumstances affecting tax capacity. Nonuniformity will not only sacrifice equity but will also create excess burdens of various types, arising from distortion of factor supply schedules and resource allocation. If incomes from some sources are taxed more heavily than those from others, the recipients of the former will be discriminated against and resources will flow from the more heavily taxed fields to the less heavily taxed ones. Administration is likewise complicated.

Second, the structure of the tax must permit minimum costs of compliance and administration consistent with effective enforcement. Otherwise, resources are wasted and equity is lost.

Third, the exemptions and rate structure must reflect contemporary consensus of thought on equity, balanced with consideration of relative economic effects of various structures.

Uniformity and ease of compliance requires the use of the global approach to income taxation, all income being summed in a single category and taxed under a single rate schedule. The schedular approach, common in southern Europe and Latin America, under which each type of income is taxed separately, suffers from several major defects: compliance and administrative costs are increased since several separate returns must be filed; attainment of progression is complicated; and rate differences are in practice arbitrary.

Attainment of the goals requires several elements:

1. A concept of income that reflects tax capacity satisfactorily.

2. A tax structure that provides uniformity of treatment of income regardless of the particular distribution of income by time period.

3. Adjustments in income for tax purposes to attain maximum conformity with desired distributional goals.

4. Uniform treatment of income earned through the corporate form of organization and other incomes.

THE DEFINITION OF INCOME

Income as a measure of tax capacity may be defined broadly as economic gain to the person during a period of time. More precisely, under the definition of Henry Simons, income is measured by the sum of:[1]

1. Consumption during the period, whether out of income (factor or transfer) flowing to the person during the period or the use of durable goods previously acquired.

2. Net increase in personal wealth during the period. This figure will be negative if consumption is financed by the use of previously accumulated reserves or by borrowing.

This rule can alternatively be stated as follows: Income may be defined as the amount a person is able to spend during the year and be as well off at the end of the year as at the beginning.

While this approach provides a more satisfactory measure of economic gain attributable to the period than any other, it has never been regarded as a workable formula for ascertainment of taxable income. The approach actually used determines inflow of money to the person during the period net of the expenses of earning it and net of any amount that reflects change in the form of assets rather than gain, and adds to this sum a few other items regarded as feasible of taxation,

[1]H. C. Simons, *Personal Income Taxation* (Chicago: University of Chicago Press, 1938).

such as realized capital gains. Other elements of income in the broad definition are not included primarily because of administrative reasons; as a consequence complete uniformity necessary for maximum equity and economic efficiency cannot be attained.

Consumption versus Production

Even under the broad Simons approach to the definition of income, as well as under that more commonly used, a major difficulty is the task of ascertaining income net of the expenses of earning it, which is the significant concept for tax purposes. This task requires delineating consumption and production activity, that is, distinguishing between activity that satisfies personal wants and activity that is undertaken to gain the income, or, under the usual approach to calculation, between nondeductible consumption expenditures and deductible business expenses. The source of the problem is the dual nature of many activities, in the sense that they yield satisfaction in themselves and at the same time are necessary to earn income. In a sense this is true of all basic consumption necessary for life and continued earning of income; in addition it is true of many expenditures of a discretionary nature. The general policy is to adjust for minimum living costs by the exemption allowed all taxpayers, since the specific items cannot be identified for each taxpayer. With dual-character discretionary expenditures, the attempt is made to delineate on the basis of primary intent of the expenditure, or to divide the amount in terms of intent. Major examples of dual-purpose activities are noted below:

Education. From the standpoint of potential effects upon the economy, the tax treatment of educational expenditures is particularly important. Failure to permit deduction of educational expenditures undertaken to increase one's income will discourage persons from seeking additional education. Unfortunately, these educational expenditures cannot be delimited from those made for other reasons, particularly for social prestige, greater enjoyment of life, or catching a husband. Since delineation is impossible, deduction, if granted, must apply to all forms of education or to an arbitrary portion. The issue is further complicated because the expenditures are frequently made by parents while the benefits are received by the children. To allow the parents to make the deduction should, however, encourage them to provide additional education for their children and allow them more funds to finance it. Current deductibility for the children would be of little use, yet the children gain the ultimate monetary benefits. Goode argues that education would most effectively be encouraged by authorizing that the capital sum of educational expenditures be made deductible, in the fashion of depreciation, from earnings in subsequent years.[2] The questions of which education to make deductible (undergraduate, graduate, technical) and which expense items to include (living costs as well as tuition, for example) further complicate the picture. Certainly no simple ideal solution is available.

Expenditures for Housework and Child Care, Particularly for Working Wives. Certain expenditures are necessitated by the earning of income by the wife. Under present law, if she does her own housework the imputed income is not taxable; if she works outside, the income is taxable but the expenses of having the work done are not deductible, except in limited instances. The problem is primarily administrative: the difficulty of separating housework expenditures actually necessitated by outside work from those that would be undertaken anyway. Likewise, in many instances the working wife is merely purchasing freedom from the drudgery of housework. The decision must be based primarily on grounds of economic effects rather than equity; if society wishes to increase the labor force, a deduction, perhaps in the form of a simple earned income credit, would be justified.

Commuting and Moving Expenses. Expenses for commuting to and from work are necessary to gain the income, given the place of residence. To the extent that all persons have certain minimum expenditures of this type, the item is presumably covered by the personal exemption. Those persons who choose to commute long distances do so voluntarily and thus the additional expenditures may be regarded as essentially consumption in nature. In some instances commuting is a substitute for paying higher rents in close-in apartments; the choice between the two is a matter of personal preference.

Moving expenses are slightly different in character, since they arise only when the person makes the decision to take another job, but they also may be regarded as voluntary. Nondeductibility was long regarded as an interference with labor mobility, and in recent years the United States has liberalized the provisions.

Travel, Entertainment, and Similar Expenses. Separation of consumption and business elements in expenditures for these purposes is difficult in principle and practice. The primary-intent rule is often employed but is neither entirely equitable nor satisfactory. The net effect is to allow persons in certain types of occupations substantial tax-free luxury consumption—although in some instances the persons would

[2] R. Goode, *The Individual Income Tax* (Washington, D.C.: Brookings Institution, 1964).

prefer not to have it—and very strict rules might reduce legitimate activity of this type.

Similar examples are found in farming and other types of small business operation. A farmer buys a tractor larger and more expensive than he needs in order to impress his neighbors or replaces equipment more frequently than is economical because he enjoys new types. Or he develops a hobby such as raising showhorses and treats the expenditures as business in nature, even though they are primarily for his own enjoyment. Administrative delineation is impossible.

In summary: no completely satisfactory delimitation of production and consumption is possible, certainly in an operational fashion. Accordingly, either some expenditures of a production nature are nondeductible, with consequent loss of optimal efficiency in production, or some persons are not taxed upon all of their income, with sacrifice of equity and distortion of activity. In designing and operating the income tax structure, a compromise, based upon careful weighing of conflicting considerations, is necessary.

Nonmonetary Income

The broad Simons concept of income includes both consumption financed by current money income and consumption occurring without current monetary outlay or equivalent money income. The latter form is of major importance in developing economies and of some importance in all.

Owner-Occupied Housing. In dollar magnitude, the most important element of nonmonetary income is the imputed rental value of owner-occupied housing. If a person places his personal savings in securities and rents housing facilities, he pays tax on the income and is not permitted to deduct rental payments, which are obviously consumption expenditures. If he purchases his own home, the income from the savings takes the form of the housing service, or, in other words, avoidance of rental payments. Accordingly, the imputed rental value is a part of his income and should logically be included for tax purposes. In practice this is not required; even Great Britain, which did provide for partial inclusion for many years, has abandoned the rule. The net effect is to give a significant advantage to homeowners, to alter the choice between rental and owner-occupied housing, and to increase the quantity of resources allocated to housing. Despite the discrimination against those persons who prefer to rent and against those in the lowest income levels who benefit very little from nontaxability of imputed rent, the present practice has very strong popular support in the United States. This attitude is partly based on the philosophy of encouraging home ownership, although there are far more equitable ways of doing so. Heavy property tax burdens on residential property offset the discrimination to a limited extent, in terms of the overall tax structure. The only other reason for exclusion is administrative: the problem of ascertaining imputed rents.

Home-Produced Goods. Goods and services produced by a person for his own use—vegetables, flowers, house repair—also constitute a portion of his income in the broad sense, and failure to include these items in taxable income favors those persons able and willing to undertake this type of activity. A person may find it advantageous to take time off from his regular job and paint his house, rather than to earn his regular income and hire a painter, to the detriment of specialization.

While inclusion of some items, such as produce of a type also sold on the market by the person (for example, milk used by a dairy farmer), is acceptable both in terms of principle and administration, taxation of other activity would encounter problems of both enforcement and principle. Detection and valuation would be difficult (the former even with goods of a type regularly sold). More seriously, much of this activity is undertaken primarily for utilization of leisure time. A person grows fruit or flowers or remodels his house because he enjoys doing so, rather than solely because of desire for the final product. If the results of this use of leisure are taxed and those of other uses are not taxed—as they cannot be—discrimination results, and persons are discouraged from undertaking this form of activity. The result of attempting to tax might be a substantial reduction in the total amount of such work and thus of GNP. In other words, the person would not have his house painted at all if he did not do it himself, nor would he buy the vegetables.

A related type of activity is housework, which the person can do herself or gain an income and hire it done. Taxation of the value would encounter insuperable problems of valuation and nuisance. Production and use of leisure are also combined in a portion of this activity. If present treatment seriously discourages housewives from obtaining outside jobs, the preferable solution is a special tax credit for working wives.

Fringe Benefits. The final important example of nonmonetary income consists of fringe benefits provided by employers: health service, parking space, free meals, discounts on purchases, company cars, luxurious offices, paid vacations, expensive dinners, and many other items. These obviously constitute income in the broad sense. Failure

to tax them favors the recipients and encourages business firms to substitute fringe benefits for monetary compensation, especially for executives. On the other hand, frequently the recipients would not be willing
to buy these services if they had to pay for them; Kleinwachter's case
of the aide who attended operas free with his senior officer but detested
them is the classic example. Or, a person might prefer to eat in a
nearby restaurant instead of in company facilities. In principle, the
activities should be included to the extent to which individuals would
buy them, but this rule is impossible to administer. Accordingly in
practice the tendency is to omit them entirely except in very obvious
instances such as housing accommodations not necessitated by the
nature of the work.

Capital Gains

One of the most troublesome areas of definition of taxable income
is the status of capital gains—increases in the value of assets held (not
including stock-in-trade). Capital gains treatment is a major source of
compliance and administrative difficulties, litigation, and continuing
controversy.

Capital Gains as Income.   Under the ideal (Simons) definition
of income, capital gains, whether realized or not, typically constitute
income. Dollars earned by stock speculation can be used to buy goods
as effectively as dollars earned by work. In fact in modern society there
is no clear distinction between many of these gains and other income.
A corporation may pay cash dividends to the stockholders, or it may
retain the earnings, the stockholders realizing on the earnings by sale
of a portion of their stock. There are only two exceptions to the rule
that capital gains constitute income. If the gain is a reflection of an
increase in the general price level by an equivalent percentage, it is in a
sense illusory and does not reflect economic gain to the recipient. Adjustment by deflation by the index of price level changes would be
possible. But equity owners benefit from inflation while many other
persons are injured and adjustments that aid the former but provide no
benefit to the latter are difficult to justify. Secondly, gains due to reduction in the market rate of interest (which raises the market value of
existing fixed-income securities) may be regarded as illusory if the
money is reinvested in similar holdings. These persons, however, have
gained increased command over goods and services, and the gains may
appropriately be regarded as income.

This point of view, that capital gains constitute income, now
widely accepted, contrasts sharply with the traditional British Common-

wealth attitude, under which income was defined in terms of a recurring flow during the period, thus excluding capital gains. Whatever merit this concept may have for other purposes, it is of little significance for taxation. Great Britain has commenced to move away from the philosophy, making short-term gains taxable in 1962. While as of 1968 Canada does not tax capital gains at all, the category is substantially narrower than in the United States (gains being fully taxable if related to a regular activity of the person), and the recent Royal Commission report has recommended full taxation of all such gains.[3]

Accrual versus Realization. Under the ideal definition of income, capital gains would be taxable as they accrue, since accrual constitutes an increase in net wealth. This approach encounters two major obstacles. The annual valuation of assets would be a difficult and time-consuming process, with inevitable inaccuracies. Preparation of tax returns would be more complex for many persons. Secondly, some persons would be unable to pay tax without selling securities, an economically undesirable consequence. Accordingly capital gains are taxed on a realization basis, that is, when the assets are sold. This basis, in turn, gives rise to two problems: the gains are much more irregularly spaced by year than they would otherwise be, and asset holders are given an incentive to time their sales of securities to minimize tax, with a strong incentive to hold securities on which gains have been made. If they are sold, less money will be available for reinvestment. This "locked-in" effect is aggravated in the United States by failure to tax gains not realized until death; elderly persons with assets that have increased in value have great incentive to hold them till death. The heirs who subsequently sell the property pay tax only on the difference between the value at the time of inheritance and the subsequent sale value.

Special Treatment. While capital gains are justifiably regarded as income, some form of special treatment is necessary in light of the objectives of the income tax structure. Particularly with the use of the realization basis, full taxation of gains at regular progressive rates would result in an inequitable burden because of irregularity, unless a general system of averaging income, discussed below, was developed. Favorable treatment has also been widely justified on the grounds of encouragement for more risky investment, providing a safety valve to protect against the adverse influence that relatively high income taxes might have upon the willingness to invest. These two arguments have been used to justify the present taxation of long-term capital gains in

[3]*Report of the Royal Commission on Taxation* (Ottawa: Queen's Printer, 1966), Vol. III, chap. xv.

the United States at a maximum rate of 25 percent (with the option of including one half the gain in regular income), and to justify continued exclusion of gains from taxation in Canada and other countries.

Unfortunately, however, this special treatment is objectionable in several ways:

1. Uniformity of taxation of income is lost; income earned from stock speculation or gains in the value of land is taxed less heavily than that from long-term investments or labor.

2. Progression in the tax structure is seriously reduced, since capital gains concentrate in the higher income groups. Over half of the income of persons with incomes in excess of $200,000 consists of capital gains, in contrast to less than 10 percent of the income of persons under $50,000, and 1.2 percent for those from $5,000 to $10,000 income.[4]

3. Strong incentive is given to convert other income into the legal form of capital gains. Closely held corporations retain earnings in the business, the owners eventually realizing on the gain by sale of the stock, being taxed on capital gains rather than dividends. Many other devices have been developed to accomplish the same results in a shorter period of time, such as "collapsible corporations." A corporation is formed for a particular construction project and liquidated immediately upon completion, the entire profit receiving capital gains treatment. Not only are tax revenue and equity lost, but business practices are distorted and substantial talent is devoted to the game of tax avoidance.

4. The operation of the tax is seriously complicated. Many rulings, disputes with taxpayers, and litigation relate to the demarkation between capital gains and regular income. Certainty of the tax is materially reduced.

At the same time the limited deductibility of capital losses in the United States (against capital gains, or against other income to the extent of $1,000 per year) discriminates against those persons having heavy capital losses (they are typically in lower income levels than those receiving gains) and increases the adverse risk effect of the tax structure.

Solution. The most obvious solution, in conformity with the goals of income taxation, is the taxation of capital gains at regular income tax rates in conjunction with a general averaging system allowing the spreading of all irregular incomes over a period of several years.

[4]See Goode, *op. cit.*, p. 195.

At the same time income tax rates could be reduced because of the greater tax revenue from capital gains. Greater overall equity and simpler operation of the tax would be attained.[5] This approach is strongly opposed by those who regard the favorable treatment as es-essential for continuation of investment in equity outlets, particularly in new and expanding businesses. This dispute is not easily resolved. It may be argued that the present safety valve is needed only because progression is too steep and marginal rates too high; if the top rates were reduced to 50 percent and capital gains made fully taxable, revenue might be maintained with no loss in incentives to invest.

Heavier taxation would also increase the locked-in effect, which, it is charged, interferes with the efficiency of the capital market in allocation of capital and increases fluctuations in security prices; persons who have made gains will not sell, and thus prices continue to rise once they start. These arguments may be questioned. The effect of locking in depends on what the persons who sell stock do with the proceeds. If they buy more stock, stock prices continue to rise. More significantly, there is no conclusive evidence that the locked-in effects of the present tax are significant, and most of the influence can be attributed to the tax-free status of gains realized at death.[6]

A proposal is frequently made to permit tax-free rollovers; that is, a person could shift from one investment to another without payment of tax, as is permitted with owner-occupied homes. The main objection, in addition to administrative complications, is the provision of further opportunity for tax deferral, with little evidence of significant benefits to the economy.

If the basic long-range solution for treatment of capital gains is not adopted—and it is not likely to be—the present United States system could be greatly improved by three changes: (1) extension of the holding period for eligibility for reduced taxation from six months to a year or longer, since special treatment for assets held less than a year has no justification and favors stock speculators as distinguished from long-range investors; (2) elimination of the tax-free status of capital gains realized at death, which is a large and unnecessary tax loophole and the chief source of the locked-in effect; and (3) broader deductibility of capital losses.

Other Questions of Taxable Income

Gifts and Inheritances. The receipt of a gift or inheritance con-

---

[5]This is the recommendation of the Canadian Royal Commission on Taxation.
[6]Goode, *op. cit.,* p. 212.

stitutes income as defined. Traditionally, however, these items have been specifically excluded from income for tax purposes and taxed separately under estate and gift taxes. This separate treatment has reflected the principle that taxes on transfer of property at death (the gift taxes being considered merely as supplements to the estate tax to prevent tax avoidance by *inter vivos* giving) are justified on a distinctly different basis and philosophy from taxes upon the receipt of income from labor or property. Death taxes have been regarded not as levies based upon ability to pay represented by the receipt of bequests and gifts but as a means of reaching windfall gains, of taxing wealth once a lifetime, and of breaking up large fortunes.[7] The last-named motive played a major role in the United States, where estate taxes predated income taxes by two decades. Accordingly, death and gift tax structures are considered in Chapter 16.

Life Insurance Proceeds. The proceeds of life insurance consist of return of capital, interest earnings, and "pure" insurance compensation. If the proceeds are received by the policyholder, only the first two elements are relevant. Clearly the return of capital is not income. Separation of capital and interest, however, is often impossible except on an arbitrary basis, especially when the proceeds take the form of an annuity. When the proceeds are received by a beneficiary, all three elements constitute income in the broad sense and no separation is necessary or possible. All are excluded from income under current policy in most countries, however, and taxed as a part of the estate. As a consequence the interest earnings are never subject to income tax, and strong incentive is given to use this form of investment of savings instead of others, an advantage stressed by the insurance companies. Satisfactory treatment is not easy to devise under present tax structures. Taxation of interest earnings to policyholders on a current basis encounters both compliance and administrative problems and the objection that the policyholder does not have direct access to these earnings. If all bequests and gifts were taxed as income to the recipient, the entire insurance proceeds would be taxable to the recipient and the problem solved, except for the deferment of tax and the typically lower tax brackets of the recipients.

Retirement Benefits. Amounts received by retired persons under social security, private pension, and other retirement programs consist partly of return of funds previously paid in by the recipient, partly of

---

[7]See C. S. Shoup, *Federal Estate and Gift Taxes* (Washington, D.C.: Brookings Institution, 1966).

earnings, and, frequently, partly of sums paid in by the employer or supplied by the government. Complete separation of the first element, which is not income, from the others, which are, is complicated but not impossible. The amounts first received could be designated as solely return of capital, although record keeping would be more complex for taxpayers. Alternatively the amounts received could be allocated on some arbitrary basis. In practice in the United States all social security benefits are exempt, as well as a portion of the receipts from private pension plans—an unnecessarily liberal provision.

Other Exclusions from Income

In the United States and many countries, veterans' benefits and various relief and welfare forms of social security payments are excluded from income under the philosophy that the amounts paid are adapted to need and would be larger if they were taxable. This policy has little justification; inclusion in income would provide simpler and more equitable treatment, even if increases in payments were regarded as necessary.

Interest on state and local bonds is likewise excluded, originally for constitutional reasons, but now defended on the grounds of the greater revenue needs of the states and localities.[8] This exclusion is highly objectionable, providing a major loophole for tax avoidance on the part of the wealthy, for whom the tax savings much more than offset the lower rate of return. Thus the persons best able to undertake risky investments are encouraged to place their funds in safe ones. The tax loss to the federal government greatly exceeds the interest savings to the states; the federal government could aid state-local financing much more cheaply in other ways. The privilege is now subject to serious abuse as local governments frequently issue tax-exempt bonds to finance private industry and thus provide firms with tax-free funds. The Treasury is currently (1968) taking steps to disallow exemption of interest on this type of municipal bond.

THE TIME PERIOD PROBLEM

Income is a continuous flow for an individual extending from the time he first earns until cessation through death or other cause. Since taxation of a person on his entire life income is not feasible, the flow must be segmented into annual sums and the tax applied separately to each sum. This procedure gives rise to problems of appropriate alloca-

---

[8]D. J. Ott and A. H. Meltzer, *Federal Tax Treatment of State and Local Securities* (Washington, D.C.: Brookings Institution, 1963).

tion by year, since allocation may affect overall tax liability and create inequity if persons with the same long-period incomes are taxed differently because time allocations of their incomes are different. There are three primary sources of the problem: use of exemptions and progressive rates, changes in tax rates, and the interest value of postponing tax liability. The third is not significant for usual incomes but is significant with capital gains and with gifts if taxable as income; the second is serious only if rates do in fact vary substantially.

Irregular Incomes and Averaging

A person whose income fluctuates sharply will pay more tax, under the usual income tax structure, than one whose income is constant from year to year, for two reasons: the loss of the value of personal exemptions in years in which income is low, and the effect of progressive rates in the years in which income is unusually high. If two persons receive $100,000 income over a 10-year period, one receiving $10,000 per year, the other the entire sum in 1 year, the latter will pay much more tax than the former.[9] A similar penalty is placed upon persons whose lifetime incomes concentrate in a few years of their lives.

There is no simple, completely satisfactory solution to this problem. Unfortunately most countries, including the United States in the past, have not seriously attempted to meet the problem at all. The United States allows carry-back (three years) and carry-forward (five years) of business losses. Limited averaging of income has been permitted since 1964;[10] Canada has been somewhat more liberal, allowing five-year averaging for farmers and fishermen, and the Royal Commission report proposes general five-year averaging. Under this approach, each taxpayer can, if he wishes, recalculate his tax liability for a five-year period, average the sum of the income over the period, and reduce the heavy impact of an unusually high income in one year. This requires considerable additional effort and has a major chance element, since a five-year block, once averaged, cannot be touched again. If the sixth year produces still higher income, the person made an irrevocable mistake in averaging the previous year. To deviate from this block rule would add still further complications.

Some years ago a system of cumulative averaging was developed by William Vickrey. The taxpayer would cumulate his total income from year to year, calculate total tax on the cumulated sum every year

---

[9]With 1967 rates and the assumption that both persons are unmarried, the first would pay $21,900, the second $55,490.

[10]Income may be averaged over the previous four years if the year's income exceeds the four-year average by more than one third and by the sum of $3,000.

on the basis of the number of years over which the accumulation had occurred, and subtract the total paid in previous years (plus compound interest) from the tentative tax to determine tax liability for the year.[11] The cumulative averaging and compound interest features would insure equal treatment of fluctuating and regular incomes and eliminate gain from postponing income realization, as well as the need for recalculation under the block averaging system and the chance element. Adoption of a general averaging system would constitute a major step toward satisfactory taxation of capital gains at regular tax rates and taxation of gifts and bequests as income. The proposal would have one adverse effect: as national income rises, tax payments would lag and the stabilization effect would be lessened. The major limitation is the apparent complexity of the proposal, which has prevented it from receiving serious attention.[12]

For the lower income groups, a simple system of allowing carry-over of unused exemptions would mitigate much of the present inequity.

Full carry-over of business losses is highly important to minimize adverse effects of the tax on risk taking and on the establishment of new businesses, which often incur losses in their earlier years.

Depreciation

Another major aspect of the time period problem is the determination of appropriate annual depreciation charges for tax purposes. Capital equipment is acquired for use over a period of years. The entire cost is obviously an expense of gaining the income received over the period of life of the equipment. The amount chargeable to any one year should, logically, equal the decline in value of the equipment for the year, or, in other words, the amount necessary to maintain intact the capital of the firm. This figure cannot be ascertained, however, and so the figure chosen is arbitrary. The manner in which the total is allocated over the years of use affects the timing of the government's tax receipts, and, in an expanding economy, the total receipts. Business firms usually find it advantageous to depreciate for tax purposes as quickly as possible; the faster the depreciation, the sooner they recover their money capital tax free, and the less total tax they will pay if they continue to expand. Also the risk of not being able to deduct the entire costs of the equipment because of a series of years of losses is reduced.

---

[11]W. Vickrey, *Agenda for Progressive Taxation*, (New York: Ronald Press Co., 1947), chap. vi.

[12]An exhaustive study of averaging is found in J. Willis, *The Mitigation of the Tax Penalty on Fluctuating or Irregular Incomes* (Toronto: Canadian Tax Foundation, 1951).

Governments initially approached the problem from the standpoint of maximizing tax revenue within the constraint of allowing complete depreciation over the life of the equipment. Long periods of estimated life and straight-line or other depreciation techniques that prevented concentration of depreciation in early years were required. Gradually, however, under pressure from business groups, increased awareness that rapid depreciation aids investment, and increased concern for economic growth, the rules have been materially relaxed, permitting acceleration of deductions.

Argument has been advanced in periods of inflation to allow firms to recover tax-free an amount equal to replacement cost rather than original cost in order to facilitate purchase of new equipment. Equity requires only the tax-free recovery of the original sum; owners of equipment bought in low-price periods benefit from its use in a high-price period and are scarcely in need of special tax favors. If tax adjustments are to be made for anyone in an inflationary period, they should favor those persons who are injured by inflation. Business firms with good profit prospects have no trouble in raising additional funds and there is no justification for taxpayers' providing funds for them.

A related question is the desirability of providing stimulus for development of oil and natural resources by special depreciation rules, known as depletion allowances. In the United States, for example, producers of petroleum are allowed to deduct an amount equal to 27.5 percent of gross income annually for depletion in determining tax liability. The justification claimed is the stimulus given firms to explore new resources, the deduction compensating them for dry holes and barren mines. The allowances are very difficult to justify, and cause, at present levels, serious misallocation of resources to these fields and discrimination in favor of developers of these resources. More rapid utilization of some types of resources is not necessarily in the long-range public interest. If the government regards a policy of stimulation of exploration as warranted, provision of subsidy for marginal exploration work would be far cheaper and more equitable. Political pressures to maintain present treatment are unfortunately very strong.

THE TAXPAYING UNIT[13]

If an income tax were proportional in rate without exemptions, tax would be the same regardless of the unit on which liability was

[13]A detailed analysis is to be found in H. M. Groves, *Federal Tax Treatment of the Family* (Washington, D.C.: Brookings Institution, 1963).

placed—the individual or family. When rates are progressive and exemptions are provided, however, the unit chosen is significant. Logically the unit should be the basic income-use, decision-making entity, which, in modern society, is typically the family. While some spending decisions are made by individual family members on the basis of their own incomes, primarily decisions are made jointly on the basis of the pooled income. If each individual in the family is taxed separately, as in the Canadian tradition, this rule is violated and the tax paid by the family unit will depend upon the pattern in which income is earned by various members of the family. Tax will be higher if the husband earns all the income than if husband and wife earn equally. Even more serious, separate treatment encourages the division of property among various members of the family to reduce income, an option not available to salary and wage receivers. Accordingly, the husband and wife should be treated as a unit, as is the practice in the United States.[14]

The problem of treatment of income of children is less easily resolved. If their incomes are not pooled and they are allowed their own exemptions as well as providing dependency deductions for their parents, a loophole for escape from tax is created and strong incentive is given to place property in the names of the children. The alternative policy, which requires the inclusion of children's income in the family income and treats the children as partial partners in arriving at the appropriate tax, as utilized in France, would avoid this problem. The formula for allocation, however, must be arbitrary; is a child to be treated as one half, one fourth, or other portions of an adult? The marginal rates on income earned by the children for labor income could be higher under this system and enforcement problems on the small incomes often earned by children (for baby sitting, etc.) would be serious. Most significantly, definition of the family unit would involve major complications and possible inequity. The primary source of the problem is the partially dependent child still living in the household; where is the line to be drawn for establishing a separate unit? Strong incentive would be given for high-income persons to become separate units as soon as possible. An age figure can be used but is by no means equitable. Despite these problems, however, this general approach is probably the most satisfactory.

A related but distinct question is the choice of relative rates on single and married persons. If the same rates are used and pooling of income is mandatory, tax will be greater for a married couple than

---

[14]Equitable treatment for the family in which there is a single currently unmarried head of a household is difficult to attain.

for two single persons with the same total income. This may be justified on the grounds that two can really live more cheaply (per person) than one, but is criticized as being inherently unfair and as encouraging persons to live together without benefit of marriage. The reverse policy, as followed in the United States, of splitting the income and thus cutting the speed of progression in half provides a great tax advantage for married persons[15] and complicates the treatment of the unmarried head of household. Some compromise is required, one that does not increase the tax liability as a result of marriage but provides only a reasonable premium for marriage in the higher income groups.

Deduction for the Taxpayer and Dependents

Under usual standards of equity, exclusion of persons with bare minimum subsistence incomes from tax and adjustment of relative tax burden on others according to size of family are regarded as desirable. Accordingly a personal exemption (credit for dependents) is provided for the taxpayer and for each dependent. The greater the size of the family, the greater are the expenses necessary to maintain a given standard of living, and therefore the lower is the tax capacity at a given income level. The personal exemption is also a significant instrument for providing progression in burden distribution within the lower income bracket subject to a proportional rate (in 1960 in the United States, 60 percent of all taxpayers were in the first rate bracket). It also excludes from tax a number of persons (mostly children) with nominal incomes. This last reason is much less significant in developed economies with extensive withholding than it was in the past, or than it is in developing economies today.

While the principle of dependency deductions is widely accepted, several precise features of the deductions are less easily defined. One issue is the choice between a tax credit and a deduction from income. With the latter, as employed in the United States, the tax savings rise with income because of higher marginal tax rates. This effect is defended on the grounds that the increase in expenditures necessitated by additional dependents is greater at higher income levels than at lower. The alternative, the credit against tax, as used in some states, provides the same tax saving at all income levels and is defended on the argument that the necessary additional cost due to added dependents does not rise with income. Since this is an equity matter, no scientific answer is possible.

---

[15]With income of $100,000, a person saves $10,310 tax by marrying (1967 rates).

Another question relates to the definition of dependents. Traditionally the category was defined on the basis of age, relationship, percentage of support, and income earned. The first was eliminated in the United States as irrelevant, and restrictions based on the remaining three have been liberalized. The problem is to distinguish between legitimate dependents and those provided with only limited support; wealthy persons can easily multiply dependents and avoid substantial tax unless there are sharp restrictions.

Another question is the size of the basic exemption figure. Theoretically the figure is presumed to be the amount necessary for an absolute minimum standard of living, under the assumption that persons below this level have no tax capacity whereas those above do. This figure is not easily calculated, however, and is not uniform geographically.[16] The figures actually chosen ($600 in the United States since 1948) have been determined largely in terms of revenue requirements. The tendency for prices to rise while the exemption figure remains unchanged results in a constant decline in the real value of the exemption.

Uniformity of the exemption figure for all dependents, as has been the practice in the United States, can be justified primarily on the basis of simplicity, but scarcely meets requirements of equity, since costs of maintaining a given level of living clearly do not rise proportionately with numbers of dependents. Many basic costs of operating a household are, at least over a considerable range, independent of the size of the family. Accordingly, the figure justifiable for the first child or other dependent is less than that for the taxpayer and spouse, and that for successive children less than the amount for the first. A flat figure encourages larger families—a goal not sought in most countries.

ADJUSTMENTS FOR OTHER INFLUENCES AFFECTING TAX CAPACITY

One great advantage of income taxation is the ability to adjust tax liability in light of various considerations affecting the relative tax capacity of persons at given income levels. While appropriate adjustments, justified primarily on equity grounds, cannot be determined scientifically, consensus of opinion on them is relatively strong.

[16]1966 U.S. Bureau of Labor Statistics data for selected cities show, with an average urban cost of living of 100, a figure of 122 in Honolulu and 111 in New York versus 87 in Austin, Texas, and 85 in nonmetropolitan areas in the South.

Medical Expenses

Expenses for medical and hospital care are distributed very un-evenly by family for reasons beyond family control and reduce tax capacity of some families drastically. Equity does not require deducti-bility of all medical expenses, but only those in excess of a certain figure or percentage of income.

The deduction is not without problems. Delineation of medical expenses encounters borderline items that give rise to questions of interpretation and potential inequity. Travel for health purposes and liquor prescribed for health reasons are examples. The United States policy is liberal, but lines, somewhat arbitrary, must be drawn. The other problem is the discretionary element in medical expenses: the choice, for example, of an expensive private room instead of a hospital ward, or between a specialist in Rochester and the local general prac-titioner. Endless visits to doctors by neurotics that waste a doctor's time may be encouraged by tax deduction. Yet censorship of the necessity of medical visits or private suites in hospitals is difficult.

Casualty Losses

Losses from fire, theft, accident, and the like in excess of insurance coverage constitute negative income, in the sense of reduction in net wealth, and should be deductible in calculating taxable income, par-ticularly if the amount is significant. Deductibility of small amounts is an unwarranted nuisance. Deductibility does favor the person who fails through negligence to take out insurance, but this is not a con-trolling objection.

Interest Paid

Much more questionable is the deductibility of interest paid on nonbusiness loans (interest on business loans is obviously a legitimate expense of gaining the income). Deductibility of interest, as permitted in the United States but not in Canada, recognizes this type of payment as a mandatory one once the obligation is undertaken and one that may be regarded as justifiable when the debts have arisen out of per-sonal misfortune. A large portion of all borrowing, however, is discre-tionary, undertaken to allow the enjoyment of durable consumer goods, vacations, and so forth sooner than otherwise, and deductibility is hard to justify. The deduction does equalize somewhat the relative tax on persons with different equities in their homes but favors the home-owner over the tenant, who has no equivalent deduction. Accordingly, the discrimination produced by the failure to tax homeowners on imputed rental value of their homes is aggravated. To disallow deduction would create a major enforcement difficulty, that of distinguishing between interest on personal and business loans of farmers and operators of small businesses. A farmer borrows to build a new house but attributes the debt to purchase of additional farmland. This is the primary reason the deduction was first granted and must be weighed against equity considerations.

Contributions to Charitable and Religious Organizations[17]

While the making of contributions may be considered to reduce tax capacity, the primary motive for the deduction is the desire on the part of governments to stimulate contributions to these organizations. For persons in higher tax brackets the net cost of making contributions is greatly reduced by the tax. Many organizations carry on welfare and community-benefit activities that governments themselves would otherwise do, at least in part. From the standpoint of a free society, preservation of private charitable activity, educational and research facilities, and similar functions has strong justification. While in the United States religious activity is not regarded as an appropriate governmental function, consensus of thought has supported indirect aid through deductibility of contributions to churches—although with a strong minority, including some church groups, opposing.

While the principle of deductibility has widespread support even though primary direct benefit concentrates in the higher income groups, two questions can be raised. Some of the activities of these eligible organizations are not ones whose goals would sustain widespread support, yet censorship of purpose except in extreme cases is contrary to the principles of freedom of activity in this sphere. The basic issue is the degree of discretion individuals should have over the allocation of tax-free income for various activities; the answer must rest upon value judgments. More significantly, the privilege of deductibility has at times been the basis of deliberate tax avoidance. Wealthy persons give business property to a nonprofit foundation whose policies they control; a small portion of the earnings is utilized for the conservation of ring-tailed gophers and the rest is used for expansion of the business enterprise. Legislation seeks to prevent such abuses, but new avenues for avoidance are constantly being developed.

---

[17]M. K. Taussig, "Economic Aspects of the Personal Income Tax Treatment of Charitable Contributions," *National Tax Journal,* Vol. XX (March, 1967), pp. 1–19, analyzes the effects of the deduction and concludes that the incentive effect of the deduction in encouraging persons to give larger amounts is limited.

Taxes[18]

Taxes paid other governmental units may alternatively be regarded as payments that reduce tax capacity, or as payments for governmental services. Deduction of them, limited in the United States to taxes paid state and local governments, is based partly on the first interpretation, but primarily is justified as a device to protect the tax resources of these governments and thus to strengthen the federal governmental structure. Without the deduction of state income tax payments, combined income tax rates would at times have exceeded 100 percent at the margin—an intolerable situation. While deductibility of sales and income taxes lessens progressivity of the tax structure, this effect can be offset by changes in rate structure. Deductibility of property taxes, however, benefits homeowners at the expense of tenants. Yet allowing deductibility of the first two types and not property taxes is geographically discriminatory because of the varying reliance on the three types of tax.

Deductibility of gasoline taxes, used in lieu of tolls, is hard to justify on any basis. Deductibility of federal taxes for income tax purposes, as once permitted, has no justification.

The Standard or Optional Deduction

The provision of a standard deduction, which the taxpayer is free to use if he prefers instead of itemizing deductions, as permitted in the United States, is primarily designed to simplify tax returns, and incidentally to lessen petty chiseling. In the United States the policy also has the effect of increasing the exemption figure at the lower income levels and of offsetting some of the discrimination against tenants, who cannot benefit from interest and property tax deductions available to homeowners. Otherwise, an optional deduction makes little sense in terms of equity; persons are allowed to deduct certain expenditures considered to reduce tax capacity, and then those not making the expenditures are authorized to deduct a standard figure in lieu of them! A simpler technique would limit the deductions to a figure in excess of an established minimum. Many taxpayers would have no deduction and others would be restricted to lower amounts, while the marginal tax rates, those most likely to influence behavior, would be somewhat lower. The difference is not great, however; under the present system taxpayers think they are getting a "break" by the deductions, forget-

---

[18]B. Bridges, Jr., "Deductibility of State and Local Nonbusiness Taxes under the Federal Individual Income Tax," *National Tax Journal,* Vol. XIX (March, 1966), pp. 1–17.

ting that if they are average taxpayers they are paying equivalently higher rates.

THE SIGNIFICANCE OF THE CORPORATION

If the concept of ability to pay is regarded as meaningful only in terms of human beings, use of the corporate form should in no way affect income tax liability. Furthermore, uniformity is necessary if income taxation is to be neutral for the choice of form of business organization and if restrictive effects on investment are to be minimized. Complete uniformity requires (1) taxation of dividend earnings to the stockholders and (2) inclusion in their taxable income of an allocated share of undistributed profits, with no tax on the corporation as such. This procedure is often called the "partnership" approach to taxation of corporate income. While this method is now authorized for certain small, closely held corporations, its general usage would encounter several major problems. First, serious allocational questions would arise, particularly when stock is held by numbers of persons for short periods during the year, and when the corporation has several types of stock issues with varying contingent claims. Second, stockholders would be taxed upon sums they do not currently receive and over whose disposition they, as individuals, have no control. Serious hardships and forced sale of stock could occur. Third, this procedure would provide no tax on earnings accruing to nonresident stockholders, a problem of major importance to the states and to countries such as Canada with extensive foreign ownership. The approach is not unusable but the obstacles are serious.

If the income tax were applied only to dividends received and corporate earnings remained untaxed until they were paid out or reflected in capital gains, as suggested by Henry Simons, undistributed earnings would be tax-free on a current basis and the postponement would cost the government substantial revenue. This approach would give strong incentive to retain larger sums in the corporation and would allow substantial tax avoidance, so long as capital gains receive favorable treatment.

Separate Entity Approach

In practice the usual approach has been to impose a separate tax on the net earnings of corporations, partly as a means of reaching undistributed profits on a current basis, partly as a reflection of the philosophy that the corporation as such has tax capacity distinct from that of the owners and accordingly should be taxed on its entire income independently of the tax on the earnings of the stockholders. This philosophy has seldom been stated with any degree of precision[19] but rests upon the separation of ownership and control in the large corporation. The large firm is an entity, both legally and economically distinct from the persons who own it, with substantial resources to which the stockholders have no access and with economic power over which they have no control. Basic decision making rests with management, which acts in terms of the interests of the corporation per se. An additional argument, particularly relevant at the state level, is that the corporation must be taxed if the state in which the property is located is to obtain revenue when the stock is owned by nonresidents.

The separate identity rule has been generally accepted in the United States, in which the corporate tax predates the personal income tax. A different rate schedule has been used, typically with one basic rate and a reduced rate on companies with limited earnings, the lower rate designed primarily to aid development and growth of small businesses. The progressive rates of the personal income tax have not been applied to corporations because of recognition that large absolute profits primarily reflect large capital investment, not necessarily high rate of return on capital. Large corporations may be widely held and small corporations owned by a few wealthy persons. Furthermore, application of regular progressive rates would encourage amoebalike splitting of corporations into many smaller ones to reduce tax, a result produced to some extent by the two-rate system of the present tax.

Consequences of the Separate Entity Approach

While the taxation of the corporation as such on its total earnings produces substantial tax revenues, the system does not conform with generally accepted standards. In the first place, a tax on all corporate earnings may in part, as explained in Chapter 8, shift forward to consumers of the products, creating a pattern of income redistribution comparable to that of a sales tax, with wide variation on different products. Certainly this is not the result intended by governments in imposing the tax.

Secondly, the portion of the tax not shifted forward constitutes a double burden on the stockholders, since it either curtails the dividends they receive or checks the increase in the value of their stock

[19]P. Studenski, "Toward a Theory of Business Taxation," *Journal of Political Economy*, Vol. XLVIII (October, 1940), pp. 621–54, provides one of the few statements.

by lessening retained earnings. The burden concentrates on the persons holding stock at the time the tax is imposed or increased, since the reduction in the selling price of the stock consequent to the reduced earnings will free subsequent owners of a portion of the burden. The defense for double taxation of dividend income on the grounds that the corporation has taxpaying ability distinct from its owners is open to serious question. The concept of tax capacity has no meaning apart from individuals, and the discriminatory double taxation of dividend recipients cannot, by usual standards of equity, be dismissed as irrelevant. Some persons have defended the corporation tax along these lines on the grounds that the overall burden distribution is progressive.[20] But this argument does not justify the discrimination, at given income levels, between dividend receivers and others, particularly recipients of interest income. Furthermore, this discrimination against stockholders increases the potential dangers of adverse effects upon risk taking and investment.

Thirdly, this approach does not provide uniform treatment of undistributed profits of corporate and noncorporate forms of business enterprise. The tax is higher under the corporate form if the owners are in low-income brackets and lower if the owners are in high brackets. As a consequence, progression does not operate in intended fashion.

Finally, the differential treatment causes distortion of economic activity and loss of efficiency, particularly in the choice between corporate and noncorporate forms of business organization. If the owners of a business are in relatively low income tax brackets and wish to use most of the earnings for personal use, incorporating will raise tax liability. On the other hand, if the owners are in high-income brackets and wish to use most of the earnings for business expansion, they will benefit from incorporation, especially if capital gains are not fully taxable. Tax saving is a major objective for many incorporations. The tax treatment also affects dividend policies of corporations. If the decision makers are subject to high current tax rates, they will pay out less than economic considerations dictate so as to postpone and perhaps eventually avoid taxes.

Methods of financing may be also affected. Since interest payments are deductible by the corporation but dividends are not, management of the large, widely held firms will be given incentive to rely more heavily on debt financing. There is little empirical evidence of

---

[20]See R. Goode, *The Corporation Income Tax* (New York: Wiley, 1951).

this consequence,[21] partly because there are strong prejudices in many firms against borrowing.

Alternatives

If the partnership approach—the only completely neutral nondiscriminatory approach, but one subject to serious difficulties—is rejected, two major alternatives to the present treatment are available:

1. Complete exemption from personal income tax of dividends received by stockholders. Under the system used for a number of years in Great Britain (now abandoned), and proposed by the Royal Commission for use in Canada, the portion of the corporate income tax on income paid out as dividends would be regarded simply as a withholding device. Stockholders would include in their taxable incomes their dividends plus the amount of corporate tax paid on these amounts and receive credit against their tax liability for the corporate tax paid, as they do now with income tax withheld on wages and salaries. This procedure would eliminate double taxation of dividend income and provide uniform treatment for the portion of corporate earnings paid out as dividends and other income, under the assumption that the corporate tax is not reflected in higher product prices. Partial use of this approach is provided by the present Canadian system whereby the stockholder receives a credit (20 percent) against personal income tax liability on dividends received.

This approach suffers from a basic defect: the possible nonvalidity of the assumption that the corporate tax is not shifted. If the corporate tax is reflected in higher prices of the products, the stockholders are not subjected to discriminatory treatment and the tax credit would free them from any tax liability. Some shifting of the corporate tax is almost inevitable and introduction of this technique would not necessarily eliminate it. Secondly, since the corporate tax would remain unchanged, any effects that it may have on corporate financing or upon investment decisions would continue.

2. Dividend-paid credit. The alternative approach would allow the corporation to deduct dividend payments in calculating taxable income for the corporate tax, which, therefore, would apply only to undistributed profits. Dividends would be taxed only at the personal income level. Accordingly the danger of providing an unwarranted bonus to stockholders would be avoided since corporations can scarcely shift

[21]J. A. Pechman, *Federal Tax Policy* (Washington, D.C.: Brookings Institution, 1966), p. 113.

taxes that are not imposed upon them, and adverse effects of the present tax on corporate decision making would be eliminated. On the other hand, to the extent that corporate management in the large enterprise stresses after-tax profit as the measure of its success, it might be encouraged to pay out larger sums as dividends than otherwise, lessening funds available for expansion. This consequence, however, is of doubtful significance. The complaint is often made that the dividend-paid credit approach is unfair to newly expanding businesses that must retain most of their earnings in order to obtain funds for growth, compared to mature businesses able to pay out most of their earnings. This argument is of questionable validity, if one views the overall picture of tax on the corporation and its owners. In one respect this approach is less satisfactory than the alternative: foreign stockholders cannot be taxed on their dividends. Accordingly, some form of special withholding tax on dividends paid to nonresidents would be required.

Neither of these alternatives provide equal treatment for undistributed profits and other income. Accordingly decisions to pay out or hold earnings will be affected by the tax position of the stockholders, in those corporations in which the decisions are made in terms of the interests of the stockholders. No method can provide uniform treatment of undistributed profits and other incomes except the partnership technique.

Any approach that reduces the double taxation of dividend income will reduce the revenue from the income tax structure as a whole. This loss can obviously be made up by a rate increase, with overall burden distributed more satisfactorily among various income recipients. This type of change, however, has little political appeal. As a consequence, the movement in the United States toward reform of the corporate tax, which attracted interest in the early fifties, has no strong political support. The defects in the present structure are recognized, but the tax is highly productive of revenue and complaints are not strong; there is a tendency to let well enough alone. Some support has developed for replacement of the corporate income tax by a value added tax.

The Special Problem of Cooperatives

The cooperative type of business organization is the most troublesome of all from the standpoint of attaining neutrality and equity. The profits of cooperatives, apart from a fixed return on the shares of the members and additions to reserves, are distributed to the customers on the basis of purchases (buying cooperatives) or sales (producer cooperatives). The basic issue centers around the nature of these distributions: are they merely offsets of overcharges for commodities bought or underpayments for produce sold, or are they essentially incomes? Should, therefore, the amounts be taxed to the recipients, to the cooperative, as such, to both, or not at all? The most logical answer appears to be that those "earnings" arising from economies in operation are not income and should not be taxed, either to the cooperative or to the recipients. If they were taxed to either or both, the cooperatives would have strong incentive to reduce their selling prices or increase their purchase prices. On the other hand, the amounts that represent earnings on invested capital and amounts added to surplus can legitimately be regarded as income and taxed in the same fashion as income earned in the corporation. While the amounts added to surplus can be, and usually are, taxed, the portion of patronage dividends arising out of invested capital cannot in practice be separated from gains from economies, and are not taxed—to the advantage of the cooperative form of organization. This issue has generated considerable emotional heat, defensiveness on the part of cooperatives, and strong complaints from their enemies.

TAX RATE STRUCTURES

The rate structure of an income tax must be based primarily upon the pattern of progression desired in contemporary society, balanced against possible adverse economic effects. Accordingly, no scientific rules can be employed to build the rate structure but a few general observations are possible. First, the elementary point should not be overlooked of insuring that the marginal rate never exceeds 100 percent, as it has in some countries at certain points in the income scale by the nature of rate tables employed. Second, since the basic rate is of primary importance in determining revenue yield, its level must be set in terms of revenue needs. Third, if the basic rate bracket is relatively wide, as it was for many years in the United States, most taxpayers will fall in this bracket and will not be subjected to progressive rates— a result that may not be desired. Fourth, high marginal rates are productive of very little revenue[22] but offer the greatest danger of adverse effects upon both work incentives (on the part of executives) and willingness to undertake risk. In addition they channel substantial high-priced talent to the task of finding ways and means of avoiding tax. The use of marginal rates up to 91 percent, as in the United States

---

[22]In 1966, only 1.5 percent of taxable income was taxed at rates in excess of 50 percent. See Pechman, *op. cit.*, p. 55.

for two decades, is extremely questionable for these reasons. In large measure the high rates reflected political window dressing, which Congress was reluctant to abandon. The Canadian Royal Commission has proposed a maximum of 50 percent.

REFERENCES

GENERAL

GOODE, R. The Individual Income Tax. Washington, D.C.: Brookings Institution, 1964.

The most complete modern study of income tax structural questions:

PECHMAN, J. A. Federal Tax Policy. Washington, D.C.: Brookings Institution, 1966.

A recent survey of federal tax policy.

Report of the Royal Commission on Taxation, vols. III, IV. Ottawa: Queen's Printer, 1966.

One of the most complete studies of income taxation ever made; much is relevant to all countries.

SIMONS, H. C. Personal Income Taxation. Chicago: University of Chicago Press, 1938.

The classic historical and analytical study of personal income taxation, with stress on the concept of income.

SMITH, D. T. Federal Tax Reform. New York: McGraw-Hill, 1961.

A more conservative approach to tax policy.

U.S. HOUSE OF REPRESENTATIVES, COMMITTEE ON WAYS AND MEANS. Tax Revision Compendium. 3 vols. Washington, D.C.: U.S. Government Printing Office, 1959.

A series of papers on income taxation by experts in the field, prepared at the request of the Ways and Means Committee.

VICKREY, W. Agenda for Progressive Taxation. New York: Ronald Press Co., 1947.

An intensive study of the features of an optimal income tax structure, still useful.

SPECIFIC ASPECTS

GOODE, R. The Corporation Income Tax. New York: Wiley, 1951.

Although out of date, this is still the most significant volume on the corporation income tax.

GROVES, H. M. Federal Tax Treatment of the Family. Washington, D.C.: Brookings Institution, 1963.

SELTZER, L. H. The Nature and Tax Treatment of Capital Gains. New York: National Bureau of Economic Research, 1951.

The classic study of capital gains problem.

Chapter 16

OPTIMAL SALES, EXCISE, PROPERTY, AND DEATH TAX STRUCTURES

While income taxation is widely accepted in developed economies as the most desirable form of taxation, use of other forms as well is considered justifiable, and these forms in fact play major roles in tax structures. These taxes have frequently been framed with little regard to the usually accepted standards of taxation, with the consequence that they interfere with attainment of the objectives of the overall tax structure. Because of their direct impact upon business firms, some of these taxes offer particular dangers of loss in economic efficiency.

SALES TAXATION

A sales tax is designed to distribute a portion of the total tax burden in proportion to consumer expenditures, in the same fashion as a proportional rate expenditure tax collected directly from individuals. If this goal is to be attained in a fashion consistent with other objectives of the tax structure, several requirements must be met. First, the tax must apply uniformly to all consumer expenditures except those for which specific justification for exclusion is established. Failure to provide uniform coverage not only creates inequity through discrimination in favor of persons having relatively high preferences for the exempt commodities, but also results in consumer excess burden and frequently complicates operation of the tax, as noted below. Uniformity in burden requires application of the tax at a uniform rate to all consumption purchases and shifting of the exact amount of the tax to the consumers. Only by this means can a sales tax produce the same distributional effects as a proportional rate expenditure tax.

Second, the distribution of burden by income class, considered in light of the overall tax structure, must be acceptable on the basis of the standards of contemporary society. Third, the tax must be neutral in its effects upon production and distribution techniques. If choice of methods of operation and organization is altered, economic efficiency is lost, unless the pretax situation was not optimal and the change brings the economy closer to the optimum. Finally, operation of the tax must be feasible, with a high level of enforcement at low cost and minimum compliance costs.

These requirements may conflict. Equity may require exemptions, which reduce uniformity and ease of administration. Administrative requirements may lessen equity. In such instances conflicting considerations must be weighed to reach a decision.

Structure of the Tax

Sales taxes may take a number of possible forms, ranging from the turnover tax on all transactions on the one hand to manufacturers, wholesale, and retail taxes and various hybrids of these on the other. Selection of the form most suitable in terms of the requirements must be based upon the circumstances of the country, in light of the relative advantages and limitations of each form.

The Retail Sales Tax. The form of tax that meets the requirements of uniformity and economic neutrality most closely is the retail sales tax, (or its equivalent, the value added tax extended through the retail level), imposed upon final sales to consumers. A tax on the final retail price, fully shifted forward, will constitute a uniform percentage of consumer expenditures upon all taxed goods. By contrast, preretail taxes, which do not include all distribution costs in the taxable price, will produce variations in the ratio of tax payments to consumer expenditures on various goods because of varying distribution margins. A fully shifted 10 percent manufacturers tax will constitute 5 percent of consumer expenditures on commodities with 50 percent distribution margins and 7½ percent on those with 25 percent margins. The turnover tax produces still further variation because of differences in the numbers of sales through which various commodities pass on the route from initial production to final consumption. Additional variation arises with nonretail taxes because of their tendency to pyramid through the use of percentage markups, which retail taxes do not do. Separate quotation and application of retail tax to the customer's bill in lieu of price adjustments increase the likelihood of uniform shifting. The retail tax can also be applied more easily to services, often rendered by small establishments, and thus provide broader coverage.

Secondly, only the retail tax is completely neutral among various distribution systems and therefore does not alter methods of doing business. Taxes levied at manufacturing and wholesale levels favor firms that transfer distributional activity forward beyond the impact of the tax in order to minimize the taxable price figure. Thus a manufacturers tax discourages forward integration by manufacturers, favoring firms performing a minimum of distributional functions and selling to wholesale distributors. Wholesale sales taxes favor the backward integrated retailer buying in large quantities at low cost. Both favor the private brand distributor, who performs many functions normally carried on by the manufacturer (research, advertising) and thus is able to buy cheaply.

Only the retail form of tax can provide equal treatment for domestic and imported goods (except in the relatively rare instances of importation by the final consumer, where equality is difficult with any tax). The problem is particularly severe with a manufacturers sales tax since the tax applies to most imported goods at a later stage of distribution than that at which domestic goods are taxed.

Thirdly, from an administrative standpoint the retail form of tax has many advantages. For subordinate units of government no other form is feasible because of the jurisdictional problem. A much higher percentage of retail sales is made within a taxing jurisdiction than the percentage of sales by manufacturers and wholesalers, and the task of enforcement against outside firms is less troublesome. In many other respects the retail tax is the simplest form of sales tax to operate. "Retail sale" is an easier concept to define in workable fashion than "manufacturer" and "sale by a manufacturer" or "sale to a retailer." Treatment of transportation and other incidental charges creates less uncertainty and discrimination with the retail tax. The retail tax also avoids the troublesome adjustments in taxable price with wholesale or manufacturers taxes designed to lessen discrimination against certain distributional channels.[1]

The retail tax yields a substantially greater revenue with a given tax rate—nearly twice as much as a manufacturers tax. Accordingly pressure to evade and resistance on the part of the taxpaying firms are lessened. Only with the retail tax can the consumer be made aware of the amount of tax he is paying, a consequence of merit for attainment of levels of governmental activities optimum in terms of the preferences of society. With the typical quotation of retail tax separate from selling price of the commodity, the taxpaying vendors are more likely to regard themselves as tax collectors rather than as taxpayers and are less likely to seek to evade tax.

---

[1]This has been demonstrated by Canadian experience. See *Canada, Report of the Royal Commission on Taxation* (Ottawa: Queen's Printer, 1966), Vol. V, pp. 13–16.

Advantages of the Manufacturers and Wholesale Taxes.[2] Single-stage sales taxes levied prior to the retail level offer only one advantage over the retail tax: the number of taxpaying firms is much smaller and these firms are typically large enough to have adequate record systems. The one significant limitation of the retail sales tax is the large number of small retailers, many with limited record systems. In the United States this has proven to be only a minor nuisance. In a country in which most retailing is of a small-scale nature, the enforcement of a retail tax is much more difficult and costly, and the case for a manufacturers or wholesale tax, or a hybrid wholesale-retail tax as discussed in Chapter 17, is stronger. Otherwise, the preretail taxes have no merit whatever compared to retail taxes, as has been demonstrated very conclusively by Canada's 40-year experience with the manufacturers sales tax. Failure to attain neutrality among various distribution channels, uncertainty, and serious complications in the operation of the tax resulting from it, and the unequal burden on various consumer purchases led the 1966 Royal Commission to recommend its replacement by a retail tax.[3]

The Turnover Tax. The turnover tax does not warrant serious consideration.[4] The discrimination against nonintegrated firms and the effects in encouraging integration produced by the "cascade" nature of the tax lessen economic efficiency, lead to strong complaints, and bring modifications that complicate the taxes beyond the possibility of effective administration. The nonuniformity of burden on various consumer expenditures is substantial and burden pattern by income group is indeterminate. Elimination of the exact amount of tax from exports is impossible, and imported goods are often favored over do-

---

[2]If a country is unwilling to use a retail sales tax, the choice between the manufacturers and wholesale taxes is not a clear-cut one. The wholesale tax (which applies to sales to retailers, whether by manufacturers or wholesale distributors) is subject to the defects of preretail taxes to a lesser degree, since the tax is closer to the final retail level. Ratios of tax to final consumer expenditures will differ less, since only variations in retail margins are relevant. Possible effects on choice of distribution channels are also less. The wholesale tax is advantageous if imports are significant, since equality of tax on imported and domestic goods is easier to attain with it than with a manufacturers tax. The wholesale tax has one major limitation compared to the manufacturers tax: when retailers integrate backward and buy cheaply at the manufacturing level, the price adjustments necessary for tax purposes to lessen discrimination are upward ones—called *uplift* in Great Britain. The firms will inevitably resist this type of adjustment more than downward adjustments permitted competitors with the manufacturers tax. The wholesale tax would be more difficult to administer in a country with large numbers of small wholesalers.

[3]*Royal Commission, op. cit.,* Vol. V.

[4]A description and analysis of turnover taxes is given in G. Schmölders, *Turnover Taxes* (Amsterdam: International Bureau of Fiscal Documentation, 1966).

mestically produced goods. The only advantage of the tax is the lower rate required to raise a given sum. Germany, the originator of the turnover tax in its modern form, abandoned it January 1, 1968, in favor of the value added tax, and the other European Common Market countries plan to make the change in the near future.[5]

The Value Added Tax. A general value added tax applies to all business firms at all stages of production and distribution, but only on *value added,* that is, gross sales less the cost of taxable goods purchased.[6]

There are two general approaches to calculation. Under the first, the firm calculates value added by subtracting from sales the costs of all goods purchased and applies the tax rate to this figure. Under the second, as used in France, the firm calculates gross tax on its sales, subtracts tax paid on purchases during the period, and pays the difference. Other things equal, the two methods will produce the same tax liability. The second method requires separate statement of tax on each invoice so that firms can calculate the total amount of tax they have paid on their purchases and facilitates cross-audit of firms. Tax paid by one firm appears as a deduction by its customers.

A value added tax extended through the retail level will produce the same revenue as a retail sales tax at the same rate, since the retail price equals the sum of the figures of value added at each stage in production and distribution. The distribution of burden will also be the same, provided that the tax is shifted forward in full. If the tax extends only through the wholesale level, the yield will be the same as that of a wholesale sales tax. The value added tax avoids the cascade features of the turnover tax and thus the discrimination and incentive given to integration.

As compared to a single-stage tax, the value added tax offers limited advantages. Since the direct impact of the tax is spread over a wider range of firms, there may be less complaint from the taxpaying vendors, especially if the rate is high.[7] A substantial portion of the total tax will be collected in the manufacturing and wholesale sectors, lessening the chances of evasion and loss of revenue. From an administrative standpoint, the tax offers a significant advantage provided the tax deduction technique is employed; since tax paid by one firm constitutes a deduction by another firm, cross checking of various tax-

---

[5]A. R. Prest, "The E.E.C. Value Added Tax and the U.K.," *District Bank Review,* December, 1967, pp. 3–21.

[6]The most complete study of value added taxation is Clara Sullivan's *The Tax on Value Added* (New York: Columbia University Press, 1965).

[7]This is particularly important in France, with a 25 percent tax rate.

payers is facilitated. If one firm shows tax paid to another firm, accounts of the latter can be examined to be sure that the amount was actually paid to the government. Freeing of producers goods from tax may be facilitated somewhat since exclusion is attained by allowing firms to deduct tax paid on all purchases for business use. With a single-stage tax exclusion requires that the vendor sell tax-free when the purchase is made for business use.

On the other hand, the value added tax is a much more complex levy than a single-stage retail or wholesale tax.[8] Firms must keep records of tax on purchases as well as tax due on sales, returns are more complex, and auditing is more complicated. Inevitably questions of interpretation about deductibility of various tax items will arise. Commodity exemptions are particularly troublesome since the effectiveness of an exemption is lost if the exempt commodity is purchased for use in producing a taxable commodity. There is no tax to deduct, and the full tax will apply to the sale of the second commodity unless special rules are provided. French experience has shown that uniform treatment of all commodities is almost essential if the tax is to work effectively. Complete and exact shifting of the tax forward to the final purchasers is less likely than with a retail tax because of the series of steps through which the tax applies. Tax liability of various competing firms relative to sales will differ according to their purchases of taxed goods during the period.[9]

Taxation of Consumption Goods Only

A sales tax is designed to distribute tax burden in relation to consumer spending. Logically, therefore, the tax should be confined to consumption purposes, those made for the purpose of satisfying personal wants, rather than for use in production. Failure to limit the coverage of a sales tax to consumption purchases produces some of the evils of preretail taxes. No longer will the tax be proportional to consumer expenditures, since the element of tax on different commodities will vary, and shifting is likely to be less uniform, with failure to shift in some instances and pyramiding in others. Firms will be encouraged to use less capital-intensive methods and produce goods for their own use

[8]The complexity is explained in detail in the article by F. Forte, "On the Feasibility of a Truly General Value Added Tax," *National Tax Journal*, Vol. XIX (December, 1966), pp. 337–61.

[9]This question has not been carefully explored. J. F. Due, "The Value Added Tax," *Western Economic Journal*, Vol. III (Spring, 1965), pp. 165–71 and W. H. Oakland, "The Theory of the Value Added Tax. II Incidence Effects," *National Tax Journal*, Vol. XX (September, 1967), pp. 270–81, consider the question.

instead of buying them. Investment may be restricted since the tax may cease to be a tax solely on consumption, and may reduce the return on savings as well. Exporters are placed at a disadvantage in competing with firms in jurisdictions not having this type of tax.

As a practical matter exclusion of all producers goods is almost impossible, because many articles can be used for either production or consumption use, and the vendor cannot determine use at the time of sale. A farmer, for example, buys light bulbs for use in his house and and his barn; neither the vendor nor a sales tax auditor can ascertain actual use of each bulb. As a consequence, the exclusion is restricted either very rigidly to physical ingredients and parts, or these items plus other major categories of producers goods such as industrial and farm machinery and fuel. Most jurisdictions could broaden their exemptions; many do not see the need for exempting producers goods and others are concerned about loss of revenue.

Exclusion of all producers goods may be somewhat easier with a value added tax than with a usual sales tax, since the vendor can be allowed to deduct tax on all purchases made for business use. But the difference is not substantial; the same tendency to deduct tax on goods bought for personal use would be strong, and certain types of businesses where the greatest difficulties arise, such as farming, would presumably not be subject to value added tax.

Tax Coverage of Consumption Goods and Other Issues

The uniformity rule requires that the tax apply to all items of consumer spending except those for which exclusion is strongly justified. But universal coverage may place a heavier burden on the lower income groups than society regards as equitable, and certain types of expenditures may be regarded as unsuitable for taxation. Exclusion of other items may be necessitated by administrative considerations.

Services. While sales taxes have often been limited to physical commodities (tangible personal property), extension to consumer services increases uniformity and lessens discrimination and regressivity, since expenditures on services rise more rapidly than income. Taxation of many services, particularly those rendered by commercial establishments also selling taxable goods, simplifies administration, since charges for goods no longer need be distinguished from charges for services. Tax can easily and justifiably be extended to such services as fabrication and repair of taxable goods, admissions, laundry and dry cleaning, hotels and motels, barber and beauty parlor service, and others of this nature. Other services, however, are less suitable for inclusion within the tax.

Exclusion of medical, dental, and hospital services can be justified on grounds of social policy, as can those for education and legal work. Taxation of rental of real property (other than transient) discriminates against the tenant compared to the homeowner. Personal services rendered by individuals rather than established commercial businesses are administratively difficult to reach. Many professional and other services are utilized primarily by business firms, and their exclusion is warranted on the same basis that producers goods are excluded from tax, as noted below. Taxation of producers services is worse than taxation of producers goods of a physical nature in one respect: firms are encouraged to provide them with their own employees.

In summary, therefore: while all services rendered consumers by commercial (as distinguished from professional or personal) establishments can appropriately be included within the tax, there is strong justification for excluding professional services and personal services rendered by individuals and those primarily provided business firms.

Exemptions. Exclusion from tax of classes of commodities lessens uniformity and creates inequity and consumer excess burden, reduces yield at a given rate, and complicates administration, since vendors must distinguish between taxable and exempt sales. However, exemption of a few major categories may be justified on equity considerations relating to distribution of burden by income group. Justification is strongest for two categories: food and prescription medicine.

Exemption of food removes much of the burden on the lower income group and regressiveness, as well as discrimination against large families compared to small. The exemption creates some operational problems, but is workable since the category of food is easily defined. The primary objection, in addition to the revenue loss (20 to 30 percent), is the luxury character of many food expenditures. Some persons concentrate their discretionary expenditures on food, just as others do on recreation, or clothes, or travel. An alternative approach to lessen regressiveness, the provision of a credit against income tax for an amount representing sales tax paid on basic necessities, avoids this discrimination and the administration problems of food exemption. The procedure is now used by several states.[10] The system is workable only if the government also has a broad coverage income tax, and even if it does, additional persons must file income tax returns in order to obtain their refunds.

---

[10]James Papke, "New Perspectives in Retail Sales Taxation," *Proceedings of National Tax Association for 1965*, pp. 258–70; Tax Foundation of Hawaii, *Hawaii's Personal Income Tax Credits* (Honolulu, 1966).

Exemption of prescription medicines can be justified on grounds of social policy, in light of the very uneven distribution of these expenditures among various families. Extension of exemption to such commodities as children's clothing or all clothing creates serious interpretative questions, complicates application of the tax, and excludes many items that are not necessary elements in a minimum living standard. Effective sales taxation cannot be built upon the principle that only luxuries are to be taxed; tax must apply to all commodities except a few major easily definable categories of substantial importance in the budgets of the lowest income groups.

Rate Uniformity. Use of a number of tax rates in an effort to improve equity of the tax and lessen consumption of certain luxuries creates the same problems as exemptions: questions of interpretation of the appropriate rate class and complications in the tasks of compliance and enforcement, as well as consumer excess burden. Theoretically rate differentiation might improve overall equity by placing more of the burden on the wealthy, but in so doing it would create other inequities through discrimination on the basis of consumer preferences. In practice differentiation is likely to so impair the effectiveness of operation that the basic objectives are not attained. The sales taxes in India are classic examples of the destruction of efficiency by the use of extensive rate variation.

Interjurisdictional Sales. In accordance with the requirement of uniformity, the tax should be the same, per dollar of consumer expenditure, whether the goods are imported or domestic. On the other hand, according to the philosophy of a consumer levy exports should not be subject to tax. To do so would place domestic producers at a disadvantage in world markets, with given exchange rates.

On trade within the country but across jurisdictional lines, the primary problem is enforcement—discovery of purchases made outside the jurisdiction. Failure to reach these transactions results in inequity and loss of economic efficiency. The states employ use taxes, making the purchaser responsible for payment on articles purchased tax-free outside the state. These are in practice collectible from the purchaser only on items such as cars that must be registered; otherwise, enforcement depends upon the ability of the states to require collection and payment by the out-of-state vendors.

Separate Quotation of Tax. If the tax is imposed at the retail level, requirement of quotation of the tax separately from the price of the product facilitates shifting of the tax by encouraging uniformity of action and avoiding the necessity for readjusting individual prices.

Furthermore, the practice encourages the acceptance by vendors of the attitude that they are tax collectors rather than taxpayers and lessens their incentive to evade tax.

Question may be raised about the reactions of consumers to high-rate separately quoted taxes. No precise answer is possible; in part the reaction depends upon past experience. For many years state sales taxes in the United States did not exceed 3 percent; now 4 percent and 5 percent are becoming common. The rate is now 8 percent in the province of Quebec, and if the proposed Royal Commission recommendations in Canada were to be accepted, the rate would reach 15 or 16 percent.

Other Questions. Development of a logical sales tax structure requires answers to a surprising number of minor questions that, if not appropriately resolved, cause loss of economic efficiency. For example, exclusion from tax of real property contracts discourages prefabrication. The full price of a prefabricated article is taxable whereas much of the labor cost will escape the tax if fabrication is performed in conjunction with installation on the job site. Exclusion of finance charges from the tax, as is common, leads firms to separate financing from other charges to lessen tax liability.

EXCISE TAXATION

As explained in the previous chapter, excise taxes find justification in a tax structure only when specific circumstances warrant:

1. Commodities whose production and use create costs to society not borne by producers, such as liquor and tobacco. An excise raises the price to the consumer and thus reduces output and prevents excessive allocation of resources. Tax rates, therefore, should reflect estimates of external costs arising from use of the commodities. In practice governments have also been motivated in their use of these excises by the very large revenue obtainable at politically tolerable rates, made possible by the inelastic demands. Inelasticity, however, lessens the effectiveness of the taxes in reducing consumption to optimal levels. In practice the rates are dictated largely by revenue considerations.

Given the intent of the levies, use of specific rates is justified, since the added social cost is presumably related to physical units, not to their value. Use of specific rates also avoids the discrimination against various distribution channels that occurs with ad valorem taxes collected prior to the retail level. The high rates warrant collecting the tax at the manufacturing level, where control is more effective. The liquor taxes are, in a rough way, progressive according to alcoholic content, the tax on distilled spirits being the highest, that on wine directly adjusted to alcoholic content, and that on beer relatively light. This policy is justified in light of the general purpose of the taxes.

The taxes are not free of criticism, however. The specific rates tend to penalize economy brands, particularly of cigarettes. The taxes on cigarettes and beer are highly regressive, the former being the most regressive major tax in the whole structure. These criticisms are not valid if the taxes are regarded as justifiable on bases other than ability to pay. The major administrative problem is bootlegging, and, with cigarettes, in some countries, smuggling. The former is a continuing problem, but one that can be kept within reasonable limits by effective enforcement.

2. Excises in lieu of charges designed to distribute the costs of a particular governmental service in relation to use as explained in Chapter 13. Motor fuel taxes are the major examples. Since payment is related to use, these taxes are justified on the benefit basis and aid in adjusting the output of the services to the preferences of the community. Accordingly, the taxes have specific rates, which simplify collection and avoid discrimination. The major problem has been the lag in yield as the price level has risen; with ad valorem rates the yield would keep pace with increases in the price of gasoline. Adjustment of rates in terms of place and time of usage would have great merit but is difficult administratively.

3. Taxes designed to free certain resources for governmental use. In periods of inflationary pressures and increased use by government of certain specialized resources, as, for example, for purposes of national defense, special excises on consumer goods using these resources would free the resources for government. Such instances are of limited significance and the taxes have an unfortunate tendency to live on beyond the period of justification.

WEALTH TAXATION

The objective of taxation of wealth is to bring the tax structure more in line with accepted equity standards by adjusting the overall tax distribution on the basis of this additional element reflecting economic well-being and tax capacity. A tax on wealth also adjusts the burden more equitably among holders of various forms of wealth, compensating for the discrimination of the income tax in favor of maximum-security and little-or-no-return investments and those with returns not easily taxed, such as imputed rent of an owner-occupied home. The wealth tax, based on the value of wealth regardless of the income from it, aids in attaining a more acceptable pattern of distribution.

Structure of a Net Wealth Tax

The objective of a wealth tax is to tax each individual (or family unit) on net assets or wealth—the total value of all property owned less debts outstanding. The contrast between this type of tax (used to some extent in the countries of northern Europe) and the usual type of property tax are substantial:

1. The tax would apply only to individuals, not to corporations, as the aim is to adjust the burden in terms of personal economic well-being.

2. All property, including cash, stocks, bonds, and other intangibles, would be included in taxable wealth.

3. All debt would be subtracted, in view of the aim to tax net wealth.

While broad coverage is obviously desirable in the interests of uniformity, some exemption would be warranted, presumably upon a family unit basis, in order to free from taxes those families that own some wealth, particularly a home, but have little current income. This is typical of many elderly persons retired on small pensions. A substantial tax could force these families to sell their homes to escape tax, a socially undesirable consequence. The exemption could be established in terms of both income and wealth, applying to wealth less than a specified figure, provided income were under the established figure. Similar considerations suggest the need for limiting the rate.

The case for progression is less strong than with income taxation, which is the best vehicle for introducing progression into the overall tax structure. A progressive wealth tax could have serious effects on closely held businesses and could aggravate the problem of defining the family unit. Progression would be justified in a country in which the tax is used as a deliberate instrument for breaking up large landholdings or other blocks of wealth.

Difficulties. The primary difficulty with any tax imposed upon wealth is assessment, in the sense of determination of value, a problem avoided with income and consumption taxes. A related problem is the potential escape of certain types of property: unregistered coupon bonds, cash, bank deposits in foreign banks, and valuable personal effects, such as expensive diamond rings. Failure to reach certain types of wealth encourages persons to shift to these forms.

Apart from these inherent problems of all wealth taxation, which limit their potential revenue, use of net wealth taxation in the United States and in many countries would encounter another serious limitation: the present tax on property is primarily a local government revenue source and the only tax the local governments can rely on for large sums of money. To supplement the tax on property at the local level with a federal tax on net wealth would raise the combined burden to unacceptable levels. Replacement of present property taxes by wealth taxes at the local level would encounter two serious obstacles. One is administrative: while the federal government could trace down a person's wealth reasonably well, local governments cannot possibly do so, since they cannot discover such items as security holdings or funds on deposit in other areas. Furthermore, to abandon taxation of corporation property, as such, would cause serious dislocation in relative revenues received by various local units. Those local government areas with substantial corporation property to which they supply governmental services would lose a large part of their property tax revenue if the corporation were owned by outsiders. Communities with numerous residents owning extensive corporate securities would benefit. This type of redistribution is not only politically intolerable but would create insuperable financial problems for areas losing revenue.

Accordingly, discussion of a net wealth tax in the United States is largely academic, merely providing an outline of an ideal tax in this field with which to compare, evaluate, and develop reforms for actual taxes on property.[11]

The Property Tax

The property tax as it operates in the United States today was described briefly in Chapter 5. The tax differs from the net wealth tax in two principal ways:

1. Tax applies to property owned by corporations as well as by individuals. In the last century, individuals were not only taxed on their real property but on intangibles as well, and therefore corporation property was taxed twice: on the real property and on the securities that reflected ownership in it. The obvious inequity of this treatment and the inability of local assessors to find securities led to abandonment, by law or practice, of the portion of the tax on intangibles.

2. The tax applies to the gross value of property without adjustment for debt.

---

[11]Experience with net wealth taxation elsewhere appears in the symposium volume "Net Wealth Taxation," *Public Finance,* Vol. XV (Nos. 3 and 4) 1960.

Rates are proportional, and in most states without exemption. The levy is regarded as an *in rem* tax against the property per se, rather than a tax against the owners; liability constitutes a legal claim against the property. A few states provide homestead exemption of owner-occupied houses up to a certain value.

Accordingly, the tax is very far removed from an optimal net wealth tax, a large part—about half—of the tax being obtained from corporations. Individuals, in turn, are taxed only on their real property and, in some states, on a few items of tangible personal property, and on a gross basis with no recognition given to debts outstanding.

This form of tax is justified on three bases:

1. Since many of the services of local governments directly benefit individuals and business firms in relation to property owned, a substantial portion of the property tax can be justified on the benefit basis. Financing of police and fire protection, street lighting, streets and sidewalks, and sewerage systems are examples. If these services were not provided by local governments, persons would have to buy them.

2. Local governments require an independent source of revenue in the interests of financial autonomy and optimal adjustment of levels of local governmental activities; the only major tax they can use is one imposed upon real property and a few other items. Some inequity must be tolerated in the light of financial necessity.

3. The substantial portion of the tax resting upon housing compensates to some extent for the failure to apply income tax to imputed value of owner-occupied housing and adjusts the overall tax burden in terms of wealth placed in this form.

Limitations. These arguments all have some merit; the benefit considerations, however, provide no justification for the portion of the property tax that finances education—the chief expenditure of local governments. But the tax suffers from a number of limitations, some being manifestations of the basic problems of all wealth taxation, but most being consequences of deviation from a true net wealth tax.

First, the tax, by striking only certain forms of wealth and not applying to others, fails to accomplish the primary goal of wealth taxation and discriminates severely against those persons who concentrate their wealth in taxable forms, particularly housing facilities. Given the present height of property tax rates, the tax places a very severe burden on persons who own their homes but have little current incomes: persons out of work, widows with small children, elderly retired persons. Persons having substantial investments in securities largely escape tax.

Second, much of the portion of the tax on corporations is likely shifted to the consumers of the products, and thus the burden is distributed in the fashion of a nonuniform sales tax, instead of resting on the owners of the businesses. Shifting is likely nonuniform, some business owners escaping and others not.

Third, the tax places a relatively heavy burden on real-property-intensive industries, particularly the railroads, and thus causes distortion of resource allocation and loss of efficiency, to the extent that the taxes on these firms exceed the additional costs of governmental services for which they are responsible. The tax has particularly undesirable results for the logging industry, encouraging firms to cut the best timber and abandon the land instead of logging selectively on a sustaining-yield basis. For all types of business, investment in real property is rendered less attractive relative to other forms.

TABLE 16–1

DISTRIBUTION OF RATIOS OF ASSESSED TO SALE VALUE,
NEVADA, 1960

Ratio of Assessed Value to Sales Value	Number	Percent
0– 9	55	0.7
10–19	1,342	17.4
20–29	3,700	47.9
30–39	2,038	26.4
40–74	529	6.9
75 and over	56	0.7
Total	7,720	100.0

SOURCE: State of Nevada, Tax Commission, Division of Assessment Standards, *Report on Assessment Ratio Study*, 1960.

Finally, the administration of the tax has been highly unsatisfactory. Assessors are typically elected and their subordinates are often chosen on a patronage basis. They have often failed to use modern appraisal methods and to reassess at frequent intervals. They have typically underassessed property despite legal requirements for use of full market value, with a consequent wider range of inequity in individual assessments.[12] Some types of property escape tax entirely. The consequences have been gross inequity in relative tax burdens, as illustrated in Table 16–1. The range is not a matter of a few percentage points,

[12]The national average in 1957 was 30 percent of sale value. See F. L. Bird, *The General Property Tax* (Chicago: Public Administration Service, 1960), p. 39.

but of differences of four or five times. The studies are not entirely accurate but give substantial proof of serious inequity. The difficulty is the product of unsatisfactory methods of selecting assessors, use of small units for assessment (townships in most of the East), and sheer inertia, rather than outright bribery or political favoritism, although the latter have not been unknown.

Reforms. Given the importance of the tax as a source of local revenue, any basic change in coverage is impossible. The primary feasible reform is improved administration. The trend has been toward higher standards, and many jurisdictions today are obtaining relatively good results. Effective administration requires trained property appraisers and use of modern valuation techniques. A number of states have sought to improve the picture by providing technical assistance, schools for assessors, and equalization among counties. Under usual equalization techniques, the state revenue department makes sample checks of the ratios of assessments to sale values in each county and adjusts the overall level to a uniform figure. This procedure does not automatically eliminate individual inequities in assessment, but brings assessment closer to full market value and thus lessens the range of inequities. State equalization also facilitates uniformity of assessment of state assessed property, usually railroads and public utilities, with locally assessed types. In some states changes in the property tax law would be desirable; a few still nominally tax intangibles but in practice do not reach them. Taxation of business inventories is troublesome administratively and leads to relocation of business activity and distortion of business practices.[13]

Site Value Taxation. Replacement of the property tax by a levy exclusively on the value of land, often called site value taxation, has long been proposed.[14] This form of tax is used to some extent in parts of western Canada, Australia, and British Commonwealth countries of East and Central Africa.[15] The basic argument is that taxation of land values will encourage more efficient use of land, since the holding of

[13]The *Wall Street Journal* of March 6, 1967, provided excellent examples, in the article "Today is Inventory Day in California," p. 8.

[14]The idea of land taxation goes back to David Ricardo; it was developed and popularized by Henry George, who called for the elimination of all taxes except that on the "unearned increment" of land; thus the plan was labeled the single tax. See his *Progress and Poverty* (1879).

In the present day, the idea of a single tax is not a feasible one. Even if governments took all earnings from land, the amount would not be adequate to meet expenditures. The single tax feature, is, however, incidental to George's basic proposal.

[15]See A. M. Woodruff and L. L. Ecker-Racz, "Property Taxes and Land Use Patterns in Australia and New Zealand," *Tax Executive*, Vol. XVIII (October, 1965), pp. 16–63.

land vacant becomes prohibitive. The land value approach also avoids the adverse effect that the taxation of buildings may have upon economic development. The principle is also defended on equity grounds, that landowners greatly benefit from increased earnings of land due to growth of the area, with little or no contribution on their part. Society is thus justified in recovering most or all of this gain. The argument has some merit, particularly for urban land in rapidly growing areas. Such a levy, however, is not adjusted to tax capacity as evidenced by wealth, but must be defended as a measure designed to recover for society the unearned gains from land ownership. A primary objection is that many municipal services are necessitated by the construction of buildings, and optimal expenditure levels will be more closely attained if buildings are subject to tax as well.

DEATH AND GIFT TAXES

The taxation of gifts and inheritances is designed to reach the taxpaying ability reflected by the receipt of gratuitous transfers. These receipts constitute income in the broad sense of the term but have typically been excluded from income and taxed under separate legislation. Furthermore, liability for these taxes is independent of the income or wealth of the recipients; bequests and gifts, per se, have been regarded as suitable objects for taxation.

Framing an optimal bequest-gift tax structure within the confines of this framework is difficult and has typically not been done systematically. Four goals are regarded as important:

1. The taxes should be progressive relative to the size of the estate or inheritance, by usual standards of society. This objective is based in part on the argument that tax capacity rises more rapidly than the sum of the bequest or gift, partly on the deliberate desire to break up large fortunes.

2. The taxes should be adjusted on the basis of the relationship of the heir to the decedent. Receipt of a bequest by a widow or minor children from the deceased spouse or parent represents less tax capacity than the receipt of a similar amount from a distant relative or unrelated person, or receipt by an adult child. The widow's or child's economic well-being is not increased by the bequest; that of other persons is.

3. The amount of tax should be the same, taking interest into consideration, regardless of time of giving or the form in which the property is given (for example, gift or bequest; trust versus direct gift).

Otherwise the tax will affect the choice of methods of giving property.

4. The tax structure should minimize adverse economic effects, such as forced liquidation of closely held businesses.

Defects of Existing Taxes. The existing death and gift taxes are defective in many ways in terms of these objectives. The taxes are progressive, but in relation to the size of the particular share or estate, not to the total amount received by a particular recipient, which is a more logical basis. Two persons inherit $500,000, one in a lump sum from one person, the other in ten $50,000 bequests from different persons. The tax will be much less on the latter than on the former. As noted below, the effective progression is also broken by the failure to integrate estate and gift taxes.

The state inheritance taxes adjust both exemptions and rates on the basis of the relationship of the heir to the decedent; in fact the states have overdone the differentiation, by providing large numbers of separate categories (adult child, minor child, brother and sister, niece, nephew, grandchild, parent, grandparent, aunt, uncle, and so forth) with little logic to differentiate tax rates among them. The federal estate tax differentiates only in favor of the surviving spouse.

The failure to integrate gift and death taxes not only interferes with progression but encourages persons to give away property prior to death. Gifts offer at least three advantages: the total sum is divided into at least two parts, thus checking progression; the gift tax exemptions are very liberal, as explained in Chapter 5; and the amount paid as gift tax is not a portion of the taxable base for either gift or estate tax purposes. The surprising discovery is that wealthy persons do not give away even more property than they do prior to death.[16]

The present taxes likewise provide strong incentive to use trusts with life-estate-remainder provisions for bequeathing property; the evidence of this phenomenon is strong. A leaves property to son B for use during his lifetime, the property passing to grandson C on B's death. Tax applies only when the first transfer is made, not the second. The consequence is the tying up of substantial amounts of property in trusts, lessening the flexibility of investment.[17] Alternatively, a person may lessen total tax liability by leaving property directly to a grandson instead of to his son, thus avoiding one application of tax.

Except for stimulating the use of trusts, the present taxes appear

---

[16]J. A. Pechman, *Federal Tax Policy* (Washington, D.C.: Brookings Institution, 1966), p. 189, indicates how relatively little property is given away prior to death.

[17]See G. J. Jantscher, *Trusts and Estate Taxation* (Washington, D.C.: Brookings Institution, 1967).

to have relatively little adverse economic effect. Special provisions in the law lessen the danger of forced liquidation of businesses, but do lead wealthy persons to keep their estates more liquid than otherwise and sometimes encourage owners of closely held businesses to sell prior to death to avoid danger of forced liquidation or overvaluation of property for death tax purposes.

Solutions. Solutions to these problems within the framework of the present taxes are not easily found, and some of them are not easily resolved regardless of the framework employed. One of the most troublesome to solve is that created by the life-estate-remainder trust. The first recipient, often the widow or children, has use of and control over the property, but in effect cannot dispose of it. Has she received income or not? Under present law gift or estate tax applies when the trust is created, but not when the life tenant dies. If the amounts were made taxable at each transfer the donor would be encouraged to give the property directly to the next generation heirs; with appropriate legal techniques much the same control over property could be maintained. There appears to be no satisfactory alternative within the framework of the present tax structure.

One elaborate plan has been devised to meet this general problem, including skipping of generations to reduce tax: Vickrey's bequeathing power approach, which would adjust the tax rate according to the excess of the age of the decedent over that of the heir, so that the burden would be the same regardless of the path the bequest followed.[18] The plan has merit within the framework of separate taxation of gifts and bequests, but its complications have precluded serious consideration.

Another alternative approach, which would integrate gift and estate taxes and make the operation of progression more effective, is the accessions tax.[19] The tax would be placed upon the donee, on a cumulative basis, on all gifts and bequests received over his lifetime from all donors, with a lifetime exemption plus a small exemption on each individual gift and bequest. The tax would therefore be related to the sum of a person's gratuitous receipts, and the taxation of gifts and bequests would be integrated. Enforcement would be somewhat more complex than that of the estate tax. The most serious problem relates to certain forms of discretionary trusts, the taxation of which might be postponed more or less indefinitely.

---

[18]W. Vickrey, *Agenda for Progressive Taxation* (New York: Ronald Press Co., 1947), chap. viii.

[19]See H. J. Rudick, "What Alternative to Estate and Gift Taxes?," *California Law Review*, Vol. XXXVI (March, 1950), pp. 150–82.

Taxation of Gifts and Bequests as Income. No matter how well gift and death taxes were designed within the present framework, certain objectionable features would persist, as a result of the divorce of the taxation of gifts and bequests from the taxation of income. One consequence of the separate tax treatment is the problem of delineation between income and gratutious transfers. An example is the distinction between graduate fellowships and assistantships, with the absurd consequence that the recipient has to pay tax only if he works for the income. Similar problems arise in distinguishing awards and prizes from payments for services, and with the tax status of business gifts to customers and employees.

Secondly, tax liability is related only to the size of the gift, estate, or inheritance, and in some instances to the relationship of the heir to the decedent, with no recognition whatever of the economic position—wealth or income—of the recipient. Thus a penniless person pays the same or more tax on an inheritance from a distant relative as a millionaire does on the receipt of the same sum from a brother. Tax capacity reflected in an inheritance cannot appropriately be considered in a vacuum, without regard to the economic position of the recipients.

Taxation of all gifts and bequests received as income would avoid the problem of delineation and make the tax treatment accord much more fully with usually accepted standards of equity. However, some qualifications would be required for equity and administrative reasons. A separate form, such as that used for capital gains, would be required of taxpayers receiving gifts and bequests, the taxable amount being transferred to the basic return. Spreading of the gift or bequest over a period of several years should be permitted to avoid severe tax penalty, unless a general system of averaging of income were employed. Small gifts would of necessity be exempted, to avoid taxing persons on Christmas and birthday presents and similar items. Finally, either all gifts within the family unit would be exempt (husband to wife, or parent to minor child), as proposed by the Canadian Royal Commission, which endorses this approach,[20] or granted a special exemption because of the lack of a clear distinction between gift and support.

This system, while avoiding some of the problems and inequities of the present policy, would not be entirely free of problems:

1. The worst difficulty would center around precise delineation between gifts and partial support of persons outside the family unit: the aged parents; the young married couple in college partially sup-

---

[20]*Royal Commission, op. cit.,* chap. xvii.

ported by their parents. Taxation of these support payments would violate usual standards of equity, but delineation of them from pure gifts would be troublesome. If the family unit rule were employed, great incentive would be provided to make gifts before the child left the unit.

2. Gifts in kind. Noncash gifts of considerable value (for example, old paintings) could create serious difficulties to the recipients and require embarrassing refusals of the gifts. The more basic problem in terms of the economy is the receipt by bequest of a large interest in a closely held business—a problem that arises now with the estate tax, and could be more serious with income tax treatment. Special provisions to allow deferment of payment would be required in income tax legislation as well to avoid forced liquidation.

3. Enforcement. While bequests are easy to detect because of the necessity for court approval of the transfer, gifts are not, even larger ones. Some evasion would be inevitable.

4. Choice in timing. Typical gifts differ from regular income in one major respect: they are optional on the part of the donor (and the donee) and they can be timed to suit the convenience of all concerned and minimize tax. Thus persons systematically giving away property to their heirs would concentrate gifts in the years in which the donees' incomes were low. This is not too serious a problem and can scarcely be avoided.

Of these problems, without question the first is the most serious. It is largely avoided under present death taxes by the high exemptions, relatively low rates compared to those of income taxes on moderate amounts, and adjustment of the exemption and rate to the relationship of the heir to the decedent. The problem is not insuperable, but meeting it would without question give rise to a number of complications in the treatment.

APPENDIX—OPTIMAL PROGRAMS OF TAX ADMINISTRATION

No tax can attain its objectives without effective enforcement. Escape from tax whether legally (avoidance) or illegally (evasion) results in loss of equity and in undesirable economic consequences. There are several requirements for effective operation of a tax:

1. A Satisfactory Law, Adapted to the Circumstances of the Country. If, for example, the tax applies to transactions that cannot possibly be discovered (for example, under a sales tax, sale of used furniture by one individual to another), evasion and breakdown of enforcement are

inevitable. Application of local property taxes to intangibles is another example. Establishment of numerous exemptions in a sales tax without precise delineation between taxable and nontaxable goods will greatly reduce the effectiveness of operation. Loopholes of various types, such as the failure to tax certain types of income coupled with ability to convert other income into the exempt form, reduce equity and distort business practice.

2. A Competent and Adequate Staff. Tax admistration is a type of activity that requires well-trained personnel. Yet all too frequently the positions have been filled on the basis of political patronage, with turnover of staff whenever the administration changes. Salaries must be adequate to attract and retain good quality personnel. Many tax administration agencies are short of staff; additional auditors would often add revenue several times the amount of their cost.

3. Provision of Adequate Information to Taxpayers. The rule that ignorance is no excuse is inappropriate in the tax field. Information should be readily available to taxpayers in comprehensible form,[21] with clear definitions of tax liability. The U.S. federal government, derelict in this regard for many years, has made great improvements.

4. Maximum Convenience for Taxpayers. The task of payment of tax should require minimum time and effort on the part of taxpayers; not only will collection be more complete but waste of resources avoided. Timing of tax payments should coincide with receipt of income; withholding for income taxes has greatly improved the convenience to taxpayers. Tax returns should be as simple and clear as possible, with request only for information that is actually needed. Requirements of notarization and of preparation of a number of copies and personal appearance at a tax office are unnecessary.

5. Adequate Control Systems. Taxpayers must be registered in some fashion, with a number provided for control purposes, as a basis for mailing return forms and ascertaining whether or not returns have been filed. With sales taxes the registration numbers also facilitate exclusion from tax of nonretail sales. Followup to insure that payments have been made and immediate contact of delinquents—those not filing—are imperative. This is particularly important when the taxpayers are vendors who collect the tax from their customers. Delinquency is a continuing problem with retail sales taxes. The delinquents are primarily small stores short of funds and personnel, but adequate

---

[21]Some of the "C" circulars of the Canadian federal sales tax are classics in incomprehensibility.

control measures can reduce the percentage from 15 percent to 3 or 4 percent in each filing interval.

6. Comprehensive Audit. While most taxpayers are honest, some are not, and most will give themselves the benefit of any doubt. Error likewise is common. Accordingly a comprehensive audit program is necessary to check the accuracy of the returns, although a detailed review of each return each year is not necessary. There are normally two elements in audit. All returns receive an office check, to ascertain obvious errors and spot those returns requiring careful review. A more detailed audit, with the taxpayer required to present evidence of deductions and with information obtained from third parties, such as employers and suppliers, is then undertaken with those returns that appear to warrant it and others selected on a random basis. With sales, excise, and some other taxes, this detailed review takes the form of field audit, the auditor visiting the place of business and checking the records of the firm and its suppliers.

With virtually all taxes, the most important key to effective audit is cross-check. A worker reports a certain wage; records of his employer are checked to ascertain the correctness of the figure. A retailer reports certain sales subject to sales tax; records of his suppliers are reviewed to ascertain the correctness of his purchase figures and thus, approximately, of his reported sales. An inherent problem with property taxation is the lack of cross-checking possibilities.

7. Effective Use of EDP (Electronic Data Processing) Equipment. Development of modern computers allows much more effective enforcement at less cost. The computer installations perform several tasks:

a) Maintaining the list of registered taxpayers and addressing return forms from this list.

b) Processing of returns and payments and preparation of statistics.

c) Ascertainment of delinquents and preparation of notices and master lists.

d) Routine checking of arithmetic.

e) Cross-checking of information obtained from various persons: of wages paid employers against wages reported by the employees; dividends paid by corporations and those reported by stockholders, and so on.

f) Ascertainment of returns that appear to warrant detailed audit, either because cross-checking reveals errors, or because various data depart from established norms. For example, with a retail sales tax exempting food, supermarkets on the average may have 15 percent of their gross sales taxable (nonfood items). The tax return of a particular supermarket shows only 5 percent of sales taxable. Obviously audit is in order; this may demonstrate that the store simply carried fewer nonfood items than other stores, but it may very well reveal evasion. The EDP equipment is also used to build up the norms from data on the returns and to analyze the data to reveal common sources of error in reporting.

8. The Use of Adequate but Reasonable Penalties. If penalties are too low, taxpayers may deliberately break the law and pay the penalty. On the other hand if they are unreasonably high, taxpayers become antagonistic to the government and administrators, and courts are likely to be lenient in application of the penalties. Reasonable penalties uniformly applied are highly effective. Automatic percentage penalties without need for court action for failure to file and other errors not involving fraud are particularly useful in enforcing payment.

REFERENCES

SALES AND EXCISE TAXATION[22]

DUE, J. F. *Sales Taxation*. London: Routledge and Kegan Paul, and Urbana, Ill.; University of Illinois Press, 1957.

Analysis of the various forms of sales taxation and structural questions.

MORGAN, D. C. *Retail Sales Tax*. Madison, Wis.: University of Wisconsin Press, 1964.

Analysis of four major sales tax issues.

Report of the Royal Commission on Taxation, Vol. V. Ottawa: Queen's Printer, 1966.[23]

An extensive review of sales taxation.

The Role of Direct and Indirect Taxation in the Federal Revenue System. Princeton, N.J.: Princeton University Press, 1964.

The article by D. H. Eldridge is particularly relevant.

SULLIVAN, CLARA. *The Tax on Value Added.* New York: Columbia University Press, 1965.

The only detailed analysis of value added taxation.

---

[22]Among the older references, R. M. Haig and Carl S. Shoup, *The Sales Tax in the American States* (New York: Columbia University Press, 1934); and N. H. Jacoby, *Retail Sales Taxation* (Chicago: Commerce Clearing House, 1938) are useful.

[23]Two specialized studies on Canadian sales taxation, both published by Canadian Tax Foundation, Toronto, were J. F. Due, *General Manufacturers Sales Tax in Canada* (1951) and *Provincial Sales Taxes* (rev. ed., 1964).

U.S. TREASURY, DIVISION OF TAX RESEARCH. "Considerations Respecting a Federal Retail Sales Tax," *Hearings of Ways and Means Committee on Revenue Revision of 1943,* pp. 1095–1272.

Although out of date, this remains one of the most complete studies of sales tax structure.

PROPERTY AND DEATH TAXATION[24]

BIRD, F. L. *The General Property Tax.* Chicago: Public Adminstration Service, 1960.

A summary of the 1957 Census of Governments data on property taxation.

LINDHOLM, R. W. (ed.). *Property Taxation USA.* Madison, Wis.: University of Wisconsin Press, 1968.

MORTON, W. A. *Housing Taxation.* Madison, Wis.: University of Wisconsin Press, 1955.

NETZER, D. *Economics of the Property Tax.* Washington, D.C.: Brookings Institution, 1966.

An intensive study of property taxation.

SHOUP, CARL. *Federal Estate and Gift Taxes.* Washington, D.C.: Brookings Institution, 1966.

TAIT, ALAN. *The Taxation of Personal Wealth.* Urbana, Ill.: University of Illinois Press, 1967.

The reports of state tax study commissions in various states contain intensive studies of property taxation. Note, for example, CALIFORNIA ASSEMBLY INTERIM COMMITTEE ON REVENUE AND TAXATION. *Taxation of Property in California.* Sacramento, 1964.

TAX ADMINISTRATION

DUE, J. F. *State Sales Tax Administration.* Chicago: Public Administration Service, 1964.

PENNIMAN, CLARA, AND HELLER, WALTER. *State Income Tax Administration.* Chicago: Public Adminstration Service, 1959.

---

[24]The classic property tax study was J. P. Jensen's *Property Taxation in the United States* (Chicago: University of Chicago Press, 1931).

PART V

Development

THE RELATIONSHIP OF GOVERNMENTAL FINANCE AND ECONOMIC DEVELOPMENT

Chapter 17

Governmental expenditure and tax policies are conditioned by the characteristics of the particular country and adapt to changes in the economy; at the same time the policies may have major impact upon the rate and path of development. Evaluation of governmental policies and proposals for reforms must therefore take into consideration the interrelationship between the policies and economic development. These issues are of particular concern to the developing economies, which seek to attain rapid acceleration of growth.

GOVERNMENTAL EXPENDITURES

The ratio of governmental expenditures to gross national product tends to rise with economic development. In countries such as the United States, Canada, France, Germany, and Great Britain, government expenditures constitute from 25 to 38 percent of GNP; the figures for the countries of tropical Africa and Southeast Asia range from 6 to 15 percent.[1] In part the rise in the ratio as GNP increases reflects rising social consciousness—increased recognition of the importance of social as distinguished from purely individual goals. A second reason is the increased need for governmental activities as the commercial sector grows and urbanization and industrialization expand. There is little need for governmental activity in a subsistence economy with most of the population of a country living in scattered villages. The development of national consciousness increases the desire for national defense activities and other manifestations of nationalism, such as participation in international organizations and development of airlines. Thirdly, rising per capita national income increases ability to support governmental activities; when the population is at bare subsistence levels, no margin is available for improved roads or other

[1]Detailed figures are given in the article by J. R. Lotz and E. R. Morss, "Measuring Tax Effort in Developing Countries," *International Monetary Fund Staff Papers,* Vol. XIV (November, 1967), pp. 478–99.

governmental services. Finally, a force that is significant for the most developed as well as the least developed economies is the lag in productivity per worker in the typically labor-intensive governmental sector behind the rising productivity in other sectors. Accordingly allocation of progressively greater percentages of GNP to government is necessary to maintain given levels of output.

Varying Levels of Expenditures

While the tendency toward growth of the governmental sector is universal, the rate of growth and the variation in the ratio of government expenditures to GNP differ among countries at comparable levels of economic development. One source is difference in ideology on the part of the population toward the role of government, in turn a reflection in substantial measure of the attitudes of the leaders. Some countries are ruled by a small group of "status quo" dominant families, who see no merit in increased governmental activities and are able to prevent the masses of the population from exercising influence upon policy, or, for that matter, from gaining sufficient education to know what progress is. Other countries are led by groups that seek to push economic development rapidly by all means that the government can devise and to educate the population to the acceptance of progress.

A second source is the ability of the government to finance increased activities. A number of factors affect this ability, but the two most important, given the level of per capita real income, appear to be the importance of foreign trade in the economy and possession of resources such as oil with ready world markets. Governments in early periods of development must rely heavily upon foreign trade as a source of tax revenues;[2] Natural resources provide both tax revenue and the foreign exchange required for expansion of many forms of governmental activity. A third element worthy of note is the emphasis placed on national defense, in turn a product of the relationships with neighboring countries and of the fear of invasion or domestic revolt.

Expenditure Patterns

Countries such as the United States that experienced their rapid growth in the era of laissez-faire, with resource conditions favoring development without the need for governmental assistance, gave little

[2] H. H. Hinrichs, *A General Theory of Tax Structure Change During Economic Development* (Cambridge, Mass.: Harvard Law School, 1966), chap. ii.

thought to the optimization of governmental expenditures in light of goals of development. The United States took some measures to aid the development of the country—early roads, transcontinental railroads, protection of settlers against Indian attacks—but without systematic planning. Aid was given to meet particular needs as they arose. In the present era the less developed areas of the world are trying hard to catch up with the more developed areas, and their governments seek to plan economic development carefully. Accordingly, governmental expenditure programs are designed in light of overall development goals, with expenditures related to development much more closely than in the developed economies.

The precise emphasis upon different types of governmental expenditures varies with the circumstances of the countries and the importance attached to specific goals:

1. *Education.* Since most countries today recognize the importance of trained manpower for economic development, educational expenditures are typically of major importance in the budget. Unfortunately, allocation of funds alone is not adequate; the most urgent need, particularly for secondary schools, is a supply of teachers. The concentration frequently placed upon primary education has been remarkably successful in increasing the number of children receiving several grades of schooling, but has created the serious "school leaver" problem. There are few openings in secondary schools, and children with limited education become dissatisfied with their ancestral villages but lack sufficient education to obtain jobs in trade or industry.

2. *Transport.* Many developing economies suffer from inadequacy of transport facilities that are required for specialization in production, industrialization, and foreign trade. Roads and in some instances railroads where the volume of traffic is heavy receive high priority in many expenditure programs.

3. *Public Health.* Disease, particularly of an endemic nature, is a primary obstacle to increased output in many tropical countries, and improved hospitals, medical facilities, and elementary instruction in hygiene are required. Unfortunately the reduction in the death rate sharply increases the rate of population growth. Greater use of birth control is as important in many countries as improved medical care for higher per capita real income.

4. *Agricultural Development.* Most developing economies rely primarily on agriculture for both subsistence and export and many could increase agricultural output substantially by the use of improved methods and, in some countries, the construction of irrigation and

drainage facilities. Many governments give priority to such projects, to agricultural extension, and to experimental work with new forms of crops. Land reform is often required for development but may be blocked by political strength of the landowning groups. Alternatively, if farms are too small, consolidation of holdings may be required for greater efficiency.

5. *Industry.* Most governments of developing economies regard industrial development as imperative, even if the country has relatively few natural advantages in this sphere. If private enterprise cannot be induced to establish the desired industries, the government, usually through development corporations, may undertake it directly or in partnership with a foreign enterprise. In this sphere, logical planning not infrequently gives way to considerations of prestige; many countries invest large sums of money in steel mills and similar industries despite serious natural disadvantages.

Constraints on Expenditure Planning

In all fields, planning of governmental spending programs in light of the development program is subject to several major constraints. One is the sum of money that can be raised domestically by taxes and other sources to finance the activities. A second is the ability to obtain foreign exchange, either through foreign loans or exports, to pay for the imports required for governmental activities. The foreign exchange gap is often a more serious limitation to economic development than is the savings gap. Various governmental activities differ widely in their import components. Primary education may require little except a few supplies; crude buildings adequate for schoolhouses are produced with local materials and labor, and teachers are trained in local schools. On the other hand, the construction of new railroads or steel mills may require importation of virtually all materials and equipment. The third major constraint is administrative: the ability to find adequate trained personnel to carry out the proposed activity.

The question of the actual effects of the governmental expenditures upon economic development can be answered only on the basis of overall effectiveness of planning, and detailed analysis is beyond the scope of this book. Needless to say, an effective program can bring rapid increase in economic development, not only raising per capita GNP but also altering the entire cultural background, bringing urbanization, higher levels of education, and breakdown of traditional ways of life. These changes, in turn, alter the tax potentials of the country and the expenditure patterns themselves. Aid to agriculture, for example, may decline in importance relative to construction of city sewerage systems, and primary education may decline relative to university work. Alternatively, badly conceived and implemented programs can impede development.

THE REVENUE STRUCTURES

Influences on Revenue Structures

Revenue structures are conditioned by many influences. The degree of "openness" in the economy—the importance of foreign trade relative to total economic activity—[3]plays a major role in early years of development. Openness not only affects the total amount of revenue the government can raise but also the form of the tax structure. Trade permits revenue from customs duties and export taxes. The domestic activity relating to export, especially if large scale, allows the early introduction of income taxes as well. The nature of export activity and its importance influence the type of tax that is feasible; oil production and mining facilitate taxes on exports or the income gained from exports to a greater extent than does small-farm agriculture. As an economy continues to expand, foreign trade usually plays a diminishing role in overall activity and has a declining influence on the nature of the tax structure.

The relative size of the subsistence and commercial sectors affects the development of the tax structure; only as persons move into the commercial sector can they pay taxes in cash. Taxes, in turn, may be used as an instrument to encourage persons to seek cash income. The nature and scale of commercial activity also influence development of taxation. Excises and sales taxes become possible only as commercial establishments reach sufficient size and maintain records adequate to permit control. The nature of manufacturing and retailing affects the choice of the form of a sales tax once commercial development allows such a tax. Development of a banking system greatly facilitates governmental borrowing. The ownership of commercial and industrial activity may also affect tax development; governments have fondness for taxing foreign owners, especially if the earnings are not being reinvested in the country. Tax policies of the home countries of the foreign corporations may also affect tax structure; failure of the home country to allow credit for tax paid other countries will restrict the development of income taxation.

---

[3]Hinrichs, *op. cit.*, chap. ii.

The level of education, which affects not only the standards of record keeping of vendors but also the ability to use a reasonably sophisticated form of direct taxation, also affects tax patterns. Another major influence is the nature of land ownership and income distribution, the two often being closely related in developing economies. The type of tax structure that develops in a feudal economy, with land owned by a few wealthy families, is likely to be different from that in a country with no private ownership of land in the strict sense and with only limited income inequality. Another influence is the location of dominant political power. If this rests with a small wealthy group, the tax structure is almost certain to be different than if power lies with a broader group of the population or with persons who stress economic development of the country rather than their own immediate tax liability.

Attitudes of persons paying taxes are likewise relevant. These cannot easily be explained, since they are in part a product of past experience and tradition. If taxes have come to be regarded as an instrument of a hated colonial power, persons will resist them much more than if they developed spontaneously out of the wishes of the people or of their hereditary and widely accepted rulers. Traditions of taxation were, despite hostility toward colonialism, carried over from parent countries to colonial offspring. The tax structures of South America show Spanish influence, and those of countries of British and French colonial background reflect influences of these two countries.

Administrative structure and efficiency condition the type of structure that develops. The more complex forms of tax cannot be used, or at least cannot operate effectively, until administrative standards have attained adequate levels. Traditions toward professionalism versus patronage in selection of governmental employees affect the attainment of an adequate administrative organization. The type of structure that develops in a federal system, with tendency toward autonomous sources for the states, may be substantially different from that in a unitary system, and the importance attached to local governments and autonomous revenue for them influences the extent to which taxes suitable for use at local levels are developed.

Finally, all tax structures are conditioned by the views of particular persons who play influential roles in their development. In the British Commonwealth countries, the attitudes of the persons who comprise Royal Commissions on taxation may influence the tax structure for a long period. While individual views are conditioned by circumstances that impose various restraints, substantial differences will be encountered among the views; and the structures will reflect these differences.[4]

These influences result in diversity among tax structures despite the cross-fertilization and mutual influence that the structures of countries exercise upon one another. This is particularly true in earlier years of economic development, where openness is a dominant influence. These influences likewise condition the change that occurs as economic and political development of a country continues. This is not to suggest that a tax structure automatically adjusts optimally in light of changing economic conditions; inertia and the opposition of groups that would be adversely affected by the change delay adjustments.[5] But these forces nevertheless exercise substantial influence on the structure over time.

Survey of these influences suggests the dangers that confront a developing country seeking to reform its tax structure. Failure to adapt the tax structure to economic, political, and administrative conditions will almost certainly end in disaster. Establishment of a sophisticated income tax before the country is administratively and politically capable of operating it effectively will mean widespread evasion and inequity, and, frequently, deliberate refusal to pay on the part of the wealthy.[6] This experience can discredit income taxation for generations to come. On the other hand excessive delay in establishment of an income tax may result in strong opposition from the higher income classes to its ultimate introduction.

Establishment of new taxes without regard to popular reactions can lead to riots, revolt, and speedy elimination of the levy. The British economist Nicholas Kaldor, well known for his "tough" attitude toward taxing in developing economies, may have been indirectly responsible for riots in several countries that accepted his proposals for drastic tax increases without adequate concern for popular reaction. Similarly, the transplantation of tax structures from one country to another without regard to differences in economic, political, and social characteristics can produce undesirable effects that may destroy the effectiveness of the taxes; this is the hazard that the tax adviser to a

---

[4]For example, the influence of M. Maurice Lauré in the introduction of the value added tax in France, and of Lady Hicks in the development of personal income taxation in Eastern Nigeria is well known.

[5]C. S. Shoup, "Tax Policies in Developing Countries," paper presented to Inter-American Center of Tax Administrators, Panama, 1967.

[6]The author has encountered one instance in recent years where the head of the revenue system had never filed an income tax return, and of course his subordinates were in no position to require him to do so.

foreign government must constantly guard against. On the other hand, continued inertia and failure to discard taxes that are no longer suitable under the changed circumstances or that could now be replaced by greatly superior substitutes may also retard development.

An Evolutionary Pattern of Taxation

Despite the varying circumstances certain patterns of development of tax structures are clearly discernable.[7] In the earliest period of economic development, characterized by a traditional subsistence economy with virtually no commercial activity, governments obtain their revenue from nontax sources, such as tribute or revenues from the domain, and from crude forms of direct taxation, including payment in goods (a portion of the crop), in labor services, and, as the use of money spreads, in poll taxes or taxes of a fixed amount per unit of land owned.

TABLE 17–1

MAJOR FORMS OF TAXES IN DEVELOPING ECONOMICS, 1962–65

	Percentage of Total Revenue			
Country	Taxes on Wealth and Income	Taxes on Imports	Domestic Indirect Taxes	Other
Panama................	25	27	14	34
Costa Rica............	19	52	15	14
Guatemala............	9	53	30	8
Ghana................	16	37	13	34
Honduras.............	14	45	26	15
Ecuador..............	14	39	22	25
Sierra Leone*.........	30	62	1	7
Uganda*..............	24	40	15	21
Nigeria*..............	21	59	6	14
Tanzania*.............	30	50	14	6

*1961–62.
SOURCE: United Nations, *World Economic Survey*, 1965, Part I, "The Financing of Economic Development," p. 27; J. F. Due, "Taxation in Tropical Africa," *Canadian Tax Journal*, Vol. X (September–October, 1962), pp. 359–66.

As commercial activity develops, governments are able to increase their revenue by taxing trade—particularly imports, which are subject to relatively easy control because they can be forced to pass through "bottlenecks" of customs houses. Taxation of imports also gains popular favor because of its protectionist influence and the concentration of the use of imported goods in the higher income levels.

[7]Hinrichs, *op. cit.*, has developed these patterns in detail.

Domestic trade is more difficult to tax until business activity and administrative standards have reached higher levels. Typically indirect taxes first take the form of excise taxes on domestic production of major articles that were highly productive of customs revenue, such as liquor and tobacco. Spain, however, introduced a general sales tax (*alcavala*) at an early stage in economic development, but most countries have been reluctant to follow this experiment. Almost universally countries that have passed beyond the subsistence level but have not reached a high level of economic development rely heavily on customs and export duties, and to some extent on domestic indirect taxes, as illustrated in Table 17–1. The only exceptions are countries with a major foreign enclave engaged in mineral or oil production; such countries may prefer to tax the income of the foreign companies rather than the exports of the products.

As economic development continues, the foreign-trade-related taxes decline in relative importance as growth of domestic production allows greater use of domestic indirect taxation, particularly broad-based sales taxes, and more effective use of direct taxation. In some instances, especially in tropical African countries, the income tax developed from primitive poll taxes. More commonly, income taxes have been introduced independently to meet increased revenue needs and satisfy the demand for greater progression in the tax structure. Personal and corporate income taxes are usually introduced simultaneously. The latter is often of primary importance at first, especially when a few large foreign-owned enterprises dominate the commercial sector, but in time this is outstripped by the personal income tax. The development of wealth-related tax varies so much among countries that generalization is difficult.

USE OF THE REVENUE SYSTEM AS AN INSTRUMENT TO AID ECONOMIC DEVELOPMENT

The primary contribution of government to economic development arises from governmental activities rather than from revenues, but the revenue structure may have substantial influence on development. Accordingly, in the framing of revenue structures in these countries developmental aspects play a major role.

Money Creation and Borrowing

The potentialities of nontax methods are limited. Since the primary obstacle to development is lack of capital goods relative to manpower and lack of worker and management skills, creation of money leads to inflation rather than to an increase in per capita real income. Most unemployment in a developing economy is due to structural features in the economy rather than to inadequate demand. There is one major exception to the rule against money creation: when it is required to offset hoarding. Because of lack of adequate savings facilities and of confidence in the security of such institutions as may exist, hoarding is a common phenomenon, and will create a deficiency in aggregate demand and therefore Keynesian unemployment. If money is created to offset the net hoarding, inadequacy in demand may be offset without danger of inflation. Hoarding, however, creates a backlog of liquid funds that could easily commence to flow into the market. Thus money creation to offset hoarding must be regarded as a temporary necessary evil.

Governmental domestic borrowing is primarily a device for mobilizing capital in view of the failure of domestic capital markets to function smoothly in earlier years of economic development. If the government does not gather in these funds, they are likely to remain idle and create deflationary effects unless offset by money creation; borrowing is essentially a safer substitute for money creation. Furthermore, governmental borrowing of the savings lessens danger of outflow of money capital from the country. Such outflow not only lessens funds available for domestic expansion but also aggravates the foreign exchange problem. As a source of revenue, domestic governmental borrowing is subject to severe limitations. The magnitude of domestic savings is likely to be small relative to governmental needs, and if governmental borrowing reduces the quantity of funds available for private investment, development may be retarded. The goal of borrowing under the circumstances is to absorb savings that would otherwise not be used for investment significant for economic development and might flow out of the country.

Governmental borrowing from foreign sources offers the major advantage of providing the country with additional foreign exchange to finance imports vital for development. The amount that can be borrowed from outside sources is, however, limited and frequently available only for major developmental projects. Foreign borrowing also gives rise to obligations that constitute a claim on both tax revenue and foreign exchange, and may lead to foreign domination of economic and political activity. Certainly foreign borrowing cannot be relied upon for any length of time as a source of funds for routine governmental expenses.

The Role of Taxation

Taxation must be the primary source of revenue in all economies. In addition to providing funds without the adverse consequences of other methods, taxation can accomplish several major results for a developing economy. First, taxes can be designed to curtail consumption, particularly of luxury goods, and to raise the overall S/Y ratio, by absorbing funds that would otherwise be used for consumption, and by providing incentive to save more and consume less. Taxes may also be used to restrict investment of types contributing little to economic development.

Second, taxes may be used to restrict imports in order to free foreign exchange for goods essential to economic development. In many economies the major obstacle to economic development is inadequacy of foreign exchange: the means to pay for imported capital equipment. Savings alone will not permit optimal capital formation if the goods required cannot be produced within the country.

Third, taxation may possibly be used to promote domestic real investment in place of hoarding or investing abroad, and, more significantly, as a means of channeling investment into uses that will make the greatest contribution toward economic development.

Fourth, taxation may increase availability of factor units in the commercial sector of the economy, particularly of labor, and bring more effective utilization of land and other resources. Developing economies are often characterized by substantial underemployment, persons working only a few hours a day in subsistence agriculture. Tax measures can be devised that will encourage these persons to enter the commercial labor market. Some countries suffer from poor utilization of land, owned in large estates and used inefficiently; taxes may bring more intensive land use.

Finally, taxation has a major role in attaining equitable allocation of the benefits from economic growth among the members of society. In some economies taxation is needed for redistribution of wealth and income to allow improved economic status of the population as a whole.[8]

Attainment of these goals will be facilitated by a high degree of revenue elasticity in the tax structure, so that governmental revenue will rise at a more rapid rate than national income without constant need for tax rate changes.

[8]In Peru, 8,760 families (one fourth of 1 percent of the total) receive 35 percent of the total income of the country. M. C. Taylor, "Taxation and Economic Development: A Case Study of Peru, *"Inter-American Economic Affairs,* Vol. XXI (Winter, 1967), pp. 43–54.

In light of these potential accomplishments—full attainment of which is of course impossible—the need for care in adjusting the tax structure in terms of goals is greater in a developing economy than in a mature country such as the United States. In developed economies, market forces have brought reasonably satisfactory economic adjustments. In developing economies they have not. Governments in these economies, therefore, feel justified in more positive use of taxes and other instruments to alter economic behavior deliberately to speed the process of development.

Compromise among Objectives

The need for sophisticated tax measures to bring desired adjustments in behavior must be tempered with the possibilities of effective administration. Developing economies lack trained administrative personnel, and the more allocated to tax administration, the fewer available for other important tasks. Tax programs can produce adverse results if they become mired in a swamp of administrative inefficiency, as have some of the tax holiday programs established to encourage development of new firms. Sophisticated tax structures designed to attain equity goals may result in gross inequity because of mass evasion. No measures should be introduced unless effective operation can be reasonably assured.

Conflicts arise among various objectives that must be solved on the basis of careful weighing of divergent elements. For example, the desire for maximum savings to allow a high rate of capital formation must be balanced with the need for protecting incentives to work and to develop businesses, and with the need for markets adequate for efficient production. High taxes restricting consumption can so dampen incentives that total labor supply falls, and they can reduce market potential so greatly that economies in production cannot be attained. In some countries the requirements for equity conflict with those for a high level of savings and investment; heavy taxes on the higher income groups may significantly reduce both capacity and incentive for savings and for real investment. Incentive considerations require the holding of top marginal rates of taxation to reasonable levels; a figure acceptable in a mature economy may have serious consequences in a developing one. Incentive effects also require that the burden on the gains from economic growth be moderate; the desire to insure equitable distribution of these gains must be tempered with the need for encouraging continued growth by allowing those responsible for growth to retain a considerable portion of their gains.

Finally the objectives relating directly to economic development must be balanced with the need for popular acceptance of tax structures, which is imperative for effective operation and for the maintenance of stability in government. Sharp increases in taxes without adequate education of the population to the need for them, use of provisions that appear to be unreasonable, and weak administration leading to widespread evasion, especially by the wealthy, create strong resistance to taxation, lessen the willingness of persons to pay correct amounts, and may lead to riots and overthrow of the government by force.

While the exact ingredients of an optimal tax structure vary with conditions, several generalizations are possible about the major forms of taxation.

The Role of Consumption Taxation[9]

The potential role of consumption-related taxation, particularly of the commodity tax form, is much greater than in a mature economy. Consumption taxes provide incentive to reduce consumption and increase savings and bear more heavily on persons who consume most of their income. They can also be employed to reduce consumption of particular goods. Secondly, consumption taxes can reduce purchases of imported goods. Thirdly, they presumably have somewhat less adverse effect upon work and investment incentives, since a person can postpone or escape tax if he saves rather than consumes. Fourthly, administration is easier than that of personal income taxes, since commodity taxes can be collected from a relatively small number of vendors. Consumption taxes may be more equitable than in developed economies, since the relatively few staple commodities that comprise almost the entire consumption of the lowest income groups can be excluded from tax. The equity argument is particularly strong if the alternative is a poorly enforced income tax evaded by high-income groups.

These advantages, however, should not be overstressed. Desire for increased consumption—strengthened by the demonstration effect[10]— is so great in many developing economies that income may be desired solely for the purposes of additional consumption. If this is a wide-

---

[9]R. Goode, "Taxation of Saving and Consumption in Underdeveloped Countries," *National Tax Journal*, Vol. XIV (December, 1961), pp. 305–22; D. Dosser, "Indirect Taxation and Economic Development," in *Government Finance and Economic Development* (Paris: OECD, 1965), pp. 127–42; J. M. Naharro, "Production and Consumption Taxes and Economic Development," in Joint Tax Program, OAS/IDB/ECLA, *Fiscal Policy for Economic Growth in Latin America* (Baltimore: Johns Hopkins Press, 1965), pp. 273–325.

[10]Awareness of high levels of consumption in other countries and among the wealthy in their own country.

spread attitude, tax on consumption will have the same effect upon factor supplies and incentives as a tax on income itself and will provide no incentive to increase saving, which is nil, tax or no tax. The ease of administration can also be exaggerated; while the number of taxpayers is small, enforcement is difficult if records are inadequate and the traditions of tax evasion are strong.

The greatest gain from consumption taxation can be realized only if the tax is differentiated by commodity. Uniform rate consumption taxes with basic subsistence items exempt may meet the standards of equity more effectively than in mature economies, but they do little to reduce inequality of wealth and income. Yet extensive differentiation inevitably complicates administration. Accordingly, while consumption taxes may play a major role, they must be supplemented by direct taxes on income and wealth if inequality is a serious problem.

Several forms of consumption taxation may be employed; each will be considered briefly.

Customs Duties. Taxes on imports have a major advantage: enforcement is relatively easy, so long as smuggling can be prevented. Duties can be concentrated on luxury products, restricting consumption and importation of luxury goods that contribute little to economic development. Rates can be adjusted according to the luxury characteristics, with items of basic subsistence exempt.

Framing a suitable customs duty structure is not a simple task. Consideration must be given to import elasticity as national income rises, with higher rates on luxury goods with high import elasticity. Uniform treatment of similar commodities is desirable, as well as use of a small number of rate categories. Capital goods essential for economic development should be free of tax, while those not essential are taxed in the same fashion as consumer goods. Excessive rates on incentive goods—those that persons urgently seek as their incomes rise above bare subsistence—must be kept to tolerable levels. Procedures that minimize nuisance and cost of customs clearance, smuggling, bribery of customs officials, and annoyance to tourists are important for the efficient conduct of trade.

Customs duties are subject to several limitations. They discriminate against individual consumers according to their preferences and the pattern of burden may become regressive if the coverage is broad. The framing of the structure of customs duties becomes more complex as import patterns diversify. Specific rates are simple to administer but become less satisfactory as development continues; they discriminate against users of the cheaper items, and their yield is not responsive to change in price levels. Ad valorem levies are more difficult to administer because of valuation problems. Avoidance of arbitrary distinctions among commodities is a never-ending problem as products and purchase patterns change. The catchall category—n.o.s. ("not otherwise stated")—is always troublesome, since new products fall into it until they are recognized and specifically classified.

The greatest defect of customs duties is their tendency to diminish in importance as a revenue source as economic development continues. Instead of facilitating their use, development tends to destroy them as a major revenue source. As the protective motive becomes stronger, revenues fall. With increased import substitution (replacement of imported by domestic goods), the ratio of luxury imports to total national product declines. The duties become less satisfactory measures of ability to pay and increasingly discriminatory in terms of consumer preferences, because some imported goods are replaced by domestic output while others are not.

Excises. The primary role for excise taxes is to replace the customs revenue lost as a result of development of domestic production of luxury items that have been major sources of customs revenue. Liquor and tobacco products are usually he major categories, plus motor fuel. Extension of excises to other major luxury items of domestic production has some merit, but causes discrimination among consumers on the basis of their preferences and complicates administration. Newly developing domestic industries may be destroyed by drastic curtailment of their markets.

Sales Taxes. A general sales tax is difficult to operate in the earliest years of development because of collection problems. There is little manufacturing, and retail vending is typically small scale. As commercial activity develops, a general sales tax ultimately becomes feasible. The broad coverage allows greater revenue potential at acceptable rates than excises, with less pressure toward evasion, less consumer resistance, and less discrimination according to consumer preference.

On the other hand, a sales tax cannot be used to restrict consumption of particular kinds of goods, as can customs and excises. Exemption of a few basic necessities, such as food, is feasible of administration, but extensive use of exemptions and rate differentiation to tax luxury goods more heavily complicates correct application of the tax and increases discrimination on the basis of consumer preferences. The sales tax must be considered as a general revenue measure to restrict overall consumer spending, not as a means of restricting the purchase of particular kinds of goods or of improving income distribution.

Form of Sales Tax. A major issue is the selection of the most appropriate form of sales taxation. Two forms may be ruled out. A turnover or multiple-stage tax is so discriminatory against nonintegrated businesses and nonuniform by commodity class that its consideration is not warranted. The apparent simplicity of the tax is a delusion; pressures of groups adversely affected by it lead to modifications that produce serious complications in its operation. If such a tax is introduced, the low rate makes change away from it politically difficult; initial introduction therefore, is most unfortunate.[11]

A single-stage manufacturers' sales tax is much less objectionable, but the limited scope of manufacturing compared to foreign trade results in serious problems in attaining equality between imported and domestic goods.[12] The valuation problem noted in Chapter 16 is difficult to solve and grows more complex over the years.

The feasible forms, therefore, are wholesale and retail taxes, a hybrid of these two, or a value added tax. In a country where retailing is conducted through market stalls, roadside stands, and peddling rather than through commercial establishments, the wholesale tax is the only feasible type, since tax cannot be collected from retail vendors. As the size of retailing establishments rises and a substantial portion of total retail sales, particularly of nonfood items, passes through the hands of larger retailers, use of the retail tax becomes possible and offers significant advantages. The tax is basically simpler to operate, applying to the actual sale price in all cases; the yield is higher with a given rate; the burden on all consumer expenditures is uniform; and treatment of exports and imports is more satisfactory. The retail tax becomes progressively easier to operate as development continues, while the wholesale tax gives rise to continuing problems, particularly in discrimination against certain distribution channels.

The best solution for countries with a large number of small retailers but a substantial portion of the total sales handled by larger ones is a hybrid type of tax collected from large retailers and from the suppliers of smaller ones.[13] A somewhat arbitrary line must be drawn between the two classes of retailers on the basis of sales volume, with

---

[11]Chile provides the best example of a high-rate turnover tax so productive of revenue that change to a better form is difficult.

[12]R. M. Bird, *Sales Taxation in Columbia* (Cambridge, Mass.: Harvard University Center for International Affairs, 1966).

[13]Honduras, Secretaria de Economia y Hacienda, Direccion General de la Tributacion Directa, *El Impuesto Sobre Ventas en Honduras* (Tegucigalpa: 1967); J. F. Due, "The Retail Sales Tax in Honduras," *Inter-American Economic Affairs,* Vol. XX (Winter, 1966), pp. 55–68. A similar tax has been introduced in Costa Rica and is being considered in other Central American countries.

only those vendors with sales above the specified figure registered for sales tax purposes. These firms buy for resale free of tax and collect and remit tax on their sales. The smaller unregistered vendors are not required to collect and remit tax but cannot buy tax free; tax is collected from their suppliers. This system admittedly provides some artificial advantage to small retailers, but so long as the rate of tax and the exemption figure are low the loss in economic efficiency is not likely to be very serious.[14]

A variant of this approach involves application of tax to all sales to retailers and taxation of all retailers (except the very small ones) on their gross margins (value added).[15] The use of effective audit programs with larger retailers, however, should make it unnecessary to precollect a part of the tax from these firms at the wholesale level.

The value added alternative has the advantage of spreading out the impact of the tax over a wider range of firms, collecting a portion at earlier stages in production and distribution where evasion is more difficult. This form also facilitates enforcement by allowing cross-checking; amounts reported as tax paid by one firm should appear on the accounts of its supplier as tax paid. On the other hand, the value added tax is much more complex in many ways than a single-stage tax and its introduction into a developing economy is a source of unnecessary complexity and nuisance. A single-stage wholesale or retail tax or combination of the two will accomplish the same result much more simply.[16]

A Spendings Tax.   An expenditure tax collected from individuals on the basis of tax returns permits greater equity in the tax structure than commodity taxes and can provide stronger pressure against inflation, since the rate can be made steeply progressive. The tax also has strong justification on an equity basis in a developing

[14]The advantage to small firms can be lessened by use of another device: intermediate-sized firms, those keeping some records, but not large enough to be made regular taxpayers, can be given special registration certificates that do not permit them to buy tax-free, but require them to pay tax on their gross margins. Tax is thus collected on sales to them by their suppliers, and from them on sales less cost of goods sold. That is, they would calculate tax on their total sales during the period, subtract tax paid on their purchases, and remit the difference. This method would insure that at least a large part of the tax was collected on transactions through these firms from suppliers, yet their margins would be taxable as well. This method would safeguard revenue and lessen loss of economic efficiency.

[15]This approach is used in Finland. See Alan Tait and J. F. Due, "Sales Taxation in Eire, Denmark, and Finland," *National Tax Journal,* Vol. XVIII (September, 1965), pp. 286–90.

[16]A value added tax may be preferable in a somewhat more developed country as a substitute for a turnover tax.

economy in which a small group of wealthy persons spends large sums on luxurious consumption instead of investing in business activity. The main problem is administrative; the tax is even more difficult to enforce than the income tax, since both income and net increases in savings must be ascertained. Taxpayers would have great incentive to conceal assets before the tax was introduced and bring them out as evidence of new savings after the tax was in operation. Successful administration in a developing economy is therefore doubtful; the experience in India and Ceylon in the short period in which the taxes were in use was not reassuring.[17]

Income Taxation

A sophisticated income tax cannot be applied effectively to a large number of taxpayers in an economy in which levels of literacy are low, most persons are dependent upon subsistence production, and the number of persons available for income tax enforcement is limited. Nevertheless, early introduction of an income tax can make important contributions to development financing. First, the income tax has the great advantage of automatic expansion in coverage and revenue as development continues. Thus the government receives an increasing percentage of national income, and the basic advantages of the tax are realized to a growing extent. The income tax contrasts sharply with customs duties, which deteriorate as development continues. The income tax meets requirements of equity more satisfactorily than other taxes so long as it can be enforced, and it is the best technique to lessen inequality of income when this is an objective of development policy. The tax can also be employed to encourage certain uses of income, such as reinvestment within the country, and to discourage others, such as sending capital abroad. If the tax is not introduced early, strongly entrenched groups may block its establishment for many decades, as they did in some Latin-American countries.

Administrative problems plus incentive considerations, however, restrict the revenue potentiality of the tax in earlier years of development. The tax can be applied successfully to wage and salary receivers and stockholders in larger businesses, recipients of interest, and owners of large businesses. Clearly the small semisubsistence farmer cannot be reached by the tax,[18] and traders, even larger ones, are a source of con-

---

[17]Only about 8,000 taxpayers were affected in India. See O. Prakesh, "An Indian View of the Expenditure Tax," *Manchester School of Economic and Social Studies,* Vol. XXVI (January, 1958), pp. 48–67. See also R. Goode, "New System of Direct Taxation in Ceylon," *National Tax Journal,* Vol. XIII, (December, 1960), pp. 329–40.

[18]Except by a flat sum minimum bracket.

siderable evasion. Yet some payment can be obtained from these groups, and continued administrative effort can bring ultimate success.

These considerations suggest the need for restricting the coverage of the tax to relatively high income levels and limiting the marginal rates to reasonable figures. Incentive considerations also require reasonable rates; high marginal rates are likely to produce little revenue but give rise to adverse incentives effects. The wealthy group in a developing economy often consists of the landowners; their wealth can be reached more satisfactorily by some form of tax on land.

Income Tax Structure.   The problems that confront a government of a developing economy in framing an income tax include those encountered in a mature economy and others as well. An example is the value of subsistence farming output; exclusion from tax is essential administratively, yet this output may comprise a large portion of the incomes of many families—in contrast to mature economies. The family unit, particularly with multiple wives and extended families, is more troublesome to handle in an equitable fashion than in mature economies. Children may become sources of earnings at an early age. In many countries, a reduction in the birth rate is highly important; obviously allowances for dependents should not be such as to encourage larger families. Taxation of capital gains is desirable, although hard to administer. In these economies capital gains are realized primarily on land, and taxation lessens land speculation and increases equity of the tax structure.

While uniformity of treatment of all income regardless of source has merit under all circumstances, some differentiation of rate according to use has greater justification than in mature economies. Tax penalties on export of capital and tax concessions for income saved and invested in development of the economy have merit if they are administratively feasible.

Simplicity in the structure of the tax is of greater importance than in economies with higher levels of education; many developing economies have unfortunately copied the complex income taxes of mature economies, making compliance and enforcement much more difficult. On the other hand, withholding has proven to be feasible and useful at very early periods of economic development.

The Personal Tax

Since income taxation in its usual form cannot be applied to the majority of the population in a developing economy, some other form of direct tax is desirable to gain revenue and to acquaint all families with the need for making direct tax payments to the government and paving the way for their eventual entry into the income tax structure. The most satisfactory approach is the graduated personal tax, widely used in tropical Africa. These taxes have several characteristics: coverage of all families (rather than individuals as such) except those exempted by local officials as completely destitute; application to all income (net, in the case of businesses) without deductions, exemptions, or allowances; assessment, at least in part, on presumptive income, as determined, for example, by the number of livestock or cocoa trees; simple graduation in rate by blocks of taxpayers (a flat money rate within each block) up to the level at which the income tax becomes effective; and administration primarily local. Families are assessed by persons familiar with their circumstances. Typically most taxpayers are subject to the basic rate (which may be the equivalent of $2 or $3 per family).

Such a tax brings almost all families within the scope of direct taxation and facilitates their integration into the income tax system as their incomes rise.[19] Yield is greater than from any alternative levy reaching most of the population, with greater equity. If honesty can be maintained, local administration increases the possibility of obtaining equitable assessment and facilitates local fiscal responsibility and financial autonomy.

The graduated personal tax is less likely to have adverse incentive effects than typical income taxes, since the rates are relatively low. When the taxes are levied upon presumptive, rather than actual, income they encourage additional economic activity, and provide incentive to subsistence farmers to move into the commercial sector to earn money income.

The only significant weakness of the taxes is the danger of inadequate administration. In urban areas particularly, it is difficult to insure that all persons pay, and in both rural and urban areas assessment may not be equitable.

Taxation of Corporate Income

Corporate income taxation is essential to reach income earned in the corporate form of business on a current basis when it is not paid out as dividends or is paid to foreign stockholders. The case for such taxation is particularly strong when the corporations are foreign owned and operate in enclaves, contributing little to the development of the country. Corporate taxation is relatively easy to administer compared

---

[19]In the Eastern region of Nigeria the personal tax and the income tax were integrated into a single tax structure.

to personal taxation and in many developing economies can make an important contribution to government revenue. Politically, such taxation has great appeal (too much in some instances) and is without doubt an ingredient necessary to obtain general acceptance of the tax structure. Given the tax laws of the home countries, the overall tax burden may not be increased, the developing economy enjoying some of the revenue otherwise going to the country of the owners. Finally, company taxation offers possibilities for directing investment along lines regarded as most important for economic development.

On the other hand, a country can easily kill the goose that lays the golden eggs. If company taxation is not held to moderate levels, investment from both domestic and foreign sources will be discouraged, and funds will merely be diverted from private investment to government. Absorption of funds that would be used for domestic investment may hamper development; absorption of those that otherwise would be paid to foreign investors and not reinvested in the country or used for investments that do not aid growth encourage development.

The exact structure of the company taxation may have a marked influence upon its developmental effects. Adjustments in the tax that lessen risk encourage additional investment activity. One of the incisive tax policies with this effect is the allowance of full loss carry-forward, so that losses incurred in early years of operation can be deducted for tax purposes from profits earned in later years. Similarly, provisions allowing rapid depreciation of equipment purchases lessen the risk that full deduction for tax purposes will never be attained. Both of these measures reduce revenue so long as the economy is continuing to expand but are justified in terms of equity and economic effects.

Tax Incentives. Special tax concessions[20] such as investment credit and tax holiday provisions may aid development. These have two major functions: (1) they lessen the impact of the company taxes upon funds and incentives for investment by reducing tax burden and (2) they provide a means to channel investment into preferred outlets. The first effect is similar to the impact of a lower tax rate. The second advantage is the more important one. For the maximum rate of economic development, investment decisions cannot be left in the hands of private investors as they can in mature economies, because some investments have greater external benefits to the economy than others. The inevitable uncertainties in developing economies bias in-

[20]See J. Heller and K. M. Kauffman, *Tax Incentives for Industry in Less Developed Countries* (Cambridge, Mass.: Harvard Law School, 1963); G. E. Lent, "Tax Incentives for Investment in Developing Countries," *International Monetary Fund Staff Papers,* Vol. XIV (July, 1967), pp. 539–643.

vestors in the direction of short-term investments and land speculation. The government may divert investment to long-term projects by adjusting investment allowances in their favor and by granting special tax holidays to the preferred investment outlets. In reverse, depreciation deductions may be disallowed on nonpreferred investments.

Such programs are not without their difficulties, as any country that has tried them knows. The investment credit approach, made applicable automatically to all firms in the industries covered, is simpler to operate than the usual tax holiday approach, but favors the capital-intensive type of investment, a policy that may be questioned in a labor surplus economy. The tax holiday approach may bog down in administrative difficulties, with long delays in granting the concessions; in practice all the requests are usually ultimately granted. The effectiveness of the overall program depends upon the ability of the government to select the most advantageous types of investment. The government always runs the risk of choking off some kinds of investment without stimulating others; investments in office buildings and breweries may be preferred to no investment at all. Tax revenue is sacrificed, much of it on gains from investment that would have been undertaken anyway. There is always the danger that adjacent countries will escalate concessions in competition with one another for industry, all in the end losing the revenue and gaining nothing.

Little attention has been given in most countries to the adjustment of company tax liability according to the use made of the earnings. Tax concessions could be made on earnings reinvested within the country (not necessarily in the same industry), with substantially heavier—but not so heavy as to kill the goose—burden on earnings transferred outside the country. Such a policy is not difficult to administer, at least for the larger companies, those that typically earn most of the total profits in a developing economy. Yet very little use has been made of the policy. The significance for development may be as great as governmental absorption of the funds, while the overall adverse incentive effects will be very much less.

Export Duties[21]

Taxes on the exportation of particular products may serve as a partial substitute for income taxes in a developing economy and as

[21]R. Goode, G. E. Lent, and P. D. Ojka, "Role of Export Taxes in Developing Economies," *International Monetary Fund Staff Papers*, Vol. XIII (November, 1966), pp. 453–503.

a means of capturing windfall gains due to sharp increases in world prices. For the former purpose, as used for example in Ghana, the tax offers the advantage of administrative simplicity; when goods are exported through marketing boards or a few large dealers, collection of tax is easier than collection of income tax from numerous small farmers. But used in this fashion, the tax is not only inequitable, since other incomes will not be taxed to the same extent, but may also have serious adverse incentive effects, shifting farmers to domestic products or to export products not subject to tax, with consequent overall loss of efficiency and foreign exchange. As a means of obtaining additional revenue from large foreign-owned producers, income taxation is likely to be more effective. The taxes may also drive persons back into the subsistence sector. On the whole, a graduated personal tax is a more satisfactory means of reaching lower income farmers and the income tax is a better way of reaching those with higher incomes.

As a means of taxing windfall gains from sharp increases in world market prices for the country's exports, export duties have greater merit. They can absorb a substantial portion of the increase in domestic incomes without adverse incentive effects. At the same time they can check domestic inflation, which will otherwise arise because the increase in incomes will not be accompanied by comparable increases in domestic production (and should not, in the interests of economic development, be accompanied by an equivalent increase in consumer goods imports). For this purpose, the export duties must have rates that are nominal so long as world prices are more or less normal but that climb steeply with an increase in prices. Since the revenues will fluctuate widely, these levies must be regarded as supplementary sources of funds available in certain periods for development purposes rather than as normal regular sources of governmental revenue.

Question may be raised about the extent to which such taxes may be shifted to foreign consumers. Under usual conditions in world markets, the answer is not at all; the net income of the producers is reduced by the full amount of the tax. Only if the country completely dominates the world market is shifting possible, and even in this instance it will be advantageous to the country only if the previous price was not the one maximizing gain to the country. These situations are rare, and any country that possesses such a monopoly must take care not to destroy its market by encouraging production in other areas or the development of synthetic substitutes.

Taxation of Property[22]

In practice wealth taxes in developing economies are primarily levies on real property, since a net wealth tax of any form cannot be administered under the circumstances. Taxation of land and other real property offers important advantages, with minimum danger of adverse incentive effects so long as the taxes are reasonable. The taxes serve to recover for the government a portion of the gain from increases in land values characteristic of rapidly developing areas. By checking increases in these values they facilitate development; sharp increases in land values tend to slow the rate of growth. Property taxes not only restrict the growth of new fortunes but may also aid in redistribution of wealth without serious incentive effects. Since the taxes are based upon the value of the property, not directly upon income, they presumably have less adverse effect in discouraging economic activity than income taxes directly related to earnings. If properly designed, the taxes may lead to better utilization of the land, since the owners will be under greater pressure to maximize revenue from it.

Urban and rural land raise different issues. With urban property, there are major questions about the exact form of tax to use. Capital value is preferable to rental because value reflects future expectations sooner than do rental figures. The rental approach is preferable from an administrative standpoint only when most persons live in rental properties. A more fundamental issue is the choice of site value taxation versus taxation of both land and improvements.[23] The former, it is argued, avoids any discouraging effect on building, makes the holding of vacant property untenable, and is particularly effective in capturing increases in land values, which are products of development, not of individual enterprise. Yet several questions arise. Property taxes are primarily local taxes and in part benefit based, and the construction of additional buildings necessitates additional services from government, for which building owners are directly responsible.

Futhermore, the failure to tax improvements may easily encour-

[22]See H. P. Wald, *Taxation of Agricultural Land in Underdeveloped Economies* (Cambridge, Mass.: Harvard Law School, 1959); and his "Reform of Agricultural Taxation to Promote Economic Development in Latin America," *Fiscal Policy for Economic Growth in Latin America, op. cit.*, chap. x. Richard Bird and Oliver Oldman (eds.), *Readings in Taxation in Developing Countries* (Baltimore: Johns Hopkins Press, 1964), pp. 402–35; N. Tanabe, "The Taxation of Net Wealth," *International Monetary Fund Staff Papers*, Vol. XIV (March, 1967), pp. 124–68.

[23]G. E. Lent, "The Taxation of Land Values," *International Monetary Fund Staff Papers*, Vol. XIV (March, 1967), pp. 89–123.

age construction that contributes relatively little to economic growth; for example, construction of office buildings appears to be excessive in many developing economies. The Uganda system of applying a somewhat lower rate to improvements than to land is perhaps the best solution, because some incentive is given to develop vacant sites, while governments receive some compensation toward the costs of the additional services necessitated by buildings.

Generalization about rural land taxes is difficult because of the many differences among countries in land ownership patterns. Where large estates are common, land taxes provide a useful supplement to income taxation in reaching the large landowners and in bringing about more efficient utilization of the land, frequently an important problem. Use of progressive land taxes as an instrument to break up large estates is of doubtful desirability, since the goal can more easily be accomplished by direct means. On the other hand, strong incentive may be given for more intensive use: for example, for shift from cattle grazing to intensive farming. By contrast, these arguments for land taxation have little relevance for peasant agriculture, especially with communal ownership of the land.

The greatest problem with both rural and urban taxation of real property is assessment: the maintenance of up-to-date values on the property. In many countries (India, parts of Central America, for example), land taxation became a dead letter because valuations were not kept up to date and became nominal. This problem has been encountered even in most developed countries. A high-quality initial professional assessment is required, perhaps by an outside group, as well as constant effort to keep the figures up to date. The task is not impossible; many jurisdictions have not faced up to the problem, or political forces have blocked reassessment.[24] Similarly, strong efforts are required to enforce collection; delinquency cripples operation of the tax, with cumulative ramifications.

REFERENCES

BIRD, RICHARD, AND OLDMAN, OLIVER (eds.). *Readings in Taxation in Developing Countries,* 2d ed. Baltimore: Johns Hopkins Press, 1967.

DUE, J. F. *Taxation and Economic Development in Tropical Africa.* Cambridge, Mass.: MIT Press, 1963.

---

[24]Improvements in India and Pakistan in recent years have brought significant increases in revenue. See United Nations, *Economic Survey of Asia and the Far East,* 1964, p. 63.

HICKS, URSULA K. *Development Finance: Planning and Control.* Oxford: Oxford University Press, 1965.

JOINT TAX PROGRAM, OAS/IDB/ECLA. *Fiscal Policy for Economic Growth in Latin America.* Baltimore: Johns Hopkins Press, 1965.

———. *Problems of Tax Adminstration in Latin America.* Baltimore: Johns Hopkins Press, 1965.

PEACOCK, A. T., AND HAUSER, G. (eds.). *Government Finance and Economic Development.* Paris: OECD, 1965.

PREST, A. R. *Public Finance in Underdeveloped Countries.* London: Weidenfeld and Nicolson, 1962.

Index

INDEX

473

This book has been set in 12 and 10 point Garamond, leaded 1 point. Chapter titles and part numbers are in 18 point Futura Medium. Chapter numbers and part titles are in 18 point Futura Medium italics. The size of the type page is 27 x 46½ picas.

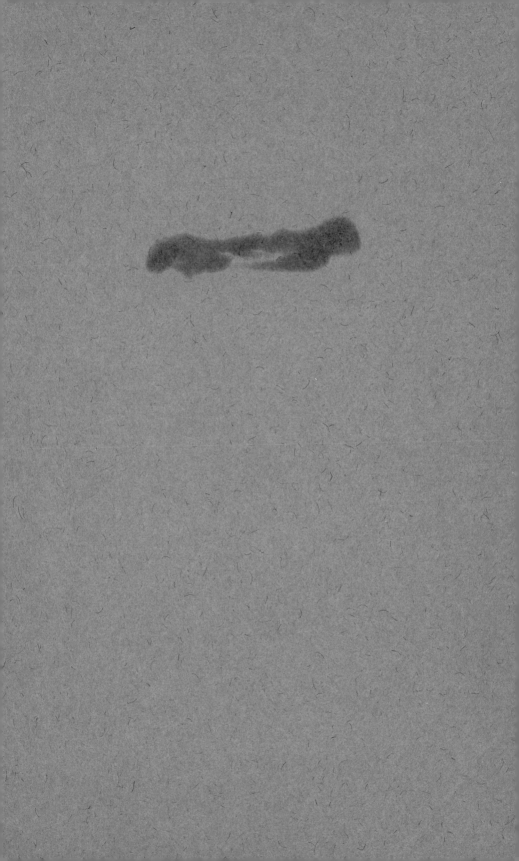

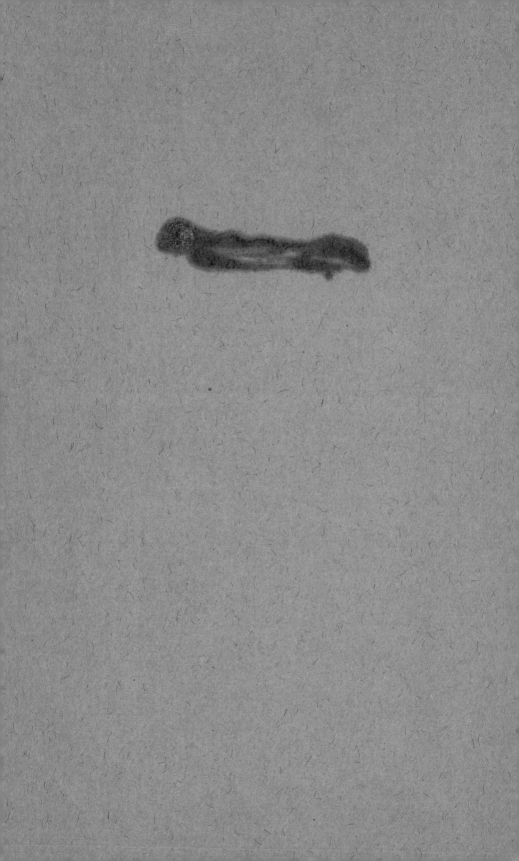

Date Due

APR 14 '78			
JAN 1 3 1981			
'MAY 4 1983			